MONEY BEYOND BORDERS

Money Beyond Borders

GLOBAL CURRENCIES
FROM CROESUS TO CRYPTO

BARRY EICHENGREEN

PRINCETON UNIVERSITY PRESS
PRINCETON & OXFORD

Copyright © 2026 by Barry Eichengreen

Princeton University Press is committed to the protection of copyright and the intellectual property our authors entrust to us. Copyright promotes the progress and integrity of knowledge created by humans. By engaging with an authorized copy of this work, you are supporting creators and the global exchange of ideas. As this work is protected by copyright, any reproduction or distribution of it in any form for any purpose requires permission; permission requests should be sent to permissions@press.princeton.edu. Ingestion of any IP for any AI purposes is strictly prohibited.

Published by Princeton University Press
41 William Street, Princeton, New Jersey 08540
99 Banbury Road, Oxford OX2 6JX

press.princeton.edu

GPSR Authorized Representative: Easy Access System Europe - Mustamäe tee 50, 10621 Tallinn, Estonia, gpsr.requests@easproject.com

All Rights Reserved

ISBN 978-0-691-28053-0
ISBN (epub) 978-0-691-28817-8
ISBN (PDF) 978-0-691-28055-4

British Library Cataloging-in-Publication Data is available

Editorial: Joe Jackson and Rebecca Binnie
Production Editorial: Karen Carter
Jacket/Cover Design: Karl Spurzem
Production: Danielle Amatucci
Publicity: Kate Farquhar-Thomson and James Schneider
Copyeditor: Holly La Fon

This book has been composed in Arno

Printed in the United States of America

10 9 8 7 6 5 4 3 2 1

CONTENTS

Preface vii

1 Introduction 1

PART I. WHAT CAME BEFORE 21

2 Aristotelian Beginnings 23

3 Renaissance of Credit 49

4 The First Global Currency 71

5 Fiat Lux 84

6 The World's Banker 96

**PART II. THE DOLLAR'S WORLD, AND
WE ONLY LIVE IN IT** 125

7 Engineering an International Currency 127

8 Dollar Dominance 153

9 Meet the New Boss 178

PART III. WHAT COMES NEXT   203

10   Outside Options   205

11   Our Currency, Our Problem   224

Acknowledgments   243

Notes   245

References   291

Index   323

PREFACE

THIS IS not the first book about international currencies. It is not even my first book about international currencies. But it is an effort to shed new light on an old topic by widening the aperture. It seeks to better understand the future by peering further into the past. Most historical work to date has focused on the international roles of the pound sterling in the nineteenth century and the dollar in the twentieth. Some recent research, such as the excellent book on the Bank of Amsterdam and the Dutch guilder by Steven Quinn and William Roberds, seeks to push the historical frontier back a century or more. In this volume, wisely or not, I attempt to recount the entire history of international currencies—the cross-border use of coins, notes, and other monetary claims—from the Lydians of ancient Anatolia, who are credited with inventing coinage in the seventh century BCE, all the way up to the cryptocurrencies of today and central bank digital currencies of tomorrow. To be clear, this book is not another history of currency and coin. It is not another history of money. It focuses squarely on cross-border use, on the use of currency, coin, and bank money in international transactions involving parties residing outside the borders of the issuing state, nation, or kingdom.

In practice this means the international use of national currencies. National governments generally reserve for themselves control of the money printing press and, before that, the mint.[1] It follows that there is a tension between the national origin of money, whose management is under the authority of a government that privileges the interests of that same nation, and the existence of an integrated global economy, whose operation rests on international monetary foundations.

Today the national currency that ranks first among equals is, of course, the U.S. dollar. The dollar is widely used in international transactions. Indeed, it is prominently used in commercial and financial transactions not just between Americans and foreigners but also among foreigners themselves—that is, among parties none of whom reside in the United States and whose transactions do not touch American shores. The dollar is used around the world. It is the financial grease in the wheels of twenty-first century globalization. But this very fact creates a tension between U.S. monetary and financial policies, which seek to advance America's national interests, and the dependence of other countries on the international financial services provided by the U.S. dollar.

Recent events place these cross currents in bold relief. U.S. sanctions on Russia following that country's 2022 attack on Ukraine made full use of the leverage America possessed because of the dollar's international role. By freezing the foreign reserves of the Bank of Russia and locking Russia out of the U.S. banking system, those sanctions exploited Moscow's dependence on the dollar and U.S. banks. At the same time, this episode triggered a global rethink of dollar dependence. Other countries contemplating even the remote possibility that they might end up not being on the best terms with the United States considered steps to avoid being in Russia's position. Their unease deepened in 2024, when Donald Trump, in his campaign for the presidency, floated the idea of unilaterally depreciating the dollar with the goal of enhancing U.S. export competitiveness. It rose still further in 2025, when Trump, as sitting president, warned the BRICS countries against attempting to develop their own currency as a substitute for the global dollar, threatening them with 100 percent tariffs if they dared take steps in this direction. In April 2025 Trump then unfurled double- and triple-digit "Liberation Day" tariffs that looked to decouple the U.S. from the global economy and unmoor the dollar from the international system. These events put on clear display the tension between the dollar's de jure status as America's currency and its de facto dominance of international financial markets.

This book is about this tension between national currencies and the international economy and how it has played out over time. The issues are long-standing. They were evident in the nineteenth century, when successive French and German governments sought to reduce their dependence on the London money market and the pound sterling by promoting Paris, Hamburg, and Berlin as international financial centers. They were apparent in the twentieth century, when the U.S. Congress created the Federal Reserve System in no small part as a way of fostering international use of the dollar. These historical comparisons may be informative as much for laying bare the differences between past and present as they are for suggesting parallels. Either way, however, it is my contention that looking back at the long sweep of history can help us anticipate what comes next.

International currency status rests on the strength and extent of the issuing country's commercial and financial links with the rest of the world: how much it imports and exports; how much it borrows and lends. It depends on the stability of its financial institutions and the liquidity of its financial markets. But that status also has political preconditions. International currencies are those of states where there exists a separation of powers and rule of law, deterring opportunistic behavior by the issuer while ensuring that creditors have voice. International currency status depends on the issuer's ability to forge durable geopolitical alliances. Central banks and governments hold and use the currencies of their alliance partners. Doing so is a gesture of goodwill. Alliance partners are seen as dependable stewards of a country's foreign balances. The government at the head of the alliance can exert geopolitical leverage for its partners to use its currency. But President Trump's tariffs and disparagement of America's alliance partners raise questions about the durability of America's international economic and financial links. Challenges to rule of law at home and U.S. alliances abroad raise questions about the political foundations of dollar dominance. These factors have prompted foreign holders of dollars to reconsider their reliance on the currency, which in turn creates questions about its dominant international position.

International currency status is not forever. To the contrary, history suggests that international currencies display something of a lifecycle. Initially, international use of a currency has convenience value for merchants and bankers of the issuing country. It eases exporting and lending, since sales and loans will be denominated in a currency familiar to those merchants and bankers, who are then relieved of the need to manage the risk that the exchange rate will move against them. The safe-haven characteristic of an international currency also works to stabilize the issuer's financial markets, since investors rush into that currency and those markets, rather than rushing out, when the global economy experiences a negative shock. These factors are positives for the issuing economy, for the growth of its cross-border transactions, and not least for international use of its currency. They reinforce the currency's dominant international position.

But international use is an additional source of demand for that currency, elevating its value on the foreign exchange market. A more expensive currency creates headwinds for exporters and lenders. That the issuer has well-developed financial markets and serves as an international financial center may encourage it to specialize, sometimes excessively, in financial transactions, at the expense of the industrial and commercial activities that are the fundamental sources of economic and military prowess. The same capacity to project economic and military leverage that makes for widespread international use of a currency can encourage foreign adventures, absorbing resources that are more productively devoted to local uses. At some point, the cost of such foreign adventures can endanger the stability of the currency itself. Erosion of the issuer's economic and geopolitical preeminence may then be followed by erosion of its monetary and financial preeminence. Some of Trump's advisors suggest that the U.S. is on the downside of this monetary cycle, where the costs to the United States of the dollar's international role exceed the benefits.[2]

But there is nothing inevitable about the downswing of the cycle. Innovation and productivity growth can more than offset any headwinds to exports from a strong exchange rate. Excessive financialization can be avoided by prudent financial regulation. The temptation to engage in foreign adventures and tendency to fall prey to damaging foreign entanglements can be resisted through the pursuit of a coherent foreign policy. International currency status is akin to an endowment of natural resource wealth. It can be managed well, in which case it is an asset for current and future generations, or it can be managed poorly, in which case it becomes a curse. It can be managed like either Norway's natural gas or Venezuela's oil, in other words.

How the U.S. manages its monetary inheritance we are about to see.

1

Introduction

IT WAS NOT RICHARD NIXON's most memorable address. That honor goes to his 1952 "Checkers" speech, when the vice-presidential nominee defended himself against accusations of financial misconduct but steadfastly refused to return one gift, the family dog Checkers. Or else it goes to the 1974 Oval Office peroration in which he announced he was resigning the presidency. But Nixon's speech to the nation on the evening of August 15, 1971, outlining "a new economic policy" was his most economically consequential. Glancing down at a sheaf of papers, his tie slightly askew, the president announced a grab bag of policies to stimulate spending and counter unemployment. These included a 10 percent tax credit for investment in equipment and machinery, repeal of a 7 percent excise on new cars, and acceleration by a year of the increase in personal tax exemptions scheduled for January 1, 1973. This was the sort of thing Americans had come to expect of an incumbent president, or at least of this incumbent president, eager to look good in the face of a general election.

But the next set of policies Nixon unveiled that evening was more startling. The president went on to lay out an array of wage and price controls across the economy. By executive order, Nixon immediately froze in place the prices American retailers posted for consumers, the rents landlords charged tenants, and the wages employers paid workers. The goal was to break the back of inflation, as Nixon put it. "The time has come," he declared, "for decisive action—action that will break the vicious circle of spiraling prices and costs."[1]

This price freeze was shocking. These were the first wage and price controls the United States had seen since the Korean War. That fact sat uneasily with the president's assertion, in the same speech, that he aimed to wind down the conflict in Vietnam. And they were a reversal of Nixon's earlier opposition to a provision in the Defense Production Act of 1970, which gave the president temporary power to combat inflation by freezing wages and prices.[2] Both the White House and Republicans in Congress had understood this effort to give the president authority over wages and prices as a political gambit by the Democrats: aware of the administration's reluctance to interfere in the operation of the economy, Democrats could then blame inflation on the president's failure to act.

Thus, Nixon's announcement represented a dramatic about-face. Not only that: It made a sharp break with both Republican orthodoxy and American ideology. Within months, this unprecedented peacetime government intervention in the operation of the economy gave birth to the Libertarian Party. The policies horrified free-market-oriented economists, who filled airwaves and publications with predictions of widespread resource misallocation and shortages of consumer goods.

Those warnings were not unfounded. With controls coming into force in midsummer, gasoline prices were frozen at seasonal highs, heating-oil prices at off-season lows. Refineries responded by shifting their mix of production, leading to fears of winter shortages of the oil people used to heat their homes. Food production saw similar distortions. Because fresh fruit and vegetables were exempt from Nixon's controls, but processed foods were not, General Foods halted production of frozen foods and focused on higher-profit product lines. Supermarket freezer cabinets soon stood empty.

Further, with the price of dressed meat now strictly controlled but the prices of live animals still unfrozen, meatpackers predictably declined to buy at uncontrolled prices what they could only sell at controlled prices. Cattle, rather than being slaughtered and dressed, were left to fatten on the farm. The problem was compounded, as such problems are, by a mysterious decline in the population of anchovies off the coast of Peru.[3] American cattlemen relied on anchovies as a much needed source of animal feed. Once the little fish became more expensive, so did live cattle, intensifying the squeeze on the meatpacking industry. Then as meat at the supermarket grew scarce, hijackers began targeting meat trucks, presumably to sell their contents on the black market. Ranchers in Utah complained of cattle rustling. Canadian packers started buying cattle in the United States, dressing it in Canada, and shipping it back to the American market, since the price freeze did not apply to imported beef.

What is most striking about Nixon's extraordinary departure in U.S. economic policy, with its wide range of untoward consequences, is that it was hardly a justified response to runaway inflation. Consumer price inflation was only running at a moderate 4 percent annual rate at the time of his speech—and it was actually edging lower relative to prior years.

The real explanation for the president's unprecedented resort to wage and price controls was different. In fact, it lay in a crisis of the U.S. dollar—and specifically in a looming threat to the currency's international status. The dollar was being unjustifiably attacked, as Nixon put it in his August 15 speech, by "international money speculators," causing its stability against other national currencies to teeter. Foreign governments, he complained, were heaping gratuitous pressure on the currency, as they rushed to exchange their greenbacks for the U.S. government's dwindling stock of gold.

In addition to imposing price controls, Nixon responded with another drastic move: he suspended the conversion of dollars into gold, a policy that had formed the linchpin of the currency's special status all the way back to 1934, when the United States fixed the dollar price of gold at $35 an ounce. This step would allow the greenback to fall on the foreign exchange market, as needed to enhance the competitiveness of U.S. exports. Wage and price controls were therefore designed to reassure American households—also voters—that depreciation would not erode the value of their dollars by increasing the cost of living. Controls also served as a useful distraction from these more far-reaching measures: suspension of the dollar's convertibility into gold, a steep drop in its value on foreign exchange markets, and a potential end to its singular international status, which together would launch the United States and the global economy into the great unknown.[4]

Not Finished Yet

Not a few observers concluded that the "Nixon Shock," the label history attaches to the president's August 15, 1971 measures, had brought the age of dollar dominance to an unhappy end. The fixed link to gold, a feature that only the dollar had enjoyed since World War II, was now consigned to the dustbin of history, as it were. No longer would the U.S. authorities make gold available to all comers, or even to the governments and central banks of friendly countries. Central banks naïve enough to hold the dollar had suffered major financial losses as a result of its devaluation. No sooner did the U.S. Treasury negotiate a second set of currency values than the dollar had to be devalued a second time, in March 1973, a second devaluation that loosed a rip-roaring inflation. A currency that had once been a beacon of stability now looked more like an engine of instability. No less an authority than the eminent economist and international monetary historian Charles Kindleberger, who had been studying these issues since the 1930s, wrote decisively in the wake of these events that the dollar was "finished" as an international currency.[5]

Hindsight tells us that they could not have been more wrong: today, more than half a century later, a majority of global exports and imports continue to be invoiced and settled in dollars. More than half of global GDP—not counting the GDP of the United States itself—is produced by countries whose currencies remain linked, in one way or another, to the dollar.[6] The dollar remains the dominant currency in international banking: the lion's share of foreign bank loans and deposits are denominated in dollars. The dollar is involved in 90 percent of foreign exchange transactions worldwide. More than half the foreign currency reserves of central banks and governments are held as dollar-denominated securities and deposits.[7]

How can we explain this state of affairs despite the Nixon shock and the trials and tribulations that followed in its wake? The dollar's ubiquity today reflects the fact that the United States remains the largest economy in the world, as it has been for more than a century. The market in U.S. Treasury bonds is the single largest and most liquid security market in the world, and it is freely open to foreign investors. Moreover, the dollar's prevalence feeds on itself. The very fact that so many importers, exporters, and investors use dollars when conducting international business makes it the go-to currency for anyone engaged in cross-border transactions.

The dollar's prevailing status as the dominant international currency confers considerable advantages on the United States. U.S. banks and firms enjoy the convenience of transacting in their native currency. Given the captive demand for U.S. Treasury securities by central banks, private financial institutions, and corporate treasuries around the world, the U.S. government can borrow at favorable interest rates. These advantages extend to foreign relations and influence. Because such a large share of foreign savings is held in dollars and so many international transactions go through the U.S. banking system, the United States possesses a formidable financial weapon. In an economic or geopolitical dispute, it can freeze the foreign dollar balances of governments, firms, and oligarchs. It can garnish their assets. By barring individuals, companies, and entire countries from transacting through the U.S. banks that are the repositories of those assets, the United States can effectively prevent those it sanctions from engaging in cross-border business of all kinds. This is what is meant by what has been referred to for more than half a century as America's "exorbitant privilege"—that the United States gains an upper hand in many ways from the fact that its currency is so widely used internationally.[8]

But for these very same reasons, dollar dependence is not an entirely happy situation for other countries. For instance, governments typically earn less on U.S. Treasury bonds than they pay when issuing their own debt securities, the low interest rate paid by the U.S. reflecting the dollar's safe-haven status. But safe-haven status is not immutable. Although the dollar has a long record as a safe-haven currency, questions are increasingly asked about the sustainability of the U.S. government's ballooning debt and, therefore, about whether the value of U.S. Treasury securities could come into jeopardy. Further, an American administration preoccupied by U.S. export competitiveness, or seeking to enhance the country's industrial self-sufficiency, could take additional steps to depress the dollar exchange rate, in the manner of Nixon, and thus erode the value of balances held abroad by foreign governments. If it continues to see other countries as rivals rather than allies, it could take more frequent recourse to sanctions, exploiting the dependence of those other countries on the dollar and exposing their financial and political vulnerability. At this point, those other countries would no longer regard the dollar as safe.

These issues are not new. Finance ministers voiced similar concerns in 1971, but President Nixon's Treasury secretary, John Connally, was unrepenting. He encapsulated their dilemma with typical Texas bravado, bluntly observing that "it's our currency but your problem."[9]

TINA (There Is No Alternative)

Connally could adopt this arrogant tone because at that time there existed no alternative to the dollar for undertaking international transactions. The situation is different today. Potential rivals to the dollar are making headway. One is the Chinese renminbi, the currency of an economy that has overtaken the United States as leading exporter and, for some countries, leading foreign investor. The day is not far away when the renminbi could circulate alongside the dollar, offering another full-fledged set of payment rails. Another potential alternative is the euro, the closest thing to a supranational currency circulating today. Yet another is a network of digital currencies—officially-sanctioned cryptocurrencies, if you will—issued by emerging-market central banks and traded on a dedicated digital platform, obviating the need to go through the dollar and U.S. banking system at all.

Actual and conceivable alternatives are not the same, though. Impediments to a real changing of the guard remain. China's financial markets are not fully open to the rest of the world. Western governments and central banks are reluctant, too, to rely on the currency of a geopolitical rival. Even nonaligned countries are of two minds about falling into China's monetary camp.[10] The euro, in its turn, punches below its weight, the euro area still lacking an integrated capital market, or "capital markets union" in eurospeak, akin to that of the United States. Some may look to a digital future, when technologists succeed in engineering a set of interoperable central bank digital currencies that can be conveniently used in cross-border transactions. But whether governments and central banks can agree on oversight and regulation of a common digital platform is another, eminently political, matter.

There are reasons to think, moreover, that reports of the dollar's demise are greatly exaggerated, so to speak. Prophecies and pronouncements of the greenback's loss of international currency status, as discussed earlier, trace back at least to Connally's day and the collapse of the Bretton Woods international monetary system following the Nixon shock. Much to the surprise of contemporaries, no discernible flight from the dollar followed that earthquake, despite the shock that reverberated from the end of the dollar's longstanding peg to gold. Thus, none of the pronouncements about the end of dollar dominance made after Nixon's measures proved true. In our fraught current environment, worries about the sustainability of U.S. debt, the polarization of U.S. politics, and weaponization of the dollar have similarly provoked angst, and talk of dollar alternatives, but little has yet changed in actual practice.

For good reason. America has outperformed other advanced countries economically. It is a leader in the development of artificial intelligence and related digital technology. The U.S. defense establishment may be challenged, but it is still preeminent in its ability to project strategic and military power. All of these elements continue to bolster the dollar's status as the dominant international currency.

How long will these advantages last? Will a rising competitor, such as China's renminbi, finally gain parity or even ascendancy over the traditionally resilient U.S. dollar? And could economic decline or disaster lead to a collapse from which the dollar does not recover? These are open—and frequently asked—questions.

One way of attempting to answer them is by tracing the arc of earlier international currencies. There have been international currencies—defined as monetary units used in transactions beyond the borders of the issuing kingdom, state, or nation—for as long as there have been currencies. Prominent ancient examples include the "owls "of Athens, named after the owl image stamped upon them, which circulated in other Greek city-states already by the fifth century BCE. Silver coins minted by Alexander the Great circulated north of the Danube and east of the Levant (present-day Syria and environs). Coins minted by Julius Caesar and subsequent Roman emperors have been found in India, Sri Lanka, and China.[11] From the fourth century CE, traders used the solidus, the gold coin of the Byzantine Empire, everywhere from Britain to South Asia. In the thirteenth century, the florin, the currency of a financially and commercially precocious Florentine city-state, circulated over a vast area stretching from England and France in the West to the Levant in the East—not just as a vehicle for trade but also as an instrument for undertaking financial transactions. Spanish pieces of eight, coined from abundant New World silver, then became the first truly global currency. Traders used Spanish silver coin in transactions everywhere from the Dutch East Indies and the Ottoman Empire to the newly independent United States, where they remained legal tender into the 1850s. They served as the primary vehicle for China's foreign trade for fully four centuries.

In the seventeenth and eighteenth centuries, the Dutch took currency internationalization up a notch. They created a pure fiat currency—as distinct from bank money one could convert into a precious metal—backed by the Bank of Amsterdam, a proto-central bank. Credits drawn on Amsterdam and denominated in Dutch guilders financed trade throughout Western Europe and beyond.[12] When merchants in London and St. Petersburg did business with one another, they first converted their local currencies into guilders, before converting guilders into the target currency, just as traders today, when making foreign exchange transactions, go through the dollar. Following the French and Napoleonic Wars, London overtook Amsterdam as the leading international financial center, and the pound sterling supplanted the guilder. In the nineteenth century, sterling was used to finance and settle a majority of the world's trade and two-thirds of its foreign and overseas investment transactions. Sterling remained a leading international currency well into the twentieth century, permanently ceding its place to the dollar only after 1945.

Strong States

What common threads do these international currencies share, and how do they grow and maintain their influence in the course of their lifecycle?

At the most basic level, currencies commanding widespread international use must hold their value. That means they must be issued by strong states, able to reliably raise resources necessary for their basic needs without resorting to debasement or inflation. The weight and silver content of Athens's owls remained essentially unchanged for centuries. The Byzantine solidus circulated at the same gold content for seven hundred years. The value of Florence's gold coin did not fluctuate for more than three centuries. Spanish silver coin held its value for going on four centuries. The British pound sterling was synonymous with the gold standard, which guaranteed its value, for much of the eighteenth and nineteenth centuries. On rare occasions when exigent circumstances forced Britain to suspend gold convertibility, the country restored it subsequently at the previous gold parity, affirming that guarantee.

Political structures underpinned this steady value: these earlier international currencies, more often than not, were the currencies of political democracies and republics. Individuals with strong interest in preserving the value of the monetary unit were represented in the senate, parliament, or other representative body. This was true of the United States in the twentieth century, but also Britain in the nineteenth, Holland in the eighteenth, and Florence in the fourteenth. In Florence, the Popolani—a coalition of merchants, bankers, and entrepreneurs—seized control of the communal government from the nobility in 1250, a date that immediately preceded the issuance of the gold florin that then came into widespread international circulation. In ancient Rome, pressure to establish the denarius system came from the Senate, where property holders were well represented. That same Senate oversaw minting and emission once the system came into full operation.[13] In ancient Athens, the coinage of a stable unit with widespread circulation coincided with the advent of democracy. These deliberative bodies applied checks and balances, limiting arbitrary action by an emperor, king, prime minister, or chief executive that might have compromised investor rights and eroded the safe-asset status of the currency.

In the modern era, this division of powers has been extended to the central bank, which serves as steward of the currency. It enjoys autonomy from politics. This has been true not only of the U.S. Federal Reserve System in the twentieth and twenty-first centuries but, de facto, of the Bank of England in the nineteenth century and the Bank of Amsterdam in the eighteenth. Before the advent of the central bank, as in early modern Florence, autonomous institutions with an interest in preserving the stability of the currency, such as Arte del Cambio, the guild of money changers, exercised political and social sway and played a similar stability-preserving role.[14]

Another distinguishing feature of strong states that issue an international currency is the administrative capacity to coin money and print notes at a high level of uniformity, inspiring confidence in users.[15] In Roman times, only Rome itself was empowered to mint gold and silver coin.[16] The Roman authorities controlled each stage, from mining the precious metals to minting the coins. Later governments took similar pains to protect the integrity of their production. When the Spanish Crown uncovered a scandal at the royal mint at Potosí, in present-day Bolivia, it wrested direct control of mint operations to prevent unscrupulous mint masters from minting subpar coin again. When Dutch traders complained of a proliferation of depreciated gold and silver coins, Amsterdam's civic leaders established a public bank to assay those coins and replace them with uniform bank money.

A similar concept applies in the twentieth and twenty-first centuries when money is held in the form of bank deposits, bills, and bonds, rather than currency and coin. As before, international currencies are the currencies of states with the administrative and regulatory capacity to ensure the stability of their banking and financial systems. Where such capacity is lacking and financial crises result, as in the United States in the 1930s, merchants and investors will conclude that the country's banking system is no longer a safe repository for their funds or a reliable source of credit. The international role of its currency will be imperiled.

Finally, international currencies are those of states with the fiscal and military capacity to defend their borders and institutions, including their monetary institutions. Where the state possesses this capacity, its currency is secure. Market participants regard it as a "safe asset," that is, as a reliable store of value.[17] International adoption of that currency is further encouraged when this military power uses its strategic capacity to defend its allies. Countries hold as reserves and use in international transactions the currencies of their alliance partners, not their rivals, as demonstrated throughout history.[18] Before World War I, members of the Triple Alliance (Germany, Austria-Hungary, and Italy) and the Triple Entente (Britain, France, and Russia) each disproportionately held as reserves the currencies of their alliance partners. In the 1960s, West Germany and Japan held and used dollars, rather than converting them into gold as they could legally under the Bretton Woods system. They did so because they valued the presence of American troops on their territory and, more generally, the security umbrella the United States provided. They feared that such conversions would hasten the withdrawal of those troops. In the 1970s, despite the collapse of the dollar's peg to gold, Saudi Arabia agreed to invest its export earnings in U.S. Treasury bonds because of the value it attached to U.S. military protection.[19] Today, South Korea and Japan hold a larger share of their foreign reserves in dollars than their economic characteristics and trade and investment links with the United States would lead one to expect, specifically because they regard the United States as a reliable political partner and value its security guarantee.

Other forms of this idea have also played out, of course. Military forces that subdue and annex foreign lands can expand the reach of a currency directly, when the metropole mandates use of its currency by a dependency, as is not infrequently the case.[20] Foreign legions and military bases also aid the international diffusion of the currency, since it is used to pay soldiers, who then use it to procure local goods and services. "Alexanders," the coins of Alexander the Great, entered circulation via the pay packets of his infantrymen campaigning abroad. Roman legions stationed from Campania to the British Isles were paid in full-bodied Roman silver coin.[21] American soldiers stationed in Europe after World War II were paid in dollars that were sought after by residents who doubted the stability of local currencies, especially those of defeated powers.

Yet even when the victorious power does not maintain troops abroad, the perceived safety of its currency is often enough to encourage foreigners to hold and use it. In turn, this captive demand allows the dominant power to fund its military at lower cost. In the 1960s, the U.S. could maintain troop deployments in West Germany and Japan partly because their governments were willing to accumulate dollars and committed to not converting them into gold, as noted. If its allies wavered, Washington could threaten to withdraw those boots on the ground. At present, many are questioning whether China's growing military and geopolitical sway will encourage other countries to hold and use its currency, and whether this will further strengthen China's geostrategic position. History does point to this possibility, thought there is no guarantee. This is because imperial reach can shade into imperial overreach—when a military becomes overcommitted to territorial expansion, it can strain a state's fiscal resources, impelling desperate authorities to debase the currency.

More generally, victory and defeat on the battlefield, and the financial stress associated with war, have more than once precipitated a changing of the international monetary guard. The French occupation of Amsterdam in 1795, juxtaposed against Britain's security as an island, hastened the transition from the Dutch guilder to the pound sterling—not least by encouraging continental financiers to evacuate to the safety of London. Yields on risky Dutch government bonds rose above those on safe British government securities and remained elevated, relative to that London benchmark, for more than a century thereafter. Defeat in World War I ended any aspirations Germany had of establishing the mark as a leading international currency. And the burdens of two world wars, by weakening Britain's financial position, drove the transition to the dollar.

From Trade to Finance

The appeal of an international currency relies not only on the efforts of the state, of course, but also on the forces of the market. Typically, the process starts when trade expands and merchants embrace a preferred currency to use in commercial transactions.[22] Once importers and exporters grow accustomed to taking and making payment in that currency, and find themselves holding balances in it, they look to put those idle funds to work. Financial transactions begin to supplement commercial transactions, as merchants who previously specialized in trade expand to provide short-term credit to firms needing working capital and, eventually, long-term loans to corporate, sovereign, and other borrowers.

There is a logic for why the commercial role of an international currency—its function in buying and selling of merchandise and commodities—comes first. All cross-border transactions carry an element of risk. But import and export transactions have the advantage that they can be settled on the spot (more or less). Borrowing and repayment, in contrast, necessarily take place over time, sometimes long periods of time. In trade, payment is made for merchandise when it is delivered. In financial transactions, there is only the borrower's promise to pay in the future when the loan comes due. A king who needed a loan might have assigned the revenues of his salt monopoly or other income to service the loan. But no higher power could prevent him from reneging on his promise and revoking the assignment of those revenues—only his desire to maintain his good reputation and access to more credit.[23]

More generally, in lending it is important to know the character of the borrower, information one can gain either through experience or from a trusted intermediary. Thus, merchants began lending across borders only when they acquired agents abroad to act as intermediaries. Those agents sourced raw materials and marketed goods, and then, based on this experience, evaluated the creditworthiness of these counterparties. Investors purchased financial claims from foreign borrowers only once these were attested to by reputable merchant banks experienced in the business. In other words, merchant bankers started out as merchants, and became bankers over time. They built on deep knowledge acquired through trade to branch into finance.

This sequence was followed in Florence starting in the fourteenth century, for example, when certain successful merchants, such as the Medici, become extravagantly wealthy. Florentine merchants importing unfinished wool from Northern Europe first convinced their suppliers to take payment in florins. With their accumulated stores of currency, they then moved into providing florin credits to foreign suppliers needing working capital, employing agents to evaluate the creditworthiness of potential borrowers. From there, they began to extend long-term loans to English and French kings. Six centuries later, the United States followed a similar sequence when authorities sought to foster international use of the dollar by creating the Federal Reserve System. The new central bank first promoted the dollar as a vehicle for settling merchandise transactions and providing trade credit to exporters and importers. It did so by making a market in dollar trade acceptances—credit instruments bought and sold by American banks to finance and settle U.S. trade. From there, those same banks, having opened foreign branches, moved into providing dollar credits to finance trade that never touched American shores. Finally, they provided dollar loans to foreign governments, banks, and corporations.

Today, this strategy is again being followed by Beijing, as Chinese policymakers seek to support international use of the renminbi. Chinese exporters and importers are being asked to first use the currency in their own trade-related settlements. As the renminbi gains ground in trade invoicing and settlements, many anticipate that the currency will be also used in cross-border financial transactions, even though Chinese capital markets are not fully open to the rest of the world.

It follows that the more a country trades with the rest of the world, the more likely its currency is to enter international use. Thus, the Athenian tetradrachm became the leading coin of the Eastern Mediterranean because Athens was a leading trader and its port, Piraeus, was a leading entrepôt center. Fast forward two millennia: sterling circa 1780 was poised to supplant the guilder as the leading international currency because London had already surpassed Amsterdam as the leading entrepôt center. In the second half of the twentieth century, the dollar was poised to replace sterling as the leading international currency because U.S. exports exceeded British exports, first modestly at the time of World War I, and then dramatically in later years.

The connections between international trade and international currency use, obviously, cut both ways. More exports encourage more international use of the exporter's currency. Equally, however, steps enabling more international use of a currency encourage more exports. In the seventeenth century, the Dutch minted large-value coins tailored to the needs of their export markets to facilitate merchandise exports and imports. Efforts by the early Federal Reserve to create a market in dollar trade acceptances were taken in response to complaints by U.S. exporters that they were handicapped by their reliance on credit sourced in London and denominated in sterling. Benefiting from the Fed's efforts, U.S. exports received a visible boost.

Innovation and Infrastructure

Trade acceptances were a financial innovation. Analogous instruments had not existed in the United States before. This points to the more general role of financial innovation in the development and diffusion of international currencies. An example is the bill of exchange. Arab merchants employed a primitive version of these promissory notes for settling accounts already in the eighth century CE, though its use at that time was confined to personal networks, limiting international credit flows. The Florentines and other Northern Italian merchants, making contact with the Levant, popularized the bill starting in the thirteenth century. Mirroring prior practice in the Middle East, early bills were simple written instructions for payment in a foreign place at a future time by an overseas branch of the merchant house originating the transaction.

But with the growth of trade, European merchants began drawing and paying bills on merchant houses with which they had no personal connection, in places where they did not possess a branch. Repeat business encouraged them to make good on their promises. When another house added its signature, or endorsement, to the bill—a practice first prevalent in sixteenth-century Italy and then when juridical authorities in Amsterdam, Antwerp, and elsewhere determined that legal protections enjoyed by the initial creditor could be transferred to a new bearer—bills became negotiable. They were bought and sold in impersonal markets by individuals lacking social or familial connections.[24] Simple promissory notes—written promises to pay a stated sum to a specified person—were thereby transformed into standardized orders to pay the bearer, whomever they may be. The locations pioneering these negotiable instruments, Florence, Antwerp, and Amsterdam, saw increased international use of their currencies. Channels for extending international credit denominated first in Florentine florins and then Dutch guilders expanded accordingly.

But these new instruments flourished, providing free-flowing international credit, only with the support of well-developed market infrastructure. The bill of exchange on London, a negotiable promissory note denominated in sterling, became the dominant financial instrument for international transactions only once the city had three key features in place: acceptance houses to attach their names and guarantees to high-quality bills of exchange, specialized brokers to buy bills from banks with excess inventory and place them with banks that had idle funds, and a central bank to backstop the market by purchasing bills when merchant banks collectively sought to offload them and no one else stood ready to buy. Although the Federal Reserve and the American Acceptance Council developed an analogous dollar-denominated financial instrument after 1914, the United States lacked a comparable ecosystem of bill brokers and acceptance houses. When the acceptance market melted down and the Fed abandoned it in the 1930s, the United States no longer possessed a market maker and liquidity provider of last resort. Hence the new instrument failed to take off. The dollar's challenge to the pound sterling was deferred.

Today, we see China similarly attempting to develop the market infrastructure needed to foster international use of its currency. It has designated one of its four big banks to function as official renminbi clearing bank for each global financial center, extended renminbi-denominated currency swaps and credits to foreign central banks, and built out the Cross-Border Interbank Payment System known as CIPS to facilitate payments. Time will tell whether this challenge to the greenback is successful, or whether dollar dominance lives to see another day.

The contrast between the Bank of England's commitment to backstop the market in the nineteenth century and the Fed's less-than-stellar support in the Depression of the 1930s underscores the importance, for the viability of any international currency, of not just a market but, specifically, a liquid market. Banks, firms, and governments gravitate toward a currency when it is easy to buy, sell, hold, and use. They favor it when the costs of buying, selling, and using it are predictably low.

Market liquidity in this sense depends on the presence of a diverse population of investors, who will not all seek to buy or sell the currency at the same time, as much as on efficient institutions to bring them together. The Dutch market displayed unmatched liquidity toward the end of the seventeenth century, when the Bank of Amsterdam began providing receipts for its customers' deposits of gold and silver. Customers could then use those receipts to purchase bills of exchange once reputable merchant bankers added their signatures to their clients' bills, guaranteeing payment. In the nineteenth century, the London money market exhibited unprecedented liquidity because of the large volume of sterling bills traded there, the presence of a diverse population of domestic and foreign banks, and the infrastructure provided by the Stock Exchange, discount and acceptance houses, and the Bank of England. The market in U.S. Treasury bills enjoys its reputation for liquidity for analogous reasons.[25]

This focus on market liquidity highlights the fact that countries that are home to international financial centers have a leg up in fostering international use of their currencies. In Florence, the Bardi, Peruzzi, and other great merchant bankers were able to attract deposits from abroad and put them to work internationally, practices that are the hallmarks of an international financial center. This resulted in greater capitalization and turnover and a more diverse investor base, key constituents of market liquidity. London was the leading nineteenth-century financial center by virtue of its ability to attract and place money abroad, where both the foreign deposits it attracted and foreign loans it extended were naturally denominated in sterling. After World War II, New York was the unrivaled financial capital of the world, the United States being the only country with open capital markets offering free access to foreign investors. When Middle East oil exporters found themselves receiving windfall profits following the 1973 Organization of Arab Petroleum Exporting Countries (OAPEC) shock, they deposited their receipts in New York and accumulated dollar reserves, overcoming reservations about U.S. foreign policy. This wrongfooted those who predicted that the end of Bretton Woods would spell the end of dollar dominance.

To be sure, oil exporters also held dollars in London, where an offshore market in dollar deposits developed in reaction against restrictive U.S. bank regulation and objections to U.S. foreign policy. Ironically, however, this unbundling of the financial center, London, from the national identity of the currency traded there, the dollar, worked to the advantage of the incumbent international currency. It created another venue, free of restrictive regulation and objectionable foreign policies, where dollars could be freely held and traded.

Downside Risk

Much as history sheds light on the rise and persistence of international currencies, it helps to explain their fall. Typically, loss of international currency status is preceded by loss of economic and strategic preeminence. The wool cloth producers of sixteenth-century Florence found themselves unable to keep pace with more dynamic Dutch and English competitors, and the city-state could no longer repel larger territorial entities on the battlefield. Both factors spelled trouble for the florin. The Dutch fishing, processing, and cloth industries experienced mounting competitive difficulties in the late seventeenth and eighteenth centuries, while the taxes needed to support an expensive military establishment grew increasingly burdensome and debilitating. A financial crisis in 1791 and a military defeat in 1795 then brought the guilder's international reign to an end. Late-nineteenth-century Britain lost economic ground to the United States and other late-industrializing economies, and two world wars saddled the country with crushing debts, rendering sterling a "zombie international currency."[26]

Widespread international use of a national currency may itself be a factor in economic and geopolitical decline. The development of liquid markets and the ascendancy of finance can draw savers to speculation in financial assets, to the neglect of practical investments in manufacturing and trade, accelerating an economy's commercial decline. The market liquidity that attracts and benefits from the presence of foreign investors is part of what makes financial investments attractive, more attractive even than investments in productive capacity. Additional demand for a country's liabilities as a form of reserves and means of payment can cause its currency to become overvalued, making it more challenging for merchandise exporters. Bankers and others who benefit from a currency's international status resist a devaluation that might slow the erosion of industrial competitiveness. In this way, international currency status may contain the seeds of its own destruction.

At the same time, these cases highlight the remarkable persistence, once acquired, of international currency status. Downfalls do not always occur right away, even once economic warning bells begin to ring. Florence's golden age spanned the early fifteenth century, after which its economic difficulties mounted. Despite this, the florin remained in ubiquitous international use for an additional hundred years and more. The Spanish economy went into relative decline in the early seventeenth century, yet Spanish silver coin remained in widespread global circulation for another two hundred years. The economic difficulties of the Netherlands dated to the mid- and late-seventeenth century, as noted, but as late as 1790 the guilder was still the dominant international currency in Europe and beyond. The economic shortcomings of late Victorian and Edwardian Britain were widely discussed already at the time, but sterling remained the world's leading international currency, except for a brief period after World War I, up to 1939. In each case, an installed base of users, together with the interest of stakeholders in preserving the financial status quo, held the incumbent international currency in place, despite other woes of the issuing economy. For that incumbent to give way, moreover, there had to exist a desirable alternative, which was not always the case.

So, what does this mean for the future of the dollar, and where does history suggest it is in its lifecycle? Perhaps this is something on which history can shed light.

PART I

What Came Before

2

Aristotelian Beginnings

A HISTORY of international money presupposes the existence of money. Prehistoric and ancient peoples used a variety of objects from nature, such as cowrie shells and lumps of metal, and manmade items such as knives, axes, and tripods as means of payment, units of account, and stores of value—the three canonical functions of money.[1] In time the need to utilize these in transactions across the borders of states and kingdoms required a degree of standardization. Hence, the development of coinage. Aristotle himself suggested that coins were invented for purposes of international trade: "When the inhabitants of one country became more dependent on those of another, and they imported what they needed, and exported what they had too much of, money necessarily came into use."[2]

Aristotle then went on to elaborate the connections between commerce and coinage, highlighting the intrinsic advantages of the latter:

> The various necessities of life are not easily carried about, and hence men agreed to employ in their dealings with each other something which was intrinsically useful and easily applicable to the purposes of life, for example, iron, silver, and the like. Of this the value was at first measured simply by size and weight, but in process of time they put a stamp upon it, to save the trouble of weighing and to mark the value.

It is hard to imagine a more modern formulation.

Observers down the generations, starting with the poet and philosopher Xenophanes, who lived in the sixth century BCE, ascribed the invention of coinage specifically to the Lydians. These early inhabitants of Anatolia around 650 BCE crafted coins out of electrum, a naturally occurring alloy of gold and silver.[3] Electrum was indigenous to the region—by the seventh century BCE, it was being panned and mined in prodigious amounts, meaning that the metal for minting coins lay readily at hand.

Gold and silver bullion, which is to say, ingots or nuggets of precious metal valued by weight, had long since circulated widely, as Aristotle noted in the passage above. In the language of numismatists, these lumps were weighed out rather than paid out.[4] But this practice posed special problems in the case of electrum, since its ratio of gold to silver varied naturally and could be manipulated by the addition of refined silver to the alloy, diluting its gold content. Assaying, or testing, a lump of electrum by scraping it on a touchstone was costly, since each scrape wore away a trace of precious metal. This method was impractical for bags of many tiny ingots and chips, as a merchant would have to assay each piece individually just to complete a mundane commercial transaction. The move to coinage—stamping the ingot with a seal and establishing a uniform weight—solved these problems by transferring the valuation function from weighing and assaying to the authority of the issuer, an authority grounded in his reputation and testified to by his stamp.

Eventually, the original problem motivating the Lydians's development of coinage dissolved, as metallurgists developed methods for separating electrum into its constituents. This allowed Croesus, the famously wealthy king who reigned over Lydia from 560 to 546 BCE, to produce distinct gold and silver coins, which eventually replaced the earlier electrum issues. But if the original problem was gone, the solution remained. Although precious metal still circulated in ingot or bullion form for use in large-value transactions, gold and silver coin became increasingly prevalent.

Though Croesus subjugated Greek cities in Asia Minor, he made treaties of friendship with Greek Islands, showing the difficulty of annexing lands separated by sea, as Lydia was a land-based power. Contact with the Lydians inspired these islands to mint their own coins, but out of the most abundant metal in Greece, silver. Aegina, Athens, Corinth, and other maritime trading cities followed suit, starting around 550 BCE.

That the practice originated in these Lydian and Greek trading cities suggests commercial motives. Transactions were smoothed by standardized coins whose value was indicated by an official stamp. Coins eliminated the need for a double coincidence of wants. Trading could now happen faster and more easily than before, in a world where merchants had expressed the value of their wares in the number of double-headed axes they commanded or took payment in lumps of bullion.[5]

Adherents to the so-called primitive view of ancient Greece argue that its economy was too backward and economic motives too subordinate to social and political norms to support robust trade.[6] Farmers were self-sufficient. Taxes were paid as a share of the harvest. Urban authorities imported only essentials such as grain and timber to feed, house, and heat city populations. Laws prescribing the use of standard weights and measures were promulgated to quash disputes and preserve harmony in traditional society. Coined money served similar functions. Authorities issued it to support the state, not the economy. It was a vehicle for collecting tribute and paying the army and mercenaries. It was an expression of the state's civic identity and political power. It was a symbol of political sovereignty, not a means to any economic end, by this view.

Coins may be an undeniably powerful symbol of sovereignty, but it is hard to deny the importance of commercial motives, namely the need for a standardized medium of exchange for transactions.[7] Starting in the fourth century BCE, Greek city-states minted fractional silver and small-denomination bronze coins suitable for day-to-day transactions but of little utility for paying taxes or tribute, and of limited use for a state paying wages to soldiers and mercenaries.[8] It is hard to imagine why officials would have bothered with this small change had they not appreciated its commercial convenience.

In practice, Greek coins, especially large denominations, circulated far and wide. Hoards have been found in Egypt, the Levant, Asia Minor, and parts of Mesopotamia not under Greek rule, where residents lacked political motives but were known to trade with the Greeks.[9] Most likely, their presence indicates they were used for trade in pottery and spices, commodities of less official concern than grain and timber, which went unmentioned in official narratives.[10]

City-states minted their own coins and insisted on the exclusive use of those coins within their jurisdictional boundaries. This encouraged individuals who received foreign coins to trade them for the local issue. Widespread adoption of a common weight, the most widely used being the Aegean standard of 12.2 grams of silver, streamlined this process.[11] A common standard allowed one to trade foreign coin for local coin straight up.[12] Still, traders doing business in multiple jurisdictions might be required to hold inventories of different coins. The desire to limit the cost of holding these balances, together with the disproportionate commercial importance of certain states, led merchants to do business in a subset of currencies, the same subset used by other merchants. This subset was what today we call "vehicle currencies."[13]

By the sixth century BCE, reflecting these vehicle-currency effects, the units used most widely included the Cyzicene electrum stater (stater being short for standard coin), the Corinth and Aegean silver staters, and the Attic silver tetradrachm (Attica referring to the larger region where Athens was located, and tetradrachm meaning four drachmas, where the drachma was a smaller silver coin used mainly for local transactions).[14] The electrum stater was used around the Black Sea where Cyzicene traders were active.[15] The Corinth silver stater circulated in Sicily and Southern Italy, where Greeks established colonies, and where the Corinthians, among the leading traders of the day, purchased grain, clothing, cheese, and pigs for local consumption and re-export. Aegina engaged in the slave trade and the transport and sale of staple commodities. Discoveries of its coins in Sicily, Egypt, and northern and southern Asia Minor then come as no surprise.[16]

Toward the Attic Standard

From the early fifth century BCE, other Greek states increasingly prized Athens's silver coins for transactions across borders.[17] Part of the attraction lay in the high quality of Athenian silver, available courtesy of the Laurion mines twenty-five miles south of the city. In addition, the weight, fineness (parts per thousand of precious metal), and even design of Athens's "owls" (the owl being the symbol of Athena, the city's patron goddess of wisdom) remained the same for centuries. The numismatist Colin Kraay argues that Athenian officials left the coin's silver content and design unchanged precisely to encourage its use in far-flung markets.[18]

Moreover, Athens was a vital commercial hub. Its port, Piraeus, ranked as the leading trading center of the Greek lands, overtaking others like Aegina, Lechaion, and Cenchreae.[19] Wheat imports into Athens from Sicily, Cyprus, Thrace, and Egypt were greater, on a per capita basis, than imports into the Netherlands at the peak of that country's Baltic grain trade in 1649—when the Dutch guilder was the leading international currency.[20] Athens's silver coins were the leading domestic export with which it financed, or balanced, its merchandise trade. Athens paid for imported timber, foodstuffs, and slaves by exporting silver coins. The reputation and wide circulation of its coins sometimes even led foreign merchants to accept them at values in excess of their intrinsic metallic content, in a foundational example of the "exorbitant privilege" that accrues to the issuer of an international currency.[21] When other Greek cities minted trade coins, they too adopted the Attic weight and fineness, since this was the standard to which merchants had grown accustomed.

Not least of its strengths, Athens boasted a large and powerful navy. In 478 BCE it established the Delian League, a military alliance of Ionian Greeks. This encouraged its alliance partners to adopt Athenian currency, since it made more sense to rely on the coinage of an ally than a rival who might revoke access, and as a show of good faith. With the coming in 431–401 BCE of the Peloponnesian War, Athens then mandated exclusive use of the tetradrachm by its subjects as a way of marshaling resources for the conflict. This simplified calculation of the tribute those subject states owed, a pressing matter in time of war. It forced the subject states to turn in their native coins, which were then reminted as the Athenian type, Athens charging a fee for the service.

Thus, we see in the adoption of Athens's currency by other Greek states all the classic determinants of international currency status: the economic size and extensive cross-border transactions of the issuer; the stability and reputability of its issue; and the political and military clout needed to influence the decisions of its economic and political partners. In time, Athens's owls were used for financing long-distance trade and related transactions across the eastern Mediterranean, the Near East, and beyond.[22]

Alexander the Great then took things to the next level. On becoming king of Macedonia in 336 BCE, he introduced silver coins based on the earlier Attic standard, but now bearing his effigy.[23] Alexander's territory, and that of his successors, stretched from the unified city-states of Mainland Greece eastward to Anatolia, Persia, Afghanistan, and even portions of India. His "Alexanders," as they came to be known for self-evident reasons, were minted by regional authorities to a high level of uniformity. These entered circulation via the pay packets of infantrymen loyal to Alexander and the kings who succeeded him.[24] Whether Alexander actively suppressed local coinages in Asia Minor and elsewhere, or whether his royal coin came to dominate because consumers and merchants preferred its high quality and uniformity, is uncertain.[25] But there is no uncertainty about that dominance. Alexanders were used not only in his lands and by his subjects but in adjoining territories by other individuals with whom those Greek subjects had contact.

The circulation of Alexanders persisted into the period of the Seleucid Empire, the Greek state that succeeded Alexander's Macedonian Empire in 312 BCE, at the conclusion of the civil wars that followed Alexander's death. Mints issued posthumous Alexanders from Macedonia and the Peloponnese to Cyprus, Egypt, and Cyrene (in modern-day Libya). Minting followed martial rhythms—rising in the run-up to and prosecution of wars—suggesting a principal motivation for coinage and emission. Local authorities, seeking to piggyback on Alexanders's reputation for soundness, minted imitations outside the empire. These were coined north of the Danube, Celtic mercenaries employed by the Macedonian army having introduced the real thing into their native lands, and north of the Black Sea, where they arrived as protection money extorted by local states and strongmen.[26] Fewer coins resembling Alexanders surfaced around the Western Mediterranean, as Greek penetration of the area was lower and fewer mercenaries were drawn from these lands.

Juno Moneta

Once Rome defeated the Seleucids in 190 BCE, Roman gold and silver coins came to be used over an even wider area than the earlier Hellenic owls and Alexanders. Still, it would take a quarter of a millennium for the entire Italian Peninsula to come under Roman rule, and another century for Rome to add Sicily, Corsica, Sardinia, and parts of Spain and North Africa as spoils of its wars with Carthage. The same leisurely pace characterized the spread of the Roman monetary standard. Rome had remained a state without a coinage as late as the third century BCE. No trace of minting activity or even of foreign coin circulating in territory under Roman control before this time has come to light. This does not mean that the Roman economy was non-monetized. From the mid-sixth century BCE, it did have a recognized metallic monetary unit, a pound of bronze, used to track prices and make payments. Aes rude, cast but unworked and unmarked lumps of bronze, functioned as a kind of protocurrency. But, indicative of their rudimentary nature, when pay was introduced for the Roman army in 406 BCE, it was still weighed out rather than paid out. This remained standard practice for the better part of two centuries.[27]

Actual Roman coin had to replace aes rude for Roman money to enter widespread international circulation, reflecting the importance of official seal and certification for international currency status. When coin was adopted widely, the circulating media comprised a mix of Alexanders, introduced into the south of the Italian Peninsula by Greek colonists and traders, and locally minted silver and bronze coins produced according to various standards. The native Roman currency, the denarius, started not as an actual coin but a unit of account—a more convenient unit than weights of bronze in which to express incomes and payments. Even then, Rome calibrated its value as equivalent to a drachma of Attic (ancient Greek) weight, reflecting the continued circulation of Hellenic coin in the south.[28] This backstory highlights that the denarius did not come to circulate so widely because Rome had an early monetary start—quite the contrary. First-mover advantage may help an international currency get a leg up, but it is not everything.

Appearance of the earliest Roman coins, full-bodied silver (where the silver content matched the monetary value) and token bronze (where the face value of the coin exceeded the value of its metallic content), coincided with the republic's expansion into southern Italy. These issues appear to have been for use by Roman quartermasters for obtaining materials in connection with building the Appian Way from Rome to Campania. To boost acceptance, they resembled already circulating Greek coin in weight and value. These issues were one-offs, struck in southern Italy itself.

The first in situ Roman mint was established around 269 BCE in the temple of Juno Moneta on the Capitoline Hill. Legend has it that the Romans had built a temple to Jupiter on the site, which became a secure place to store precious metal. When the Gauls overran Rome in 390 BCE and attempted to seize the hill, they disturbed a flock of geese. The geese's honking alerted the guards, who successfully repelled the invasion. In thanks, the Romans built a shrine to Moneta, the goddess of warning. This tale of warning and protection made the Capitoline a logical place to situate a mint. Juno Moneta continued to feature on minted coins as late as the Middle Ages—and the name of course has given us terms such as money, monetize, and mint, all derived from the Latin.

Initially, this new mint concentrated on issuing aes signatum, six-pound bronze bars with no mark of value but embossed with a symbol indicative of their origin. That symbol was typically a detailed portrait of cattle—a reminder that early Romans considered livestock the standard of value. Numismatists regard aes signatum as transitional units between aes rude, those earlier cast lumps of bronze, and coined money. One-pound bronze coins soon followed, but these were awkward to use in everyday transactions even when cut up into twenty-fourths. Minting remained sporadic until the Punic Wars, starting in 264, when production ramped up. Again, we see here, and throughout history, how war acts as a catalyst for the provision and spread of a currency.

Rome and its allies in this fight for control of Sicily and southern Italy also minted silver to finance their campaign. Booty seized in fighting provided the material for large-scale silver coinage.[29] Circulation of the unit, the didrachm (the name indicating its worth, namely two Greek drachmas—again reflecting the Roman tendency to emulate the Greeks), spread first to the Apennine areas of Italy (mountainous ranges running down the spine of the peninsula), and most fully to the southern Apennines where fighting was intense and Hellenistic coin familiar. Because local communities where Roman-allied troops were stationed bore the responsibility for their maintenance and pay, these communities either acquired Roman-style coin or minted it themselves.

The standard unit, the silver denarius, was finally issued on or around 213 BCE.[30] War once more provided the spark: Rome was now engaged in a fight for survival with Carthage. When Hannibal invaded in 218, he inflicted devastating losses on the Romans. Desperate to provision its troops, Rome debased the didrachm, reducing its weight and purity. The quadrigatus, a lighter coin containing less silver, replaced it.[31] After 213, when Roman troops finally gained the upper hand, officials saw the need for a currency reform if they did not want to lose widespread acceptance of their issuance. Booty derived from battlefield victories again supplied the raw material.[32] The denarius was introduced at a rate and weight of 7 denarii per ounce of silver, 84 per pound. In addition to the denarius, Rome minted half and quarter denarii, three denominations of gold coins, and low-value bronze coins.[33] As in Greece, the effort devoted to providing small-denomination coin indicates an active commercial economy and the state's interest in promoting it.

From Unit of Account to Means of Payment

Still, this proved something of a lackluster start. Early efforts to operate a full bimetallic standard with active circulation of both gold and silver coin appear to have failed. With gold in short supply, Rome abandoned gold coinage for the time being.[34] In the first half of the second century BCE, it produced only coins of common and inexpensive metal, mainly bronze assēs.

But the denarius remained the unit of account, and its coinage revived around the middle of the second century BCE, coincident with the period of Roman expansion. From this point, finally, it began to circulate widely. The denarius was used to denominate and physically settle trade throughout an empire that at its zenith commanded the Mediterranean basin and stretched from Scotland in the northwest to Russia in the northeast, and beyond the borders of the empire proper.[35] The geographical scope of the empire reflected the development of an effective military and administrative bureaucracy, one of the historical prerequisites for international currency status. Conquering and administering more provinces meant receiving more tribute in denarii. Stationing legions and administrators throughout the empire promoted the circulation of Rome's currency when soldiers and bureaucrats were paid in coined money and the army's furnishers received the same.[36] Circulation of the denarius across the length and breadth of the empire, and even beyond the territory Rome formally controlled, attests to the relationship between international currency status on the one hand and the ability of a dominant economic and military power to project commercial and political influence on the other.

To ensure quality, only Rome was now authorized to mint silver and gold coin. Rulers confined lesser authorities to minting bronze subsidiary coin conforming to Roman weights and standards. To ensure adequate supplies, Rome controlled the mining of precious metal to boot. Coinage came officially under the authority of the Senate, which received reports from boards of junior magistrates overseeing the mints. The *tresviri*, as these magistrates were known, regulated the minting and purity of gold and silver coins to minimize fluctuations in their relative value. They limited emission and maintained inventories to regulate the provision of different coins, allowing gold coin, previously scarce, to reenter circulation. Their interventions resembled remarkably the much later operations of a central bank overseeing a bimetallic monetary standard and similarly acting to maintain the circulation of both gold and silver coin.[37]

Thus, even in this early period we see all the core requirements for a widely accepted international currency, namely quality assurance, regulated provision ensuring adequate but not excessive supply, political checks and balances, and geopolitical security for the issuer, at least after 202 BCE with the end of the Second Punic War.

Subsequent military successes expanded the ambit of the denarius still further. In the second century BCE, denarii arrived in Spain

(Hispania as it was known), traveling along with Roman troops, and eventually displaced local bronze and silver circulation. It took longer in eastern portions of the empire for Roman silver to displace native silver coins, though the result was much the same. This disparity in time for the two regions may have resulted from weaker trading links or from populations in the east being slower to assimilate (slower to come to see themselves as Romans).[38]

In both the west and east, nevertheless, the initiative stuck. Julius Caesar and subsequent generals, who battled Pompey and his followers for twenty years, minted the silver denarius in large numbers, now along with its big brother, the gold aureus. Caesar cemented the loyalty of his troops by doubling their pay and financed the wage bill by minting an enormous quantity of coin. He and subsequent Roman campaigners produced aurei and denarii not only in Rome but also in Spain, Sicily, Africa, Syria, Asia Minor, and Greece.[39] Salaries for soldiers were paid out mainly in silver, standard pay for Caesar's legionaires being a silver denarius a day (from which food and living expenses were deducted, making net pay somewhat less). Caesar famously carried a mobile mint on his military expeditions to more readily pay his legions in coins. His financial attentiveness and on-demand coin-making ability played a key role, it is said, in maintaining the morale of the troops when he prepared to cross the Rubicon and march on Rome.[40]

Ultimately, denarii and aurei introduced in the course of these military campaigns largely replaced local coinages in Western Europe, mainland Greece and, with passage of a century or so, much of the Levant. They remained the basis for international circulation across the empire and beyond for the better part of five centuries.

From Military to Mercantile

This take on the spread of the denarius emphasizes the martial aspect. Roman money was used to pay Roman soldiers. It traveled with Roman armies. Their booty provided the material needed for its emission. Events on the battlefield provided impetus for its diffusion, for its debasement in the wake of military setbacks, and for currency reform and standardization that made for widespread acceptance.

This, of course, conveys only part of the story. As in Greece, the other part was trade. The literature on trade and monetization in the Roman Republic and Empire parallels that on Greece. Early analyses questioned the existence of a market, much less an international market. Individuals at the time did not exchange goods and services in expectation of income or profit, it was thought. Rather, their circulation was based on norms of reciprocity and redistribution, that is, on social relationships and political priorities. Production in Republican and Imperial Rome, in this view, was dominated by self-sufficient households.[41] When trade took place, it was local and small-scale. Wealth derived not from entrepreneurship and investment but from control of land and taxation by powerful political interests.

The skepticism of the early primitivists, as this school of thought came to be known, extended to denying a meaningful role for money, including in international transactions. When hoards of Roman coin were unearthed, historians writing in the primitivist tradition questioned whether their owners amassed them from trade and investment, transactions facilitated by international money. Silver denarii discovered north of the empire had been used, they argued, for tribute payments buying off barbarian tribes. Coins, once received, were used not for commercial purposes but for ransom, blood money, dowry, and heirloom payments, or for ornamental purposes.[42] When a hoard discovered in China contained the mintage of thirteen separate emperors whose collective reign spanned two and a half centuries, numismatists conjectured not that this indicated ongoing commercial relations but rather an ambassadorial gift or the trove of a Mongol or Persian plunderer.[43]

Contradicting the primitivist view is evidence of a dense network of Roman trade girding the Mediterranean and the east in the period of the republic and even more under the empire. The Romans had better transportation technology than the Greeks, including cargo ships of unprecedented size, capable of long voyages. Their largest vessels rivaled the carrying capacity of the largest wooden ships plying the route between Europe and the East Indies in the sixteenth and seventeenth centuries.[44] Political unification of the Mediterranean Basin under Roman rule further encouraged commercial activity. It enhanced the security of property rights, prohibited merchants from selling adulterated goods, and strengthened contract enforcement. Together, these measures stimulated economic growth, albeit of the extensive variety; they supported larger populations rather than higher living standards, in other words. They fostered economic integration through trade in grains and other staple products.

To steps Roman authorities took to protect the rights of producers, consumers, and merchants, one might add as a factor benefiting trade the establishment of a uniform currency. Uniformity meant that merchants, when accepting payment in monetary form, knew what they were getting. On rare occasion, it allowed them to make payment across space without requiring physical movement of awkwardly heavy and valuable coin or bullion. On agreement between the parties, coin could be provided in one place against sales and receipts in another, avoiding the costs and dangers of having to physically transport the metal long distances. Coin thus began to shade into credit, anticipating developments shaping markets in international currencies in more modern times.[45]

None of this commercial history denies a role for the state, but demonstrates that state and market worked together. Provinces paid an annual tribute to Rome, which the state then distributed to those engaged in the execution of public works. Recipients used their income to purchase art, land, wine, and slaves, among other items.[46] Tribute flowed from the Roman treasury back to the provinces when wages were paid to the legions and food and equipment were purchased to sustain them. The existence of a uniform, widely accepted currency greased the wheels of this circular flow.

Since Rome's trade did not end at the borders of the empire, neither did the circulation of its currency. Denarii have been found in India, Sri Lanka, China, and other extra-Roman locations. Despite controversy about their origin, the dating of these coins coincides with the arrival in Europe of merchandise from these same parts of Asia. The dates of

Roman coin found in India coincide with the arrival in Europe of Indian spices, ivory, pearls, semi-precious stones, and silk. Coin evidence suggests that this eastern trade spanned three and a half centuries, from the end of the first century BCE to the final days of the Roman Empire, and that it centered on southern India while occasionally penetrating the north of the subcontinent. Trade between the Roman Empire and Asia reached its apogee during the Pax Romana, the centuries after 27 BCE when few military conflicts disturbed the Silk Road. The presence of Roman coin in India and corresponding absence of punch-marked Indian coin in Europe suggests that the West ran trade deficits with the East and settled them in its own currency, again underscoring the international status of the denarius. Adjusting the number of coins for their weight and value indicates that these trade deficits were largest in the reigns of Emperors Tiberius (14–37 CE), Claudius (41–54 CE), and Nero (54–68 CE), although the movement of coin continued after Nero.[47]

Because Roman trade with the East transited Alexandria, we have evidence on details of payment. Egypt had a highly developed bureaucracy that generated written contracts and receipts, which are a detailed source of evidence. It had a hot, dry climate, so written records, in the form of papyri, survived there, while virtually nowhere else in the Roman Empire. These sources document how goods imported from India transited the Red Sea, were shipped overland to the Nile and Alexandria, and then continued to market via the Mediterranean, waterborne shipping having cost advantages relative to overland transportation. Coin used for their purchase moved in the opposite direction.

Critically, Egypt itself had a closed currency system; it had possessed its own silver coinage from the time of the Ptolemaic kingdom (from 305 BCE).[48] Unlike other provinces, it was allowed to retain this closed system even when absorbed as a province of the Roman Empire in 30 BCE; the circulation of denarii and aurei was forbidden in Roman Egypt.[49] Egypt's own currency, not being well-known, did not circulate elsewhere, as hoard evidence and its absence tend to suggest. Hence traders seeking to purchase merchandise in the East had to assemble the requisite coins in Rome or at another imperial mint. These were placed in sealed bags of standard weight containing a specified number of coins and shipped to Alexandria, where their arrival was recorded before they were conveyed further east.[50] That denarii found in individual hoards in India frequently have an identical backside (technically, a reverse), as if they came from the same batch, suggests that they were selected and assembled expressly for this purpose.[51]

These hoards again remind one of the "exorbitant privilege" of a country that issues the leading international reserve currency, meaning the ability of that country to run merchandise trade deficits because of robust foreign demand for its assets. In principle, Rome might have settled its trade with Asia with lumps or ingots of precious metal. But given the complexity of weighing bullion and assaying its purity, the same weight in metal would have commanded less merchandise. Trade costs would have been higher. Trade volumes would have been lower.[52] Sealed bags of coins of reputable weight and purity facilitated these long-distance transactions.

Rise and Fall

The empire and the denarius reached their maximum extent around 117 CE, after which much of Mesopotamia was lost. Edward Gibbon, in his classic treatment of the fall of Rome, emphasized the corrosive effect of Christianity and loss of traditional values in its demise. These developments, he argued, raised questions about the emperor's divine status, allowed church leaders to intrude into politics, and destabilized prevailing modes of governance. The Roman state, as it aged, became more bureaucratic and less cohesive. The republic's democratic traditions, which had allowed the Senate to check excessive emission and deter debasement of the denarius, gave way to rule by one man, whose imperial whims, including over money, could go unchecked. Rule of law waned, and corruption grew more pervasive, as land became increasingly concentrated in the hands of a few large estate holders. Groups on the fringes of the empire aspiring to form states of their own forced Rome into even more frequent and costly wars. Holding the empire together, much less expanding it, required the upkeep of 160,000 Roman legions, along with auxiliaries and mercenaries recruited from provincial populations. Provisioning and paying such a large army required levying taxes equal to fully a quarter or even possibly a third of national income.[53] Heavy land taxes encouraged evasion by large estate owners, often in cahoots with the functionaries responsible for collecting their payments, who, more often than not, were themselves large estate owners. This in turn placed an intolerable burden on other individuals and institutions subject to taxation.

Yet recent scholarship looks to different forces, including some connected to Roman coinage and its international circulation, as causes of Roman decline. Kyle Harper has pointed to the role of environmental factors and emerging infectious diseases, in particular.[54] Trade connections, boosted by international acceptance of the denarius, allowed for the arrival of pathogenic microorganisms. Unprecedented urbanization, made possible by the importation of food, timber, and other essentials of city life, accelerated the spread of germs and disease. Less favorable climate owing to volcanic eruptions and solar cycles depressed agricultural yields, resulting in worsening nutrition that increased susceptibility to infectious disease. In turn, adverse climate events and pandemics reduced supplies of agricultural labor and military manpower. The state struggled to meet the financial requirements of an empire with extensive infrastructure, administrative, and military needs. Merely staffing the military grew challenging.

We saw in chapter 1 how international currency status can lead to excessive financialization and loss of competitiveness, resulting eventually in economic, commercial, and even monetary decline for the country that holds it. The Roman case points to an additional mechanism: the international acceptance of the denarius promoted trade and urbanization that led to pathogenic disruption.

Another hypothesis, even more directly connected to coinage, is that background pollution from silver mining resulted in cognitive damage to the population. Silver is extracted from lead-rich ore, a process that emitted as much as 4,600 tons of lead annually in Rome, possibly raising lead levels in the blood of Roman inhabitants by as much as five micrograms per deciliter and causing a drop of two to three IQ points in Roman individuals.[55] Immune system impairment linked to low-level lead exposure could have also contributed to the devastation of the Antonine Plague, which killed 5 to 10 percent of the Roman population. If this is correct, then pollution as much as pandemic was responsible for Rome's imperial decline—pollution that flowed, ironically, from none other than the empire's monetary precocity.

Slippery Slope

Whether inflation and currency debasement, by undermining the finances and morale of the citizenry, played a further role in the decline of the empire is contested. The process started under Nero, emperor from 54 to 68 CE, who debased the denarius to ensure that both gold and silver remained in circulation at the prevailing mint ratio. Denarii used in transactions became worn as they passed hand to hand, shedding weight and metal. Having no ready mechanism for recalling, melting, and recoining the existing circulation, Nero instead reduced the weight of new denarii to match the diminished weight of coins in circulation.[56] He adjusted the weight of the aureus correspondingly to maintain the prevailing ratio of twenty-five silver coins per gold coin, resulting in a 4 to 6 percent reduction in weight.[57]

This first adjustment was only a technical correction, responding to the continued circulation of older, worn denarii. But having opened the door, Nero walked through it. The emperor faced mounting fiscal pressures on multiple sides: an ambitious program of infrastructure investment focused on canal building, the great fire of 64 CE that required large swaths of Rome to be rebuilt, construction of his extravagant three-hundred-room Domus Aurea palace, and costly wars on several fronts. Although Nero might have preferred to relax the state's resource constraint by simply coining new denarii, silver coin and bullion were fast disappearing into the German lands, where these were the most desired form in which to hold wealth. As these circumstances drove the price of silver relative to gold above twenty-five to one (it now took more than an ounce of gold to obtain twenty-five ounces of silver), it became unprofitable to coin denarii at official weights and prices.

Burdens on the state treasury thus led Nero to seek ways of relaxing the constraint. His solution, predictably, was further debasement. While the aureus remained full-bodied, he added copper to the denarius, returning its emission to profitability. Together with the earlier decision to decrease its size, the coin's silver content now shrank by as much as 25 percent. This operation was disguised, since the official ratio of twenty-five denarii per aureus did not actually change. The denarius was effectively transformed into a token currency with a face value greater than that of its actual metal content. Having abandoned its bimetallic standard, Rome now operated on a gold-coin standard with a token silver-copper hybrid coin circulating alongside.

Roman historians argue that this amounted to the first step down an economic slippery slope, along which the denarius was progressively debased and confidence, including that of foreign holders, was lost. This interpretation is not entirely fair to Nero. Nero's mint did not emit copious amounts of coin in the manner of a government seeking to maximize seigniorage revenues. Inflation remained muted—historians estimate it as running at less than 1 percent per annum—because of the limited emission of new coins.[58] The economy was becoming more monetized, allowing more coin to be minted without pronounced inflationary effects.[59] The number of denarii paid to the legions did not increase, as one would expect in a scenario of serious inflation and debasement. In addition, the new weights and fineness put in place by Nero's monetary reforms remained intact for decades. The Finnish historian Gunnar Mickwitz detected no pronounced changes in economic behavior on the part of individuals, of a sort that would indicate major disruptions from inflation. A more recent historian, Ramsay MacMullen, echoes Mickwitz's conclusion.[60] Although, as the twentieth century's John Maynard Keynes put it, invoking Lenin, there may be "no surer means of overturning the existing basis of society than to debauch the currency," Nero's currency modification did not rise to the level of debauchment.[61] There is no evidence that it was central to Rome's decline and fall.

Still, debasement was not without consequences. Given little change in Roman prices and no change in the unit of account, imported commodities and merchandise did grow more expensive, analogous to the effect of a modern currency devaluation. This narrowed Rome's deficit with the East and helped stanch the drain of silver from the empire. It is said that international currency status requires the issuer to run trade deficits with the rest of the world, since other economies must sell a surplus of commodities to that issuer to get their hands on its currency.[62] Nero's debasement made it more difficult for other economies to do so. Pre-reform coins are abundant in Indian hoards, but Nero's post-reform coins are nowhere to be found.[63] Indirectly, then, Nero's fiddling with the denarius may have been the first stage in in the currency's loss of international status.

Nero's successors observed his strategy of debasement and, with the passage of a century and more, were not deterred by his unhappy end. As the Roman historian Gareth Harney writes, "While [Nero's] changes were minor at first, a disturbing precedent was set: emperors now realized that they could cover their debts through debasement."[64] Septimius Severus (193–211) sought to secure the army's support by raising its pay. Doubling payments to the legions required him to slash the silver content of the denarius to 50 percent.[65] Subsequent emperors followed his lead: by the time of Gallienus (260–68), silver content had plunged to 5 percent. Under Claudius Gothicus (268–70), it was a mere 1 percent.[66] Inflation accelerated, although by how much is hard to say. We do know that Gallienus paid his troops twice as much as had his predecessor Valerian, which provides a rough gauge of the magnitudes.[67] The situation became dire enough that older coins were hoarded or melted down; the economy was flooded with near-worthless new denominations. During the disastrous reign of Honorius (395–423), Rome was occupied by the Visigoths, and the western empire splintered. It turned out that debasement, if controlled at the outset, could become a slippery slope after all. Given a couple of centuries, the international role of the denarius was no more.

The Dollar of the Middle Ages

But even the splintering of the empire did not signal the demise of the Roman state as a source of international currency. Diocletian (284–305) divided the empire into east and west, and Constantine I (306–37) moved the imperial capital to Byzantium, renamed first New Rome and then Constantinople. Constantine reformed the civil and military administrations, was scrupulous about maintaining a balanced budget, and issued a large gold coin, the solidus, to signify the strength of his regime. At 4.5 grams, the solidus, known in Western Europe as the bezant (solidus for *solid* gold, bezant for *Byzantium*), was the largest gold coin in the world, with an alloy up to 99 percent pure, the most achievable given the technology of the time.[68] All these characteristics made it ideally suited for large-value, long-distance transactions. Diocletian had minted the coin in small amounts as a replacement for the aureus but was hamstrung by the limited availability of gold.[69] Starting in 312, Constantine vaulted it to center stage, issuing it big time. A Christian, Constantine solved the problem of gold scarcity by forcing open the empire's pagan temples and melting down their treasures, thereby providing the material for his coins in a true God-versus-mammon moment. His legions became known as "soldiers" by virtue of the solidi in which they were paid.

But widespread acceptance and circulation of the solidus depended on more than just the coin's impressive appearance and the ubiquity of Constantine's troops. It rested on the reputation of Byzantine officials for fiscal probity and fair administration of taxes, on which the political legitimacy of the Byzantine state fundamentally rested.[70] The provision of justice was an important legitimizing function of the Byzantine emperor, and the concept encompassed monetary and fiscal justice. Byzantine administrators developed an efficient tax administration focused on land taxes.[71] They attached considerable importance to the value and stability of their coin.[72] Like any leading international currency, the solidus was thus backed not only by a unitary monetary system but also by the state's strong and stable fiscal accounts and a political commitment to their maintenance.

The solidus benefited further from Byzantium's fortuitous location, on the European side of the Bosporus Strait, at the entrance to the Black Sea, which allowed the empire to control trade in all directions at a time when the Silk Road and caravan trade were especially active. Indeed, the revival of trade in the fourth century owed much to Constantine's success in restoring monetary stability. A stable monetary system helped to revitalize financial activity, which was actively intermediated by bankers and money changers belonging to the guild of the *trapezitai*. The existence of this guild of money changers itself indicated the cross-border nature of much of that banking.[73] Their activities rejuvenated Byzantium's commercial networks, first in the Mediterranean Basin and then beyond.[74] Those commercial networks became a conveyor belt for the spread of Constantine's gold coin. This, then, provides a powerful example of the reciprocal interaction of an international currency in promoting trade, but also of the growth of trade in promoting international use of that currency.

By the fifth century, the solidus was utilized in trade everywhere from Britain to India.[75] Merchants employed it around the Mediterranean and in transactions with the Baltic, German and French lands, and Syria-Palestine, at least prior to the monetary reforms of 'Abd al-Malik (more on which later).[76] Like Rome before it, Byzantium imported more merchandise and commodities from the East than it exported. And like Rome, it settled the difference using its imperial coin.[77] The popularity of the solidus persisted because its integrity persisted: its weight and composition remained stable for seven centuries.[78] In time, it crowded out other gold coin in high-value transactions. Other issuers found it hard to compete even when they sought to masquerade by placing on their own coins a portrait of the Byzantine emperor. The medieval historian Robert Lopez summed it up when he referred to the solidus as "the dollar of the Middle Ages" and went on to assert that the currency surpassed even the U.S. dollar of the 1950s "in stability and intrinsic value" (the 1950s being when Lopez was writing and when the dollar stood head and shoulders above other currencies).[79] Were Lopez alive today and able to see the dollar's subsequent trials and tribulations, he would be even more impressed, no doubt, by the stability of the solidus, literally for centuries.

The Umayyad Alternative

Another eminent monetary historian, Carlo Cipolla, while conceding that the gold solidus reigned as the dominant currency from the fifth through seventh centuries, objected however that it was forced subsequently to share its international role with the Muslim gold dinar of ʿAbd al-Malik, the fifth Umayyad caliph from 696 CE. The Umayyad Caliphate, the second caliphate formed after the death of the Islamic prophet Muhammad, extended from Morocco and Iberia in the west to portions of modern-day Afghanistan in the east. The solidus and dinar, when newly minted, varied slightly in weight; ʿAbd al-Malik's dinar was lighter to match the weight of worn solidi already in circulation. (The numismatist Philip Grierson posits an alternative explanation, namely that the weight of the full-bodied solidus was not well-adapted to the system of weights and measures prevailing in the Arab world. Grierson argues that ʿAbd al-Malik's intent to create a coin that weighed exactly twenty Arabic carats, where a carat was a standard unit of weight derived from the seed of the carob tree.[80])

In terms of appearance, the two coins differed mainly by whether the reverse was stamped with a cross (the solidus was while the dinar obviously was not). ʿAbd al-Malik no doubt saw the advantages of a coin that otherwise resembled the solidus, and which might therefore find quick acceptance as a unit of account and means of payment. But he took offense to Christian iconography.[81] He therefore adopted the same design while removing only the horizontal bar from the cross; the result resembled a pillar or herdsman's staff.[82] The name "dinar" was similarly intended to reassure those unfamiliar with locally coined money, resembling as it did the Latin "denarius."[83] Once the coin gained wide acceptance, including beyond the borders of the caliphate itself, the imagery on the front changed to text along the lines of, "There is no god but God, he alone, Muhammad is the messenger of God."[84] In fact, similar phrases, while now familiar from Islamic religious texts, do not actually appear in the Quran itself.[85] It thus can be argued that the spread of the dinar throughout Muslim lands played a role in the creation and diffusion of the orthodox Islamic creed.

The dinar was minted in Damascus, North Africa, Spain, and Egypt. It became the dominant unit in Muslim lands stretching from present-day Morocco and Portugal in the west to present-day Iran in the east, in the same way the solidus dominated throughout Christendom. Both coins were used in trade between their issuing kingdoms and neighbors, and both circulated across the Mediterranean.

Decline and Fall Once More

The dinar and solidus both saw their ends as international currencies amid military defeats, another example of the pattern that recurs throughout history.[86] A central tenet of Umayyad ideology was expansion of the state through war against non-Muslims.[87] But maintaining a continuous war footing drained the caliphate's treasury and limited the resources available for commercial activity. Crushing taxes fomented discontent, violent resistance, and even civil war. Fighting multiple opponents proved "materially unrewarding," in the understated words of one historian of the caliphate.[88] The more territory the empire conquered, the further from their home base it became necessary to station fighters, and the more the costs associated with maintaining them. Endless campaigning sapped morale, and bad went to worse when the Umayyads were unable to defeat a reinvigorated Byzantium, the Central Asian Turks, and Khazars, all of whom mobilized against them. Imperial overstretch once more.

The end finally came when the Umayyads and their successors, the Abbasids, could not repel the advancing Mongols, resulting in the caliphate's collapse in 1258. Also reliant on trade, the Mongols minted gold and silver coins, emulating earlier local and regional issues to smooth interaction with merchants and facilitate payment of taxes. But following the death of Genghis Khan, the Mongol Empire split into four regional khanates, and the currency similarly split into four regional issues. From this point, no uniform standard existed to facilitate transactions with other groups and other parts of the world.

The Byzantine economy faced its own equally daunting, and ultimately fatal, challenges. Land traditionally tilled by peasant farmers granted title in return for their military service became increasingly concentrated in the hands of large estate holders, not unlike the trajectory in Rome centuries before. Agricultural productivity stagnated, and newly powerful estate owners gained leverage to extract concessions, including tax exemptions, from the imperial administration. For town-dwellers and country communities still forced to pay taxes, the state's levies became increasingly onerous.[89] Officials farmed out tax collection to private agents and civil servants, who were authorized to keep for themselves receipts above their assigned quotas. Predictable resentment toward these impositions spurred tax revolts and evasion. Infrastructure investment became disproportionately concentrated in Constantinople, where residents had the loudest political voice, starving the regions. Guild organizations weakened and even broke down entirely. Maintenance of the navy fell into neglect, as fiscal resources were funneled to pay for the opulence and grand display favored by the Byzantine court. Complicating matters externally, the seafaring merchants of Venice and Genoa had superior mastery of maritime violence, what is sometimes called piracy, which they leveraged to crowd out Byzantine traders.[90]

Finally, there was a role for the currency. Byzantium had kept the weight and purity of the solidus stable for 700 years, while its rivals repeatedly debased their currencies. The solidus became overvalued, causing Byzantine exporters and merchants to fall behind their Italian and Muslim rivals. Jumping ahead a millennium or so, this is not unlike arguments about the United States and the dollar—that the dollar is chronically overvalued on foreign exchange markets due to the appetite of foreign governments and central banks for dollar reserves, disadvantaging American exporters seeking to compete internationally.

But as in the case of the United States today, it is important to bear in mind that these economic woes were not exclusively about the currency. Fundamentally, they were the products of fiscal underperformance, inadequate infrastructure investment, and political self-dealing by the wealthy and well-connected. Lessons from thirteenth century Byzantium for twenty-first century America, one might say.

For this combination of reasons, a previously vibrant Byzantine economy became increasingly sclerotic. Geostrategic problems followed, as economic stagnation undermined Byzantium's military capacity, and extensive military action came with sharply rising costs. In the ninth century Byzantium fought wars with the Abbasids and Bulgarians, followed in the tenth century by raids and retaliation along the Byzantine-Arab border and battles over Bulgaria and Crete. Hiring mercenaries to augment native troops tripled an already large military budget between 775 and 1025.[91] Nonetheless, Byzantine forces proved unable to prevent the Pecheneg Turks from crossing the Danube in 1046, and Constantinople was obliged to sue for an expensive peace.

Faced with this disaster, Constantine IX (1042–55) looked to alter the currency to ameliorate financial stress. He reduced the size of newly minted coins, along with their gold content, in a disguised effort to economize on wages paid to the military.[92] Soldiers received the same weight in coin as before, as they could see, but its purity was now diminished, something they may have failed to appreciate, at least initially.[93] Subsequent emperors resorted to this stratagem repeatedly. The numismatic evidence suggests that the gold content of the solidus may have been chipped away by the end of the eleventh century to just 10 percent of its initial level.[94]

This was a painful comedown after seven hundred years of monetary stability. It rendered merchants reluctant to accept the solidus in payment even when weighed, since they could no longer be sure about the quality of the alloy. A monetary reform in 1092–93 simplified and stabilized the coinage, but the prestige of the solidus had been lost. Military defeat, in the form of conquest of Constantinople by the Crusaders in 1204 and loss of two-thirds of the empire's territory, once again ended international use of a currency.

Persistent but Not Eternal

Repeatedly in the ancient and medieval periods, then, military and mercantile influences combined to encourage the use of the leading power's monetary unit in its transactions with other political entities—in what today we would call international transactions. Circulation of these monetary units across wide geographic areas was remarkably persistent. But that same wide geographic circulation set in motion forces resulting in the loss of economic and monetary dominance. It supported trade that, whatever its other merits, exposed native populations to plague and pestilence. Coining precious metal entailed mining and refining, which could be a source of lead poisoning and cognitive impairment. While gold coin for paying legions and mercenaries was yet another mechanism through which circulation of that unit could spread to new regions, its ready availability might also entice emperors into unsustainable military adventures.

But if international currency status in the ancient and early modern periods was strikingly persistent, it was not forever. When the rising commercial powers Genoa, Venice, and Florence sought currency with which to grease the wheels of trade, instead of adopting the solidus, they issued gold coins of their own. By the third decade of the fourteenth century, the imperial administration of Byzantium itself, when accounting for the payment of rents, expressed them in Venetian gold ducats.[95] A new stage in the development of the international monetary system was clearly underway.

3

Renaissance of Credit

IF THE BYZANTINE SOLIDUS was the dollar of the Middle Ages, then the Florentine gold florin was the greenback of the Renaissance. It circulated from in England in Europe's northwest to the Crusader States of the Middle East.[1] Its appeal lay its stability, seeing no significant change in its gold content or appearance for fully three centuries.[2] The florin enjoyed acceptance as payment wherever Florentines traded, and Florentines traded everywhere. In terms of its underpinnings—the stability of the issue and the transactions undertaken by the issuer—the florin resembled the international currencies that preceded it.

It differed, though, in one particular and important aspect: its role in banking and finance. Florence pioneered modern banking, and international banking specifically. Florence's widely branched international banks developed out of multi-branch holding companies, sometimes referred to as business systems or partnership networks, that Florentine merchants founded to source inputs and market products across Europe and the Levant. Over time, these multi-branch merchant houses evolved into widely branched merchant banks, Their far-flung financial operations widened the domain of the florin.

The Florentines did not invent double-entry bookkeeping, the modern accounting device enabling bankers and merchants to keep systematic track of revenues and expenditures, or the bill of exchange, the promissory note that became the main vehicle for borrowing and lending. Venice laid claim to the former, while Arab merchants had long employed an instrument resembling the latter.[3] But the Florentines elaborated these contracts and conventions. When using them, they denominated their entries in florins. Their loans and payments to producers, traders, kings, popes, and crusaders they similarly delivered in florins. Importantly, this was the case even when the transaction entailed no actual movement of physical coin.

Thus, when one speaks of the florin as an international currency, one must refer not just to tangible coin but also to bank money. The same is of course true today. When we speak of the dollar as an international currency, we mean its physical manifestation—namely, hundred dollar bills—but even more importantly, its virtual equivalent: dollar bank deposits and securities held by foreign entities both in the United States as well as in overseas centers such as London, reflecting the presence there of the Eurodollar market.[4]

What is true of the dollar today was true of the British pound sterling and the Dutch guilder, the two international currencies that immediately preceded the greenback. They circulated, including outside the political jurisdiction where they were issued, in the form of tangible currency and coin but also as intangible bank money. This same substitution of bank money for coin had not occurred previously, at least on any significant scale. It was not prevailing practice in ancient Greece and Rome or medieval Byzantium. Since credit markets were rudimentary, money meant coined money or, absent that, bullion. Thus, Florence was the innovator. The florin marked the transition from ancient and medieval practice where actual coin of the realm was the predominant international means of payment, store of value, and unit of account, to the modern world where bank money predominates—and where cross-border payments are made not only in conjunction with purchases and sales of commodities and manufactures but also to serve as vehicles for purely financial transactions, what today we call international capital flows.

Commerce and Campaigns

In the thirteenth century, commerce and military campaigns remained the primary mechanisms for the international diffusion of currencies, as had been true for a millennium and more. The florin's rise then represents a surprising historical twist, since Florence was a leader in neither domain. As a city-state, it lacked the vast hinterland needed for assembling and projecting military force. It possessed few iron reserves or coal deposits, and its forests were depleted. It lacked the coastal access advantage of Venice and Genoa. Its Arno River was navigable only by small craft, and the outlet to the sea was occupied by Pisa. Thus, when Florentine merchants imported wool from England, they relied on Genoese shipping.[5]

Similarly, Venice, not Florence, served as the principal entrepôt center connecting the Byzantine Empire with western Europe. Genoa and Pisa cultivated links to southern France, Moorish Spain, and North Africa while competing with Venice in the eastern Mediterranean. Venetian and Genoese merchants imported spices, perfumes, and semiprecious stones but also manufactures, including ceramics, rugs, metalwork, paper, and silks, from the Byzantine and Muslim empires, while exporting raw materials such as timber, metals, and furs sourced in Europe's regional markets. Florence finished and exported wool, but that was the extent of its international commercial reach.[6] When merchants from Florence ventured into the eastern Mediterranean, they traveled aboard Pisa's ships and under Pisa's flag, Pisans possessing trading privileges in the Byzantine Empire and the Crusader States of the Middle East.[7]

Still, Florence was not untouched by the expansion of commercial activity on the Italian Peninsula in the high Middle Ages (after 1000 CE).[8] The city's principal commercial and industrial asset was ample free-flowing water suitable for cleaning and dying wool. The Florentines developed a finishing industry based on importing wool from northern and western Europe, putting this out for spinning, weaving, and dying, and then marketing the resulting cloth at home and abroad.[9] They now participated in the more general growth of these activities. The physical expansion of the city suggests that this tendency was well underway in the twelfth century. By the early thirteenth century, references to Florentine merchants and their wares appear up and down the Italian Peninsula. In 1211 Florentines are recorded at the Champagne Fairs, Europe's commercial crossroads, where they engaged in foreign exchange transactions, anticipating their later specialization in finance.[10]

Coin changing hands at the Champagne Fairs was silver, as gold was scarce in Western Europe since the eighth century. Some gold coins of Byzantium and the Muslim lands, described in chapter 2, eventually reached Europe, although serial debasements and the inevitable wear and tear did not enhance their popularity. But the low worth of circulating silver eventually became inconvenient with the rising value of wholesale transactions. Venice relieved this constraint in the early thirteenth century by minting a large silver coin, aptly named the "grosso," equal in value to twenty-four silver denarii and suitable for paying wages to shipwrights and other craftsmen.[11] The impetus and opportunity to mint it are said to have sprung from a contract to provide transportation for those going on the Fourth Crusade (1202–4). The crusaders paid Venice twenty tons of silver in ingots, a portion of which went toward hiring shipwrights to build the fleet. The twenty-four-denarii coin was an appropriate unit for paying their wages.[12] The crusaders had agreed to pay more, on the order of twenty-eight tons, but fell short of raising the entire sum. The Venetians accepted the deal when the crusaders agreed to attack a rival trading city, Zara (the modern-day Croatian city of Zadar), on their way to Constantinople.

But while the grosso and other coins minted to the same standard—by Pisa, Lucca, Sienna, and Florence—were helpful, they were still inadequate for wholesale transactions, including long-distance trade. The latter would require gold coin.

At this point, gold fortunately began flowing into Western Europe from West Africa, the Arabic East, and the Hungarian mines of Kremnica, in present-day Slovakia. As early as 1217 the King of Hungary began shipping gold ingots to Venice to pay for galleys for the Fifth Crusade. With the development of trade relations between Venice and Hungary, the flow of precious metal quickened. Although Hungary sent the Italians other exports—one Florentine merchant purchased Magyar horses that he sold at a profit—the Italians exported a wider range of products, reflecting their ability to source these across the Mediterranean and beyond.[13] Hungary ran a trade deficit in other goods, which it settled by shipping gold. Nor did Venice long maintain its monopoly of Hungarian trade, as illustrated by the example of Florence's Magyar horses; competition from other Italian city-states was simply too great. Those other city-states similarly saw inflows of Hungarian gold.

Florence, Genoa, and Lucca all appear to have minted gold coins on or around 1252.[14] Venice was the principal recipient of gold inflows but focused on refining that gold into bars, delaying its minting of gold coins until as late as 1284.[15] Florence preceded it in this development, launching its coin-minting operations three decades earlier. In that interim, Florentine coins became the standard. Other Italian city-states, when following, matched the fineness and weight of the florin.

Why did the Florentines move so quickly? It is not as if they were aware of and anxious to capture the exorbitant privilege of issuing a gold coin that could serve as international currency. In fact, they initially minted the florin to make domestic trade and production more convenient.[16] Clothiers sourcing wool from multiple markets in Northern Europe and the western Mediterranean sold it to spinners in the Florentine countryside. The spinners in turn put their thread out to master weavers with expensive looms who required helpers to operate them. One story goes that master weavers received payment per roll of cloth, and one gold florin equaled payment for one standard roll.[17] After cleaning, stretching, and dying, processes that might also entail payment in gold, the finished rolls were shipped to market, including to gold-using parts of the eastern Mediterranean. It made sense for wool manufacturers to use the same unit for their outlays that they received in payment, since this minimized hassle and risk. In this way, a coin minted in response to domestic imperatives came into international use.

Relatedly, it made sense for Florentine merchants to use this same gold coin when purchasing unfinished cloth in Flanders and Brabant; doing so matched their revenues and costs. Recall that gold was scarce in northwest Europe, while silver was relatively abundant. With gold going for a high price, northern European cloth exporters happily took payment in this form. Already in the 1280s, use of the florin radiated along an axis running north from Tuscany to Champagne and Paris, and from there to Flanders and Brabant, as well as south to Rome, Naples, and the Kingdom of Sicily. As international commerce expanded, so did the international domain of the currency. Other city-states able to access specie sufficient to mint gold coin of their own similarly copied the florin's size, fineness, name, and even distinctive fleur de leis symbol. The florin was now effectively, in the words of the economic historian Robert Lopez (who we met already in chapter 2), "supra-national tender."[18]

The *Commenda* and Its Limits

Given simultaneous steps by Florence, Genoa, and Lucca, followed in short order by Venice, why did the Florentine issue become the standard? It is tempting to point to the florin's stability, though at this early stage such stability was not a given. At least as important were steps communal authorities proactively took to promote use of the currency. For example, they provided leather purses sealed with official red wax and stamped with the value of the contents, inspired presumably by the earlier Roman practice of using sealed purses when shipping coin to Egypt and further east. Florentine purses could contain as many as a thousand coins, making them useful for large-value transactions.[19]

The most fundamental factor supporting international take-up of the florin, however, was the flourishing Florentine business network. Though latecomers to international trade, the Florentines expanded their cross-border operations vigorously. In doing so they created the largest, mostly broadly branched business organizations the world had yet seen. And the florin was the natural vehicle for the numerous transactions, foreign as well as domestic, these organizations conducted. Accordingly, it swiftly became a vehicle currency for foreigners transacting with these same commercial entities.

Traditionally, Italian merchants had organized such long-distance trade using *commenda* contracts.[20] These were one-off agreements between a sedentary investor, the *commendator*, and a traveling associate known as the *tractator*.[21] In some cases the *tractator* added capital of his own, conventionally half as much as provided by the *commendator*. In this case the contract was known as a bilateral *commenda* (in contrast to the unilateral *commenda*, where the *tractator* provided no capital). The *commendator* might provide instructions regarding the transactions to be undertaken or leave it to the *tractator* to exercise his judgment. The *tractator* would carry coined money to the Champagne Fairs or another market, purchase goods there, and sell them, often but not necessarily at his home base. Revenues would be used to return the capital to its provider, and residual profits would be split. In a bilateral *commenda*, profits were divided fifty-fifty, while the *commendator* suffered two-thirds of any losses. Under a unilateral *commenda*, the *commendator* received three-quarters of the profit and bore all financial losses, while the *tractator's* losses were limited to time and labor.

One can see the appeal of this arrangement. It exploited the different strengths of the traveling salesman and financier. The partnership relaxed financial constraints on the traveler. Sharing profits incentivized the traveler, superior to paying a fixed wage or salary in a setting where an investor could not readily keep an eye on his efforts.

But one can also see drawbacks. The agent might expend less than optimal effort, since he captured just half of the returns to effort supplied.[22] He also had limited incentive to build a reputation for excellence, since renewal of the contract remained an open question. In the absence of an ongoing relationship, there was the danger that the *tractator* might abscond with the funds. Limiting the contract to a single traveling partner and investor also constrained the scale of the undertaking. It increased risk and limited diversification compared to a partnership where investors held shares in multiple ventures.[23]

In the thirteenth century, responding to the challenges of organizing a growing volume of trade across lengthening distances owing to the late medieval commercial revolution alluded to above, the Tuscans developed workarounds for these problems. Partnerships entailing multiple investors and voyages were established for seven years, ten years, and longer. These allowed for diversification, risk reduction, and ongoing commercial relations missing from earlier forms. Partners were limited initially to members of a single extended family. Once they admitted outsiders, investors could sell their shares to other investors before the end of the fixed period. Effectively, this entity prefigured the modern joint-stock corporation.[24]

Rather than contracting with a *tractator* for each voyage, the partners now hired specialist shippers to transport their goods to point of sale.

They posted resident agents in each market where merchandise was purchased. These specialist shippers effectively formed the logistics division of the enterprise, while the resident agents were the seed of branch offices, as they eventually became. Larger partnerships had multiple branches, one in each major market of Europe and the Middle East. Now that the partners had permanent representatives in major markets, their agents no longer had need to gather in a central meeting place. These innovations thus coincided with the decline of the Champagne Fairs.[25]

Advent of the Business System

The Florentines could not yet claim leadership in these innovations; credit for them goes to the Genoese, Venetians, and Lucchese. Their leadership took shape at the next stage, starting in the 1370s. Critical for the subsequent circulation of the florin across Europe, Florentine merchants created groups of partnerships. Known as "companies," each partnership had separate shareholders but remained connected to other members of the business group through ongoing commercial relationships. Not incidentally, the word "company" comes from the Italian *compagnia*, in turn derived from the *compagni* or companions joined together in the partnership. These entities have been variously described as business systems, partnership systems, company agglomerates, and holding companies.[26] Whatever the label, they comprised several legally autonomous partnerships, each with a separate set of books but linked to a controlling owner, family, or set of partners. Legal separation provided financial protection; if one partnership failed, it did not threaten other healthy entities. Linkage might take the form of a holding-company arrangement where the controlling partnership owned portions of the other partnerships, as in the case of the Medici family. Each partnership had its own manager—perhaps a junior partner, perhaps a salaried employee. In principle, managers were in constant communication with the controlling partner, who had final say over operations, though in practice the slow speed of communication gave managers considerable day-to-day autonomy.[27]

Francesco Datini is sometimes credited with this organizational innovation. The son of a modest taverner, Datini lost his parents to the Black Death at the age of thirteen. Not atypically for an impecunious teenager, he apprenticed to a shopkeeper in Florence. But he then carved out a position for himself as a trader in Avignon, the seat of the pope, where he dealt in armor and daggers for the knights of the Papal Court. When the papacy returned to Italy, Datini followed, moving to Prato, where he entered the cloth trade, before returning to Florence, the base from which he established a set of legally separate trading partnerships.

Datini was an accomplished trader, although his detractors paint him as imperious and arbitrary for withholding payment from artisans he employed, and as distrustful of his partners, to whom he meted out high-handed treatment. Multiple biographies have centered on him, inspired no doubt by his achievements as a merchant and entrepreneur, but more concretely by the exceptional quality and quantity of the documentation he left behind.[28] In any case, scholars have pointed to at least three experiments with partnership systems more-or-less simultaneous to his, all in Florence, suggesting that this innovation was more a product of the city's fertile milieu rather than the invention of a singularly creative entrepreneur.[29] Given their rapid adoption, these organizational innovations—replacing one-off contracts with ongoing business relationships and developing an elaborate division of labor—enhanced Florence's commercial footprint, which in turn enhanced the footprint of the florin.

In the fourteenth century, at their height, three Florentine partnership systems—those of the Bardi, Peruzzi, and Acciaiuoli families—were by far the largest and most articulated business organizations of the day.[30] They had scores of agents across Europe and the Middle East. They managed offices in Paris and London in Europe's northwest, in Spain and Tunis in the western Mediterranean, and at Constantinople in the East. Their span of control extended not just across vast physical distance but over the wide range of products they traded.

Operations such as these gained several advantages from the new organizational structure. First, it enabled the coordination of the activities of different companies in different business lines, each of which depended on others for their profitability. For example, a clothier who relied on a single autonomous supplier for an essential dyestuff faced a potential hold-up problem, where that supplier might use his leverage to extort a share of the clothier's profits. Having a common controlling partner helped to eliminate this danger, in the same way it is eliminated in a modern vertically integrated corporation.[31]

Second, partnership systems allowed partners to reap the benefits of vertical integration while protecting the assets of one group from the liabilities of another. These were not yet limited-liability partnerships, where each partner was responsible for only his pro rata ownership share of the company's liabilities.[32] Already, however, separating different unlimited liability companies shielded the assets of one partnership from the bankruptcy of another. The dramatic failures of the 1340s, when the Bardi and Peruzzi went under due to failed loans to Edward III of England, highlighted the value to investors of this decentralized structure.[33]

Third, partnership systems were a way of pooling credit and relaxing financial constraints. Companies involved in the same partnership system borrowed and lent to one another as needed to conduct profitable business. A common controlling partner or partners provided a conduit for sharing information. This headed off another peril of business: that a manager or one set of partners might borrow opportunistically and put someone else's money unnecessarily at risk.[34]

Liquidity Starts at Home

To come into widespread international use, a currency must be stable, and it must be the preferred habitat of agents engaged in a substantial volume of transactions. The florin checked both these boxes. The operators of the mint, members of the Arte del Cambio (guild of moneyers), answered to the Popolani, an interest group of merchants, bankers, and entrepreneurs who sealed their control of Florence's communal government in the final decades of the thirteenth century and had a strong interest in maintaining a stable currency. And the city-state's sophisticated business systems were the motors for vigorously expanding international transactions.

In addition to those requirements, an international currency must be liquid: it must be easy to buy, sell, and transfer at a low cost and predictable price. Ideally, this would be true not only of coins and bank money. It should also be the case for interest-bearing near monies, such as government securities denominated in the same currency.

Typically, liquidity starts at home, in a dense market rich with local-currency transactions and assets. Here, Florence's local bankers played a catalytic role. This is another reminder that the florin first rose to prominence as a unit used for domestic transactions and only later acquired its leading international role.[35] Some local bankers, interacting as fellow members of Arte del Cambio, took the opportunity to form partnerships, sometimes larger commercial partnerships also involving nonbankers. Other local bankers might be one-man shops who used brokers to connect them to borrowers. We can think of these local bankers as akin to the community bankers who supplement the activities of large, nationally branched commercial banks in the twenty-first-century United States. They accepted demand deposits, which they safeguarded on behalf of their clients.[36] They offered payment services enabling a customer to pay his bills in the manner of a twenty-first-century bank making automatic monthly payments to a customer's credit card company. Where the customer was an employer, they paid his workers at the end of the week. Small disbursements would be paid in coin, which the banker held under lock and key.[37] Larger payments for purchases of merchandise could be executed through a transfer of credits on the banker's books or between different banks, in the manner of the modern interbank clearing market.

Although they charged fees for these services, local bankers earned their main income by loaning and investing funds. They extended unsecured credit—unsecured by anything other than a promise to pay—to bakers, weavers, and other artisans, for periods as long as a year. This promise to pay, once written down, was what came to be known as a promissory note. Local bankers almost certainly charged interest on their loans, though there is little evidence of this, since any such indication could have been used against them in a legal complaint, given thirteenth- and fourteenth-century prohibitions on manifest usury, their term for the practice of publicly lending on interest.[38] In practice there were ways of disguising interest payments: these might be recorded as a gift from a client to his banker, for example. In addition to extending unsecured loans, bankers might provide advances to holders of the municipality's (in contemporary parlance, the commune's) debt securities (the Monte Comune) or to those with claims on the public dowry fund (the Monte delle doti), if the investor in question required cash prior to the next regularly scheduled coupon payment.[39] They might invest in these debt securities themselves, betting on an increase in their price in the same way a twenty-first-century bank purchases Treasury bonds for its own account. All this augmented the liquidity of the city-state's nascent money market.

From Local to International Banking

Whereas local bankers attracted deposits from city residents, Florence's great merchant bankers attracted deposits from abroad, including from wealthy clerics and notables who were customers of their branches in other Italian cities and in foreign commercial centers as far afield as London. By the end of the thirteenth century, the largest Florentine partnerships, the Bardi and Peruzzi, had international reputations for offering secure deposits and sizable returns. Unlike demand deposits attracted by Florence's local bankers, these were time deposits, contracted for a fixed term, analogous to modern certificates of deposit. Depositors received the equivalent of interest at the end of the period, at a rate of 7 to 8 percent. The interest paid was purportedly at the discretion of the firm to avoid charges of usury, but in fact it was negotiated in advance.[40]

Taking deposits leveraged the capital of the partners, whose core business might lie in trading textiles and managing property, as in the case of the Medicis. They could use the funds to purchase additional raw wool and unfinished cloth, or the money might allow the partners to branch into new business lines. After advancing credit to suppliers in the manner of a commercial partnership, merchants next began providing loans to unrelated parties, first to simple inn- and shopkeepers, in competition with local bankers, and then to kings and cardinals, where they had the field to themselves. As they expanded, what started out as a subsidiary line of business became their principal activity. At this point, Florentine merchant bankers became bankers, pure and simple. And since funds deposited with a branch in one market could be lent by a branch in another, they became international bankers as well.

With these widely branched banks now maintaining accounts on their clients' behalf, they were positioned to provide payment as well as credit services. A Florence-based merchant importing unfinished cloth from Flanders could instruct his bank's home office to transmit to the bank's branch in Bruges an order to purchase merchandise. The branch manager or his designate would complete the purchase and arrange to ship the merchandise back to Florence. He would pay purchase and shipping charges in local currency.[41] The account of the Florentine merchant at the home office would then be debited the corresponding number of florins, where the bank would have used the market exchange rate with an adjustment for profit.

This was now a straightforward accounting transaction. No coin had to move to complete the purchase so long as flows of goods and services in the two directions netted out. It also avoided the risks from storms and piracy when shipping gold by sea, and the cost of armed guards and insurance when transporting it overland. Thus it became a more widespread application of the selective practices utilized by the Romans, among others, in earlier eras.[42] Neither was there the need for a foreign-exchange transaction so long as the foreign branch had local-currency funding on hand.[43]

Such arrangements worked smoothly when the client's bank had a branch and resources in the relevant foreign market. They worked, in other words, when the transaction remained within a single business organization. But completing an interbank transfer required another approach. In this case the transaction entailed negotiating a bill of exchange. With a bill, a merchant in Florence seeking to import merchandise could initiate the transaction by instructing his bank to transfer florins to another Florentine merchant with the relevant connection. In return, the first merchant would receive a bill payable in foreign currency that he could send to the exporter, who would take it to the second merchant's bank. This bank would then pay the exporter in foreign currency. The bank would have debited the second merchant's foreign account but added a corresponding credit to his domestic florin account, embedding its fee in the exchange rate used for the conversion.

Florentine firms, with their elaborate networks and acquaintance with international financial transactions, were the foremost players in this market. They did not limit their participation to transactions in which Florentines were principals; they might equally provide services for transactions that did not involve Florence or its residents. Some Florentine firms established branches in foreign markets precisely to provide this service to third parties. Florentines themselves might do little or no business in the commodities and merchandise exported to and imported from the markets in question. Once there, however, commercial opportunities presented themselves. In earlier instances, Florentine merchants engaged in trade had been encouraged to branch into related financial services. Now, engaging in the business of financial services encouraged them to branch into trade. Both self-reinforcing connections expanded the ambit of the florin.

Next, it was only a small step from using the bill of exchange as a form of trade credit for financing an underlying commercial transaction to using it as a credit instrument for conducting a purely financial transaction. Instead of using a bill to pay for merchandise, one could use the bill as principal for extending a loan. Given religious prohibitions on usury, the bill might still look like payment for merchandise. But the merchandise was fictitious. A bill of exchange conveyed in the other direction, executed typically after two months (the average travel time for an imagined roundtrip between Florence and Bruges, as needed to complete the fictitious commercial transaction), completed repayment of the credit, again with adjustment of the exchange rate to add an implicit interest charge.[44]

This interest payment compensated the banker for extending the credit but also for the exchange risk associated with the loan. Since the banker would be taking in florin and paying out foreign currency in the first transaction, while receiving foreign currency while paying out florin in the second, there was a risk that the exchange rate would move against him in the interim. Bankers with specialized knowledge of the operation of foreign exchange markets were best able to manage this risk. Given their prominence in the market for bills, Florentines became leading participants in the foreign exchange trading centers of Venice, Geneva, and Lyons.[45]

Banker to Kings and Princes

Florentine merchant bankers next escalated from providing credit to foreign merchants in the overseas market cities where they did business to extending credit to the municipal governments of those same cities, and to the kings and princes to which residents of those cities were beholden. Sovereigns borrowed for day-to-day expenses, for waging military campaigns, and for buying allies. In 1336–37, King Edward III of England borrowed more than 1.5 million florins from the Bardi, Peruzzi, and other Florentine houses to pay subsidies to his allies, such as the Duke of Brabant and Emperor Louis IV of Bavaria.[46] The Florentines transferred the funds in bullion and coin. The wide acceptability of the florin meant that the duke and emperor welcomed its use as a vehicle for this financial transaction.

Loans to rulers and governments were invariably large, increasing the reward but also the risk. Trade credits and commercial loans could be extended to multiple parties, thereby offering a degree of diversification, but large loans to sovereigns created dangerous portfolio concentrations. Loans by the Bardi to Edward III in the four years from 1328 to 1331 may have averaged 15 percent of the family's total assets.[47] Unlike credit extended under the guise of commercial transactions, which was self-liquidating, kings and princes borrowed for longer periods, to finance military campaigns and for other purposes. This allowed more time for the unexpected to happen and for good loans to go bad.

Sovereigns anxious for funding might put up the crown jewels as collateral—a credible commitment, since a monarch's reputation would be fatally compromised should they lose them to their banker.[48] But the possibility of these dire consequences made the practice exceptional. More commonly, bankers took a lien on a source of state income such as customs duties, port tolls, seigniorage, or salt tax revenues. Ofttimes the banker administered the collection of these duties directly. Not infrequently he did so more efficiently than the state itself, merchant bankers already operating large organizations with multiple agents disbursed across space. Bankers possessed commercial, financial, and organizational expertise. Direct administration put them in a position to independently verify a claim that royal revenues were insufficient to service and repay what was borrowed. A creditor assigned customs duties levied at a port physically held the customs seal, meaning that no merchandise could be exported or landed absent his oversight.[49]

The problem being that a royal concession, once granted, could always be revoked. If a sovereign did decide to stop paying, there was no higher earthly power to which to appeal. In the worst case, default by a sovereign could put the entire house at risk, as happened to the Bardi and Peruzzi when Edward III defaulted in 1345.[50]

So why did Florentine bankers pursue this risky business? The answer is straightforward: lending to sovereigns was immensely profitable, notwithstanding the risks. The healthy double-digit interest rates paid by fourteenth-, fifteenth-, and sixteenth-century sovereigns compensated for instances when things went sideways. The historian Edmund Fryde painstakingly reconstructed the effective interest rate on loans by the Bardi to Edward III in 1328–31, estimating that these rates averaged 26 percent. The magnitude of this risk premium is striking, given that 1328–31 was a period of peace when one might expect that all would go well. Rates paid by English kings in times of war, when lenders might demand an even larger risk premium, ranged up to 40 percent.[51] Understandably, bankers found these high rates difficult to resist. On balance, realized returns incorporating defaults and debt service interruptions compared favorably with returns on alternative investments.[52] Even prominent defaults and bankruptcies did not deter new bankers from entering the field when a regime gained ground on the battlefield, the personality occupying the throne changed, or an errant king promised to mend his ways.

Tuscan bankers also developed strategies for mitigating these risks. They lent for short periods, forcing a king to repeatedly renew his loans. For the sovereign, borrowing for short periods and running the risk that a loan might not be rolled over, something that could create problems for the treasury, or even worse, on the battlefield, was a way of signaling that he intended to pay. For the bankers, it helped to distinguish worthy borrowers.[53]

Bankers also formed consortia, what we would call syndicates. The Riccardi of Lucca arranged syndicated loans for Edward I, transferring portions of the principal to fourteen other merchant banks, in an early example of the originate-and-distribute model.[54] This cohesive coalition of bankers did double duty as a mechanism for penalizing defaulting sovereigns. When creditors agreed that none of them would resume lending until the borrower made a good-faith effort to settle his debts, it strengthened their negotiating position. A credible threat to bar the borrower from the market would make default less tempting in the first place. The Genoese famously employed this kind of cartel arrangement when lending to Philip II of Spain. The Florentines would have been aware of the practice.[55]

Along with immediate monetary returns, lending to sovereigns had other attractions. The bankers and their wares might receive safe passage while transiting the country. Where the sovereign's license was required to do business, a loan could raise the odds of this being granted. Where a firm sought a franchise to operate a mint, mine, or port, to monopolize sales of a product, or to receive exemption from an export tax, a loan could similarly grease the wheels. Edward I, who placed a tax on English wool exports, first offered the export tax revenues as collateral for a series of loans, but then allowed eight Florentine firms to administer that tax, a position they leveraged to gain de facto monopoly control of the English wool export trade.[56] Edward II permitted the Bardi to export wool free of charge as quid pro quo for additional loans. Edward III took the practice a step further, granting the Bardi and Peruzzi a formal monopoly on the export of wool to southern Europe.[57] A century later, in 1462, the Medici were able to partner with the papacy for the exclusive right to market alum mined at Tolfa.[58]

Moreover, where a firm ran a trade imbalance with a kingdom that might otherwise have to be settled in bullion and specie, the interest income thrown off by the loan might obviate the need for costly specie shipments. Canonical examples were the Florentines' fourteenth-century loans to English kings, which generated income sufficient to finance shipments of English wool to southern Europe.[59] In this way, the financial advantages conferred by the florin reinforced the Florentines' commercial predominance, which in turn redounded in favor of their currency.

At the Papal Court

As illustrated by the Medici's partnership with the papacy, the Florentines complemented their early engagement with English kings with an equally deep relationship with the curia. Edward I and II had revenue streams in distinct parts of the English kingdom, which the Florentines anticipated and administered. The papacy levied taxes on dioceses throughout Europe and similarly needed help with their collection and transfer. In the second half of the thirteenth century, Florentine merchants positioned themselves at the center of these transactions. When Pope Innocent IV (1243–54) imposed levies on the English church and crown, there was no one better to oversee their transfer to Rome than the Florentines, who were already deeply enmeshed in the English economy.[60] It is surely no coincidence that the deepening involvement of Florentine companies in the papal finances took place in the 1250s, at the same time as the minting and wide availability of the gold florin.[61]

Florentine bankers having demonstrated facility at these activities, the papacy tasked them with assembling and transferring ecclesiastical revenues elsewhere in Europe where Florence also had agents and branches. Over time, the Florentines became even more deeply implicated in the church's economic and financial affairs. Pope Urban VI (1378–89) was desperate for funding following the Western Schism, when a rival pope, Clement VII, set up his own court in Avignon, taking much of the Catholic Church's administrative apparatus and treasury with him. The bankers were eager to service Urban's needs. Once the connection was made, it persisted. For much of the fifteenth century, Florentine bankers occupied the office of the depository, the entity responsible for day-to-day financial transactions, taking deposits and making payments on behalf of the Papal Treasury (what was known as the Apostolic Chamber).[62] Such payments included transfers to princes fighting Turkish incursions into Christendom; these payments were most efficiently executed by bankers with widely branched networks and international experience. The bankers made other payments on behalf of the Chamber, charging a commission for the service. They advanced loans to the treasurer, both short-term credits to fill temporary gaps between income and spending and long-term loans to finance ongoing projects, including military action. While the former were extended at an interest rate of 10 to 12 percent, the latter could command as much as 20 percent, due to their greater risk.[63] Loans were collateralized, as usual, by securing first lien on and administering customs duties, port tolls, the salt monopoly, the mint, and other revenue streams. Reflecting the prestige attached to the office of the depository, services provided to the Papal Treasury thus opened the door to other lucrative banking and commercial activities.

The Medici made the most of their papal connection. Their branch in Rome generated more than half of all earnings of the Medici Bank in the early fifteenth century.[64] Having learned from their predecessors' involvement with Edward III of the dangers of concentrated exposures, the Medici formed consortia to spread the risk. Starting in 1526, they helped the curia place long-term debt securities with individual investors, administering the periodic interest payments.[65] Securitization diversified the risk of papal lending still further. There would be no more catastrophic failures like those that had toppled the Bardi and the Peruzzi.

The City-State and Its Limits

With the development of more sophisticated and costly military technologies and the rise of territorial states, Florence as a city-state found its position growing shakier, strategically and politically. Piero de' Medici's surrender in 1494 to the forces of King Charles VIII of France, in which he unilaterally relinquished Florentine territories in return for peace, was only an especially vivid manifestation of the general predicament. The Italian wars of 1494 to 1559, in which various princes contested their claims to Italian cities and regions, threw food production and grain imports in and around Florence into disarray. Invading armies carried the plague that infected the region in 1527–31, resulting in the death of as much as 25 percent of the city's population.[66] Marauding troops terrorized the trade routes to and from northern Europe along which money and credit customarily flowed. The burden of taxation was ratcheted up, not just to field Florence's troops but also to subsidize those of the papacy with which the city was allied.

By the sixteenth century, for this combination of reasons, Florence fell into decline.[67] Politically, the city moved away from its republican traditions, becoming more of a principate along the lines of Imperial Rome, in which the Medici exerted arbitrary powers and where patronage mattered more than economic initiative or financial acumen.[68] Instead of seeking out new opportunities, a calcified elite sought to protect markets and prerogatives where they had an existing stake.[69] As the Renaissance historian Eric Cochrane put it, the "restlessness, the dissatisfaction, and the sense of independence that may have in part been responsible for the vitality of Florentine culture in the past had now given way to quiet, satisfaction, and servility, and to the conviction that not much was left to do but to sit back and enjoy what had already been accomplished."[70]

The sad reality was that Florentines found it increasingly difficult to compete with producers in the Low Countries and England, given the ready access of these newcomers to high-quality raw materials and technical skills, the latter not least of Florentine craftsmen now seeking more remunerative employment abroad. A sclerotic bureaucracy of a long-entrenched wool guild resisted adaptation, causing the productivity of weavers to stagnate.[71] In response to competition, clothiers shifted toward silk and luxury cloth, albeit with limited success, since other producers were moving upmarket as well. Meanwhile, powerful financial interests invested in a strong florin resisted all talk of debasement that might have improved the competitiveness of the city's merchandise exports. By the seventeenth century, Florence had lost its Spanish, French, southern Italian, and Levantine markets.[72]

Meanwhile, wealthy Florentines invested in the Monte Comune and Monte delle doti rather than new commercial undertakings. With pressing financial needs, the communal government issued an abundance of debt to sate these demands, stymying potential progress. "The high returns on public debt," one historian observed, "drew capital that might otherwise have been invested in new businesses, financing the economic growth and structural change that Florence's economy badly needed at this time."[73] Rather than investing in industrial and commercial concerns, the Medici and their friends cultivated connections and favoritism at the papal court, where they could make quick profits. Yet even in Rome, the relative position of Florentine banking declined in the face of competition from other Italian city-states.

Now, in addition, there were the Germans, who repurposed the best of the Florentines' innovations. The Fuggers, an Augsburg-based family firm, started, like their Florentine predecessors, in the textile trade and branched into international banking. Jakob Fugger, who took an already thriving family firm to the top of the commercial and financial leagues and became the wealthiest person in history, expressly modeled his mercantile and financial practices on the earlier innovations of the Florentines.[74] Among other practices familiar in Florence, Fugger pioneered the use of double-entry bookkeeping north of the Alps. He and his descendants developed a network of agents across Europe, an efficient logistics system, and close contacts with European courts, the curia, and the pope, all in the manner of Florence.[75] The Fuggers competed for the right to administer transfers from the German church to the papacy. "Augsburg is akin to a German Florence, and the Fuggers must be viewed as equals to the Medici," wrote one sixteenth-century Renaissance scholar.[76] The Genoese, meanwhile, also challenged the Florentines as providers of financial services to the Apostolic Chamber. And it was of course the Genoese and not the Florentines who, for better or worse, dominated lending to Philip II of Spain.

At the end of the day, there was no fundamental reason why a small city nestled in the hills of Tuscany should have dominated the international monetary landscape indefinitely. For centuries, the Florentines commanded that landscape by marrying cross-border trade and finance, becoming leaders in international banking. Their period of high influence marked the transition from the world in which international currency was synonymous with specie to one where international finance centered on disembodied transfers of bank money. But as larger, better-situated economies adopted similar practices, other currencies were able to challenge the florin's international role.

An interesting question is whether Florence's success at international banking itself contributed to the economy's relative decline. The Florentine economy, some historians have suggested, became excessively financialized.[77] Up-and-coming entrepreneurs pursued banking instead of the wool and silk trades that were Florence's commercial bread and butter. A powerful financial elite dead set on a strong florin resisted debasements that might have enhanced the competitiveness of merchandise exports. The bankers did well, but workers did not, with consequences that included widening income inequality and weakened social cohesion.[78] International currency status had costs as well as benefits. Florence and the florin illustrated both aspects.

4

The First Global Currency

ALTHOUGH THE Florentine florin circulated across Europe and even penetrated the Levant, the coin never reached other parts of the world. It was left to the Spanish silver dollar to become the first true global currency. One could hardly overstate how radically the discovery of silver in Peru and Mexico transformed the global monetary landscape. Precious metal deposits on this scale had never been unearthed before. For three centuries, Spanish New World silver dominated other coins used in commercial transactions. Spanish silver financed trade and enabled payments around the world. The sixteenth-century silver avalanche, the influx of silver coin and specie from Spanish America, touched every inhabited continent. It displaced local monies in China and other economies in an early instance of what is now known as currency substitution.[1]

The strongest effect of New World silver lay in promoting the interaction of continents. No region known to Europeans was shielded from its effects. Exports of coined Spanish silver financed imports of luxury goods from Europe for consumption by Spanish colonists, but equally, New World imports of silk from Asia for use by Mexican weavers. Spanish pieces of eight, referred to also as Spanish dollars and Spanish pesos, were the vehicle for payments by European merchants to Indian and Chinese exporters, enabling Europe to settle its trade imbalance with the Asian continent. Merchandise imported from Asia through this silver exchange was then re-exported to Africa as part of the European and transatlantic slave trade. In these ways, coined Spanish silver forged the first age of globalization.

Precursors

This said, the New World silver discoveries were not alone, or for that matter even first. The 15th century had seen other important silver discoveries in the Austrian Tyrol and Bohemia. Starting in the 1430s, a bullion famine on the back of falling mine output resulted in four and more decades of deflation. Other prices fell relative to that of coined silver, whose value, set by the authorities, remained relatively stable. This change in relative prices made prospecting and mining more attractive.

Specifically, it provided an incentive for diffusion of the Saiger process for separating silver from copper, which was adopted in Germany starting in the mid-fifteenth century, enabling less pure ores to be exploited.[2] The *Saigerprozess* involved mixing silver-containing black copper with lead, casting it into cakes, and heating those cakes above the fusion point of lead but below that of copper. Silver-rich lead would flow out, leaving copper behind. In a second stage the cakes were retreated in a drying furnace, purifying them of lead. Whether the process was developed in the fifteenth century or even earlier is disputed.[3] There is no question, in any case, that the rise in the relative price of silver encouraged its further adoption, as well as stimulating the introduction of drainage tunnels and horse-powered drainage pumps, permitting the construction of deeper mine shafts.

Buoyed by these innovations, Europe's silver output quintupled between the 1450s and the 1530s.[4] This amounted to five times the quantity of silver exported from the Western Hemisphere to Seville in the same period, the arrival of New World bullion and coin not yet being fully underway.[5] After European silver output peaked in the 1530s, Japanese production and exports took up the slack. Japanese miners developed their own version of the Saiger process, an ash-blowing technique known as *haifuki*.[6] Like their European counterparts, rising silver prices prompted them to invest in systematic surveying methods and install drains, pulleys, and pumps. By the end of the sixteenth century, Japan accounted for 30 percent of world silver production. Japanese silver reached China on Portuguese ships, and other parts of the world through the combined efforts of Portuguese traders and Chinese smugglers.[7]

Thus, the specie shortage that hindered the emergence of a global silver standard was on its way to resolution even before New World silver came on stream. Merchants, workers, and governments were growing accustomed to using silver in transactions. On its arrival, New World silver therefore found a ready reception.

Silver City

Japanese and European output was then dwarfed by the production of the mines of Potosí, in the present-day Bolivian Andes, and Zacatecas, in the Viceroyalty of New Spain, present-day Mexico. From a mere 20 percent of European output in the decade ending in 1535, New World silver output surpassed Europe's in the 1560s and doubled it in the 1570s.[8] In the sixteenth century, Potosí's rich seams accounted for 60 percent of silver production worldwide. The city swelled to a population of 200,000, larger than London and Amsterdam, despite its location at an elevation of 13,000 feet. Between 1500 and 1800, Spanish mines, led by Potosí, produced 150,000 tons of silver, a majority of newly mined global supply. A significant portion accrued to the Spanish Crown, explaining how a middle-sized state with otherwise limited natural resources would control a sizable portion of the world's landmass.[9]

Initially, operations at Potosí concentrated on surface ores, which were crushed by mills powered by mules or water wheels. Crushed ore was then smelted in blast furnaces along with lead, in a process familiar to the Germans and Japanese (Spanish mine operators in fact imported German technicians to provide relevant expertise).[10] Silver extraction and exports quadrupled again following introduction of the so-called patio process in 1570.[11] Attributed to a Sevillian merchant, Bartolomé de Medina, this technique involved mixing crushed ore with mercury, salt, copper sulfate, and water, and then spreading the resulting slurry on a stone courtyard or patio.[12] After some weeks, silver ore amalgamated with the mercury while separating from other elements, and impurities were washed away. The residual silver was then pressed into bars, which were heated in furnaces, vaporizing the remaining mercury. The bars were recast and stamped to indicate their weight and fineness. The royal coat of arms was affixed, at which point the Crown took 10 percent, reflecting its sovereignty over subsoil rights.[13]

Though nominally private, mining and refining operations were public-private partnerships. The Royal Treasury supplied inputs such as mercury and gunpowder at subsidized prices. To ensure adequate water supplies, the Spanish Viceroy Don Francisco de Toledo constructed reservoirs linked to Potosí by an elaborate network of aqueducts and canals. (Construction and maintenance, while related, were different matters. Poor maintenance of the reservoirs combined with heavy rains to cause a catastrophic flood in 1626, which drowned 350 souls.) More accurately, the viceroy commissioned the construction of the reservoirs and canals, while indigenous Andeans drafted into service performed the actual work. Consolidation of this forced-labor draft, known as the *mita*, was another contribution, as it were, of the viceroy. Able-bodied men in villages within a zone defined by travel time to the mines were required to provide one of every seven years to the mines, receiving modest compensation. The institution declined in the eighteenth century, before Simón Bolivar abolished it in 1825.

Minting operations, on the other hand, were carried out by private agents. Agents purchased their offices, receiving in return a salary and additional compensation proportional to the number of coins minted. Office holders followed standards the royal authorities set and enforced through periodic inspections. In 1497 a set of royal decrees defined the real as the basic unit of denomination, with a silver content of 93 percent and a weight of 3.383 grams. Eight reales were the equivalent of one peso piece; hence the nomenclature "pieces of eight."[14] These specifications remained in place, essentially unchanged, until the 1730s—a remarkably long span given the military and political turbulence of the period.[15] Spanish rulers evidently understood the advantages, in terms of seigniorage and otherwise, of a dominant international currency. They understood further what was required to obtain one.[16]

Coins were minted by cutting silver bars into blanks and embossing a design using a hammer and die.[17] Inevitably, the resulting coins were irregular, rendering them susceptible to clipping—that is, to being shaved to remove a portion of their silver content. Another risk was that unscrupulous mint masters might substitute lower-grade silver, heavy in impurities, since this permitted them to mint more coins from a given amount of silver, which in turn meant more compensation.

A notorious case of transgression occurred at Potosí itself, which was further removed from royal surveillance than more accessible mints of Bogotá, Mexico City, Lima, and Seville. In the 1640s, a period of declining mine output, Potosí began producing bars with less silver and more copper than permitted by royal regulation. Their pinkish tint gave them away, as did the fact that the volume of coins produced rose even while silver output fell. Assayers and the public realized that the silver content of the resulting pieces of eight was less than advertised, leading them to accept coins with the Potosí mark only at a discount.

In the case of a debasement, when silver content was reduced by decree, that reduction was at least uniform. In this instance of debasement by stealth, by contrast, the extent of the reduction was variable and uncertain, with even more damaging consequences for acceptance of the currency. This reduction of silver content, moreover, came at the expense of the Crown.[18]

Predictably miffed, King Philip IV commissioned an investigation by Francisco de Nestares Marín, a renowned inquisitor. (Here, of course, inquisitor means not only one who makes inquiries but also an official of the Spanish Inquisition, tasked with prosecuting heresy and other offences against Catholic doctrine.) Nestares Marín was known for courage and incorruptibility, an important point because previous investigators had been bribed or scared off. In the course of his three-and-a-half-year-long investigation, Nestares Marín was threatened by hired thugs, shot at, and survived a poisoning attempt. Mint officials blamed their workers, who included indigenous Andeans conscripted by the *mita* as well as African slaves. Those enslaved persons, it turned out, were among the star witnesses, since, as Kris Lane, a leading historian of Potosí put it, they had little to lose.[19] Nestares Marín's inquiries ultimately led him to conclude that the rot started at the top—that Francisco Gómez de la Rocha, a one-time coca merchant who had moved from drug trade to broking silver before becoming municipal magistrate of Potosí, and Juan Ramírez de Arellano, the head assayer, were the masterminds of the scheme. Granted special powers not just to investigate but also punish, Nestares Marín had the two men summarily executed.[20] Rocha was tortured and garroted, his body strung up in the open as a warning. This was one way of maintaining the integrity of a monetary unit.

From this point the Crown took more systematic control of operations at Potosí and other royal mints. Poor-quality coins were recalled, over-stamped to indicate their reduced value, or melted down. Re-minted coins were distinguished by a design featuring the Pillars of Hercules instead of the Jerusalem cross as before (hence "pillar dollar," as the new coin came to be known). Through these Herculean efforts, as it were, confidence in Spanish silver coin revived.[21]

Unnatural Experiment

The Potosí debasement provided a natural experiment illustrating the real's global reach and consequences for globalization. As the scandal unfolded, merchants stopped accepting Spanish silver imprinted with the now notorious Potosí "P." They questioned the value of coins produced by other Spanish mints, such as that of Mexico City, and the purity of Spanish silver bars. Castilians paid their taxes in devalued Potosí coin, undermining the ability of the Crown to support troops stationed abroad. Other states, starting with Genoa in 1642, banned suspect Spanish coin, threatening to imprison those seeking to pass it. On April 1, 1650, giving in to reality, Philip IV recalled the debased Potosí coins, subjecting their holders to a 37.5 percent tax.

But the damage was done. Royal officials had no way of compelling the return of coin held outside the empire and faced stiff resistance from Spanish subjects insofar as some Potosí coin might turn out to be full-bodied. Traders complained about shortages of reputable coin. With less money chasing the same quantity of goods, the Great Inflation or Price Revolution of the preceding century and a half petered out in the

1640s, or soon after. (Pinpointing the date is hard, the statistical record being incomplete and the lags between money and inflation being long and variable.)

As inflation gave way to deflation, international commerce slowed. Although estimates of global trade for this period are rough and ready, one duo of economic historians, Kevin O'Rourke and Jeffrey Williamson, estimate that the rate of growth of intercontinental trade fell by a third, in volume terms, between the first and second halves of the seventeenth century—that is to say, in the fifty years before and after the Potosí scandal and Philip's decree.[22] Nothing better illustrates the lubricating effects of an international currency and the damage wrought by its disappearance.

Following this interruption, and with the Crown's reform efforts, minting resumed at a faster pace than before. By the end of the colonial era there were a total of seven active mints in Spanish America. The Crown also expanded existing mint facilities, reflecting its appetite for income.[23] As a result, coinage of Spanish American silver rose by a factor of five in the eighteenth century. Global trade expanded at twice the rate of the century before, again according to the estimates of O'Rourke and Williamson. Massive quantities of a universally accepted international means of payment was not the only factor contributing to this rebound, but it played a vital role.

Agent of Globalization

The Spanish minted two-thirds of the New World silver they mined before exporting it to other parts of the world. Perhaps 90 percent of these coins were pieces of eight.[24] At Potosí, where more precise records were kept following the scandal of the 1640s, the ratio of mintage to silver output was even higher; it rose still further in the eighteenth century, when the Crown installed mechanical stamping machines and other improved minting technologies.[25] Silver not minted in the New World was shipped to Seville, per royal decree, where the mint transformed two-thirds into coin, the balance remaining in the form of bars. In addition, a significant quantity of New World silver, both coin and specie, was smuggled to England, France, Italy, Germany, and the Low Countries, where it commanded higher prices than in Seville, the smugglers including Spanish officials and merchants themselves. Some ended up in the hands of the Fuggers, those erstwhile competitors of Florence's bankers.[26] Much of the rest found its way to the Crown's Genoese bankers, who took it as collateral for loans negotiated to pay the Spanish Empire's troops and suppliers in the Low Countries.[27]

From Europe, coined silver was then re-exported to Asia, with help from Portuguese merchants and, starting in the seventeenth century, the English and Dutch East India Companies. Additional New World silver reached Asia via the Pacific, conveyed there by the Manila galleons. In China, Spanish silver coins circulated alongside local copper coins and private paper notes. In India, reflecting their uniformity and perceived high quality, they circulated by count, as opposed to having to be weighed in each transaction in the manner of other coinage.

New World silver exports, like the mining and refining that enabled them, were privately organized with royal assistance. Private ships licensed by the Crown, carrying silver procured by their owner-operators, made up the treasure fleet, the convoy system linking the New World with Mother Spain. Some 75 percent of silver arriving in Cadiz and Seville in the sixteenth and seventeenth centuries and 85 percent arriving in the eighteenth century took the form of private shipments.[28]

The Crown similarly regulated the Manila galleons plying the route between Acapulco and the Spanish East Indies. Royal authorities determined the timing of voyages, taxed Chinese goods when they entered the Philippines for transshipment and then taxed them again on landing in Acapulco. The galleons made one or two round trips a year, transporting silver from Mexico to Manila and returning with silk, jade, spices, and porcelain for local consumption and re-export to Europe.[29] In the same way Roman construction of large cargo ships had been conducive to international use of their currency, Spanish development of even larger ships capable of carrying two thousand tons of merchandise and five hundred men provided a powerful vehicle for the international and intercontinental diffusion of Spanish silver coin.

Why so much silver ended up in Asia is no mystery, which is not the same as saying that the reasons are fully understood. Simply put, silver, which had utility in transactions, was scarce in Asia but abundant in Europe and the Americas.[30] In the early sixteenth century, when New World silver first began arriving in Europe, the gold-silver price ratio was 1:6 in China but 1:12 in Europe.[31] This created an obvious arbitrage opportunity. Europeans assembled silver coin and shipped it to Asia in return for gold and other merchandise.[32] Europe's comparative advantage in the extraction and export of silver was strong: as much as 90 percent of European cargos destined for China in the sixteenth through eighteenth centuries, by value, consisted of silver coins. For cargoes destined for India, the comparable figure approached 80 percent.[33]

Although trade led to convergence over time, the relative price of silver remained 50 percent higher in China than Europe in the early eighteenth century. This persistent divergence created continued arbitrage opportunities for merchants and traders but also for miners and refiners. The mining output of the Americas rose four- to five-fold in the eighteenth century in response to sustained demand for silver money from the Dutch and English East India Companies for use in their trade with Asia.[34]

By 1750, gold-silver price ratios in Europe and Asia had finally converged, eliminating the arbitrage motive. Yet the eastward flow of silver continued unabated. (This is the part that is less than fully understood.) A possible explanation is that Europe had a comparative advantage not just in mining but also in minting.[35] Lacking an indigenous source of silver coin, China acquired coin from Europe and its American colonies.[36] China had previously imported specie from Japan, as noted. It used those ingots for high-value transactions. With the growth of Chinese exports and commercialization of the Chinese countryside, however, uncoined silver became increasingly awkward as a unit of account and means of payment. Ingots had to be weighed and assayed, services for which silver masters charged a fee.[37] Spanish dollars were a convenient alternative.

Hence most silver imported into China in the four centuries after 1500 took the form of Spanish silver coin, which dominated the high-value circulation and provided the basis for China's foreign trade. The silk and spices Europeans brought back from the East were then re-exported to Africa, and traded for slaves and gold.[38] Cotton piece goods that the Europeans purchased in Bengal with silver went on to be traded in the Moluccas for spices exported to Europe.[39] In this way Spanish silver coin forged links between Europe, India, and China and served as the agent of a wider globalization.

Piasters of Eight

Spanish silver, then, fully deserved its reputation as the first global currency. Pieces of eight cost more than the silver within them, their value boosted by their uniformity, external certification, and reputation for holding their value.[40] They were plentiful and easy to access, and their global circulation made them handy for transactions. The coin's profusion of different names (pesos in Spain, Spanish dollars in the English-speaking world, piasters in France) is another indication of their global extension. Spanish silver pieces were used throughout their home regions of Spanish America itself, of course, where they were the sole recognized form of legal tender, but also everywhere from Batavia (present-day Jakarta), the capital of the Dutch East Indies, to the island of Réunion off the African coast and the port cities of the Ottoman Empire.

As early as the sixteenth century, Spanish silver coins were the principal means of payment for international transactions in East Asia, and Southern China especially.[41] When the Dutch and English East India Companies pushed their governments to mint their own versions of the real, China's traders rejected these imposters as less reputable, disapproving of their more variable weight and silver content.[42] Instead, they wanted only Spanish coin. Canton Maritime Customs, established in 1685 to regulate trade and navigation of the Pearl River Delta, took payment from foreign vessels in pieces of eight. French, Danish, and Swedish traders active in Canton in the eighteenth century paid for merchandise exclusively in silver pesos.[43] When American merchants arrived in China in 1784, their interlocutors would not sell to them on credit or accept their bills; they demanded Spanish dollars. Spanish dollars circulated as de facto legal tender in Singapore, Penang, and elsewhere in East

Asia well into the nineteenth century.[44] In South Asia, where multiple metallic currencies circulated, the silver peso was the reference unit against which exchange rates between them were fixed. Local currencies might coexist with the silver real. But even where the former were used for petty transactions, the latter dominated international trade.

No case better illustrates the extraordinary staying power of Spanish silver than the United States. England banned the export of silver coin to its North American colonies and prohibited them from coining money of their own. Hence the colonies turned to pieces of eight, minted in Mexico and obtained via trade with the West Indies. Although each North American colony made its own money of account, the colonists referred to Spanish dollars when calculating exchange rates and used pieces of eight for their commercial transactions.[45] When in 1792 Alexander Hamilton introduced the one-dollar coin of the recently independent United States, he sought to encourage its acceptance by assaying the silver content of a set of worn Spanish dollars and setting the weight and fineness of the new U.S. dollar to trade at par with that average.

Yet even once Hamilton established a mint in Philadelphia and the federal government began producing coins of its own, Spanish silver continued to dominate. Foreign merchants still preferred the old coins when purchasing U.S. goods for export.[46] Correspondingly, an act of Congress on February 9, 1793, recognized Spanish milled dollars as legal tender. Elevating their status was meant to be a temporary measure, only in effect until the new mint got up and running. But when the mint struggled to produce adequate quantities of silver coin, Congress extended the Spanish dollar's legal tender status repeatedly, in 1806, 1816, 1819, 1823, 1827, and for a final time in 1834. At this point Spanish and Mexican silver coins still accounted for a quarter of all the coin circulating in the United States.[47]

The U.S. Coinage Act of 1857 finally banned foreign coins as legal tender, the California gold rush having solved the problem of inadequate specie for large denomination coins, and the mint developing the capacity to produce copper-nickel cents. So-called free banks emitted paper banknotes in denominations of $1 and higher, and the Nevada silver rush beginning in 1858 then made it possible to mint growing numbers of silver dollars. Providing another impetus for the ban, immigrants who arrived in the United States in the 1840s brought with them not just their luggage but also a bountiful mishmash of unfamiliar monies, somewhat to the dismay and confusion of those already living in the country.[48] Hence the 1857 act, and offer by the mint to exchange "two bit" (two reales) coins for twenty-five U.S. cents, and pieces of eight (known by this time as Spanish dollars) for one U.S. dollar.

Even then, the New York Stock Exchange continued to quote prices in eighths of a dollar. The practice proved remarkably enduring: the New York exchange shifted to full decimalization only in 2001.

Losing Its Luster

Universal acceptance of Spanish silver coin—its position as not just an international currency but as the first true global currency—lingered even after the Spanish empire went into decline. Historians situate Spain's relative economic decline as beginning in the sixteenth century, but Spanish silver's global dominance survived for at least another two hundred years.[49]

That dominance disintegrated finally in the early nineteenth century in the disorder following Latin American independence, when the Crown lost control of its mints in Mexico and Potosí. Clashing armies disabled or destroyed recently installed steam engines at mines at Cerro de Pasco, in the Peruvian highlands. Mine shafts filled with water once pumps were idled, and miners were enlisted to fight wars of independence.[50]

The Western Hemisphere's new republican governments established successor mints where they could. These churned out both full-bodied and depreciated coin, though in declining quantities compared to Spanish silver's seventeenth- and eighteenth-century heyday. The silver peso was still minted in Mexico, but no longer in a single centralized mint in Mexico City. Royalists and insurgents had minted their own provisional coins during the independence struggle to underwrite commerce and pay troops. As internal travel grew hazardous, severing the royal mint in Mexico City from the provinces, branch mints started up, first in

Durango, Guadalajara, Guanajuato, and Zacatecas, and then elsewhere. This decentralized approach continued into the post-independence period, not always with positive consequences for the quality and uniformity of the resulting coinage.

Mexican silver pesos no longer flowed to Spain, since between 1823 and 1836 Mexico and Spain were in a de facto state of war. They went instead to the United States, where they augmented the currency supply, and to Britain and France, where they contributed to the reserves of the Bank of England and Bank of France. Britain having extended loans to commercial and mining enterprises in Mexico, coined silver was used to service these debts. Better-off Mexicans who had accumulated their wealth in the Spanish period worried about their new country's precarious politics, and used coined silver as a vehicle for parking their savings in London, inaugurating the now long-standing Latin American tradition of capital flight.[51] Some of their silver ended up in the hands of English merchants and bankers, who used it to finance merchandise and commodity imports from Asia, continuing centuries-long practice.

But with uniformity and external certification no longer guaranteed by a formidable, long-established power, acceptance of the once-coveted silver started turning to rejection. Following China's defeat in the First Opium War (1839–42), the European powers minted their own trade dollars to use in their trade with the country. There could be no clearer indication of how far Spanish, now Mexican, silver had fallen.

5

Fiat Lux

NEW WORLD silver extraction peaked in the seventeenth century, after which production fell into decline. Fortunately, from a monetary standpoint, it left other options in its wake, most notably bank money and bills of exchange. The Florentines and others had long since used bills to settle cross-border transactions, as depicted earlier, including with suppliers in the Low Countries. The Dutch, familiar with the practice, took it to new heights. Starting in the seventeenth century, they created a pure fiat currency, as distinct from bank money convertible into specie. The Bank of Amsterdam managed the new currency, operating as a de facto central bank. In effect, the Dutch elaborated earlier Italian experiments with bank credit, although they made the leap of delinking credit from precious metal. The Dutch invented their bank money for domestic reasons, but what started out domestic did not stay domestic. In time, the bank money of the Netherlands came to dominate coin and bullion, including that of the Spanish, as a mechanism for financing trade, extending cross-border loans, and otherwise executing international payments.

From a sixteenth-century perspective, odds seemed low that the Netherlands would develop into a commercial powerhouse or that Dutch bank money would become a leading vehicle for cross-border transactions. Amsterdam was a commercial backwater. While the Dutch controlled the nearby Baltic trade, their commercial sway extended no further.[1] Merchants and investors there still formed antiquated trading partnerships to underwrite single voyages. They dissolved these when the ship returned, the cargo was sold, and profits were distributed, as had been the practice for centuries. The organizational costs of these arrangements were considerable, for the same reasons that the costs of *commenda* contracts in thirteenth-century Florence were considerable.[2] Italian merchants had long since graduated from this awkward start-and-stop process. Dutch firms, in contrast, continued to lack of the continuity of the great Italian merchant houses well into the sixteenth century.[3]

Moreover, the monetary landscape of the early Dutch Republic was chaotic. Multiple mints in multiple provinces produced a jumble of coins, with additional coins of neighboring authorities circulating alongside. Philip II, who on becoming King of Spain in 1556 inherited the Netherlands, made a futile attempt to impose order on this chaos. Philip quickly placed restrictions on Dutch mint masters, as part of a broader effort to centralize administration of the provinces. In 1557 he introduced a new silver coin, the eponymous Philipsdaalder, to take precedence over the others and promote uniformity. But these arrangements collapsed in 1572 with the Dutch Revolt against Philip's centralizing policies. Holland and Zeeland seized local mints and, to fund their militaries, pumped out debased coins. Other provinces, losing silver, responded in kind.[4]

Following the final confederation of seven Dutch provinces in 1588, the newly formed Dutch Republic had fully fourteen operating mints and a bewildering array of full-bodied and depreciated coins. "The competition among these mint masters was in most cases to the detriment of the fineness and weight of the currency," as the Dutch monetary historian J. G. van Dillen politely put it.[5] Small mints beyond the boundaries of the Republic and hence beyond the reach of its regulation supplied yet additional varieties of gold and silver coin, passing them off as full-bodied—or at least as no more debased than already circulating media. By the close of the sixteenth century, more than eight hundred coins enjoyed de facto legal tender status.[6] Dutch moneychangers did business in literally a thousand different gold and silver units.[7]

Order from Chaos

By this point, Dutch merchants had had enough. Seeing commerce held back by monetary disarray, Holland introduced high-value gold coins for use in its trade with the Baltic. Other provinces, inspired by its example, followed in issuing trade coins tailored for use in the Baltic, the Levant, and other parts of the world. Possessing efficient minting technology and organization, the Dutch successfully exchanged their trade coins for imported agricultural goods and other commodities.[8]

Merchant investors engaged in long-distance trade meanwhile began organizing as shareholders and directors. Managers responsible for day-to-day operations now reported to boards of directors representing the shareholders as a group. This sounds strikingly familiar to modern ears, as this was a modern-looking corporate form, more so even than the holding company form developed by the Florentines in the fifteenth century. Next, in 1602, a permanent trading entity, the Dutch East India Company, or VOC, was established with a charter from the Dutch Parliament, transferable shares, and a twenty-one-year monopoly on Asian trade.[9] Just as merchants in Florence had moved from contracts governing individual voyages to standing partnerships sponsoring multiple sailings, the Dutch now established permanent trading companies, aided by the patronage of the state.

The VOC served as a conduit for the movement of Dutch currency and credit between Europe and Asia. It carried Dutch and Spanish coin from the Netherlands, much as the Manila galleons carried pieces of eight from Acapulco.[10] The VOC also transported silver bullion to Asia, where it minted silver coins bearing the company's imprint.[11] In fact, silver coins and ingots constituted the bulk of the cargo on the VOC's outbound ships.

The VOC and other such partnerships (the Dutch West India Company, for example) helped to enlarge the Dutch trade network from the Baltic and the Atlantic coasts of Spain, France, and Portugal to Italy, Russia, the Levant, West Africa, the Americas, and Asia. The Dutch used their proprietary trade coin to buy up cotton, silk, porcelain, textiles, tea, pearls, ivory, and above all, spices. Use of the coin expanded in parallel with Dutch commerce, in the familiar historical pattern of finance following trade.[12] Dutch mints accommodated this demand by creating large-value coins tailored to purpose: the leeuwendaalder for trade with the Levant, the silver dukaat for trade with the Baltic, and the silver ducaton for trade with the East.[13] They made the coins mainly out of Spanish silver, brought to the Netherlands directly from Spain or with intermediation by England once the Spanish and English signed the Treaty of Madrid, ending the Anglo-Spanish war and reestablishing trade relations.[14] Previously the VOC had sent Mexican and Sevillian pieces of eight to its outpost in Batavia to finance purchases of pepper and other commodities. Over the half century following the advent of the ducaton, it shifted to carrying and using Dutch rather than Spanish money.[15]

These coins traded at fixed prices against the bank money of the public banks of provinces, foremost among which was the Bank of Amsterdam. Impetus for founding the bank in 1609 had been the need to straighten out the messy domestic currency situation. But international implications followed. The Bank of Amsterdam held gold and silver on behalf of Dutch merchants, crediting their deposit accounts. It accepted reputable, full-bodied gold and silver trade coins at their official rates, while assaying other coins and crediting the depositor's account according to their precious metal content. In this way, it worked to transform a confusing, heterogeneous array of coin into uniform bank money. Although deposits at the bank bore no interest, the City of Amsterdam guaranteed their security, extending the municipal equivalent of deposit insurance. The bank's customers could withdraw bullion on demand, whether to make payments or for other purposes, paying a transaction fee of 1 percent or slightly more. This fee compensated the bank for the cost of melting and reminting low-quality coin, as depositors naturally preferred high-quality trade coin when withdrawing their funds.

Once deposit accounts became commonplace, it was convenient to complete a transaction by instructing the Bank of Amsterdam to transfer funds from one account to another, saving the 1 percent charge. This bank giro system (where "giro" means direct transfer of funds among deposit account holders) gained critical mass once the Dutch authorities decreed that bills of exchange of more than 600 guilders (from 1643, more than 300 guilders) should be paid exclusively through the bank.[16] Already in 1625, after just fifteen years of operation, the Bank of Amsterdam listed upward of 1,350 deposit accounts.

Given Holland's proliferating commercial connections with other states and provinces, what was convenient for Dutch merchants was equally convenient for merchants based elsewhere. Correspondingly, Amsterdam became the hub of global foreign exchange and credit markets. More bills of exchange were traded on Amsterdam than on any other financial center.[17] Only bills on Amsterdam, denominated in guilders, were accepted throughout the Baltic and Russia.[18] Merchants in third countries lacking direct financial links with one another similarly settled their transactions in Amsterdam using the guilder. The economist and economic historian Eli Heckscher noted how the English, principal importers of timber and naval stores from Sweden, obtained credit and settled their accounts not in London or Stockholm but in Amsterdam.[19] Average daily turnover on the Amsterdam foreign exchange market was an astounding 2.5 billion guilders, four or five times the Republic's GDP.[20] By comparison, the Bank for International Settlements estimates for 2022 that global foreign exchange market turnover averaged $7.5 trillion, or less than a third of contemporaneous U.S. GDP.[21]

The remarkable volume and range of these transactions reflected not just the security of Bank of Amsterdam deposits but also their liquidity and stability. The bank intervened regularly in the market, buying and selling coin and bullion to ensure that bank money traded one-to-one for coin.[22] This allowed merchants to make payment with equal ease in coin or giro transfers, since recipients were indifferent between the two. The bank's interventions constituted early recognition that liquidity was crucial for the operation of a central money market, and of an international money market in particular. It acknowledged that liquidity did not take care of itself. The Bank of Amsterdam's interventions thus marked a significant step in the development of international financial markets, echoing all the way into the present. Its interventions institutionalized this liquidity-provision function, a function that in time would become standard practice for central banks supporting the operations of an international financial center and international currency.

Payment on Receipt

The Bank of Amsterdam, recall, stood ready to buy and sell coins in exchange for credit balances held in its deposit accounts, charging a fee of 1 percent for the withdrawal of coins. Starting in 1684, merchants received both guilders and a receipt when depositing high-quality gold and silver coins. Possession of the receipt allowed them to repurchase exactly the same coin deposited previously for a fee of just a quarter percent for silver and a half percent for gold.[23] The bank fashioned this receipt system as part of a tightening of internal controls; it allowed the bank to more easily trace the provenance of deposits of gold and silver.

The implications, initially unanticipated, were far-reaching. Deposits and giro transfers became more attractive for those possessing a receipt, since these financial claims were now convertible into silver and gold at even lower cost. This dramatically expanded the use of bank transfers. Better still, receipts were transferable, so depositors with no immediate need for coin could sell them on the secondary market. The purchaser could redeem coin from the bank so long as he had an account containing at least a matching amount.[24] This means of payment was highly sought after, since receipts were fungible, had a low fee, and guaranteed the type of coin that could be redeemed. Traditional withdrawals without receipt, which still cost 1 percent or more, fell into disuse and soon were abolished.

Importantly, coin deposited before 1684 for which the account holder had received a corresponding amount of bank money now became property of the bank. Not having received a receipt at the time of deposit, the account holder could no longer redeem bank money for gold or silver. In technical terms, his bank money, which was no longer convertible into specie, became a de facto fiat currency. This is not to say that depositors minded, given the stability and wide international acceptability of Bank of Amsterdam deposits.

These arrangements supported a growing range of financial transactions centered on Amsterdam and denominated in guilders. Bank money was more liquid, safer, and easier to transfer than large gold and silver coins. It therefore was more attractive for making international payments.[25] Bank funds under receipt could be used to purchase bills of exchange and earn interest, thereby deepening the market in bills. Merchant bankers with reputable customers added their signatures to their clients' bills, guaranteeing payment on maturity.[26] Metals dealers, prominently including twenty-five to thirty German Jewish firms, used receipts to import precious metal, instructing their agents in other cities to purchase full-bodied coins with bills drawn on Amsterdam.[27] In this way Amsterdam became the center of global specie markets. A huge flow of coins were deposited in the bank under receipt. At the height of this system, in the mid-eighteenth century, fully a quarter of all newly produced New World silver flowed through the bank.[28] Today the Netherlands Bank, the central bank of a small country of seventeen million residents, remains among the top ten gold-holding central banks. The roots of this exception trace back to the seventeenth century and the Bank of Amsterdam's receipt system.

The geographical span of the Amsterdam money market was enormous. By the early eighteenth century, the firm Andries Pels & Sons, at that time Amsterdam's largest merchant bank, did acceptance business with clients in scores of European countries.[29] From providing short-term acceptances, Dutch financial firms moved next into underwriting long-term loans, in much the way the Florentines moved from trade credit to sovereign lending. Their first long-term loans were mortgages on plantations in the Caribbean and Surinam, serviced out of product consignments controlled by the initiating merchant-banking houses. They then securitized these loans and sold them on to other investors.[30] After 1750, similarly structured loans were floated on behalf of Denmark, Sweden, Austria, Russia, and Poland by Dutch merchants who developed trade relations with these economies before branching into banking.[31] In 1782, a loan was organized for the young United States, a self-declared independent republic still at war with Britain and with little in the way of a financial track record. The new nation was desperate for the funds to pay troops, buy weapons, and otherwise sustain the war effort but lacked the tax system needed to mobilize that funding at home. Arranged by John Adams, the future U.S. president and then minister plenipotentiary to the Netherlands, the Dutch loan bore a

5 percent rate of interest, ran ten years to maturity, and was in the impressive amount of three million guilders.

At this point, Amsterdam and the guilder had unquestionably taken center stage in the international monetary system. Amsterdam had the lowest interest rates in Europe, reflecting the unmatched liquidity of the market and the security associated with the receipt system. Interest rates were low, in modern parlance, because of the guilder's safe-asset status.[32] The obligations of merchants and bankers in other countries were readily converted into drafts on Amsterdam, the market there being deep and liquid and the exchange rate being stable.[33] Come the mid-eighteenth century, the exchange rate on Amsterdam—meaning that between the guilder and other currencies—was quoted more widely than any other exchange rate. Economic historian Marc Flandreau and his colleagues, in their exhaustive catalog of eighteenth-century foreign exchange transactions, find quotations for the guilder in a staggering 84 percent of all financial centers worldwide.[34] The one place to which the guilder's reach did not extend was Latin America (apart from Surinam), where Dutch trading companies failed to penetrate and Spanish silver continued to dominate.

For all its activity, the Bank of Amsterdam remained less than a full-fledged central bank, in that it did not issue currency notes, though its receipt system fairly approximated them. Nor did it act as a lender of last resort. But as a dependable provider of liquidity, it supported the operation of a deep capital market capable of financing a massive volume of cross-border transactions spanning much of the world.

Unhappy Circumstances

As few expected the Dutch rise to prominence, few anticipated that these happy circumstances would soon come to an unhappy end. Although the Dutch traded extensively, growing French and English competition progressively eroded their commercial predominance. Dutch policymakers pursued aggressive military and diplomatic action to protect their trading links, battling foreign armadas and negotiating commercial treaties. But like sixteenth-century Florence, which lost to larger regional states on the battlefield, the Dutch lacked the wherewithal to contend with better-resourced French and British forces. Taxes to support the military grew heavier, weighing even more on economic growth. Already in the late seventeenth century, problems beset the fishing and processing industries. By the mid-18th century, cloth manufacturing, facing stiff French competition, was in decline. Where in 1671 the cloth industry of Leiden had produced 139,000 pieces, by 1750 output had fallen to 54,000 pieces, and by to 1775 41,000 pieces.[35] Mirroring Florence before it, Dutch manufacturing suffered the consequences of excessive financialization. Instead of investing in industrial enterprises that would have strengthened the economy, the rentier class used their wealth to speculate in West Indian mortgage securities. They invested in British funds, as shares in the British East India Company, the Bank of England, and the South Sea Company were known.[36]

The Republic's entrepôt trade was then dealt a blow by the English Navigation Acts and their counterparts in other countries, which taxed or prohibited recourse to Dutch shipping. Baltic trade, traditionally a Dutch preserve, stagnated as bulk products such as grain, salt, and herring gave way to trade in manufactures, few of which the Netherlands produced at scale. There were expedients: resorting to commission trade, which involved receiving goods for sale from foreign producers and purchasing goods on behalf of foreign buyers, enabled Dutch shipping and commerce to defend market share. Smuggling was another creative response to the Navigation Acts and allowed Dutch merchants to avoid heavy English taxes on imported tea. Rising merchant banks such as Hope & Co. focused on finance. They funded traders, foreign as well as domestic, and lent to governments. Companies such as Hope, as contemporaries often referred to it, were international from the start.[37] The founder of the Dutch Hopes, Henry Hope, had moved from Scotland to Rotterdam in the 1660s to broker trade between Holland and England. The start-up being unsuccessful, he moved back to London, pursued there by his Dutch creditors. After the family settled its debts, Henry's son Archibald returned to Rotterdam, first resuming the firm's English trade and then expanding it to the Americas, to which Hope transported British colonists, via Rotterdam, and from which they sourced plantation goods. Hope participated in the slave trade, arranging for the transportation of West Africans to those same Caribbean plantations, and becoming actively involved in plantation management. A branch of the family moved to Amsterdam at the beginning of the eighteenth century and then diversified from trade to lending, first to plantations in the West Indies, where they had property and with which they already had trade relations, and then to governments.

From 1772, owing partly to its own growth and to the exit of competitors in the financial crisis that year, Hope became the leading merchant bank in Amsterdam. At this point its capital equaled that of the Bank of Amsterdam. This, then, offers another example of the Florentine and then Dutch path of starting out as a merchant, moving into merchant banking, and then becoming bankers pure and simple.

Extend and Pretend

These strategies helped, but they did not slow the inroads of fierce French and British industrial and commercial competitors into struggling Dutch trade. The difficulties of the VOC, the most important economic enterprise of the day, then brought the economy's problems to a head. In its heyday in the late seventeenth century, the VOC had monopolized global trade in cinnamon, nutmeg, cloves, and pepper, shipping these and other products to Batavia and then on to Europe, where they could sell for upwards of triple their purchase price. But lucrative markups were unsustainable when the British East India Company and other new competitors entered the same field. The VOC pivoted to selling cotton, silk, tea, and coffee. It integrated backward, raising coffee on its own plantations in Java. But the British responded by adopting similar strategies, moving into these markets as well. The French imported coffee from the West Indies. Sweden, Denmark, and Austria established Asian trading companies, which they funded, with no little irony, by borrowing on the Amsterdam market. The VOC next attempted to offset falling profits by expanding the scale of its operations, borrowing to finance new investments. Ultimately, however, more ships financed by taking on more debt did not make for more profits. They instead made for financial fragility.

The Bank of Amsterdam had not been created to act as a lender. Its founders intended it to serve as a repository for gold and silver and to provide a uniform currency. Over time, however, the merchants and city council members overseeing its operation pressured it to lend to the city government and, more ominously, to the VOC. Amsterdam's governing council had mixed motives, since council members were investors and even directors of the East India Company.

As late as 1778, the VOC religiously repaid what it borrowed from the Bank of Amsterdam out of the proceeds of its annual auctions of colonial produce.[38] But the Fourth Anglo-Dutch War of 1780–84 strained its finances to the breaking point. This conflict grew out of the British Royal Navy's interference in Holland's trade with the rebellious American colonies. (Amsterdam's willingness to finance the U.S. loan negotiated by John Adams had not helped to smooth relations.) British interference escalated with the declaration of war: as a result, the VOC's shipments fell in 1780 to their lowest ebb in a century, the antiquated Dutch fleet being no match for the formidable British Navy.

Given the fixed costs of maintaining ships, fortresses, plantations, and staff, the VOC doubled down on borrowing from the Bank of Amsterdam. And for the first time, it rolled over rather than repaying earlier loans.[39] Depositors began to question whether the bank would recover the principal it had lent to the company, initiating a downward spiral. They responded in the manner of panicked depositors everywhere, running on the bank by presenting their receipts and demanding gold and silver coin in return. The bank's gold and silver reserves fell alarmingly, from more than seventeen million guilders in 1776 to less than eight million in 1783.[40] With its reserves of gold and silver dwindling, the bank was no longer able to intervene in the market to keep bank money stable in terms of specie.

The crisis management that followed was almost comical for its futility. In a classic instance of what bankers today refer to as "extend and pretend," the Bank lent the VOC an additional 2.5 million guilders in 1782 to put off the day of reckoning, and with the hope that, if things went wrong, the government of Holland would bail it out. Wrong they promptly went: in 1784, under the Treaty of Paris, which ended the Fourth Anglo-Dutch War, the English gained the right of free trade with the Dutch East Indies. Anticipating additional losses, the VOC stopped servicing its debts. When the Bank of Amsterdam attempted to stabilize the value of bank money and restore investor confidence by again selling guilder coins, its reserves fell precipitously. The French Revolution relieved the pressure temporarily. Gold that normally would have flowed to Paris now flowed to Amsterdam instead; the Bank of Amsterdam, if no longer an entirely safe haven, was at least a safer haven than any comparable French repository. But the respite did not last. In 1790, experiencing renewed withdrawals, the Bank was forced to raise the price of gold coins, effectively devaluing bank money.

In 1791, a desperate Amsterdam City Council authorized the issuance of six million guilders worth of bonds to recapitalize the Bank. While the sum was impressive, only 40 percent of the funds actually went toward recapitalization, the balance being diverted to the city's own pressing financial needs. The city council was effectively lending to itself; 60 percent of its 1791 bonds were essentially fictitious. Inadequate recapitalization, as a negative signal, was worse than no recapitalization at all. Depositors continued withdrawing coin from the Bank and, when possible, shipping it abroad. The bank now lacked the resources to maintain the liquidity of the Amsterdam market and ensure the availability of trade finance. The city for its part lacked the resources to recapitalize the bank. Increasingly, merchants in search of funds looked elsewhere, namely to London.

In 1795, the death knell sounded when French forces occupied the Netherlands, and Dutch commerce collapsed. As in earlier historical cases, from ancient Rome to medieval Byzantium, financial collapse followed. The partners in Hope & Co., the most important Dutch merchant bank, fled to England. In the upheavals that followed, French, Austrian, Danish, Russian, Spanish, and Swedish governments suspended their debt-service payments to Hope & Co. Some governments repudiated their obligations outright. The international role of the guilder, like the Dutch Republic itself, was no more.

6

The World's Banker

WHEN THE HOPES FLED AMSTERDAM IN 1795, they moved to London in lieu of another continental financial center. London had several attractions for the financially minded. It was safely beyond the reach of the French. The city was poised to supplant Amsterdam as the leading international financial center. It did not hurt, of course, that the British government, welcoming the Hopes' expertise and even more their gold, sent a Royal Navy frigate to accompany them across the Channel.

London's origins as an international financial center traced back to the sixteenth century, when English overseas trade increased and the Royal Exchange, the commodity exchange considered the city's first formal financial institution, was founded. The Glorious Revolution then encouraged investors, including Dutch investors, to hold British consols, the perpetual bonds birthed there in 1751.[1] Investors were so encouraged by the creation of a constitutional monarchy, where the power to approve government borrowing and raise taxes was vested in Parliament, where bondholders were directly represented.[2] In addition, the country developed a party system in which creditors were embedded in a larger coalition, the pluralistic Whig Party, amplifying their influence and enhancing the credibility of English credit.[3]

By the eighteenth century, England had developed a dynamic and highly articulated financial system. It had a liquid market in consols, whose prices rose and fell with economic and financial conditions. The Royal Exchange was complemented by additional commodity exchanges, whose operation enabled merchants financing imports and exports to accurately value the underlying collateral. A maritime insurance market grew up in Lloyd's Tavern, supporting shipment of those commodities. Private bankers collected deposits, discounted bills of exchange (providing advance payment before the date the bill was due), extended loans to brokers, and acted as agents for provincial banks. Closer to Westminster, bankers in the West End managed funds for the Crown and landed aristocracy.

In the eighteenth century, these bankers worked hand in glove with their counterparts in Amsterdam.[4] Packet boats carried mail between England and the Netherlands twice weekly. When an English merchant-manufacturer wished to import linens from Germany, print them locally, and export them to North America, he could instruct his bank to arrange with a correspondent in Amsterdam to pay his German supplier.[5]

Changing of the Guard

In the final decades of the eighteenth century, as industrialization spread from textiles to other sectors, the balance began to shift. London bankers now provided international credit directly. Although the Dutch extended their pioneering loan to the U.S. government in 1782, Britain financed the bulk of U.S. trade. Over the subsequent century, international financial transactions originating in London and denominated in sterling rose to the point where the city and the pound dominated trade and investment finance worldwide. London took over as the "clearing house of the world," the sterling bill of exchange becoming the closest thing to "a form of 'international currency.'"[6] Banks in London bought and sold sterling bills, allowing merchants at home and abroad to finance imports on credit, and to receive payment for exports in advance of the settlement date. The turnover of bills in London rose five-fold between 1840 and 1913. A growing number of those bills financed trade that never touched British shores. On the eve of World War I, most bills originated and traded in London were for foreign or, more precisely, overseas transactions.

What was true of trade was equally true of finance. Sterling was the most important currency for international bonds, a majority of which were underwritten by London-based investment banks.

The French and Napoleonic Wars accelerated this changing of the guard, Amsterdam-based bankers such as the Hopes not being alone in abandoning the continent for London. British expatriates made the same migration along with native bankers based in Paris, Amsterdam, and other continental financial centers. Prominent among them was Walter Boyd, a stereotypically adventurous Scotsman who started his career in the French capital, providing banking services to English tourists and foreign diplomats, including Thomas Jefferson, before branching into speculative investments in securities and foreign exchange. Boyd fled Paris for London in 1792, following abolition of the monarchy and just ahead of confiscation of the property of his firm, Boyd, Ker & Co., and issuing of arrest warrants for his partners. Within a couple of years in his new milieu, he was a leading financier of the English Crown and its foreign allies.

Traders from Hamburg, Berlin, Leipzig, and Hanover, some but not all of Jewish origin, also gravitated to London, drawn to its climate of religious toleration, much as they gravitated toward Amsterdam in previous centuries for similar reasons.[7] This wave likewise brought with it notable figures. Seventeen-year-old Johann Heinrich Schröder arrived from Hamburg in 1802 in advance of Napoleon's occupation of his Hanseatic hometown. He was soon doing booming business smuggling British goods in violation of the Continental System (Napoleon's blockade on the import of British goods into French-controlled territories).[8] The firm he founded, J. Henry Schröder & Co., became one of the nineteenth century's top merchant banks.

The most famous example, no doubt, was Nathan Mayer Rothschild, sent by this family from Frankfurt to Manchester in 1798 to arrange exports of cotton goods to the continent. Known for his brusque manner and even more for his ready cash, Rothschild started out buying up large quantities of textiles, which he shipped directly to markets across Europe, cutting out the middlemen who traditionally dominated this trade. Soon Rothschild was advancing funds to those same Midlands manufacturers and continental importers. After a decade accumulating wealth, he moved from Manchester to London and from commerce to finance, using family connections to move funds on behalf of the Crown, paying its troops abroad, and transferring English subsidy payments to the country's European allies.

That Rothschild relocated to Manchester to work in the textile trade is indicative of other attractions of Britain besides the natural protection from French occupation provided by the Channel. Burgeoning mechanized textile production supercharged British exports. London had surpassed Amsterdam as a trading center already in 1780, gauged by the number of ships entering and leaving its port. This marked a drastic shift from a century before, when the Dutch merchant marine accounted for fully half of all European shipping and the value of Dutch exports was twice that of the British. British exports rose further during the French and Napoleonic Wars, energized by martial disruptions to the country's continental European competitors and manufacturing growth in the Midlands. Although France seized the occasional English ship, the cost of naval insurance fell during wartime, testifying to the Royal Navy's rule of the seas.[9]

Real Bills

London's emergence as the preeminent financial center and sterling's status as the leading international currency reflected the operation of a dense network of institutions. Along with the metropolitan banks, organized commodity exchanges, and insurance markets developed in earlier years, there had now sprung up investment banks specialized in underwriting bonds for governments and railways. Overseas banks established by London merchants in foreign commercial centers provided trade credit and ancillary services. Foreign and overseas banks headquartered in Western Europe and the Commonwealth opened London branches to place their clients' money there. London had an organized Stock Exchange, and a nascent market in Treasury bills (short-dated Treasury securities), which would grow in importance as time went on. There was the gold standard to limit exchange risk, and the Bank of England, which in time would assume lender-of-last-resort responsibilities. All of this with the Royal Navy to ensure safe passage.

London had not always been so internationally oriented. Bills of exchange, the most popular financial instrument, remained for many years entirely domestic. They had long been familiar to London merchants and bankers, courtesy of the Italian merchant-financiers resident there in the thirteenth and fourteenth centuries.[10] Like others exposed to Italian finance, the English were quick to grasp how these practices, employed by foreigners for cross-border payments, might also be used in domestic transactions.

But the bill of exchange only came into its own in the eighteenth century when two developments collided: the rapid growth of production and trade, and a shortage of silver for commercial transactions. This story featured none other than Sir Isaac Newton, England's premier scientist. Newton was appointed Warden of the Royal Mint and then, upon the death of incumbent Thomas Neale, was made Master. He had been recommended for the post to solve a set of troublesome problems, including drunkenness among mint masters and the counterfeiting and clipping of small-denomination silver coin. There was also a subtler issue. The Master was responsible for setting gold and silver prices at levels where it was profitable to coin both metals and keep them in simultaneous circulation, gold for high-value payments and silver for everyday commercial transactions.

Newton took his post at the mint seriously, deploying his prodigious mathematical skills and making extensive calculations to ensure his plans would work. Unfortunately, the key calculation, in which he attempted to set the relative price of gold and silver at an appropriate level, went awry. Specifically, Newton did not factor into his calculations the massive gold discoveries that had just occurred in Minas Gerais, inland from Rio de Janeiro. With Brazilian specie flooding into Europe courtesy of Portuguese traders, the market price of gold dropped below Newton's official price, leaving the mint swimming in gold but denuded of silver. Silver was exported to Asia, all but disappearing from the British Isles. This left only gold, which was still too valuable for many commercial transactions, and copper, minted to provide small change, which posed the opposite problem.[11]

In the absence of metallic alternatives, merchants dispatched written instructions to their banks. In time these private orders were standardized. Then they became negotiable, meaning one could sell them to third parties. At this point they became bills of exchange, in other words. These instruments, popularized in the wake of Newton's gaffe, became the standard vehicle for settling commodity and merchandise transactions. The main way of obtaining credit from a bank was, similarly, by discounting a bill of exchange.[12]

Neither uniformity nor negotiability was achieved overnight. Written payment instructions began as idiosyncratic orders by merchants and banking firms. Their format varied by circumstance and location; only in time did they acquire a standard form. Likewise, negotiability, which transferred to the bearer the rights and juridical protections of the originator, was established gradually. A primitive version of the principle had developed in Antwerp and Amsterdam in the sixteenth century, as noted in chapter 5, but English courts continued to question its validity.[13] Hence the take-up of bills was slower in England.

Toward the end of the eighteenth century, English jurists finally began recognizing the negotiability of domestic credit certificates.[14] Even then they hesitated to extend the principle to "accommodation paper," bills accommodating a merchant's need for short-term credit. In a typical accommodation transaction, one firm drew on a second firm an odd amount that approximated payment for goods that could feasibly be shipped to the second firm. When the bill came due, the process was reversed, and the credit was repaid with interest.[15] But the commercial transactions underlying these transactions were entirely fictitious—the goods never in fact existed.

The illusion was needed because strictly financial transactions fell afoul of the real bills doctrine. According to this principle, variously attributed to John Law and Adam Smith, market participants should draw bills and create credit only when purchasing and selling real, existing goods.[16] Real bills were essential for settling commercial transactions, which made the economy run, so issuing them was well and good. "Fictitious" accommodation bills drawn for purely financial purposes, in contrast, only encouraged speculation, bubbles, and busts, adherents to the doctrine argued, resulting in costly dislocations.

English jurists were beholden to the real bills doctrine. Consequently, over the course of the eighteenth century, they extended negotiability only to a range of real but not fictitious bills. The bearer, to enforce his claim, still had to cite an actual, underlying commercial transaction. In the nineteenth century, with a growing need for credit, England did begin to allow negotiability for accommodation paper—the holder simply had to document that there was an underlying transfer of funds.[17] Reality was finally acknowledged in 1836, when the law was reinterpreted to treat accommodation paper in the same manner as real bills.

Innovation and Infrastructure Once More

The development of a liquid market in domestic, also known as inland, bills of exchange accompanied this evolution. Transactions in inland bills rose from £2 million in 1700 to £30 million in 1775 and £477 million in 1815—that is, by a remarkable 250 times.[18] British GDP meanwhile increased by a factor of five, according to the best available estimates.[19] This rise in the ratio of bills to output indicates a financial revolution of the first order.

An elaborate infrastructure for issuing, trading, and investing in bills supported this revolution. At its center were London's banks. Many of these banks had goldsmith origins, goldsmiths holding their customers' specie and plate for safekeeping and putting them to work as short-term loans. Rather than lending out actual specie, however, goldsmiths made their loans in the form of notes, which they promised to convert into gold on demand, in this way anticipating modern banking practice. Merchants quickly figured out that it could be more convenient to pay one another by transferring these notes instead of physically conveying coins, and a fledgling system of bank credit developed. By 1700, forty goldsmith-bankers were active in London.[20] Following this example, members of other trades started to establish their own banks. By 1800, London was home to seventy banks, some substantial in size.

In contrast, a multitude of small banks, more than seven hundred in number, dotted the countryside beyond London. Many of these makeshift operations, which began appearing in the 1750s, were little more than "jumped-up shopkeepers with no knowledge of banking principles," according to Wilfred King, an early historian of London's financial markets.[21] Here King was channeling Lord Liverpool, who complained in 1825—not a good year financially, as we will see—how "any small tradesman, a cheesemonger, a butcher, or a shoemaker, may open a country bank."[22]

Among other activities, such as accepting deposits, extending loans to local farmers and shopkeepers, and managing estates for absentee landlords, these country banks issued notes, which statute permitted so long as they had no more than six partners.[23] This was an incentive to stay small, creating to what to all appearances was a highly atomized banking system. Appearances were deceiving, however, since there were also the integrating operations of London's banks. Country banks relied on London correspondents to make payments on their behalf. To this end, they maintained interest-earning deposits with their metropolitan agents. These connections linked financial conditions in the countryside and the capital. A country bank might instruct its agent to buy bills on its behalf, putting its deposits to work. Insofar as such bills originated elsewhere, this linked financial conditions across regions.

Specialized bill brokers appeared next. These brokers obtained bills of exchange for banks that wished to discount them—that wished to purchase them at a discount before they matured and earn a return on the difference between their purchase price and face value. Equally, brokers accommodated banks needing cash by taking bills off their hands. Early bill brokers were small-scale operators, often failed bankers. Such were the origins of Thomas Richardson, engaged in bill broking from 1802, who was joined by John Overend in 1805 and Samuel and John Gurney in 1807. Following Richardson's death in 1827, the firm became Overend & Gurney, the leading bill broker of the day.

Initially, brokers such as Richardson dealt with city banks. When rapid inflation hit during the Napoleonic Wars, however, city banks turned from discounting bills to investing in government bonds. Usury laws capped the interest rate on discounts of bills at 5 percent, while bonds had no such limit.[24] Facing a dearth of metropolitan demand for their broking services, Richardson and his colleagues instead looked outside the capital for bills to discount and banks seeking discounts.[25]

In doing so, they provided a link between country banks in industrializing regions where funds were scarce and agricultural regions where they were abundant. A bank in an agricultural area, seeking to invest in bills, might obtain these from a broker, while a bank in an industrial area, with more customer demand than it could meet, might sell bills through this channel. In this way a regionally fragmented banking and financial system was knit more closely together.[26]

Bill brokers earned their commission, typically one-eighth percent of the value of the bill, by attesting to the quality of the notes they dealt.[27] Brokers, therefore, had to specialize even more than banks in assessing the creditworthiness and reliability of borrowers. Their transactions came with no formal financial guarantee; that is, the discounting banker had no legal recourse against the broker. For surety, one had only the reputation of the broker for exercising good judgment and knowing what he was doing.[28]

The discount market thereby developed into a kind of daisy chain. A bank might discount a bill on behalf of a merchant, then rediscount it at another bank with the intermediation of a broker, after which it might be rediscounted again, depending on the cash needs of the bank currently holding the instrument. The largest player in this market was the Bank of England, privately owned but with monopoly privileges and a special relationship to the government.[29] The Bank acted as discounter of last resort—a source of cash when liquidity in the discount market dried up. In this way it extended the more limited market-making activities of its predecessor, the Bank of Amsterdam, which did not discount bills.[30]

Within 24 Hours of Barter

The financial squeeze in 1825 that so excited Lord Liverpool demonstrated the importance of the Bank of England's role. In the earlier wartime period, 1797 to 1821, when gold convertibility was suspended and the bank was temporarily relieved of the obligation to pay out gold at a fixed price, it had been able to purchase bills freely. But once convertibility was restored in 1821, its purchases were limited by its gold reserves. Those reserves plunged from £14 million in 1824 to less than

£3 million in September 1825. This predicament resulted from the bank's own prior lending policy, which had been lax. Among other measures, the Bank had increased its note issue, lengthened the period over which it advanced money by rediscounting, lent against mortgages, and purchased government securities.[31] Its moves encouraged spending, including on imports, which drained gold from its reserves.

Worried that gold convertibility might be threatened, the Bank suspended its rediscounting operations. In September it sold securities from its portfolio, actively pulling liquidity from the market.[32] No less an authority than Nathan Rothschild saw this as the catalyst for the crisis that followed.[33] Banks seeking to raise liquidity by rediscounting bills at the Bank of England were stranded. On December 12 the failure of Pole, Thornton & Co., a prominent London bank, ignited runs on other financial institutions. Pole had allowed itself to become dangerously overcommitted in the earlier boom. When country banks with their own problems repatriated correspondent balances held at Pole, the bank found itself unable to meet the withdrawal demands of its depositors. These included one extraordinary, especially ill-timed £30,000 withdrawal, which suggests that someone knew something.[34]

Crisis management fell ironically to Pole's newly minted junior partner, twenty-five-year-old Henry Sykes Thornton, son of Henry Thornton (1760–1815), the English banker and parliamentarian popularly credited with originating the concept of lender of last resort. Young Thornton appealed to his more experienced connections, who were sympathetic. In response to their prodding, the Bank of England provided Pole with a secret loan of £400,000, but this was now too little, too late. Pole was forced to close its doors within a week. Being a leading London agent for country banks, its troubles sent shockwaves, leading to the failure of forty-three of its country correspondents across England, Wales, and Scotland.[35] In turn, their collapse led to bankruptcy for a substantial number of nonfinancial firms, and to runs on other country banks. Desperate for liquidity, these recalled their London deposits, threatening the stability of the entire financial system.[36]

Also threatened was the convertibility of sterling into gold and, by extension, the pound's newfound international role. Although the Bank of England had raised its discount rate from 4 to 5 percent on December 14, this was too little, too late, as well. The Bank's gold reserves, already disconcertingly low, continued to fall, indicating a lack of confidence in the bank's ability, or at least willingness, to prioritize the maintenance of gold convertibility. At the height of the crisis, in mid-December, Britain was "within 24 hours of barter," meaning that the Bank faced the imminent exhaustion of its gold reserves.[37] The option of suspending sterling's convertibility into gold was debated and narrowly rejected at a contentious five-hour cabinet meeting on the evening of Friday, December 16. Disaster was averted only when the weekend intervened, allowing time for Nathan Rothschild, acting as private lender of last resort, to mobilize substantial sums of gold in France and deposit them at the Bank.[38] It is also claimed that the Bank fortuitously discovered a previously forgotten box of uncirculated one-pound notes, augmenting its cash and enabling it to resume lending.[39]

Free to act, the Bank now purchased, discounted, and extended advances on everything that moved. Among those claiming credit for the turnaround was Vincent Stuckey, head of Stuckey's Bank and, as it happened, maternal uncle of Walter Bagehot, the English financial journalist who subsequently elaborated the elder Thornton's ideas, developing modern lender-of-last-resort doctrine.[40] (More on Bagehot appears later.) This injection of credit eased financial conditions, though it was too late to help banks and companies that had already gone under, or to prevent further economic fallout. Output and employment fell sharply. Commercial bankruptcies more than doubled between 1825 and 1826. Brick production, an indicator of construction activity, declined by 30 percent.[41] But the convertibility of the pound sterling into gold, at a fixed price, only recently restored following the French and Napoleonic Wars, survived to see another day. The newly acquired international role of the pound sterling and the London money market, if tarnished, survived as well.

The remaining London banks, having learned an important lesson, responded by increasing their cash reserves. But unwilling to see their cash lie idle, they lent that cash to bill brokers "on call," meaning on terms that allowed them to demand, or call for, repayment at any time. Brokers used these funds to buy and hold bills for their own account, earning profits on the difference between what they paid for loans and earned on bills. As their discounting operations expanded, they came to be known as discount houses.

Starting in 1830, the Bank of England acknowledged this reality by agreeing to rediscount bills not just for city banks but also for dealers and investors in bills. Four such broker-dealers, including Overend & Gurney, gained access to the bank's discount window. In this way the Bank repaired the reputational damage suffered in 1825. It affirmed its role as discounter of last resort.[42] Assumption of this role was critical for assuring the liquidity of the market in sterling bills, liquidity being a key attribute of an international currency.

International Banking

At this point, London's banking system went international. Leading agents in this evolution were the merchant banks that dealt in highly reputable bills, to which they attached their name and guarantee in return for a fee.[43] Their high-quality securities were known as acceptances, the banks in question as acceptance houses.[44] (The name derived from the practice of writing "accepted," together with the name of the accepting house, across the face of the bill.) The most prestigious were Baring Brothers and N M Rothschild & Sons, the first specializing in trade finance, the second in lending to sovereigns. But there were also others. From the 1820s, these acceptance houses opened branches abroad to originate foreign bills. Different houses specialized in different regions and commodities, reflecting their origins as merchants.[45] They provided a financial link between London and the rest of the world.

In addition to these overseas branches of major acceptance houses, self-standing joint-stock banks were established in London starting in the 1830s to provide financial services to specific countries and regions. These specialized banks were founded by merchants and financiers with knowledge of specific parts of the world. Examples included the Bank of Australasia (1835), the Colonial Bank (1836), and the Bank of British North America (1840). By 1860 there were fifteen overseas banks with 130 branches.[46]

Overseas banks had a registered head office in London, although they did most of their business abroad.[47] In Australia, New Zealand, Canada, and South Africa, where they had the field to themselves, they provided the entire range of financial services, taking deposits and making loans as well as accepting bills of exchange, which they discounted via their London offices or those of their correspondents. In Asia, where they competed with local banks, they specialized in trade finance, a field in which they had particular expertise. Rediscounting bills in London enabled them to accommodate their customers' considerable needs for credit.

Much as London-based banks and bankers opened branches abroad to originate business, foreign banks and bankers opened branches in London to gain access to its money market. The number of foreign banks with London branches rose from three in 1860 to seventy-one in 1913. In the 1860s and 1870s, banks from Australia, Canada, and New Zealand, followed by continental European banks such as Crédit Lyonnais and Deutsche Bank, all opened branches in London. Japan-based Yokohama Specie Bank opened a London subbranch, which provided limited services to its customers, in 1881. France and the United States may have been the main markets for Japan's exports of silk and tea, but finance for that trade was obtained via sterling bills discounted in London by Yokohama Bank.[48]

Even more numerous than foreign bank branch offices were foreign correspondent relationships. Foreign banks established such relationships with London banks, where the London bank held sterling deposits of the foreign bank while making and accepting payments related to the imports, exports, and sterling investments of the clients of that correspondent. On the eve of the Great War, more than 1,100 banks worldwide had correspondent arrangements in London.[49] This allowed banks in countries that did insufficient business with one another to justify investing in direct financial links to instead settle their transactions indirectly, on London, using sterling bills.

Like Water over a Causeway

In this way a market originally centered on inland credits came to be dominated by foreign bills. The bill of exchange, arising in the British Isles as a vehicle for payments between England and Italy several centuries earlier, thus returned to where it started. Bills on foreign merchants, endorsed by London acceptance houses, were now drawn on every part of the world. Many were "foreign on foreign" bills financing trade involving no British merchant that never touched British shores. By 1855, 37 percent of bills drawn on London were for international transactions. By 1870 the foreign share increased to 47 percent. By 1893 it reached 55 percent, and by 1913, 65 percent.[50] This shift was tied to rapid growth in foreign bills, which doubled in value between 1893 and 1913.[51]

Because of London's dominance of trade finance, the English financiers who dealt in acceptances could insist that these be denominated in sterling, wherever they originated.[52] Because trade credit was in sterling and transactions were settled by transferring sterling between correspondent bank accounts, importers and exporters outside Britain were incentivized to maintain sterling deposits. Since their revenues were in sterling, they borrowed in sterling, matching the currency denomination of their assets and liabilities. In this way sterling's dominance of trade finance spilled like water over a causeway into dominance of investment finance. Sterling's distinct functions, as a mechanism for financing trade, as a vehicle making payments, and as a form in which banks could hold their liquid reserves, reinforced one other. This complementarity worked to cement the currency's international role.[53]

Once habituated to London and sterling, foreign investors sought other opportunities, starting in the market for Treasury securities. Traditionally, the British government had met its short-term financial needs by relying on Exchequer bills, instruments of up to five years' duration, which the Treasury issued twice a year, in fixed denominations and carrying coupons, with little reference to market conditions.[54] Their cumbersome and illiquid nature depressed market demand for these securities—a limited demand that showed up in yields. The French government could place twelve-month Treasury bills with a preannounced interest rate of 1 percent, despite possessing a less well-developed money market. In contrast, to successfully place Exchequer bills, England's Treasury had to offer 2 percent.

To remedy this situation, Sir Stafford Northcote, Prime Minister Benjamin Disraeli's chancellor of the exchequer, turned to Walter Bagehot, editor of *The Economist* magazine. Publication of his *Lombard Street* in 1873 had catapulted Bagehot to the leading financial sage of his day; William Gladstone described him as "a sort of supplementary chancellor of the exchequer."[55] Bagehot had experience in banking, where he had become familiar with the commercial bill of exchange. His father had served as vice chairman of Stuckey's Bank, of which his uncle was chairman. (Recall the earlier discussion of that uncle's role in the crisis of 1825.) A country bank with a large branch network in its home county of Somerset, Stuckey's focused on discounting commercial bills and investing in bonds. The young Bagehot joined the firm as secretary to the management committee in 1855 and rose to head the bank's Bristol office before transitioning to journalism. Even then he continued to attend meetings of the directors of the bank.[56] His views informed by that Stuckey's experience in discounting bills, Bagehot recommended creating short-term Treasury securities that resembled as closely as possible already-circulating bills of exchange. Interest rates on these short-term Treasury bills should match those on bills of exchange, he suggested, and Treasury bills should be issued regularly, like commercial bills. The result was the Treasury Bills Act of 1877 (coinciding, as it happened, with the year of Bagehot's death) and a growing volume of Treasury bill issuance and demand.[57]

Foreign investors, especially foreign banks, liked these Treasury bills since the market was liquid and they could readily convert the proceeds into gold. Treasury bills attracted not only continental European and American investors but also those in Japan, starting when the Bank of England intermediated the Chinese war indemnity in 1895. In that episode, Japan's Finance Minister Matsukata Masayoshi convinced his prime minister that the Chinese indemnity should be paid in pounds sterling, which were as good as gold, and even more easily transferable.[58] The indemnity was financed by a loan to China from the Russian government, this being the nature of nineteenth-century alliance politics. The funds were shifted through a set of internal transactions at the Bank of England. They first moved from the Russian finance minister's account to an account listed as "Chinese Minister," and from there, on the date of the first indemnity payment, to an account headed "Japanese Minister." The order for £11,008,857 authorizing the first installment was the largest bank check in the history of the world.[59] That the Bank of England served as the vehicle for this transfer and that the principal amount was denominated in sterling again testifies to the international financial centrality of London and its currency.

Investors could find still more adventure trading on the Stock Exchange, which listed not only shares but also the bonds and debentures of foreign governments and corporations. Banks lent to brokers against the collateral of securities; the associated earnings enabled those banks to pay higher rates of interest to foreign depositors. More intrepid foreign holders of sterling could purchase stocks and bonds directly, the liquidity of the market ensuring that they could get out as easily as they got in. Their transactions focused on Britain's own Treasury bills and bonds, which had unusually deep and liquid markets. Over time, however, they came to encompass other securities, including those of foreign and colonial governments and foreign railway, industrial, and mining companies. By 1913 fully half of all securities listed on the London Stock Exchange, on many of which interest was payable in sterling, were foreign.

Thus, while London and sterling, by providing short-term credit for trade and finance, constituted an important link between home and foreign money markets, they also linked home and foreign security markets, mobilizing funds for long-term investment. With government bonds, railway bonds, and other securities trading in multiple national markets, it became standard practice when prices diverged to sell a security in one market and buy it in another until the price differential disappeared. These arbitrage transactions were profitable because they could be settled at low cost in "finance bills," which instructed the investor's bank to transfer funds between centers. By 1913, 60 percent of prime, or first-class, bills in London were finance bills, indicative of

London's centrality in these arbitrage transactions.[60] Just as the market in inland bills had once knit together British regions formerly with disparate financial conditions, these arbitrage transactions financed in London progressively integrated formerly disparate national capital markets, enabling the first age of financial globalization.

Sovereign Setbacks

Through all this, charging for acceptances remained the single most important source of income for Britain's leading investment banks. Barings earned 50 percent of its profits from acceptances in 1830, 75 percent in 1850.[61] But Rothschild and Barings also had lines in underwriting securities on behalf of foreign governments, railways, and mining companies. This was a new departure. In the eighteenth century, England had been a foreign borrower, not a lender: prior to 1780, the Dutch purchased a large fraction of the English government's debt, while the British purchased little if any of Holland's.[62] The Dutch curtailed their investment in English government securities during the Anglo-Dutch War of 1780–84, for understandable reasons, substituting French securities. But with their incomes now rising, the English finally had the wherewithal to fund their government's debt, and then some. Come the nineteenth century, Britain became not merely a capital exporter but the leading capital exporter worldwide.

The process of becoming head lender got off to a rocky start in 1794–95 when Walter Boyd of the London house Boyd, Benfield & Co., recently arrived from Paris as seen earlier, arranged a £3 million loan on behalf of Austria, an ally of the government of King George III. Starting in 1794, shortly after Britain went to war with France, Boyd developed a personal relationship with the English prime minister, William Pitt. Before long, it was said of Boyd's relationship to the minister that he was "zealously attached."[63] Boyd leveraged the connection to organize loans for financing the army, navy, and home defense. Rivals complained that they were shut out of the competition and that Boyd used his political connections to cut a sweetheart deal.[64] Despite their frustrations, the Austrian loan followed on these earlier issues to the British Crown.

Initially, Boyd had difficulty in finding willing investors in the Austrian issue, as is often the case with a novel asset class. Placing a second Austrian loan in 1797–1800 proved easier, though personal financial distress forced Boyd to bow out. He had borrowed in order to finance risky investments in the expectation that his property, confiscated by the French government, would be restituted. When this expectation was disappointed, he went bankrupt.[65]

Still, capital flight from the continent due to the French wars meant that there was ample investment finance available in London. Also important was that the British government guaranteed these groundbreaking foreign loans.[66] Austria's geopolitical circumstances were fraught, but these loans, and the second loan in particular, commanded only a modest interest-rate premium.[67] These guarantees are a reminder that the British market in foreign loans had its origins in more than the brainwaves of clever investment bankers. In addition, its development rested on government support.

As it turned out, the Austrians stopped paying interest on the debt, forcing the British government to pay the interest in their stead and make the bondholders whole. Starting in 1816 and especially in 1821–22, lengthy restructuring negotiations took place between the two governments (restructuring negotiations always being lengthy). These involved such worthies as Prince Klemens von Metternich on the Austrian side and Lord Castlereagh and the Duke of Wellington on the English. The Austrians invoked the good offices of Salomon Rothschild, urging him to write his brother Nathan, in the hope that the well-connected (and now naturalized) English Rothschild would intervene with the British government on their behalf. Whether owing to the good offices of the Rothschilds or for other reasons, negotiations were successfully concluded in 1823, and arrears were swept away. In the end the British Treasury received £2.5 million on an original principal amount of £6.2 million, and accumulated interest of more than £17 million.[68] This served as a reminder that, notwithstanding the attractions of the market, sovereign lending was risky.

Another sign of England's takeover from the Dutch appeared when the London branch of Hope & Co. partnered with Barings to fund

America's Louisiana Purchase to the tune of $11.25 million (£2.5 million).[69] Partnered is the right word: the relationship between the two banks was cemented when Thomas Baring's daughter Dorothy married one of Hope & Co.'s most important traders.[70] The transaction was financed by issuing a block of 6 percent bonds. Bonds financing the French war indemnity, extended in 1817, then signaled "the real beginning of London's ascendency with regard to international loans."[71] Barings and Hope again acted as brokers, receiving a commission of 12 percent when investors purchased the bonds.[72] The high return speaks to the attractions of the business, notwithstanding the aforementioned risks.[73]

Next up was the Prussian state loan of 1818, marketed by Rothschild. Overseen personally by Nathan Rothschild, this loan was issued in sterling, not thalers, with interest payable in London as well as other financial centers. It featured a sinking fund, a standard provision in British public debt markets since the eighteenth century, under which the Prussian government progressively retired the principal by making regular transfers to London, to be used to purchase bonds, thereby removing them from the market.[74] Although Nathan Rothschild invested for his own account, his firm primarily worked, like Barings and Hope, to organize and distribute the loan, attaching its good name and its reputation for financial probity. That a loan to the government of Prussia, funded largely by residents of Prussia, was organized in London and denominated in sterling affirmed the international status of Britain's capital and currency.[75] Evidently, the financial world already regarded sterling as a stable currency and an attractive vehicle for international investors, even though the Prussian loan predated by three years Britain's restoration of gold convertibility, suspended during the French and Napoleonic Wars.

The race to export British capital was now on. In the 1820s it focused on bond issues for the new republics of Latin America. This was the interregnum between the English canal and railway building booms, and investors trained their eyes elsewhere, toward the New World. Latin America's newly independent governments claimed glorious economic prospects, though in fact they borrowed less for economic and commercial development than to fund their militaries and fend off regional rivals. Ambitious promoters pointed to the region's silver riches. Exuberance was such that the London Stock Exchange had to lease additional room to accommodate legions of new foreign security jobbers and brokers.[76] (Jobbers were dealers who acted as market makers; they quoted bid and ask prices and bought and sold securities to make those prices effective. Brokers were specialists in particular securities who placed orders for their clients.)

Latin American governments accounted for fully £17 million of the £25 million of foreign government securities sold in London between 1822 and 1825. The first such loan, on behalf of Gran Colombia in 1820, was underwritten by Herring, Graham and Powles. The first Chilean loan in 1822 was arranged by Hulett Brothers, the first Peruvian bonds by Thomas Kinder. These were reputable London names, though not quite so reputable as Rothschild and Barings.[77] An additional £3 million was raised by Latin American mining companies, visions of vast mineral wealth dancing in investors' heads.[78] Again, Barings and Rothschild were not underwriting these loans, but more aggressive London houses such as B. A. Goldschmidt & Co. and Barclay, Herring, Richardson & Co.

With governments borrowing for military campaigns rather than ports and warehouses, questions would predictably arise about capacity to repay. These were the bonds whose prices, when they collapsed, triggered the crisis in 1825. Mining stocks were at best highly speculative. British investors new to the game may not have appreciated, or even have been aware of, the damage incurred by these mines, especially in Peru, during the wars of independence.[79] The principal underwriters of these shares, Goldschmidt & Co. and Barclay, Herring, Richardson & Co., went belly up in 1826, after several years when mining companies had little to show in the way of ore, let alone profit.[80]

This Latin American adventure set back London and sterling. Commissions as high as 12 percent, on offer to aggressive London underwriters, were nonetheless hard to resist, so the market, after only a brief pause, started up again. Loans were organized in the 1830s for U.S. states, in the 1840s for foreign railways, and in the 1860s, once earlier Latin American defaults finally were settled, for a range of foreign governments. London and sterling played an outsized role in the export of capital throughout the period, all the way up to 1913. The British economy amassed a vast pool of savings for placement abroad, not only the savings of Britons themselves but also those of foreign investors. Foreign and overseas banks with offices in London, together with British merchant banks possessing agents and correspondents abroad, provided channels through which foreign funds were attracted into sterling for reexport around the world. This was an important generalization and extension of practices in Amsterdam in the eighteenth century. Amsterdam had drawn funds mainly from Holland and its environs, limiting the market's scope. London and sterling, in contrast, drew funding from around the world, projecting their financial influence from the regional to the global.[81]

For their part, houses such as Rothschild and Barings with a reputation for probity—prior at least to the 1890 crisis when defaults on Argentine loans dented the image of the latter—gathered information on investment prospects and signaled quality by attaching their names to the borrower's prospectus. They formed syndicates with other banks to spread the risk of underwriting large loans, as the Italians had done in earlier centuries.[82] They worked with the Stock Exchange to list bonds in good standing.[83] This ensured the provision of timely information on prices, smoothing the operation of secondary markets. The liquidity of those markets was further enhanced by the activities of an expanding class of jobbers who specialized in different securities, held substantial inventories of the latter, and thereby ensured that large orders could be placed without significantly moving the price or endangering the liquidity of the market.

First Among Equals

Although London was undeniably the dominant financial center and sterling the dominant international currency, they were not alone. Between 1840 and 1870, French capital exports underwritten by Paris-based *haute banques* approached British capital exports in value.[84] These French banks resembled their British merchant bank rivals except for their greater reliance on deposit funding. But where British capital flowed to other continents, the French *haute banques* channeled capital mainly to other parts of Europe.[85] The importance of Paris as a regional financial center and the franc as a regional currency then declined with France's defeat in the Franco-Prussian War of 1870–1, after which French investors sold their foreign securities in favor of *rentes* funding French indemnity payments, which offered a relatively generous yield of 6 percent. Germany emerged as a consequential creditor following its unification and the foundation of Deutsche Bank and Dresdner Bank, also in 1870–1.[86] These "Great Banks," with their extensive access to deposit funding and multiple business lines, became prominent players in international security markets, arranging loans to governments and railways and recommending securities to their clients. Private bankers such as M. M. Warburg of Hamburg and Mendelssohn & Co. of Berlin hung on as subsidiary players.[87]

Efforts to rank creditor countries by their importance are complicated by holes in the historical record.[88] One heroic reconstruction suggests that Britain made more than half of all outstanding foreign loans in 1825 and two-thirds in 1870. On the eve of the Great War, British overseas investments totaled more than twice those of France and three times those of Germany.[89] London remained the leading international financial center and exporter of capital, buoyed by cumulated experience, government support, and a dense network of financial institutions providing unparalleled secondary-market liquidity.[90]

Regarding that liquidity, Canadian banker L. D. Wilgress put it well: "In times of strain especially, London is the only place where money can be found at all times for loans."[91] In addition to London's diverse population of investors, Wilgress emphasized also "another factor . . . making London the settling place for international indebtedness," namely "the fact that it is the only free gold market in the world. That is, it is the only place where all forms of medium of exchange are immediately and unquestionably convertible into gold."[92] Elsewhere, central banks and governments employed so-called gold devices to limit the conversion of currency into gold. The German Reichsbank, in periods of strain, converted its notes into underweight coin. It allowed conversion only in Berlin, requiring noteholders, regardless of where they lived, to bring their banknotes there. The Banque de France raised the selling price of gold bars and insisted on converting its notes into five-franc silver pieces instead of gold.[93] It required commercial banks requesting gold to post commercial paper as collateral, increasing the cost of redeeming notes. The U.S. Treasury—America not possessing a central bank until 1914—varied the premium at which it sold gold bars. Sometimes it refused to sell them at all. When the U.S. gold standard was under stress, as in 1895–96, it encouraged commercial banks to limit credit to individuals seeking to export the metal. In Switzerland, another country without a central bank, in its case until 1906, the authorities instructed banks to limit gold conversion by keeping only one teller window open, having tellers count out notes slowly, and encouraging tellers to be as rude as possible.[94]

The Bank of England made little use of these devices.[95] That one could "immediately and unquestionably" convert sterling into gold thus enhanced the currency's appeal. The credibility of Britain's commitment to convertibility, in modern parlance, was important for sterling's international status. Again, it had not always been so: in 1847 and 1857, circumstances had forced the Bank of England to temporarily suspend conversion of its notes into gold. These suspensions, the first due to a harvest failure and commercial crisis, the second due to a bubble and bust in railway shares, cast some doubt on whether sterling was indeed "immediately and unquestionably" convertible. In time, the Bank put these doubts to rest. In the aftermath of both suspensions, it restored gold convertibility at the earlier parity.[96] This rule of restoration at the previous parity inspired confidence in the stability and convertibility of sterling even in periods when the stability in question was lacking.[97]

In the Last Resort

These practices were severely tested during the Overend & Gurney crisis of 1866 and the Baring crisis of 1890. Overend & Gurney, recall, was a renowned financial firm, one of few broker-dealers with direct access to the Bank of England's discount window. Its failure in 1866, like many financial failures, had multiple causes. The most straightforward explanation is the assumption of management responsibility by a new generation of partners, who oversaw the extension of risky, poorly secured loans to desperate customers, and who more generally fell down on the risk-management job.[98] Those partners had recently expanded the firm's business from bill broking to financing foreign plantations and commodity speculation, among other dubious activities. They hired one Edward Watkin Edwards to oversee these new business lines, allowing him to earn fees from both the borrowers and investors backing the loan, which gave him an obvious incentive to approve as much credit extension as possible. A perfect storm of failed loans, falling commodity prices, and collapse of the stock market rendered the firm insolvent in 1866. Rumors of its insolvency became widespread in April, when partners in the firm put their personal estates up for sale to meet their liabilities. Then on May 10, a note was plastered on the bank's door stating, somewhat theatrically, that "we regret to announce that a severe run on our deposits and resources has compelled us to suspend payment."[99]

The Bank of England allowed Overend & Gurney to fail. The firm was insolvent, of course, which was reason enough to let it go under. But in addition, the Bank wished to set an example to discourage excessive risk taking by other lenders. At the same time, the Bank worried about contagion. Overend & Gurney's failure sparked a crisis in which panicked depositors, fearing that the rot was more general, withdrew their funds from other banks. The Bank of England was compelled to discount large numbers of bills, and to purchase bills outright, to prevent the money market from collapsing, even at risk to its gold reserves.

Barings was an even more renowned firm, the largest merchant bank not just in London but the entire world. As we have seen, its business model had come to rely increasingly on fees from foreign loans for governments. Good intermediary it was, Barings held those loans on own balance sheet until they could be securitized and sold on to retail investors. In 1890 it was caught out when its largest client, Argentina, lapsed into default following a bad harvest and a coup. In this case, the impetus for the bank's very extensive exposures came not from a new generation of bank managers but a new generation of competitors. A set of aggressive French and German banks had sought to steal away Barings' most important customer by offering to market large loans on concessional terms. Barings, to protect its market share, felt compelled to respond in kind.[100] The threat to the bank when Argentina stopped paying led to a scramble for liquidity and runs on other banks thought to have claims on Baring Brothers.

The Bank of England saw Barings, unlike Overend & Gurney, as too big and too connected to fail. It lent the firm £7.5 million in cash—cash that creditors receiving payments from Barings might present at the central bank in exchange for gold.[101] Whether these steps would strengthen confidence, allowing gold convertibility to be maintained, or precipitate additional capital flight as investors sought to get out of sterling before convertibility was suspended and the currency was allowed to depreciate was, for the moment, uncertain.

Yet, in both cases—Overend & Gurney in 1866 and Barings in 1890—funds flowed toward sterling rather than away, given confidence that any suspension would soon end and the pre-suspension price of gold would be restored.[102] This stabilizing flow demonstrated sterling's now firmly established position as an international currency and London's reputation as a safe haven. Investors viewing the future through the lens of this history bet that if the Bank were again forced to halt convertibility, it would again restore the prior value of sterling in terms of gold, if not sooner, then later. Losses on sterling today would be offset by gains tomorrow. To the extent that capital flowed into sterling in anticipation of subsequent steps, those flows might avert the need to suspend convertibility in the first place—hence the absence of currency depreciation even in the difficult circumstances of 1866, when Overend & Gurney failed, and 1890, when Barings came to the brink.

The 1866 precedent was especially important for the stability and liquidity of the money market. While the Bank of England had acted previously as a lender and liquidity provider of last resort, it had done so inconsistently. In 1825 its policy of rationing credit to the discount market had threatened financial collapse, and it was able to resume rediscounting only when Nathan Rothschild rescued the rescuer. In 1847 and 1857, providing liquidity had required suspending convertibility, which was problematic. But in 1866, for the first time, the Bank combined last-resort lending with a high discount rate.[103] In the wake of Overend & Gurney's failure, it raised its discount rate from 7 to 10 percent. Investors now saw that high rate as promising attractive returns rather than signaling weakness. By attracting gold from abroad, it eliminated the need to suspend.

In addition, the Bank of England minimized the problem of adverse selection—the problem that discounting at a high rate would attract only to the riskiest borrowers. Only they would be prepared to offload their liabilities at otherwise prohibitive cost. To avoid losses, the Bank screened potential borrowers. It provided emergency liquidity only to discounters who were well-capitalized, diversified, and in possession of high-quality collateral.[104] This was a modified version of the Bagehot dictum to "lend freely at a penalty rate." It involved lending, to paraphrase Bagehot, somewhat freely at a penalty rate. The Bank's selective provision of liquidity capped the "internal drain" of funds from the money market, while the high discount rate reduced the "external drain" of gold from the bank's reserves.[105] In this way, it successfully reconciled internal and external stability.

The result was a virtuous circle where a liquid money market backed by the Bank of England turned sterling and London into safe havens for foreign funds, while the resulting safe-haven flows supported the development of a still larger, more liquid money market. Revealingly, many bills rediscounted by the Bank of England in the 1866 crisis were claims on foreigners, consistent with this picture of safe-haven flows. Further consistent is the fact that investors who kept their funds in sterling did better than those who chose to cut and run.[106] Its actions in 1866 provided the template for Bank of England intervention in subsequent periods of strain. So reassured, foreign funds continued to flow into London for placement around the world, further assuring sterling's position as the dominant international currency.

Future Foreshadowed

Sterling's position was not impregnable, of course. When the Boer War with the Transvaal and Orange Free State erupted in 1899, the British Treasury needed to borrow abroad for the first time since the Seven Years War of 1756–63. It placed portions of its National War Loan of 1900 and three subsequent Boar War loans in, of all places, New York.[107] The United States in the mid-1890s had swung from importing to exporting financial capital, reflecting rising incomes and larger savings, together with the sheer scale of the American economy, which was now unsurpassed.[108] This shift and Britain's Boer War loans signaled a new impending change of the monetary guard.

In addition, concerns had arisen about the health of the British economy, specifically worries that it had become too financialized. The best minds were being drawn into finance rather than industry—at least when they were not drawn into politics or the foreign and colonial service. Increasingly, Britain exported capital at the expense of investing at home. Low rates of domestic investment compared to Germany, France, and the United States meant slow growth of output and productivity. A high exchange rate lured financial business to London, as it had previously to Florence and Amsterdam, but disadvantaged British manufacturers. With other economies, and not just the United States, growing faster, it was no longer clear that Britannia possessed the military might to beat back threats to its empire. Other powers began to test it, most brazenly the Germans in North Africa.

In the fifteen years leading up to World War I, about half of capital exports from the United States went to foreign direct investments in rubber plantations in Sumatra and copper mines in Latin America. The other half funded Britain's war loans and bonds issued by Japan to finance its 1904–5 war with Russia.[109] But the United States still lacked a central money market like that of London. In a country devoid of bill brokers, acceptance houses, and a central bank to act as lender and liquidity provider of last resort, U.S. financial institutions placed their idle funds in the stock market, via loans to stockbrokers, despite the fact that, if the need arose, recalling them might create as many problems as it solved. For international finance, in any case, U.S. exporters still relied on London.

While there was no immediate threat to sterling's reign, the writing was on the wall. To challenge the currency, the United States needed only to develop a liquid market in dollar trade credits, known in Anglo-American parlance as an acceptance market. That market, to remain liquid under all circumstances, required a backstop. This in turn implied the need to create a central bank.

PART II

The Dollar's World, and We Only Live in It

7

Engineering an International Currency

PAUL MORITZ WARBURG was an unlikely emissary for internationalizing the dollar. Born in Hamburg of a German Jewish family, Warburg settled in New York in 1902 at the age of 34 before becoming a naturalized U.S. citizen nine years later. He spoke English with a German accent and wrote in his adopted language with effort. But within four years of becoming a permanent resident, Warburg was the leading spokesman for creating a U.S. central bank, penning articles in *The New York Times* and speaking to large audiences on the need for monetary reform. His advice was sought by Nelson Aldrich, Republican senator from Rhode Island and leading American monetary reformer, following the perilous 1907 financial crisis. That crisis had revealed the fragility of a financial system lacking an institution to act as lender of last resort to banks in distress. Resolving the crisis had required the good offices—literally as well as figuratively—of J. P. Morgan, the wealthiest person in the country. (One is reminded of how another singularly wealthy individual, Nathan Rothschild, had rescued the British financial system in 1825.) Morgan assembled New York's leading bankers in his library, pocketing the key and locking them in until the bankers with stronger balance sheets agreed to support their weaker brethren.[1] This episode, in which the survival of the entire U.S. financial system depended on the voluntary intervention of a single private citizen, drove home the limited liquidity and tenuous stability of the New York market and the absence of public support. It showed why foreigners, and indeed Americans, resisted reliance on the dollar to finance and settle cross-border transactions.

In the wake of this sobering experience, Congress duly established a National Monetary Commission to weigh reforms. To inform the commission's deliberations, Warburg contributed a lengthy study of European banking and finance.[2] He highlighted the advantages gained by European countries from possessing a market in standardized trade credits backstopped by a central bank. He also listed the disadvantages to the United States owing to the absence of analogous arrangements, which rendered American exporters heavily dependent on British finance. In 1910 Aldrich invited Warburg to the secret meeting of bankers and economists on Jekyll Island, Georgia, where they sketched the outlines of what became the Federal Reserve Act.[3]

President Woodrow Wilson appointed Warburg to the Federal Reserve Board in 1914. He served as vice-governor (vice-chair in our modern parlance) until 1918, using his position to plump for a market in dollar-denominated trade credits. In 1919 he founded the American Acceptance Council, an advocacy group for drawing institutional investors into the country's nascent market in trade acceptances, as those trade credits had come to be known. In 1921 he organized the International Acceptance Bank of New York to engage in this business. International Acceptance Bank developed into the largest acceptance-holding institution in the world, rivaled only by the Federal Reserve Bank of New York. By the end of the 1920s, due in no small part to Warburg's influence, the dollar rivalled sterling as the leading currency in which trade credits, used to finance import and export transactions, were drafted and discounted.[4]

Bold-Faced Arguments

Warburg compensated for his lack of linguistic fluency with deep knowledge of financial markets and close connections with the banking elite. He had joined M. M. Warburg & Co., his family banking firm, in 1891 following internships in shipping and banking in London and Paris.

He knew the market in bills of exchange in London and on the European Continent.[5] In 1895, not yet 30, he married Nina Loeb, daughter of Solomon Loeb, cofounder of the New York investment-banking firm Kuhn, Loeb & Co. In 1902 he became a partner in the firm, where he came under the wing of Jacob Schiff, a senior partner interested in advancing the international role of the dollar.[6] Among other things, Schiff had played a key role in the war loan Japan's government floated in the United States in 1904, one of the first significant foreign government loans marketed to American investors.[7] Schiff now encouraged a reticent Warburg to publish his internationally oriented proposals for banking and monetary reform.

The crisis in 1907 bold-faced Warburg's arguments about the defects of the American financial system.[8] It showed that the United States, because it lacked a money market, was singularly prone to financial crises. European banks, when they had excess liquidity, used it to discount bills, enlisting the help of specialized bill brokers. Because those banks were experienced in evaluating bills and attached their guarantees to high quality paper, investors traded their claims with confidence. Moreover, European money markets were populated by a diverse collection of banks that, at any point in time, encountered different commercial conditions. Hence European banks were not all apt to buy or sell bills at the same time. Their diverse demands thus worked to smooth the price of acceptance paper. And in the unlikely event of a major imbalance between credit supply and demand, they could turn to a central bank to rediscount their bills and act as liquidity provider of last resort.

In America, however, bankers' acceptances endorsed and guaranteed by reputable acceptance houses did not exist. The National Banking Act of 1863 had not authorized nationally chartered banks to guarantee the acceptances of customers engaged in foreign trade. The framers of that act had focused on creating a uniform currency and expanding the market for U.S. Treasury bonds, the Union Government needing a liquid bond market to help meet the costs of the Civil War. Trade finance, which was at this point a lower priority, could be left to acceptance houses in London. State banks, private banks, and investment banks, for their part, provided only very small amounts of acceptance credit.[9]

Firms needing short-term accommodation, but lacking the wherewithal to obtain it in London, issued single-name promissory notes backed only by their individual signature and guarantee—that is, by their personal promise to pay. Although credit reporting agencies such as R. G. Dun & Co., forerunner of today's Dun & Bradstreet, sprang up to evaluate the creditworthiness of these issuers, invariably the information they provided was incomplete. Deprived of further guarantees, other investors hesitated to purchase these promissory notes from their initial holder. As Warburg put it, promissory notes sat on the books of the initial holder as a "dead instrument and a nonliquid asset."[10]

In particular, the "idiosyncratic character" of these notes left banks reluctant to purchase them as a way of putting to work their idle funds.[11] Instead the banks lent their excess funds, subject to recall, to stockbrokers and dealers against liquid security collateral. Those brokers and dealers then put this money to work in the stock market, using it to fund their customers' purchases of stocks and bonds.

Danger arose from the fact that the banks' call loans, as these investments were logically known, could be recalled at any time. The consequences could be devastating, given the pyramided structure of U.S. banking. This National Banking System—the framework for U.S. finance prior to the advent of the Federal Reserve—encouraged banks in rural areas to hold reserves with so-called reserve city banks, which then held them with central reserve city banks, notably in New York. By its nature, the business of those rural banks was highly variable, following nature. The demand for agricultural credit rose in the spring planting and fall harvest and crop-moving seasons relative to other times of the year. This shared agricultural cycle fostered highly synchronized demands for loans.[12] Banks in rural areas, receiving credit requests from their agricultural customers each spring and fall, recalled their reserve-city deposits. Central reserve city banks, seeing an outflow of deposits, called in their brokers' loans. Wall Street investors were forced to liquidate their security holdings, weakening the market. If other problems intervened, the market might do more than weaken; it might crash. The collapsing value of stock market collateral could then threaten the solvency of the systemically important banks that had extended brokers' loans. And unlike in Europe, the United States possessed no agency to backstop the banks. It lacked a central bank, in other words.

Financial Earthquake

In 1907 this exact sequence of events played out with a vengeance, validating arguments Warburg had made in *The New York Times* at the beginning of the year. The trigger, one year removed, was the 1906 San Francisco earthquake and fire. British fire insurance companies typically relied on international diversification to spread risk.[13] The leading British firm, Royal Exchange Assurance, epitomized the practice. It earned more income from foreign fire premiums than from premiums paid by British residents.[14] But that level of diversification was no protection against a disaster of this magnitude. British firms had underwritten fully half of all fire insurance policies in San Francisco.[15] As those British insurance companies discharged their obligations to their policy holders, capital and gold flowed out of Britain, forcing the Bank of England to raise interest rates. In an even more dramatic step, the Bank stopped discounting U.S. bills to preserve its dwindling reserves. It also encouraged British joint-stock banks to limit their discounts of American paper.[16]

The predictable result was financial stringency in the United States. Exporting became more difficult for American firms as trade finance dried up. Together these adverse conditions precipitated a sharp recession in the spring of 1907. It is hard to imagine a clearer illustration of Warburg's arguments about the downside for the United States of relying on foreign financial markets and foreign currency trade finance.

In the fall of 1907, the harvest and crop-moving season brought more financial strain, and a failed plot to corner shares in the United Copper Company exacerbated the situation. The architect of the copper scheme was Fritz Augustus Heinze. Known as Augustus to his friends, Heinze was an American-born, German-educated mining engineer dubbed one of the three Copper Kings of Butte, Montana. One of those larger-than-life figures who appear not infrequently in the annals of American business, he was physically imposing, "weighing 200 pounds, with the torso of a Yale halfback, muscle of steel, and a face of ivory whiteness, lighted up with a pair of large blue eyes."[17] Ladies had an eye for Heinze, Heinze for the ladies. Along with a reputation as a hard drinker and womanizer, Heinze became known for encroaching on the mining claims of other prospectors. His preferred method at his Montana Ore Purchasing Company was to drill sideways, burrowing under his neighbors' terrestrial properties. Heinze claimed justification under Montana's so-called apex law. This contested provision allowed a mine owner to exploit a vein that surfaced or reached its highest subterranean point on his own land and to continue exploiting it even when that vein stretched under a neighbor's property. To defend against complaints of claim jumping, Heinze employed more than thirty lawyers at a time and saw to the appointment of friendly, politically connected justices to oversee cases brought by his aggrieved neighbors.

In 1906 Heinze sold his Montana Ore Purchasing Company for $12 million. The buyer was Amalgamated Copper Co., a competitor against which he had notoriously deployed his sidewise burrowing techniques.[18] Twelve million dollars was less than Montana Ore had been valued previously. In challenging Amalgamated Copper, Heinze had taken on a massive trust formed by principals in John D. Rockefeller's Standard Oil Company, who tied him up in endless, costly lawsuits. Still, $12 million more than sufficed for a graceful financial exit by someone who just fifteen years earlier was a salaried mining engineer living in a small log cabin.

Heinze now installed himself in a suite of rooms at the Waldorf Hotel in New York, where he threw lavish dinner parties and hatched schemes with dubious business partners, including the notorious Charles W. Morse. Morse's Maine-based family business was harvesting ice and shipping it to points south, notably New York. Morse built his personal fortune by buying up the available ice houses and driving other suppliers out of the market. He allegedly gifted shares of his American Ice Company to New York City Mayor Robert Van Wyck and Tammany Hall boss Richard Croker, enlisting them in his scheme. Having seized monopoly control of the ice market in New York City, the Iceman, as he was known, set out next to do the same for freight shipping. The Iceman became the Steamship King. From there it was a small step to becoming a banker.

Having found a kindred spirit and financier, Heinze applied the same aggressive tactics that marked his career as a mining engineer to new endeavors in the field of finance. Borrowing funds from the Mercantile National Bank, now controlled by Morse, he set out to develop fresh copper holdings. Heinze's company, United Copper, the rump of his operations in Montana, raised additional capital by selling shares on the curb market, that is, outside the organized New York Stock Exchange. United Copper was a blind trust, where shareholders had little information about the underlying assets. Its mineral reserves being unproven, shareholders were betting on Heinze's reputation as a successful entrepreneur and mining engineer.

When unproven reserves remained stubbornly unproven, Heinze turned his attention to a different kind of scheme. Together with his brothers Otto and Arthur, for whom he had conveniently set up a brokerage firm, Augustus sought to corner the market in United Copper shares. These had become a target for short sellers, understandably so, given the company's lack of tangible assets. Driving up the price of United Copper shares by buying them on the open market could force those short sellers, who had borrowed shares in order to sell them, to cover their positions. That is, short sellers who had anticipated buying back shares at lower prices in order to return them to their rightful owners would now have to purchase them instead at higher prices. In practice those short sellers would have only one option: to purchase shares from Heinze and his brothers who, as the sole source of those shares, could charge what they pleased.

The brothers financed their purchases of United Copper shares by again borrowing from Mercantile National Bank and other financial institutions controlled by their associates. The scheme went awry, however, when the price of United Copper shares fell rather than rising. The Heinzes had evidently underestimated the number of short sellers and the difficulty of cornering the market. Panicked depositors, seeing the failure of the scheme, ran on Mercantile National and then on other institutions linked to the brothers and their associates, notably the Knickerbocker Trust, the third-largest trust company in New York City.[19] Charles Barney, the president of the Knickerbocker, had personal dealings with the Heinzes' business associate Morse. The

Knickerbocker was a major shareholder in Morse's Western Ice Company, and Morse had bought up a block of Knickerbocker shares, having been encouraged by Barney to think he might become a director. Although Barney and Knickerbocker did not participate directly in the Heinzes' effort to corner the market in United Copper shares, all this was nonetheless enough to panic the institution's creditors and lead the Knickerbocker's directors to fire Barney.

Additional banks and trust companies, to defend against runs, now recalled their brokers' loans. The stock market crashed by 50 percent from the previous year's peak, while the interest rate on call loans soared to triple-digit levels. This in turn catalyzed fears of further bank insolvencies, precipitating additional runs. Once again, Warburg's assessments proved correct: these events amply illustrated his arguments about the destabilizing connections between the call loan market and financial conditions.

Morgan to the Rescue

Given the pyramided structure of the U.S. credit system, in which banks in agricultural regions held deposits in reserve-center banks, which in turn held deposits in central reserve-center banks, panic spread uncontrollably. For emergency assistance, distressed banks and trust companies were forced to rely on J. P. Morgan. Treasury Secretary George B. Cortelyou, alerted to the problem by Morgan and his partner George Perkins, deposited Treasury funds with distressed national banks.[20] But the resources available to the Treasury on short notice were inadequate for the task. Moreover, this coordination between the House of Morgan and the U.S. Treasury was criticized by, among others, William Jennings Bryan, for enabling Wall Street bankers to lend out at high interest rates money provided by the Treasury for free.[21] All the more reason for pushing ahead with monetary reform.

Morgan, when asked, had refused to rescue Knickerbocker Trust. The institution had large illiquid loans to construction companies erecting office buildings and electricity plants, assets unlikely to do well in an economic slump.[22] In addition, President Barney's association with

Morse and the Heinzes cast a shadow over the Knickerbocker's reputation, not to mention its balance sheet.

A despondent Barney, now ex-president of Knickerbocker Trust, shot himself. *The New York Times* covered the suicide sensationally, asking how Barney reportedly had the strength and clarity of mind to call his lawyers, change his will, and adjust his other business affairs between inflicting the wound upon himself and passing away. The afternoon papers covered his death even more sensationally, quoting A. Foster Higgins, Barney's successor as president of the Knickerbocker, to the effect that Barney shot himself because Mrs. Barney was about to divorce him over an affair with a woman "whom he described as the friend of a French prince."[23] The notoriously loquacious Higgins later denied making the statement, or at least making it for quotation.

Following the Knickerbocker's failure and runs on other banks, there then ensued the famous locked-library episode, when Morgan orchestrated a lifeboat operation for other distressed intermediaries. Together, these events raised questions of whether a private individual should be entrusted with these weighty public-policy decisions. Importantly, they also directed attention at Warburg's case for the government to create a central bank to institutionalize lending in the last resort. That Britain skated through the 1907 crisis unscathed reinforced Warburg's arguments.[24] The contrast highlighted his point about acceptances being safer than the stock market as a place for the banks to park their idle funds.

Internationalizing the Dollar

By 1913, then, there existed two interconnected rationales for reforming the U.S. financial system. First, something needed to change in order to guard against the financial instability to which the country was chronically prone, analogous crises having occurred on numerous prior occasions.[25] Stability might be enhanced, Warburg suggested, by building a European-style money market on which to buy and sell acceptance credits, providing an alternative to the tumultuous call loan market as an emplacement for banks' excess funds. Doing so would attenuate the destabilizing connections between bank liquidity and the stock market. Establishing a central bank to rediscount acceptance paper promised to further limit seasonal swings in interest rates. By dampening money market swings, this central bank would provide an "elastic currency," in the antiseptic language of the Federal Reserve Act. Financial stringency would be relieved.

Second, these reforms would limit the dependence of American exporters and investors on foreign financial centers such as London and foreign currencies such as sterling, reducing the costs and risks of foreign trade and promoting the international advance of the dollar. When a U.S. importer needed trade credit, it asked its bank for foreign exchange with which to pay the foreign exporter. That bank would source sterling from a correspondent bank in London, sterling being the currency customarily used in trade and payments.[26] But involving this second bank added cost and time. There was also the risk attached to an obligation denominated in foreign currency.[27] If a U.S. bank incurred an obligation in London, borrowing sterling while funding itself (that is to say, taking deposits) in dollars, it would pass on the risk of this currency mismatch as a cost of doing business. For exporters and importers, this represented an additional expense. This expense, and no less the symbolism, rankled: "The commissions paid by American business to London bankers to finance United States foreign trade came more and more to be labeled 'tribute,'" one historian observes.[28] Although the gold standard was intended to limit exchange rate risk and fluctuations, this was cold comfort when there were doubts about the ability of the U.S. to stay on gold, as there were in the last decade of the nineteenth century and first decade of the twentieth.[29] This situation was very different than in Britain, where the stability of the gold standard was an established fact.

A market in dollar trade acceptances promised to reduce these risks and costs by allowing American banks to do business entirely in their native currency. A dollar acceptance market had obvious appeal to U.S. financial interests, who wished to compete with London for international business. That the Federal Reserve Act included authorization for member banks to open foreign branches to better originate international business suggests that this second rationale—elevating the international role of the dollar—was more than a subsidiary concern.

The result was a reformist coalition of exporters, financiers, and politicians all seeking to improve the efficiency of the country's financial plumbing.[30] After much debate, catalyzed by the 1907 crisis, reform followed with passage of the Federal Reserve Act in 1913.

But how quickly New York and the dollar would overtake London and sterling was yet to be seen. Most observers anticipated that it would take time to build up a liquid market in trade acceptances. It had taken decades, even centuries, after all, for London to acquire the relevant expertise.

For the United States, World War I hastened the process. It accelerated the transition from sterling to the dollar, much as the French and Napoleonic Wars accelerated the transition to sterling from the guilder. London's centrality in the acceptance market meant that British acceptance houses, bill brokers, and joint-stock banks all had extensive trade-related claims outstanding when war erupted in August 1914. The outbreak of hostilities, by upending trade, dimmed the prospects for repayment and weakened those London-based financial institutions. Even when a transaction was complete, a foreign government might block transfer of the associated receipts to the British investor holding the bill. In addition, British banks had extended call loans to brokers for use in the bill market, and these loans were now imperiled by the peril in which the brokers found themselves.

The specter thus arose of depositor runs and defaults by British brokers and dealers. Seeking to hoard gold, British banks paid out their deposits in Bank of England notes rather than one-pound gold coins. The Bank was forced to work overtime to convert its notes into gold. Lines formed in Threadneedle Street in front of the building, exciting yet additional deposit outflows and forcing the authorities to close the banks.[31] Although the banks reopened after four days, the episode raised doubts about whether depositors would be able to immediately and unconditionally convert their sterling notes and deposits into gold.

Hence the concerted action of the authorities, while dodging the worst, planted doubts about the liquidity and surety of the London money market. The Bank of England lent more than £30 million to distressed bill brokers but, with its gold reserves running low, had to obtain a Treasury letter authorizing it to disregard its normal gold cover ratio—the first time in nearly half a century the Bank had taken this step.[32] The government declared a moratorium on payment of outstanding bills, raising further questions about the liquidity of sterling instruments.[33] On August 13, to quell those doubts, it instructed the Bank to discount all bills presented to it, while forsaking all right of taking legal action against the holder, the understanding being that the Treasury would compensate the Bank for losses. This removed uncertainty about the liquidity of bills. It specifically removed the illiquid bills of foreign debtors from the market, at government expense. These actions prevented the failure of major players in the acceptance market but, given uncertainty about how long this extraordinary support would last, rendered market participants wary of underwriting new acceptances. By October the volume of acceptance business had diminished to a small fraction of prewar levels.[34]

From this point, the sterling acceptance market recovered. Its recovery was incomplete, however, for three reasons. First, wartime disruptions depressed British exports, leaving less trade to be financed.[35] This presaged the postwar new normal, where unlike before 1913, Britain lost its place as the world's leading trading nation.

Second, discounts of bills for trade between third countries (so-called foreign-to-foreign bills) fell sharply when the British authorities closed the agencies and branches of Austrian and German banks and liquidated their affairs. European banks seeking to discount bills turned to Amsterdam, the Netherlands remaining neutral during the war. This was a peculiar if temporary reversion to eighteenth-century international finance, when Amsterdam was the leading center. For their part, banks in Latin America and, to a lesser extent, Asia now turned to the United States, also officially neutral until 1917.[36] For the first time, exports of coffee from Brazil to Italy were financed by New York, in dollars, in an instance of what would eventually become standard practice.[37]

Third, and most importantly, government borrowing crowded out business in sterling trade acceptances. The result was "a reorientation away from the international arena by the City of London."[38] UK Treasury bills in circulation rose more than seventy-fold between the outbreak of the war and 1919. Banks that might have lent cash to brokers for investment in commercial and finance bills or that might have invested in bills directly now saw a shortage of such paper but an abundance of Treasury bills. Given the options available (and unavailable), they invested in Treasury securities instead. The change persisted: Treasury bills continued to account for more than half of the total value of bills held on the London money market all through the 1920s and 1930s.[39]

This market in British Treasury paper, moreover, was almost entirely domestic. Foreign banks, including those of neutrals such as the Netherlands and the United States, avoided as much as possible holding UK Treasury bills, given new uncertainty about the British exchange rate. The shift from acceptance paper to Treasury paper was disproportionately a British phenomenon. Looking to the longer term, it was far from clear that these Treasury securities, with their tenuous link to international trade and payments, would appeal to foreign investors and support an ongoing global role for sterling.

Enter the Fed

The U.S. Federal Reserve Act authorized member banks to accept bills of exchange of six months or less in amounts up to 50 percent of their capital, so long as the bills grew out of import and export transactions.[40] Limiting this privilege to trade-related transactions revealed the priorities of the framers of the Federal Reserve Act, who wanted to promote international use of the dollar. Encouraging the largest, strongest financial institutions to pioneer this market aligned with those priorities, since the largest, strongest institutions were internationally active.[41] Once the market was safely up and running, the act could be amended to allow discounting bills for domestic shipments and for providing warehouse storage. Doing so would motivate additional banks to enter the market.[42]

Importantly, Section 13 of the Federal Reserve Act authorized regional Reserve Banks to rediscount acceptances on behalf of Federal

Reserve member institutions. This opened the door to active rediscounting akin to that provided by the Bank of England. Whether the Fed was in fact prepared to walk through this door was yet to be seen, however.

Taking advantage of a provision in the Federal Reserve Act allowing national banks to branch abroad, National City Bank, the most aggressively international U.S. bank, opened a branch in Buenos Aires even before the outbreak of World War I.[43] National City's president, Frank Vanderlip, had been present at Jekyll Island, along with Warburg, Aldrich, and others, when plans for a central banking act were effectively laid. He would have been vocal about this foreign-branching provision. By the end of 1916, the Federal Reserve Board had licensed forty-six foreign bank branches and subbranches, all but two operated by National City Bank.

But if National City was the pioneer, it was not without rivals. In 1920 the Fed reported that National City had eighty-one branches abroad, while its leading competitor, J. P. Morgan & Co., operated eighty-eight foreign branches.[44] A pair of umbrella organizations enabled additional banks to establish foreign branches: the American and Foreign Banking Corporation, in which small national banks pooled their capital, and the Mercantile Bank of the Americas, which facilitated the foreign operations of Brown Brothers, J. W. Seligman & Co., and the Guarantee Trust Company.[45] Meanwhile, foreign banks set up agencies and subsidiaries in New York to compete for dollar-denominated international business, in this way mirroring the migration of foreign banks to London starting in the 1860s.[46]

The value of dollar acceptances also rose strongly starting in 1918, suggesting that the institutional innovations Warburg and others pioneered were bearing fruit. Their level then fluctuated seasonally, rising in the summer and fall crop-moving seasons before declining in the winter, mimicking the seasonal fluctuation of interest rates before the war.[47] Acceptances also fluctuated with the business cycle, declining in the 1921–22 recession before recovering.[48] By the second half of the 1920s, the value of dollar acceptances rivaled the value of sterling acceptances, falling only somewhat short of the latter in 1927 and 1928 and exceeding it in 1929.[49]

This simple metric suggests that the American and British money markets and their respective currencies had reached a position of parity. Yet this image is deceptive. On multiple dimensions, American institutions continued to lag. The United States lacked experienced acceptance houses to assess the quality of bills and attach their guarantees. As a result, dollar acceptances were not as uniform as their sterling equivalents, and the American market lacked liquidity. The United States suffered from the absence of specialized bill brokers to make a market in acceptance paper.[50] Many banks that dipped their toes into the market in its early years concluded subsequently that the rewards did not justify the risks. As they dropped out, a small handful of New York-based institutions came to dominate transactions.[51] For liquidity, the U.S. market relied heavily on the good offices of the Federal Reserve System, something, as it turned out, that was not to be taken for granted.

This became apparent in 1931, when the Fed withdrew from the market. Where the Reserve Banks had held a majority of outstanding dollar acceptances in the late 1920s, their share fell sharply in 1931, before declining further from there, to virtually zero in 1934.[52] The American Acceptance Council, which had been created with considerable fanfare in 1919, quietly wound up operations in 1936. Most of the gains made by the dollar as an international currency were now abruptly given back.

Shattered Glass

It is tempting to see this decline of Federal Reserve rediscounting as a simple matter of supply and demand. With the American economy's descent into the Great Depression and the collapse of its international trade, the supply of trade acceptances fell sharply. Risk-averse investors shifted toward short-term assets, including thirty- and sixty-day acceptance paper. Since these bills were self-liquidating (since they evaporated when they matured), few were left for rediscount by Reserve Banks.[53] Moreover, market rates of interest fell relative to Reserve Bank buying rates, which were administratively set and slow to react, so few eligible bills were offered to the Federal Reserve for discount.

But the Fed's all but complete withdrawal from the market also reflected an ideological split between the system's founders. Not only Paul

Warburg but also Carter Glass, a prominent Democratic member of Congress, claimed paternity of the Federal Reserve System. Glass was a stubbornly self-taught financial expert who made banking his signature issue on entering the House of Representatives. By 1913, he had risen to chairmanship of the House Committee on Banking and Currency and played an instrumental role in passing the Glass-Owen Federal Reserve Act.[54] Glass had decided to enter politics on hearing a speech by presidential candidate William Jennings Bryan in 1896 and shared Bryan's distain for banks. President Woodrow Wilson observed that Glass, channeling that antipathy, "snarled the Federal Reserve Act through Congress out of one side of his mouth." Wilson reportedly went on, "Think what he would have done with both sides."[55]

Glass and his advisor, Dr. Henry Parker Willis, formerly a professor at Washington and Lee University and a correspondent for the *Journal of Commerce*, drafted a bill providing for a highly decentralized central banking system. In contrast to Warburg, who as a denizen of New York was happy to see a unitary institution situated in that city, Glass and Willis feared that powerful New York banks might capture the new central bank. Hence they preferred a more decentralized design. Glass took the idea to an extreme, proposing twenty regional banks, each with extensive policy autonomy. He opposed the idea of a central coordinating board to encourage these regional banks to work together. Ultimately, Glass's proposals were tempered by President Wilson, who insisted on limiting the number of reserve banks and adding a Washington, D.C.-based Federal Reserve Board to provide a modicum of central control. Warburg, who had a back channel to the White House courtesy of Wilson's campaign manager and advisor, Edward Mandell (Colonel) House, heavily shaped Wilson's modifications of the Glass Plan.[56]

So revised, the Glass-Owen bill specified that only the central bank would issue money, and that its liabilities would be backed by gold and liquid commercial paper. This last provision opened the door to the Fed rediscounting acceptances, no doubt to Warburg's satisfaction. Glass noted grudgingly that this provision allowing for rediscounting was added to the bill following compelling testimony by Warburg to the Senate Banking Committee.[57] However, Glass successfully insisted that the bills in question would be self-liquidating. They would roll off the balance sheets of the Reserve Banks at the completion of the underlying transaction in merchandise or commodities. This provision complied with the real bills doctrine, seen in chapter 6, which nineteenth-century central bankers and their early twentieth-century descendants often subscribed to. The doctrine held that banks should provide credit as needed for legitimate commercial transactions, but no more. This aligned with Glass's suspicion of concentrated financial power. The Virginian feared that permitting the central bank to rediscount finance bills not tied to commercial transactions would enable big New York banks to leverage their balance sheets and manipulate the financial system and the Federal Reserve to their advantage. Here he differed from Warburg's more expansive vision informed by the role of finance bills in European money markets and of European central banks in ensuring their liquidity.

Matters changed once Warburg joined the Federal Reserve Board. The Federal Reserve Act was amended to permit discounting of finance drafts.[58] In 1924 a further ruling then made foreign dollar acceptances payable in the United States eligible for Federal Reserve open market purchase and rediscount when endorsed by a member bank.[59] Between 1927 and 1929 the level of foreign acceptances now rose strongly, alongside the robust growth of foreign trade. By 1930 foreign acceptances made up a third of all outstanding dollar paper.[60] The dollar acceptance market was now financing the commodity and merchandise transactions of foreign as well as American merchants and producers, signaling the dollar's assumption of a consequential international role.

For Glass, these innovations deviated dangerously from the real bills doctrine. He predictably blamed speculative excesses on Wall Street on the rediscounting of finance bills by the Federal Reserve Bank of New York, the leading adherent to the Warburg doctrine.[61] Glass bore a personal grudge against Warburg, who frequently received credit for the design of the Federal Reserve Act, dismissing him as "a maniacal and earnest foreign bore."[62] He now set out to eliminate Warburg's amendments. At his volition, the Senate launched an investigation into the acceptance market in 1931; Glass chaired the relevant subcommittee.[63]

This provided a pulpit from which he could argue that central bank manipulation had spawned the boom and bust resulting in the Great Depression, and from which he could advocate a return to the real bills doctrine.

Specifically, Glass and his fellow committee members pointed to the large numbers of foreign dollar acceptances issued by German banks and discounted by the Federal Reserve. These facilitated the short-term capital inflows Germany used to finance its balance of payments deficit.[64] But that deficit was unsustainable, and the arrangement increasingly resembled a Ponzi scheme. If U.S. banks hesitated to roll over their maturing credits and provide more, German debtors would be unable to repay. It turned out that Glass had a point. This was precisely what happened in 1931, causing the acceptance liabilities of German banks to be frozen and inflicting losses on U.S. banks. Glass was quick to cite this as evidence of dangerous and indiscriminate Federal Reserve support.

But if Glass's assessment of the risks had merit, his recommendation—that the Fed should curtail its involvement in and even withdraw from the acceptance market—was excessive. Responding to his criticism, the Reserve Banks sharply reduced their operations. Capitulating to the real bills doctrine, they discounted only the realist of real bills. They more strictly scrutinized whether the acceptances they purchased and discounted were self-liquidating. They kept their bill-buying rates high to signal their dedication to prudential standards. For their part, member banks, uncertain now whether the central bank would act as a liquidity provider of last resort, grew more cautious about purchasing acceptances.

This resulted in a sharp fall in the share of dollar acceptances held by the Reserve Banks and a veritable collapse in the value of acceptances issued in New York. Where acceptances in London and New York, and hence in sterling and dollars, had been equal in value in the 1920s, by 1934 the level of dollar acceptances was barely half the level of sterling acceptances. Some observers opined that the Federal Reserve stepped out of the market because it was no longer necessary to mother the business. But the collapse in the value of dollar acceptances following its exit suggests, to the contrary, that rediscounting by a central bank prepared to act as market maker of last resort was vital for a liquid market. This was something the UK possessed. No longer the United States.

In the end, Warburg achieved only part of what he set out to accomplish. He oversaw the creation of a dollar acceptance market in New York that at its height originated as much credit as London. But that market had fragile foundations. The United States lacked acceptance houses to guarantee credits and bill brokers to make a market.[65] High costs and risks rendered dollar credit competitive only where U.S. commercial and financial interests had the best information and strongest representation, which in practice meant in connection with America's own exports.[66] Such liquidity as the dollar acceptance market possessed rested on the shoulders of the Federal Reserve, whose support was fickle.

Sterling-Dollar Competition

British acceptors, meanwhile, did not stand still. British banks had extended their reach into Central Europe, given how German banks suffered in the post–World War I period of inflation and could lend only at high interest rates. Banks from Japan and elsewhere opened additional London branches, affirming the city's international role. To be sure, British trade was stagnant, depressing the single most important source of demand for acceptance credit. To maintain the customary volume of business, banks and brokers turned to finance bills. Competition from Treasury bills remained, since the British government continued running deficits and financing them with short-term debt. But the Bank of England, unlike the Fed, was steadfast in its support for the acceptance market.[67] The 1930s only served to confirm, as informed observers had predicted, that the sterling money market remained first among equals.[68]

The picture for foreign loans looked similar. Already in 1914, National City Bank, on opening its foreign branch in Buenos Aires, had underwritten a $15 million loan to the Republic of Argentina.[69] U.S. foreign lending surged ahead of British lending in the 1920s, as the American economy and U.S. financial institutions asserted their strength. U.S. commercial and investment banks, the former operating through securities affiliates, dived into the underwriting business. In the second half of the 1920s, at the height of the postwar lending boom, the value of foreign government bonds issued in New York and denominated in dollars was more than twice the value of overseas government securities issued in London and denominated in sterling.[70] To all appearances, the dollar had supplanted sterling in the foreign loan market.

Here too, however, appearances were deceiving. By the end of the 1930s, two-thirds of dollar loans had lapsed into default. Sterling loans fared better, having been underwritten by more experienced investment bankers and extended to Britain's Commonwealth and Empire. In the 1930s, Britain continued extending sterling loans to these faithful borrowers, if at lower volumes than before. U.S. gross capital outflows and the role of the dollar in long-term foreign finance, in contrast, fell off to virtually zero.[71]

Again, the explanation for the contrast harks back to World War I. Before the war, U.S. loans to foreign governments were exceptional, as described earlier. Hostilities then fueled an unprecedented burst of lending to European governments by U.S. bankers and the American public. National City Bank extended loans to the French and Russian governments in 1914, J. P. Morgan & Co. to France and Britain in 1915. The bonds were then marketed to eager American investors.[72] U.S. banks next began lending to Latin American governments, again placing their bonds with obliging retail investors. Once America declared war in April 1917, foreign lending to the allies was undertaken directly by the U.S. government. The Liberty Loan Act, which followed once America entered the war, meant acquiring federal government claims on allied governments, again denominated in dollars. The Liberty Bonds financing these operations whet the appetite of additional American investors for government securities.

U.S. banks were prohibited from lending directly to foreign governments and corporations while the country was at war. In their stead, the federal government extended official loans to allied countries. It continued even after the armistice, crowding out private finance.[73] Starting in 1920, private dollar lending to foreign governments, railways, mining companies, and other corporations finally recovered, rising strongly for five successive years. The United States, its economy growing, had a large pool of savings available for investment abroad. Europe, in contrast, was still in financial turmoil, which discouraged saving. European reconstruction required extensive finance. There was a logic, in other words, for why American funds financed European investment.

The UK too was a net lender, reprising its prewar role. Its reconstruction-related investment needs were fewer than those of Continental Europe, meaning that it had funds for foreign investment. British banks had experience in identifying creditworthy borrowers, rendering their sterling loans attractive to domestic but also foreign investors, including Americans. Between 1920 and 1924, U.S. investors purchased the equivalent of $17 million dollars of sterling loans to foreign governments.[74] Thus the prewar arrangement, whereby London, as international financial center, attracted foreign investors whose funds were put to work by British underwriters, survived the war intact. In the first half of the 1920s, the value of foreign government securities issued in the UK and denominated in sterling was 57 percent the value of dollar securities issued in the United States.[75] This is a reasonable measure of the relative importance of the two countries and currencies in global capital markets. Both currencies possessed consequential roles, although for the moment the dollar was *primus inter pares*.

The relative importance of U.S. foreign lending, and hence of the dollar, rose further in the second half of the 1920s. In part this was for lack of competition: sterling loans to foreign borrowers fell off at mid-decade and were slow to recover. Britain struggled to return to the gold standard at the prewar parity against gold and the dollar. The Bank of England kept interest rates high to attract gold and limit capital outflows, seeking to restore that parity, as finally happened in 1925. It kept its rates high to ensure that the dollar exchange rate was maintained. Its high interest rates made investing in domestic fixed-income securities more attractive and had the intended effect of keeping British savings at home, but at a cost to sterling's international role.

In addition, the UK imposed informal restrictions on foreign lending to discourage capital outflows that might have taxed the Bank's gold reserves. The government vetted proposed bond flotations, used moral suasion to discourage them, and discriminated against foreign (as opposed to Dominion and colonial) loans.[76] These policies did not enhance the international role of London and sterling—to the contrary. Ironically, a policy designed to privilege the city, namely restoring the prewar gold parity, worked to its disadvantage.

Tsunami of Finance

U.S. foreign lending reached its apex in 1927–28. In these two years, dollar loans to governments totaled more than two and a half times their sterling equivalent.[77] U.S. lending to Europe rotated from financing reconstruction and stabilization to underwriting infrastructure investment and general government spending. Loans to Latin America likewise financed both public works and current expenditures. Contemporaries spoke of a veritable tsunami of foreign investment as aggressive new underwriters entered the fray. To give an idea of the environment, a 1932 U.S. Senate postmortem undertaken to investigate these foreign loans reported that at the height of the boom, twenty-nine representatives of American underwriting institutions competed for loans to Colombia's central and municipal governments.[78]

Unsurprisingly, the quality of bond issues varied. Established names like J. P. Morgan & Co. and Kuhn, Loeb & Co. had experienced representatives in the field. By the end of the 1920s, they had been engaged in foreign lending for years. New entrants, in contrast, lacked comparable experience and personnel. They pursued foreign lending for its high interest rates and generous underwriting fees, not unlike their English predecessors in the Latin American lending boom of the 1820s. To negotiate with governments they relied on contractors, hired guns whose compensation depended on the volume of business originated, not the subsequent performance of the loan. Lacking the reputation of a Rothschild, Baring, or Morgan, these new underwriters were prepared to attach their names to risky bond issues and flog these to individual investors. The borrowers' side also had its problems, to be sure. With such substantial amounts of money on offer, the borrowers understandably found temptation hard to resist.

More precisely, large amounts of money were on offer until the middle of 1928, when the Fed tightened. Concerned by gold losses and stock market speculation, the Open Market Investment Committee (OMIC), the Fed's policymaking arm, raised its discount and buying rates on acceptances from 3.5 percent to 5 percent.[79] To ensure that the market felt the higher interest rates, it sold $400 million of securities, leaving just $80 million in the OMIC portfolio.[80] Observers warned of "a more vigorous upward movement of interest rates than in any year since the post-war inflation period."[81]

Higher interest rates and tighter credit conditions were intended to discourage brokers' loans and put a lid on stock market speculation. This they now did, albeit with devastating consequences starting in 1929. Higher rates were also designed to attract short-term capital from abroad, or at least to prevent capital from flowing out to other countries. Here too the Fed's higher rates achieved their aim. However, not just short-term flows, the intended target, but also long-term lending was hit. After running at $530 million in the second quarter of 1928, U.S. capital exports plunged to just $120 million in the third quarter. Dollar lending to Germany, the single largest destination of U.S. foreign investment, fell off a cliff. This was an early warning that the dollar's international status rested on central bank support—support that was not to be taken for granted.

U.S. foreign lending remained depressed in 1929. Germany, Poland, Argentina, and Brazil saw their economies turn down in 1928 and early 1929, even before the United States. It is no coincidence that these were the first countries to feel what became the Great Depression; their economies depended heavily on dollar funding, which had now evaporated. Doubts arose about the ability of governments to repay their existing obligations, much less service new ones. U.S. lending revived modestly in 1930, when interest rates and enthusiasm for investing on Wall Street declined, but this fell far short of the halcyon days of 1927. Then, in 1931, widespread defaults by foreign borrowers totally demoralized the market.

When called to testify before the Senate Committee on Finance in 1932, spokesmen for the banks submitted lists of loans by country and year. These revealed that the quality of foreign loans had deteriorated as the 1920s progressed. Default rates were highest on loans originated toward the end of the decade, when competition between rival underwriters was at its peak. The performance of foreign bonds also varied by issuing house. Investors in issues sponsored by J. P. Morgan and National City Bank saw 14 percent of their bonds lapse into default. For nine other banking houses, the comparable share was 63 percent.[82] Both patterns indicated an overheated market increasingly dominated by inexperienced lenders. They pointed to the continued limitations of New York as an international financial center and the dollar as an international currency.

Sterling Endures

While two-thirds of foreign dollar bonds defaulted in the 1930s, the same was true of a much smaller fraction of sterling bonds of overseas governments and corporations. A majority of British overseas loans were to the Dominions and Empire. Economic hardships notwithstanding, these entities faithfully serviced their debts. Investors in sterling bonds suffered losses on loans to Europe and, especially, Latin America, but not on imperial obligations.[83] Reflecting their continued good standing, Canada, New Zealand, India, and South Africa contracted new sterling loans in London all through the 1930s.[84]

It helped that Britain did not experience banking crises like those in the United States starting in 1930. One might say that it was not for lack of trying. In fact, British merchant banks experienced a serious liquidity crisis in the summer of 1931. Having accepted bills for Central European merchants, their balance sheets were damaged when these were frozen by exchange controls and the negotiation of standstill agreements with Austria, Hungary, and Germany.[85] The difference from the U.S. case was the Bank of England's ready response. The Bank understood that the acceptance houses were too big and connected to fail. Indeed, a nonnegligible fraction of the Bank's directors, from the governor down, came from the ranks of merchant banks. Starting in July of 1931, the central bank made sweeping purchases of securities on the open market. In August and September, it resisted calls to raise its discount rate despite a narrowing margin between Bank rate and market rates, and despite continuing gold losses.

On Friday, September 18, those gold losses finally forced the Bank of England to suspend the operation of the gold standard, a decision Parliament ratified the following Monday. It may be exaggerating to say that the Bank of England prioritized the stability of the English financial system over maintenance of the gold standard. Officials wanted both. In the end, however, they sacrificed sterling's gold standard parity while ensuring the survival of the banks.[86]

Once conditions normalized, the Bank of England was able to cut its discount rate to 2 percent, inaugurating an era of "cheap money." Low interest rates enabled the banks to finance their operations more easily. This contrasted with the situation in the United States, where the Fed raised its policy rate following Britain's suspension of gold convertibility to defend its gold reserves, and where it halted its expansionary open market operations in August 1932 for fear of abrogating its gold standard rules. Sterling's credibility may have suffered from Britain's abandonment of the gold standard in September 1931, but any such costs were outweighed by the benefits of preserving financial stability.

Given that stability, London continued to attract fresh funds from Europe.[87] The number of foreign bank offices in London rose further in the 1930s, in contrast to the situation in New York.[88] British banks continued to lend abroad, unlike American banks.[89] Although sterling was no longer on the gold standard, other countries still pegged to the currency, not only members of the Commonwealth and Empire but also other British trading partners, in Scandinavia and elsewhere.[90] And countries pegging to sterling used the currency in payments and continued holding reserves in that form.

Hence the liquidation of foreign exchange reserves by central banks, prompted by the post-1930 eruption of financial instability, was disproportionately a liquidation of dollars. Where sterling and the dollar were coequal as reserve currencies on the eve of the Great Depression, the dollar now fell back. The economist Robert Triffin estimated that the dollar accounted for less than 20 percent of global foreign exchange reserves come 1937.[91] All this underscores the role of central bank and government support, and not just private market structure and expertise, in the establishment and maintenance of international currency status.

Transition Deferred

The 1920s and 1930s were a transitional period when international currency status was contested. The United States made strides in internationalizing the dollar. It created a central bank to enhance the liquidity of the market in dollar claims and authorized U.S. banks to branch abroad. For a time, it assumed the mantle of the leading foreign lender, where U.S. loans were naturally denominated in dollars.

With hindsight, it is tempting to see this as the point when sterling lost its preeminence as an international currency and as the dawning of the age of dollar dominance. The reality was more complex. Much of the ground the dollar gained in the 1920s, it gave back in the 1930s, when the Fed abandoned its backstopping role and the United States succumbed to financial instability. The dollar's challenge to sterling was rebuffed. Or, to be more precise, the challenge was abandoned by the United States itself. The country now had the infrastructure in place to support a dominant international currency. Just not the policies.

The period following World War II would be different.

8

Dollar Dominance

WHERE PAUL WARBURG'S family had a long history in banking and finance, Harry White, the second significant architect of the global dollar, hailed from more modest origins. White was born in 1892, in Boston, to Jacob Weissnovitz and Sarah Magilewski, who immigrated from Lithuania in 1885.[1] Sarah died in 1901 after birthing seven children, of whom Harry was youngest. Jacob started out peddling hardware and crockery, unexceptionally for an Eastern European immigrant. He made a success of the business, opening four hardware stores under the moniker J. White's Sons.

Young Harry was not especially tall, handsome, or athletic. But he was ambitious and driven, and what he lacked in sharp appearance he made up for with sharp elbows and a sharp tongue. In this respect he was the opposite of the reserved, soft-spoken Warburg.

White spent several years clerking and managing a branch of his father's business and taking courses at Massachusetts Agricultural College. With America's declaration of war on Germany in 1917, he volunteered for army service. With a mercantile background and a Mass Ag course in military science, he was commissioned as a first lieutenant and stationed as a supply officer in France. Once discharged, he moved to New York to avoid again being consigned to the hardware store. White then worked for a public-service organization aiding orphans before enrolling at Columbia University in 1922 to pursue a degree in government.

So began a remarkable academic and public-policy journey. Finding Columbia and the discipline of government uninspiring, White transferred to Stanford University and economics. Ten years older than his classmates, he gained a reputation as one of the economics department's more accomplished and outspoken students. On graduating, he moved back to Boston where Harvard admitted him as a doctoral student. Foreshadowing his subsequent policy work on the structure of the international monetary system, White completed an award-winning dissertation on the French franc and the balance of payments in the gold-standard decades before World War I under the direction of the eminent international economist Frank Taussig.

Receiving the David A. Wells Prize for best dissertation in economics was no guarantee of academic advancement, however. It was certainly no guarantee at Harvard, whose president, Abbott Lawrence Lowell, was averse to granting Jews permanent faculty positions. After languishing on a series of annual contracts, White left in 1932, at the age of forty, for a professorship at Lawrence College in Appleton, Wisconsin. A paper-mill town overlooking the Fox River, Appleton no doubt felt like a backwater to a born-and-bred Bostonian who had seen "Gay Paree." The opportunity to escape came in 1934 in the form of an invitation from Professor Jacob Viner of the University of Chicago, then serving as advisor to the Roosevelt administration. Viner, like White, was a student of Taussig. Like White, he had grown up in a working-class Eastern European immigrant family, which made for an immediate affinity.

Viner was advising Treasury Secretary Henry Morgenthau and, at one remove, President Roosevelt on a program for reconstruction of the U.S. banking and financial system following the crises of the early 1930s.[2] Since abandoning the gold standard, Roosevelt had been formulating dollar policy on the fly, deciding by how many cents to raise the dollar price of gold each morning while taking his breakfast of orange juice and eggs in bed. In his summer position as advisor to Viner, and then as principal economic analyst and assistant director in the Treasury's Division of Research and Statistics, White sought to regularize the process. In November 1935, in one of his first acts as a permanent Treasury employee, he drafted a thirty-nine-page paper modestly entitled "Monetary Policy." This sketched the outlines of a brand-new international monetary system that combined the stability of the prewar gold standard, thereby encouraging the recovery of cross-border finance and trade, with flexibility for U.S. monetary policy, whose importance had been highlighted by the disaster of the Great Depression. Sketched is the right word, for at this point White's design for a new international monetary system was, to put it charitably, incomplete. Still, in its broad strokes White's outline anticipated the breakthrough plan he brought to the Bretton Woods international monetary conference in 1944.

In the summer of 1935, White led a fact-finding mission to London, where he encountered the renowned Cambridge economist John Maynard Keynes. Nine years White's senior, Keynes had been working on international monetary matters for years. He had analyzed exchange rate regimes and international monetary standards in three monographs, his 1913 *Indian Currency and Finance*, 1923 *Tract on Monetary Reform*, and 1930 *Treatise on Money*. Keynes famously opposed Chancellor of the Exchequer Winston Churchill's return to gold at the prewar parity in 1925. No one commanded more authority on international monetary matters than the Cambridge don. It would not be long, during World War II, before Keynes and White would lock intellectual horns over how to reform the global monetary and financial order.

In 1936 White, after returning home, advised the U.S. Treasury on the Tripartite Agreement, a mixed exchange rate accord that permitted the French franc, then in crisis, to be realigned downward against sterling and the dollar, while avoiding competitive devaluations by the United States and the United Kingdom. This was a prelude, in a sense, to the compromise between exchange rate stability and policy flexibility that White would advance in 1944.

Never-Never Land

There matters stood on the eve of World War II. Exchange rate policy occupied a never-never land between the gold standard of the 1920s and the manipulated exchange rates of the 1930s. As a potential fixed point, policymakers were eyeing the dollar, which the United States repegged to gold in 1934, now at a higher price of $35 an ounce.³ Unlike other countries, America shunned capital controls and made monetary gold freely available to foreign central banks. This encouraged the belief that the gold-linked dollar might become the sun around which other currencies revolved.

For the moment, however, the dollar was less of a sun than a black hole absorbing everything around it. As war clouds gathered in Europe, investors fled to the safety of New York.⁴ With the decline of U.S. foreign lending and collapse of the market in dollar trade acceptances, these flows were a one-way street, running solely from Europe to America. Other countries suffered reserve losses, leaving them in no position to peg their currencies to the greenback except behind the cover of exchange controls, which rather defeated the purpose.

When World War II broke out, the Allied Powers mobilized their remaining gold and foreign exchange to purchase desperately needed commodities and materiel from the United States. This shoveled even more gold into the coffers of the U.S. government and U.S. banks. Despite passage of the 1941 Lend-Lease Act, which authorized the federal government to supply the Allies on credit, by the end of the war America harbored fully two-thirds of the world's monetary gold.

The story of wartime planning for postwar monetary reconstruction has been told many times.⁵ (Actually, such planning was underway well before the United States entered the war. Recall how White was writing memos and papers on the subject already in 1935. In 1941 he now began transforming those memos and papers into what became the White Plan for postwar monetary reform.) The Bretton Woods Conference of 1944, where Keynes and White aired their differences and these plans came to fruition, had precedents in a series of nineteenth-century monetary conferences and again in the London World Economic Conference of 1933.⁶ More precisely, Bretton Woods had precedents in a series of *failed* monetary conferences, primarily because there had been no dominant country to drive them, and no consensus on desirable reforms.

Now, however, America was in the driver's seat. The country's massive gold reserves were unrivaled. Its currency was a beacon of stability.

The question was whether the United States, finding itself in an unfamiliar position of leadership, could forge a consensus about desirable features of the postwar exchange rate system that allowed Bretton Woods to reach a more successful conclusion than those earlier international monetary conferences.

White, who would be instrumental in answering that question, was known for unconventional views. He had advocated expansionary fiscal policies in the 1930s, when politicians such as Franklin Delano Roosevelt and economists from Viner on down remained wedded to the principle of balanced budgets. He expressed a peculiar admiration for the Soviet economic system. There also arose a question of whether he was a communist fellow traveler or even a Soviet spy, although pursuing this would take us too far afield.[7] But on monetary matters, White remained stolidly conventional, squarely in the scholarly and public-policy mainstream. In his dissertation on the French gold standard, he had concluded that the arrangement worked reasonably well in the decades prior to World War I. A feature key to its smooth operation, he wrote, had been the large gold reserves of the Bank of France. These were not unlike the large reserves now held by the U.S. Treasury Department.[8] France's ample reserves had served as a buffer: the Bank of France was able to let gold flow in and out without having to engineer sharp changes in interest rates or otherwise disturbing the economy. White's analysis rendered him confident that the United States, now with even larger reserves, would enjoy analogous freedom of monetary action even if the dollar were again pegged to gold. He was convinced that again basing the monetary system on gold was essential for confidence, financial stability, and open trade; pre-World War I French history had demonstrated as much. "[G]old is the best medium of international exchange yet devised," White wrote in an unpublished 1942 paper. "[Its] superiority . . . rests on the common experience of nations which has revealed time and again in many quarters of the globe that a country with adequate gold can engage more freely and effectively in international trade and finance."[9]

The difference now was that only one currency, the dollar, had a realistic prospect of being convertible into gold after the war. It also followed, of course, that a monetary role for gold would in turn imply a unique and dominant international role for the dollar.

British-born Keynes was similarly known for unconventional views. His government now tasked him with fighting a rearguard action to preserve Britain's place on the global stage and, no less, its financial stability. This meant securing authorization for his government to retain, following the conclusion of hostilities, wartime controls on international financial transactions, such as restrictions on the ability of residents to purchase foreign exchange and transfer capital abroad. And it was not only controls on the actions of British residents that mattered. Britain had built up enormous liabilities to its Commonwealth and Empire. Sudden liquidation of these claims by those authorities, as might happen in the absence of controls, could bring the financial house of cards crashing down. Hence, for Keynes, it was critical to secure authorization for the retention of controls on international capital flows. In the exchange of plans prior to the conference and at Bretton Woods itself, he was fortunate to receive a sympathetic hearing, on this one issue at least, from White, who in his dissertation had seen pre-1914 international capital flows as a destabilizing force.[10]

Given Britain's wartime damage and diminished export competitiveness, not to mention its unsatisfactory 1920s experience, Keynes also sought to preserve the prerogative for governments to change their exchange rates. Here, however, he butted up against White's commitment to pegged currencies, which the American saw as critical for rebuilding trade.

Fortunately, at this conference, unlike its predecessors, agreement was ultimately reached. The result of discussions was a compromise: governments could change their exchange rates only with the prior approval of other governments, to be negotiated through discussions in a new international forum, what would be the International Monetary Fund (IMF). But the agreement made no provision for sanctions or other recourse in the absence of approval. Keynes took this to mean that countries desperate to devalue, even if taking diplomatic heat for not securing foreign agreement, could forge ahead unilaterally.

One issue yet to be resolved when delegates convened at Bretton Woods was the international role of the dollar. A decision to single out the dollar as the cornerstone currency in the new system, the only currency with the same official status as gold, would effectively underscore the diminished role of sterling. The United States alone would serve as banker to the world, borrowing short and lending long. It would enjoy artificially low interest rates on U.S. Treasury bonds accumulated and held as reserves by governments and central banks around the world.

Moreover, nothing guaranteed that the United States would provide dollar liquidity adequate for the needs of an expanding world economy, since it had rather decisively failed at this job in the 1930s. Even if it did, its growing dollar liabilities would eventually come to exceed its specie reserves, undermining confidence in the fixed dollar price of gold. There was nothing new about this problem: critics of the 1920s gold-exchange standard had warned of this destabilizing eventuality.[11] But where in the 1920s there had been multiple sources of international liquidity, now there was only the United States. This trained all eyes on the American balance of payments and the possibility that at some point U.S. gold reserves would no longer suffice for the country to make good on its exchange rate commitment.

Keynes's solution to this dilemma was to create a synthetic credit instrument, convertible into gold and emitted by a multilateral organization. His proposed unit, bancor ("bank gold" in French, so named perhaps to resonate with White's admiration of the French gold standard), would be used to settle commercial transactions. A country exporting more than it imported would accumulate this bancor up to a prespecified limit, at which point discussions would commence about the need for a change in its exchange rate. Each country would be allocated an initial stock of bancor to get trade up and running. New allocations would meet the needs of an expanding world economy, thereby preventing both a 1930s-style deflation and a dangerous imbalance between U.S. foreign dollar liabilities and U.S. gold reserves.

Bretton Woods

These were the matters hashed out at the conference at the Mt. Washington Hotel in Bretton Woods, New Hampshire, in July 1944. The hotel had been closed for the duration of the war, and had fallen into a state of disrepair. It was now hastily reopened and refurbished. The Roosevelt administration chose the venue as an escape from the stifling summer heat of Washington, D.C., for its seclusion, and for the fact that New Hampshire was represented in the Congress by Republican Senator Charles Tobey, whose support as ranking minority member of the Senate Banking and Currency Committee would be needed for ratification of a new international agreement. Tobey was an isolationist, who in the 1930s had allied himself with the aviator Charles Lindbergh and the America First Committee, of which Lindbergh was the most prominent member. Prior to Pearl Harbor, Tobey had ferociously criticized U.S. support for Britain and the other Allies. (*Time* magazine, when describing his opposition to the Roosevelt administration's supportive measures, called Tobey "a rumpled, furious man with a vivid imagination and a hound-keen nose for trouble."[12]) U.S. entry into the war changed the political lay of the land. When seeking reelection in 1944, Tobey faced a primary challenge from the internationalist wing of the New Hampshire Republican Party. To establish his own internationalist bona fides, Tobey could point to his success at bringing the global monetary and financial conference to Bretton Woods. He even got himself appointed as a member of the U.S. delegation.[13]

The result was a singular circus. Members of the Soviet delegation installed themselves in the hotel's subterranean bar.[14] Members of the Chinese delegation narrowly escaped being shot by a farmer who mistook them for a Japanese expeditionary force. Forty-four nations were present. This international color notwithstanding, everyone knew that the central negotiation was that between the UK and the United States, past and future international monetary powers that had been exchanging postwar monetary plans for years. The United States would be contributing the single largest share of funds to the new international clearing bank, soon to be named the International Monetary Fund. How much America contributed would in turn determine how much other countries could draw. The United States preferred to limit the size of those drawings, since it anticipated having to bankroll the new organization. British negotiators anticipated that the UK would be prominent among the borrowers, so they argued for a more generously resourced Fund. Keynes supported his arguments with rhetoric and logic, while White backed his with power and finance.[15] It was no surprise, in this light, that the American position won out.

The final Bretton Woods Agreement allowed signatories to retain restrictions on cross-border financial transactions, reflecting Keynes and White's shared skepticism of unregulated capital flows. In contrast, it would require countries to restore full freedom to buy and sell currencies for trade-related transactions following a transitional period of no more than five years. This mandate to restore the convertibility of currencies for merchandise transactions reflected the expectation on the part of American policymakers that the United States would become postwar exporter to the world.

Exchange rates would be pegged, as White insisted, but adjustable, as Keynes required. Given the difficulty of squaring this circle, no explicit criteria for adjusting pegged rates were specified. The agreement stated only that a country might apply for approval to change its exchange rate to correct a "fundamental disequilibrium" in its balance of payments, while leaving this key term carefully undefined. The maximum the United States would contribute to the IMF to help other countries meet their exceptional balance of payments needs was $2.5 billion, far short of Keynes's proposal for $23 billion and only cosmetically above White's opening bid of $2 billion. Finally, there would be none of Keynes's bancor. Instead, there was a privileged role for the dollar. The Americans had the lever of nonmilitary Lend-Lease aid, the U.S. initiative launched in 1941 to provide assistance to Allied countries fighting Nazi Germany. Even an implicit threat to curtail it was enough to force London to kill off Keynes's funny money.

Alternative A

The Joint Statement of British and American negotiators, presented to other delegations at Bretton Woods, spoke at White's insistence of exchange rates expressed in terms of gold, akin to the link established by the United States in 1934, when the dollar was repegged at $35 an ounce. During the first week of the Bretton Woods Conference, the U.S. team tabled a so-called "Alternative A" text referring to exchange rates "expressed in terms of gold, as a common denominator, or in terms of a gold-convertible currency unit of weight and fineness in effect on July 1, 1944." Gold-convertible currency was code for the U.S. dollar, the only currency that might be strong enough to be convertible following the war. This opaque phraseology was intended to assuage critics like Keynes who opposed singling out the dollar for special status. But when Alternative A was taken up by the Bretton Woods subcommittee concerned with monetary matters, its members, in an exceptional fit of clarity, agreed that references to "gold as a common denominator . . . or gold-convertible currenc[ies]" could be replaced by "gold as a common denominator or in terms of the United States dollar."[16] White pounced; he and his aides worked through the night, revising the draft IMF Articles of Agreement. Preoccupied with his involvement in the subcommittee on the World Bank, the IMF's sister institution, Keynes learned of the change only after leaving Bretton Woods.

Thus, the Bretton Woods Agreement acknowledged what no international agreement had done before, namely that the international monetary system would be organized around a single national currency. The dollar would be the unit by which other currencies were now measured. It was the de facto and de jure international unit of account. Financial contributions to the IMF (members' subscriptions, in the parlance of the Articles of Agreement) would be proportional to their reserves of gold and U.S. dollars, not their reserves of gold and foreign exchange overall.[17] Permitting countries to keep their currencies inconvertible was unavoidable under the circumstances, but this meant that governments and central banks, when accumulating reserves, would be accumulating dollars, the only freely usable reserve asset.[18] And since dollars dominated official transactions, they would dominate private transactions of banks and firms as well.

Tempting as it might be to ascribe this outcome to the fact that Keynes was distracted by his responsibilities to the World Bank, the roots of dollar dominance ran deeper. America's commercial, financial, and military strength was unrivalled. U.S. industry supplied two-thirds of all Allied military equipment during the war. The Allies depended on America for Lend-Lease aid and understood that they would depend on it for reconstruction aid after the conclusion of hostilities. History showed how geopolitical leverage worked to support international currency status. And in the latter stages of World War II, U.S. geopolitical power and influence had no real challengers, except the Soviet Union, which was no monetary and financial power. Two oceans separated America from its German and Japanese enemies, rendering dollar bonds and deposits secure. The advent of the Cold War and the Soviet acquisition of nuclear weaponry made oceans less relevant, but this would only highlight America's own nuclear arsenal and its leadership in the development of weapons technology. Only America had liquid financial markets open to the rest of the world. Only it had those crucial ample reserves of monetary gold, buttressing confidence in the convertibility of its currency.

Circumstances thus endowed the United States and the dollar with all the characteristics—economic and financial but also political and geostrategic—required for international currency dominance.

But it is hard to play poker when you hold all the cards. For countries to use dollars, they had to possess dollars.[19] This was another lesson of international monetary history. As explored earlier, in the fourteenth century, lending by the Bardi and Peruzzi had bestowed upon merchants, kings, and popes the florin needed to finance cross-border transactions, in turn enhancing the currency's international role. In the nineteenth century, loans on the British money market had provided foreign firms and governments with sterling balances for use in international transactions, placing the pound at the center of the global payments system.

Now, in the wake of the war, however, economies were disorganized, and governments were less than creditworthy. Banks and other institutions of the money market could not be relied on to redistribute gold and dollars presently in the hands of the United States. Instead, the U.S. government, starting in 1948, determined that it had to transfer dollars through the Marshall Plan, if the Bretton Woods system—and for that matter the Western alliance—was to survive. To be sure, the goal of the Marshall Plan's architects was not simply to ensure the dominance of the dollar. It was to support economic reconstruction and political stabilization in Europe, expand markets for U.S. exports, and beat back the Soviet threat.[20] But by providing $13 billion of official aid, the United States equipped its partners with the dollars needed for essential imports. This prevented post-World War II Western Europe from having to retreat into barter, as had Central Europe in the 1930s. Thus, the Marshall Plan was critical for cementing the dollar's international role. It allowed Europe to rebuild its capacity to export, further augmenting its dollar reserves. Were other countries denied dollar reserves, there would have been no meaningful international role for the currency. In a sense, the Marshall Plan reflected a lesson U.S. officials learned in the 1920s but forgot in the 1930s—namely that markets left to their own devices will not secure a currency's international role. Official support, both financial and political, is also a necessity. Through the Marshall Plan, the United States delivered just this. It provided more than four times the foreign reserves the recipient countries could have drawn from the IMF.[21]

Dollar Shortage to Dollar Glut

Still, this aid did not solve the problem of the dollar shortage overnight.[22] A scarcity of dollars with which to purchase oil and other essentials from the United States continued to preoccupy European policymakers and threaten the stability of the Bretton Woods system well into the 1950s. Acknowledging the chronic nature of the problem, the United States acquiesced to measures by other countries discriminating against America's exports.[23] To husband its scarce foreign exchange, the British government restricted the sale of refined oil products of American-controlled companies from 1949 through the mid-1950s. These restrictions applied not just in the UK but throughout the sterling area, the residual collection of colonies, Commonwealth countries, and trading partners that pegged to the pound and held their external assets in that form.[24]

Then in 1951 eight European countries established a Coal and Steel Community that removed barriers to trade in coal, coke, pig iron, steel, and scrap iron while retaining restrictions on imports from the United States. Again Washington, D.C., acquiesced. This last measure turned out not to be so temporary; in 1957 the group became the European Economic Community, which worked to establish free trade among its members while continuing to tax imports from outside. The U.S. economy was growing robustly, and its trade remained in substantial surplus all through the 1950s. Hence any costs to the American economy could be disregarded. Nonetheless, the episode effectively served as a reminder that with exorbitant privilege comes exorbitant responsibility.

Currency values were realigned in September 1949, thanks to the flexibility afforded by the Bretton Woods Agreement. Countries accounting for two-thirds of world trade devalued against the dollar, typically by 30 percent. This qualified as "the greatest adjustment of exchange rates that ever took place in so short a period," in the words of the Dutch economist Jacques Polak, assistant director and soon-to-be monetary guru of the IMF.[25] Devaluing cheapened Europe's exports, rendering them more competitive. Again the United States acquiesced in the adjustment, understanding that the dollar shortage, if allowed to persist, might jeopardize economic and political readjustment in Europe and endanger the international role of the greenback itself.

European countries had been running trade deficits with the United States, rendering them short of dollars and chronically dependent on U.S. aid. With these devaluations, their trade swung into balance.[26] By late 1951, Polak could trumpet that the dollar problem, if not entirely solved, had "come much nearer to solution."

What neither Polak nor others anticipated was how the dollar shortage would now give way to the opposite problem: a dollar glut. By the end of the 1950s, in an article that saluted the concept of the dollar glut in its title, another leading international economist, Albert Hirschman, wrote, "The emergence of a sizeable deficit in the United States balance of payments during 1958/59 seems to have definitely settled the great debate of the last fifteen years about the existence of a 'chronic' dollar shortage."[27] Production had recovered, enabling European countries to reduce their dependence on merchandise and commodities imported from the United States; meanwhile, European exports had gained competitiveness. Regional integration enhanced supply-side efficiency. It allowed European countries to specialize in what they did best—Germany in the production of capital goods, its partners in the production of consumer goods. The consequent strengthening of trade balances allowed European countries to earn more dollars.

Additionally, an outflow of finance from the United States had begun.[28] In the second half of the 1940s money had flowed in the opposite direction. Capital had continued to flee Europe, reflecting doubts about economic and political stability. Now, however, domestic political settlements, which involved forming governments from which communist parties were excluded, renewed investor confidence. Following the 1949 devaluations and the strong recovery of European production, capital flows turned around. Countries retained controls on such flows, as they were entitled under Bretton Woods, but those controls were less than watertight. In any case, European officials had less angst about the potentially destabilizing consequences of capital flows when funds were flowing in rather than flowing out. Governments, central banks, and commercial banks devoted a portion of their foreign dollar receipts to accumulating reserve balances, relieving the earlier reserve scarcity.

They held some of those dollars on deposit not with U.S. banks—but in London and other European financial centers. In an ironic sense, the existence of these dollar deposits outside the United States, what were known as Eurodollars, itself derived from America's singular monetary leverage. In 1956 the USSR, fearing that the United States would respond to its invasion of Hungary by freezing its dollar deposits, shifted custody of those dollars from New York to London and to Moscow Narodny Bank, an English limited liability company owned by the Soviet government.[29] Moscow's fears were not unjustified: in 1948, in response to the seizure by the new Soviet-style Czechoslovak regime of the property of American citizens, the U.S. Treasury had blocked the withdrawal of $20 million of Czech gold from the Federal Reserve Bank of New York.[30] By shifting legal custody of its U.S. dollars to an English bank, the Soviets now placed them beyond U.S. legal reach.[31]

Other countries followed suit once European financiers figured out how to put those dollars to work in the lending market. Free of statutory ceilings on U.S. interest rates, those financiers could offer attractive rates of return. British bank regulators appreciated the parallel with the nineteenth century, when London functioned as a central money market, attracting funds from abroad and lending them to foreigners. They saw the growth of the Eurodollar market as a way for London to again compete with New York as an international financial center. The difference now was that London did its international business not in Britain's own currency, the pound sterling, but in dollars, reflecting the greater global circulation and acceptance of the latter.

U.S. policymakers worried that this growing pool of offshore dollars weakened their monetary control. It undermined their ability to cap interest rates, and it facilitated capital outflows by encouraging lending and investment abroad. From the viewpoint of U.S. regulators and monetary policymakers, growth of this offshore market was a mixed blessing.

But the one respect in which the implications were not mixed was the international role of the dollar. Although the Eurodollar market operated beyond U.S. regulatory reach, its growth only enhanced international use of the greenback. It provided investors in dollar deposits more attractive returns, encouraging them to hold and use the currency. And it reassured them that their holdings were safe from U.S. diplomatic meddling.

Triffin's Dilemma

The more immediate threat to the dollar's international role originated elsewhere, namely in the growing disproportion between the number of dollars in foreign hands and the size of U.S. gold reserves. This point was made by Robert Triffin, a Belgian-American economist who served in virtually every consequential monetary and financial organization of the period.³² Triffin, like Isaah Berlin's hedgehog, knew one big thing, which he repeated at every turn. Namely, once official foreign dollar holdings exceeded U.S. gold reserves, the fixed dollar price of gold would be in jeopardy.³³ This moment was inevitable, given a growing world economy, a commensurate increase in the need for international liquidity, and inelastic global gold supplies. Eventually, U.S. gold reserves would experience the equivalent of a bank run. Governments and central banks, seeking to redeem their dollars for gold at the prevailing price before U.S. gold reserves were exhausted and the cupboard was bare, would rush to present their dollars for conversion. This run would precipitate a massive shift from dollars to gold, like the shift from foreign exchange to gold in 1929–31. With only so much gold to go around, the deflationary consequences would be severe, again as in that earlier episode. This was the first horn of Triffin's dilemma.

But the alternative appeared no better. If the United States used capital controls or other measures to limit the accumulation of dollars by foreign central banks, finance would be inadequate to support international trade and payments. As in Triffin's other scenario, global growth would be strangled.³⁴ Hence the dilemma.

Having lived through Germany's World War I occupation of Belgium and coming of age in the shadow of fascism, Triffin was a pacifist—a "peace-monger" as he put it. As a young man and university student, he had witnessed Belgium's unsatisfactory return to the gold standard in the 1920s, which led first to economic overheating and then a disastrous slump. The experience left him skeptical of conventional accounts of the smooth operation of the gold standard, including that of White.³⁵ Like Keynes, Triffin saw gold as a barbarous relic. At the same time, however, he saw the dollar-based Bretton Woods system as unstable and untenable.

As a born and bred internationalist, Triffin's solution was to resurrect Keynes's bancor as an alternative to gold and the dollar.³⁶ Bancor was progressive, civilized, and international. Triffin saw it as part of the "long march of mankind toward its unity and a better control of its own fate."³⁷ In an early formulation, dating to 1960, Triffin imagined a system in which countries held gold and gold-convertible deposits at the IMF.³⁸ IMF members would be obliged to accept those deposits when taking payment from one another. The IMF would allocate deposits to its members using a quota system—roughly speaking, according to country size—and increase their supply to meet the needs of the expanding world economy.[39] It would guarantee their convertibility into gold at a fixed price, eliminating the bank-run scenario and solving the confidence problem.

At this stage, Triffin did not explain the crucial aspect of where the IMF would get the gold needed to make good on its guarantee. He may have had in mind amending the Fund's Articles of Agreement—its constitution—to oblige governments to deliver it. But this only substituted a new dilemma for the old one. At some point, gold-convertible deposits at the IMF would exceed gold in the Fund's hands even if its members collectively transferred all their gold holdings to the organization. Triffin also suggested that the United States should prohibit other countries from holding dollars as reserves as a way of compelling them to substitute the IMF's synthetic monetary unit. But neither did he explain how to achieve this happy result.

Not for the first time, an ambitious plan for an artificial international unit to replace the global dollar fell afoul of political resistance and logical problems. National leaders balked at giving up the power to regulate global liquidity and its international distribution to a multilateral organization. American officials had little enthusiasm for plans for downgrading the dollar, as its widespread international use was too convenient for U.S. banks and firms. It did not help, of course, that Triffin's plan remained incomplete, or that his description of the transition during which the dollar would be withdrawn from international circulation was less than clear.

A breakthrough of sorts occurred in 1965, when Henry Fowler, newly appointed as U.S. Treasury secretary, stepped in and acknowledged that something should be done. An unassuming Virginian who looked and spoke the part of a country lawyer, Fowler was a pragmatist, which was what the circumstances required. Official foreign dollar holdings had just crossed Triffin's red line, where they exceeded U.S. gold reserves. America's share of the free world's gold now tallied just a third, down from two-thirds after World War II. The point was not far off when the dollar's convertibility into gold at a fixed price would be at risk. In February 1965, French President Charles de Gaulle had held a press conference where he attacked the privileged role of the dollar in the Bretton Woods system, which he saw as allowing American companies to buy up factories and other European assets on the cheap. The not-so-implicit threat was that the French government might liquidate its dollar reserves and, in so doing, ignite a run on U.S. gold stocks by other governments.

No less than U.S. President Lyndon Johnson expressed nervousness about the prospect. Johnson therefore tasked Fowler with setting up a special working group to weigh remedies.[40] Fowler's high-level group of officials from the White House, Treasury and State Departments, Council of Economic Advisors, and Federal Reserve considered steps to ensure an adequate supply of liquidity to the global economy while at the same time limiting U.S. vulnerability to hostile monetary action. It cautiously floated the creation of another new international reserve asset, not to replace the dollar, as Triffin had proposed, but to supplement it. This new source of liquidity might relieve the pressure on the American balance of payments—no longer would the U.S. have to run deficits to meet global demands for international liquidity—but without supplanting the dollar's existing role.

Fowler unveiled the U.S. proposal on July 10, 1965, in a speech to the State Bar Association in Hot Springs, Virginia, population five thousand, a home field where he was apt to get a sympathetic reception. The secretary's modest demeanor and the modest venue notwithstanding, the speech drew wide media attention and dramatic reactions for its implications for the dollar's international role. *Time* magazine placed the secretary on its cover under the banner "The World's Need for Money: Should the Dollar Be Almighty?"[41]

Again, officials hesitated. The French were unsympathetic. De Gaulle and his advisors preferred raising the $35 gold price; they insisted on devaluing the dollar, in other words.[42] The more ambitious among them, such as the economist and French presidential advisor Jacques Rueff, advocated restoring a gold standard along nineteenth-century lines. Other advanced-country governments suggested assigning oversight of the new monetary unit to the Group of Ten, an ad hoc club of internationally minded industrial nations, as a way of pushing back against developing countries pressing for unlimited creation of the new form of international liquidity.[43]

U.S. support now turned the tide.[44] It took some negotiating, but agreement in principle was reached in 1967 to create the new monetary unit. It was to be known, awkwardly, as Special Drawing Rights, or SDRs, to avoid the connotation that it was a form of international money that might supplant the dollar.[45] SDRs would not substitute for dollars; they would only supplement them. The IMF's Articles of Agreement were suitably amended. A first modest allocation of 9.3 billion SDRs, valued at $9.3 billion U.S.—note the continued dollar link—was doled out in 1970–72.

Dilemma Deferred

One might think this event heralded a dramatic change in the global role of the dollar, but one would be wrong. In fact, there was only a continuation of earlier trends. The initial 1970 installment of $3.5 billion SDRs was a drop in the bucket. It did not even begin to dent global dependence on the greenback. Official foreign dollar holdings circa 1970, by comparison, were $50 billion, total external dollar holdings about $70 billion. In the five years between Fowler's volte-face and issuance of the first tranche of SDRs, U.S. foreign dollar liabilities continued to rise, and U.S. gold stocks continued to dwindle. By the end of 1970, the country's monetary gold stock had declined to just $11 billion.

Seeing the writing on the wall, governments had already begun resorting to expedients, as governments are prone to do. To curb capital outflows and gold losses, the United States imposed a tax on Americans' purchases of foreign securities. U.S. corporations were encouraged to limit their overseas investments. Voluntary gave way to compulsory with the adoption of a Foreign Direct Investment Program restricting outward corporate investment. Fowler even proposed taxing spending by American tourists abroad at rates as high as 30 percent.[46]

In 1968 the United States and six other advanced countries then abandoned their collective commitment to maintaining the world market price of gold at $35 an ounce.[47] No longer would they sell gold at this price in London or any other market. Under a new two-tier system, central banks and governments would make gold available at this price only to other central banks and governments. The price was set free to fluctuate on the London gold market. The earlier expectation had been that the price of gold could never fall below $35 an ounce, although it could rise above that level were the United States forced to devalue. Now, the thinking went, the market price could move both ways, eliminating the one-way bet and prompting speculators to think twice.[48] Critics of the change warned that if the market price rose too high, central banks might redeem gold from the United States at $35 an ounce and sell it on the market for a profit. Fears also arose that limiting the conversion of dollars into gold was the first step down a slippery slope, at whose bottom the U.S. Treasury might no longer offer convertibility at a fixed price even to foreign central banks and governments.

Those fears came true when the bottom was indeed reached in 1971. By the summer, U.S. gold reserves had sunk further to $10 billion. West Germany remained committed to not exchanging dollars for gold as a quid pro quo for U.S. maintenance of troops and military facilities on its territory. Chancellor Ludwig Erhard had pressured Bundesbank President Karl Blessing not to sell dollars already in 1963 to avoid the danger that the United States might respond by withdrawing troops from German soil. Blessing had then written a letter to Fed Chair William McChesney Martin reaffirming this commitment in 1967.[49] President Nixon and his advisors were confident that Japan would likewise exercise restraint, but doubts remained about the others.

Rumors circulated that the United States might devalue preemptively to stem gold losses, enhance the competitiveness of its exports, and bring down an uncomfortably high rate of unemployment.[50] On the second Thursday of August 1971, the British authorities, concerned to avoid capital losses in the event of dollar devaluation, asked the New York Fed whether it would provide "cover" for Britain's $3 billion of dollar reserves. British and American English not being identical, it was unclear whether the British were requesting that the Fed compensate them for losses if the dollar was devalued, or whether they were asking for $3 billion of cash on the barrelhead. In the translation of Paul Volcker, Nixon's undersecretary for international affairs at Treasury, the Brits were asking for the entire $3 billion.[51] At the New York Fed the interpretation was that they wanted only compensation for potential losses, not payment of the entire principal in gold.[52] But either way, the jig was up.

Volcker, a long-time New York Fed economist and commercial banker before joining Treasury, had been planning for this eventuality for years. More accurately, Volcker had been working on how to avoid this eventuality—how to defend the dollar against pressure for a devaluation. In a series of memos, he argued for the creation of additional SDRs to meet the world's liquidity needs, together with revaluations of Germany's deutschmark and the Japanese yen to restore international competitive balance. The United States, Volcker argued, would then be better able to maintain the $35 gold price. American officials could claim that they had not devalued; rather, Germany and Japan had revalued.

Anticipating his subsequent incarnation as inflation fighter in chief, Volcker hoped that Fed Chair Arthur Burns would raise interest rates to restrain spending and further strengthen the balance of trade. Revaluation by Germany and Japan would make imports into the United States more expensive and, in the absence of Fed action to dampen inflation, there might be pressure for wage and price controls, which were not his preferred policy option. But in deference to the Fed, Volcker downplayed this last aspect, writing only in general terms about the need to rein in inflation.[53] Reflecting doubts that Burns and the Fed would take concerted action, the next versions of Volcker's plan conceded the point and added a temporary wage and price freeze to prevent higher import prices from feeding through into inflation. Volcker skirted the question of for how long those controls might stay in place.

Lone Star

At this point, Volcker's "action paper" made its way onto the desk of John Connally (who we met in chapter 1). A Democrat, albeit increasingly alienated from the left wing of his party, Connally had taken over as Treasury secretary when Nixon sought to give his cabinet a bipartisan veneer following Republican losses in the 1970 midterm elections. Nixon was in thrall to Connally's bold personality and saw the Texan as the ideal replacement to David Kennedy, his all-but-invisible predecessor at Treasury. The president hoped that a more forceful Treasury secretary might clear the deck of troublesome international monetary issues prior to the 1972 election.[54]

Connally made up for a lack of training in monetary affairs with supreme self-confidence and diplomatic smarts. By instinct and nature, he favored a bold plan, although, as his biographer put it, he had not the faintest idea what that bold plan might be.[55] Volcker's recommendations provided an answer, so Connally ran with them. In this case, running meant pressuring Germany, Japan, and other countries to revalue their currencies. To this end, Connally proposed a temporary surcharge on U.S. imports, to be removed once there was agreement on the new set of currency values.[56] Volcker, a free trader, criticized the surcharge as distasteful coercion. He dropped it from his action paper multiple times, but the secretary put it right back in. Connally agreed to maintain the $35 gold price valued by Volcker as a symbol of stability but insisted on closing the "gold window"—that is, suspending the U.S. obligation to pay out gold to official foreign counterparts at that price. Foreign leaders would have to agree to suitable reforms of the international system before the window was reopened, and they were again allowed to exchange their dollars for gold.[57]

The U.S. position was hammered out at a meeting of Nixon and his advisors at Camp David over the long weekend of August 13 to 15, 1971. Connally and Volcker attended for Treasury, but representatives of the State Department were not invited, the president and his aides suspecting that State, more concerned with foreign relations than international finance, would not defend the new U.S. policies to other governments. George Shultz, head of the Office of Management and the Budget; the full Council of Economic Advisors; and Fed Chair Burns were all present. The principals knew that news of their discussions about gold and the dollar could excite the markets. On departing for Camp David, they were warned not to tell their wives where they were going. On arriving, they were instructed to avoid all but the most essential telephone calls.

The back and forth was intense. Burns objected to closing the gold window, warning that this would panic financial markets. Shultz, true to his background as a professor at the University of Chicago, opposed wage and price controls on philosophical grounds. Volcker reiterated his opposition to the import surcharge. But Connally was steadfast and, as always, persuasive. At the end of three days, the group adopted the essentials of Connally's plan.

At 9 p.m. on Sunday night, prior to the opening of financial markets, Nixon delivered his Oval Office speech laying out the key provisions. The gold window was closed until further notice. Connally's import surcharge would go into effect, giving the secretary a lever in his negotiations with foreign counterparties. Wages and prices would be frozen for ninety days so that Nixon could claim that he was serious about defeating inflation.

With the gold window closed, the yen and most European currencies were left to float against the dollar, some freely but others subject to central bank intervention, each according to the preference of their governments. Developing countries sought to maintain their customary dollar pegs but widened the margins within which their currencies were permitted to fluctuate.[58] Volcker flew off in a commandeered U.S. Air Force jet to reassure the Europeans and Japanese. The IMF's executive board held emergency meetings. The Group of Ten countries convened a series of ad hoc summits. It was at one of these G-10 confabs in late November that Connally dropped his notorious "our dollar, your problem" line.

The French, long critical of the dollar's global dominance and wedded to a monetary role for gold, were especially reproving. Seeking to mend fences, Nixon met French President Georges Pompidou halfway, as it were, in the Azores, where he attempted to personally negotiate a new dollar-franc exchange rate. Nixon arrived on a specially outfitted Boeing jet, the same one in fact that had carried the casket of the late John F. Kennedy back from Dallas to Washington, D.C. Pompidou one-upped him by arriving on the Concorde. Nixon then stayed up most of the night to watch his adopted home-town football team, the Washington Redskins. Such were the advantages of having a dedicated high-speed communications link, although the sleep deprivation did not enhance Nixon's acuity at the bargaining table. The French president did not want his finance minister and political rival Valéry Giscard d'Estaing sitting in on discussions, so neither could Connally, who was banished to a primitive military barracks for the duration. Nixon ended up taking advice on exchange rates from his national security advisor, Henry Kissinger, who was something of an economic duck out of water. This was a turnaround from the Camp David meeting in August, when the State Department and the rest of the national security apparatus were not invited.

The package was tied up at a G-10 meeting at the Smithsonian Institution on December 16, three days after the conclusion of the two presidents' Azores bilateral. Following a personal inspection, Connally approved the venue, the Smithsonian "Castle" completed in 1855, as suitably historic. After three days of deliberations, it was agreed that the official dollar price of gold would be raised from $35 to $38. Effectively, the dollar would be devalued by 8.6 percent against currencies with unchanged pegs to gold, such as France and the UK. The strong currency countries, Germany and Japan, would revalue against the dollar by 13.57 and 16.90 percent, respectively. These figures made calculations of equilibrium exchange rates look more precise than they actually were. For example, the formula proposed by Connally had Japan revaluing by 17 percent, down from his earlier demand that the country revalue by 25 percent. But the Japanese recalled how when they returned to the gold standard in 1930, they had also revalued the yen by 17 percent. This was immediately followed by the economy's descent into the Great Depression and rise of the military faction in Japan. When the Japanese vice minister explained that 17 percent was toxic, Connally offered 16.90 percent, and the Japanese took it. Still other countries maintained their dollar rates unchanged.[59]

In return for these concessions, Connally agreed to remove the import surcharge. To discourage speculators from betting on additional devaluations, in the Smithsonian Agreement, as the outcome of this negotiation was forever after known, the bands within which currencies could fluctuate were widened from ±1 percent, the most permitted under the original Bretton Woods Agreement, to ± 2.25 percent. Speculators who got it wrong stood to lose as much as 4.5 percent of their bet if a currency moved from the top of its band to the bottom, or vice versa. Officials hoped that market participants would now think twice before betting against a currency. Events would show this to be at best a weak deterrent.

The change in the trade-weighted dollar exchange rate was on the same order as the change in the price of gold, roughly 8 percent. This was less than Connally had called for but the most he could obtain. Whether the new rate would stick, and whether the change in currency values would prove powerful enough to shift the U.S. balance of payments from deficit to surplus, only time would tell. Volcker, for one, was pessimistic about the prospects.

Nothing more was said about reopening the gold window. Connally was certain to refuse, and his refusal would cast a shadow over what President Nixon lauded as "the greatest monetary agreement in the history of the world." Ministers agreed only to continue discussing steps to remove the overhang of unwanted U.S. liabilities by creating additional SDRs. The dollar was devalued and diminished. Its convertibility into gold having ended, it was exceptional no more.

9

Meet the New Boss

THE QUESTION then became what would take the place of the dollar. And the answer was: the dollar.

In the fallout of the Smithsonian meeting, this answer seemed far from ordained. Dollars held by the Bank of Japan had just lost 17 percent of their value. The Deutsche Bundesbank had just suffered capital losses of 13 percent on its dollars. The unthinkable having happened once, it was not unreasonable to think that it could happen again. 1972 being an election year, Arthur Burns and John Connally wanted to avoid tightening monetary and fiscal policies. Nixon and his aides, H. R. Haldeman and John Ehrlichman, had just launched a campaign to get Burns to lower interest rates. Nixon blamed the Federal Reserve for his defeat in the 1960 presidential election and did not want to repeat the experience. To this end, Nixon's White House Plumbers (a group formed to deal with press leaks) became leakers themselves: they spread rumors that the president might expand the Federal Reserve Board to include more compliant members if Burns took his time lowering interest rates. They planted stories with United Press International that the Fed chair had hypocritically requested a pay raise despite urging the public to comply with the administration's wage and price controls.[1] Connally stepped down from Treasury in May 1972 to head up Democrats for Nixon, but policy barely moved under his successor, George Shultz. The budget deficit remained large.[2] The now lower dollar did not even deliver the hoped-for improvement in the balance of trade. Because devaluation rendered both imports and exports more expensive—and because imports exceeded exports—the deficit widened further.[3] There were good grounds for doubting, in other words, that the 1971 devaluation would be the last.

In March 1972 the Congress, to affirm the status quo, passed a bill validating the increase in the official gold price from $35 to $38 an ounce. In principle, this raised the value of U.S. monetary gold reserves for use in redeeming devalued dollars, the hope being that doing so might restore the confidence of foreign investors. But since the gold window remained closed, the bill "had no practical effect," in the measured words of *The New York Times*.[4]

The SDR had gotten off to a modest start in 1970–72 with $9.3 billion of issuance. But its valuation now was uncertain. Initially, SDRs were valued in dollars and, via that convention, as a constant amount of gold.[5] But the gold content of the dollar had lost its stability. Whether SDRs would still be worth their weight in gold was now an open question.[6]

It appeared unlikely, in any case, that the international community could agree on additional SDR issuance. The French preferred actual gold to paper gold. U.S. officials, from Paul Volcker on down, were at loggerheads about increasing the supply of an international asset that might further diminish the dollar's standing. Low-income countries insisted on linking SDR allocations to their development needs, arguing that any resources thereby created should go to them. Advanced countries remained staunchly opposed, on equally self-interested grounds, to targeting an allocation in this manner. They feared that a new allocation could usher in inflation, since low-income countries were apt to spend their SDRs instead of hoarding them. Globally, inflation hovered above 6 percent. Augmenting the supply of SDRs, which governments could use to chase after imports, threatened to add more fuel to the inflationary fire.

For the moment, the SDR sat "trapped in an IMF stalemate of vetoes," as Charles Kindleberger put it in the same passage where he declared the dollar finished.[7] Not until the end of the 1970s were disagreements finally ironed out and was there approval of another modest allocation. In the meantime, the United States continued running trade deficits, which it financed by transferring more dollars to the rest of the world. Rather than growing, the share of SDRs in international reserves worldwide shrank from 5.9 percent at the end of 1972 to a mere 2.9 percent at the end of 1978.

In principle, central banks might have substituted deutschmarks, yen, and Swiss francs for unwanted dollars. Given the limited size of the German, Japanese, and Swiss economies, however, having investors pile into their currencies would have had the undesirable effect of driving up price levels in these countries. German policy makers feared both that capital inflows would unleash inflation and that deutchmark revaluation would disrupt the fragile progress of European integration. Officials in Tokyo saw yen appreciation as threatening Japan's export drive. Already in 1971, the German government prohibited sales of money market paper to nonresidents and reimposed an earlier ban on the payment of interest on the bank deposits of nonresidents. In 1972 it added a cash deposit (*Bardepot*) scheme requiring residents who borrowed abroad to make a concurrent 40 percent non-interest-bearing deposit at the central bank. When investors found ways to sidestep these measures, the German government resorted to direct controls.[8] The Japanese government likewise reinstated controls on foreign purchases of yen-denominated securities.[9] Switzerland restricted sales of franc-denominated bonds to nonresidents, followed Germany in banning interest payments on nonresident franc deposits, and eventually even set negative interest rates on those deposits.

Economic Gambles

The notion that the Bretton Woods system would recover its bearings with only modestly different exchange rates and wider fluctuation bands appeared increasingly far-fetched. Within months of the realignment of exchange rates negotiated at the Smithsonian Institution in December 1971, the British pound, the weak link, was driven out of the system. The 1967 devaluation of sterling, supported by restrictive policies, had temporarily strengthened the British balance of payments.[10] This, together with slack demand, meant that the UK was not among the countries compelled to devalue in 1971. But those same restrictive policies made for unhappiness on the home front, with sluggish growth, rising unemployment, and a restive public. Prime Minister Edward Heath, anticipating a general election in the near future, tried jolting the economy by tabling tax concessions and public spending increases, while also expanding the money supply. (The money supply increase was a government initiative since the Bank of England, having been nationalized in 1946, took marching orders from the Treasury.) Heath's plan constituted "one of the greatest economic gambles in modern history," in the words of a prominent historian of the period.[11] There was no little irony in the fact that a Conservative Government was now advocating Keynesian policies. Electoral politics make for strange economic bedfellows.

Anthony Barber, Heath's fearless chancellor of the exchequer, presented the budget to Parliament in March 1972. (Notably, Barber had served in the Royal Airforce in World War II, was shot down and imprisoned in a German camp, and repeatedly tunneled out in events that inspired the film *The Great Escape*.) He now stood before the body and emphasized that the government placed employment growth above other priorities, including exchange rate stability. Barber boldly asserted:

> Members of this House will agree that the lesson of the international balance of payments upsets of the last few years is that it is neither necessary nor desirable to distort domestic economies to an unacceptable extent in order to maintain unrealistic exchange rates, whether they are too high or too low. Certainly, in the modern world I do not believe that there is any need for this country, or any other, to be frustrated on this score in its determination to sustain sound economic growth and to reduce unemployment.[12]

The markets took Barber at his word. Finance immediately began flowing out of the UK in anticipation of devaluation. By mid-June the flow had grown into a flood, forcing sterling to the bottom of the ± 2½ percent fluctuation limits against the dollar specified by the Smithsonian Agreement.[13] European central banks intervened in the foreign exchange market, but to no avail. Thursday, June 22, saw the largest one-day capital outflow in the history of the UK. Left with no choice, the government allowed the pound to float or, more precisely, to sink out of the Bretton Woods system, in what was effectively the third post-World War II devaluation of sterling, after those of 1949 and 1967.[14] This time there would be no going back—not until 1990 when Prime Minister Margaret Thatcher made her fateful decision to enter the European Monetary System.[15]

And if the pound could fall out of the reconstructed Bretton Woods system due to a British decision to prioritize domestic demand and politics over exchange rate stability and international commitments, then what was to prevent the United States and the dollar from following? A Commerce Department release announcing a record U.S. trade deficit in early 1973 did not reassure.[16] Nixon's pressure on the Fed to goose spending bore fruit: the M2 money supply (a broad measure encompassing currency and both demand and time deposits at banks) rose by 12 percent in 1972. Good for the president's reelection, bad for the exchange rate and America's external accounts.

At this point, the U.S. authorities could have signaled their support for the dollar. Charles Coombs, head of currency trading at the New York Fed, argued that a well-designed foreign exchange market intervention might succeed in stabilizing the currency. It would do so by inflicting losses on "dollar bears," short sellers who had borrowed dollars, immediately sold them, and contracted to repurchase them at lower prices in the future. An earlier intervention undertaken by the Fed following sterling's devaluation, Coombs observed, had indeed succeeded in "squeezing the bears" and stabilizing the greenback.[17]

But the decision to intervene rested with the Treasury, on whose behalf the Fed acted.[18] Treasury, recall, was now headed by George Shultz, a Chicago colleague of Milton Friedman. Shultz, like Friedman, was a believer in floating exchange rates and skeptical of intervention. Shultz's Treasury instructed the Fed to hold fire. Shultz dispatched his ever-ready undersecretary Volcker to Bonn, Paris, and Tokyo to explore whether the Europeans would agree to another change in currency values. Although the trip was supposed to be secret to avoid exciting speculation, Volcker's six-foot, seven-inch frame made him hard to miss.

News of his visit leaked on Saturday, February 10, sparking a panic and forcing the major foreign exchange markets to close the following Monday.

Volcker, unlike Shultz, was a fixed-exchange-rate man, so he negotiated another 10 percent devaluation of the dollar while the markets remained closed. This bought policy makers a few weeks. But with the United States showing no inclination to adjust policy or intervene on the foreign exchange market, the new rate did not hold. On March 1 the Bundesbank, desperate to prevent the deutschmark from appreciating further, purchased $2.7 billion worth of dollars in the largest single-day foreign-exchange-market intervention to that point in history.[19] The next morning the Bank of France was forced to buy $600 million in just the first ninety minutes of trading. Once more Paris and other European foreign exchange markets were closed. Central banks abandoned all intervention, leaving exchange rates to find their levels. For the dollar, that level was lower. The greenback sank to the bottom of its Smithsonian fluctuation band, from where it dropped further. European currencies floated up from their pegged rates against the dollar, some separately, others jointly. The Smithsonian Agreement breathed its last.

No Path Forward

Nor was there a clear path forward. In the messy days following, some called for a new Bretton Woods Conference, but the conditions that made the 1944 conference a success—a dominant country to provide leadership, and an intellectual consensus on the outlines of a new system—no longer existed. Instead of convening the hundred-odd members of the IMF, governments gathered a select group of twenty country representatives to discuss reforms of the international system.[20] When its members reached an impasse, this Committee of Twenty made way for another supposedly temporary body, the ironically named Interim Committee—ironic because it continued to meet for another twenty-five years.[21] Given uninspiring progress in these larger committees, Shultz convened the Library Group (so named because members met in the ground-floor library of the White House), a coffee klatch of finance ministers from the U.S., UK, France, and West Germany. Japan joined in later in 1973, making it the Group of Five (G-5). In 1977, with the addition of Italy and Canada, it became the Group of Seven. But members of this smaller grouping similarly struggled to find common ground. The most on which they could agree was that the Bretton Woods system of currency pegs had crumbled. Accordingly, the IMF's Articles of Agreement were amended to replace the signature commitment to maintaining "a system of stable exchange rates" with a commitment to "a stable system of exchange rates."[22] Rearranging the words of the Articles smacked of rearranging the deck chairs on a certain ill-fated ocean liner.

The dollar, though, had not lost its luster entirely. In October 1973, with the outbreak of the Yom Kippur War, the Organization of Arab Petroleum Exporting Countries (OAPEC), angered by American support for Israel, retaliated by embargoing oil exports to the United States. It then doubled the price of crude, only to double it again in January 1974, after which oil prices moved still higher.

For the oil producers, surging prices meant higher export earnings and enormous surpluses. This largess came with one problem—namely, where to invest all the money. Notwithstanding U.S. support for Israel, the answer once more was the dollar. Liquidity and returns evidently trumped foreign policy concerns for Middle East petrostates.[23] Petrodollars, as their investments came to be known, were placed in U.S. Treasury bonds and dollar bank deposits, onshore but also in Eurodollar markets, indicative of tensions between the Arab countries and the United States—dollar deposits in Europe being beyond the reach of the U.S. authorities. Petrodollar inflows pushed the dollar higher: by early 1974 it had risen by 25 percent against the German deutschmark and Swiss franc compared to the previous July. Not for the last time, the dollar, its safe-haven status intact, benefited from macroeconomic volatility and geopolitical uncertainty, even volatility and uncertainty to which the United States itself contributed.

U.S. and European banks put those dollars to work as syndicated loans to developing countries—loans similarly denominated in dollars. Shultz paved the way by abolishing remaining U.S. controls on foreign lending in 1974, in one of his last acts on exiting the Treasury.[24] Throughout, the dollar remained the principal conduit for cross-border capital flows. The United States was still the single largest merchandise importer and exporter. Trade in commodities, not least oil, was invoiced and settled in dollars. It made sense for countries that exported commodities to borrow in dollars, since this matched the currency composition of their assets and liabilities. Only the market in U.S. Treasury securities had the depth and liquidity needed to digest such a large capital inflow. Only U.S. money-center banks, which did business in dollars, had the balance-sheet capacity and organizational wherewithal to arrange large loans for sovereign borrowers.

Crisis? What Crisis?

Still, not all was well on the U.S. economic front, to put an understated gloss on the point. Inflation accelerated sharply after 1973 in the period earning the title "The Great Inflation." 1977–78 saw a marked decline in the dollar exchange rate. Between early 1977, with the inauguration of the Carter administration, and October 1978, the eve of midterm elections, the dollar lost 13 percent of its value against other currencies.[25]

A thirteen percent dip was enough to throw observers off balance. Against the backdrop of a dollar exchange rate that had been stable for nearly four decades and had remained so as recently as 1971, some perceived this sharp loss of value as a full-blown dollar crisis.[26] Carter and his advisors, led by Treasury secretary Michael Blumenthal, had a more measured response; in their view, a weaker dollar was not undesirable. On the upside, it could counter sluggish growth and strengthen the balance of payments at the same time. But the currency's decline got out of hand when Blumenthal began opining publicly on the subject. In truth, many of the secretary's statements were relatively anodyne. In October 1977 he observed that the "relatively small" appreciation of the Japanese yen and German deutschmark would not be enough to reduce the U.S. trade deficit, implying that more foreign currency appreciation and dollar depreciation were in the cards. He told the Organisation for

Economic Co-operation and Development (OECD) that exchange rates should "play their appropriate role" in international adjustment.[27] Still, these were statements that left room for interpretation. If the adjustment of the U.S. external accounts remained incomplete, one could fairly infer that depreciation of the dollar, in the view of Blumenthal and other U.S. officials, was similarly incomplete. Justifiably or not, Blumenthal gained a reputation for favoring a weaker currency. As in the case of Anthony Barber before him, the markets took him at his word.

For the Carter administration, the weak dollar was an embarrassment. For the Federal Reserve, it was a troublesome source of inflation. By early 1978, U.S. officials concluded that something should be done. The Treasury negotiated a currency swap line with the Bundesbank, which allowed the Fed to intervene in the foreign exchange market, using deutchmarks to buy dollars.[28] Foreign central banks simultaneously sold their currencies to support the dollar. The greenback recovered briefly, but it resumed its prior fall as soon as these operations ended. Turnover on foreign exchange markets had risen strongly in the 1970s in response to more frequent fluctuations.[29] Together with the limited firepower of central banks and governments, this rendered intervention even less effective than before. Investors understood that the Carter administration, wishing to support economic growth, was reluctant to tighten fiscal policy, and that the Fed, for similar reasons, hesitated to raise interest rates. As Volcker, now president of the Federal Reserve Bank of New York, subsequently put it, "Foreigners sensed that for the Carter administration a stable dollar was a much lower priority than growth and jobs."[30]

Foreign exchange market intervention not backed by changed policies consequently provided only temporary relief.[31] Given tepid growth, there was little appetite for changed policies, so the dollar continued its fall. Henry Reuss, chairman of the Joint Economic Committee and leading congressional voice on currency matters, cautioned, "We must not panic," a statement all but guaranteed to provoke panic. The press wrote of a "collapsing" dollar and "wild routs on the currency and stock exchanges."[32] Blumenthal blamed groundless negative sentiment, what he called a "a psychological semi-panic not due to the underlying situation."³³

The fact that central banks and governments continued to hold the bulk of their reserves in dollars, now rapidly losing value, led to talk and even a little action around reform. At the annual meeting of the IMF in the fall of 1978, the Interim Committee finally agreed to another allocation of SDRs.³⁴ But this second allocation, like the first, was meager; in 1982, when it was complete, SDRs still accounted for just 5.8 percent of total reserves. Some debated the idea of a Substitution Account through which dollar reserves might be exchanged for SDRs, after which those dollars would be retired from the market. But a Substitution Account, for neither the first nor the last time, was a bridge too far. As with Triffin's earlier plan to exchange dollars for IMF deposits, it posed too many technical and political difficulties.³⁵

By October 1978, the dollar's fall had risen to the top of the Carter administration's worry list. Anthony Solomon, Carter's sagacious Undersecretary of the Treasury for Monetary Affairs, warned that the collapse, if allowed to continue, could threaten the stability of the U.S. banking system.³⁶ On Monday, November 1, Carter and Blumenthal, in cooperation with the Fed, launched a surprise attack on currency speculators—the kind of "bear squeeze" Charles Coombs had recommended in 1973. Carter's economic advisors met in secret the preceding Saturday and then maintained their normal weekend social schedules of cocktail parties. To avoid the press corps, the president flew back from Camp David on Sunday evening under cover of darkness.

The emergency package announced Monday morning doubled down on earlier interventions. It expanded swap lines with foreign central banks and accelerated Treasury gold sales as a way of mopping up dollars. An innovative element was the issuance of $10 billion of German deutschmark and Japanese yen-denominated Treasury bonds ("Carter bonds" as they inevitably came to be called). Issuing these signaled that the administration was prepared to put its money where its mouth was, since the cost of servicing and retiring them would skyrocket if the dollar fell. The biggest step came from the Fed, which raised its lending rate by a startling 100 basis points. This was its largest interest-rate hike since

1933, when the dollar was hit by the speculative attack that drove the United States off the gold standard.

These measures made clear that the administration had made stabilizing the dollar a priority. They effectively squeezed the dollar bears, who dropped out of the market to lick their wounds. The currency reversed course, rising between November 1978 and June 1979 by 6 percent on a trade-weighted basis.

Volcker Shock

This episode again showed that actual changes in policy, not just cosmetic interventions and "open mouth" operations, were required to stabilize the dollar. But stabilizing the currency was not enough to stabilize public opinion. 1979 brought a dismaying second round of oil-price increases, this time against the backdrop of strikes by Iranian oilfield and refinery workers. An offshoot of Nixon's temporary gas price controls remained in place, and Carter's policies of allocating petroleum to refineries by executive order resulted in gasoline shortages, lines at the pump, and disruptive, even violent demonstrations by truckers. With consumer confidence weakening and the Fed's higher interest rates beginning to bite, the expansion of U.S. spending slowed to a 1 percent annual rate.

By June, the president's approval rating had dropped to 30 percent. Just a fifth of Americans approved his handling of the economy.[37] On July 15, in an ill-fated Oval Office speech, Carter spoke of a crisis of confidence afflicting the American people.[38] Echoing Treasury Secretary Blumenthal's earlier comments, he cast America's problems as more psychological than real. Within days of the speech, Carter reorganized his cabinet. This reshuffling was designed to create the impression of a fresh start. Carter accepted the resignation of six cabinet members, including Blumenthal, who the president's inner circle blamed for the furor over the dollar.[39]

Blumenthal's dismissal created the need for a new Treasury chief. After Reginald Jones of General Electric, Thomas Clausen of Bank of America, and Irving Shapiro of DuPont all turned the job down, Carter shifted the sitting Fed chair, G. William Miller, to Treasury. He then filled the vacancy at the Federal Reserve Board by nominating Volcker, now four years into his term as president of the New York Fed.

Volcker was known for his support for a stable dollar. In his years on the FOMC, he had acquired a reputation as a committed inflation fighter.[40] Bringing down inflation was now understood, including by Carter, to be a precondition for restoring confidence in the currency.

The new chair traveled in his first official trip to the annual meeting of the International Monetary Fund in Belgrade, Yugoslavia. There he was greeted by not very veiled criticism of U.S. policy from foreign officials. Arthur Burns, who knew of what he spoke, gave a downbeat speech lamenting the limited ability of central bankers to control inflation and currency values in the face of political pressure. Volcker drew a more positive conclusion. He resolved that the first order of business was reining in inflation, political pressure or not. Leaving for Washington, D.C., while the Belgrade meeting was still underway, he hoped to avoid detection but was again betrayed by his tall stature. Arriving home, he called an extraordinary Saturday meeting of the FOMC. So began the concerted tightening that eventually brought the Fed's policy rate to 19.1 percent and broke the back of inflation.

Volcker's assault on inflation set the dollar off on another roller coaster ride. Between September 1979 and Volcker's emergency meeting, and early 1985, when the currency peaked, the trade-weighted dollar appreciated by almost 50 percent.[41] Sky-high U.S. interest rates will do that: they act as a financial magnet, attracting capital from abroad.[42] But more than just tight U.S. monetary policy supported the dollar; in addition, there was an extraordinarily loose fiscal policy. The Reagan administration's 1981 tax cut (the Economic Recovery Tax Act) lowered personal income tax rates from 70 to 50 percent at the top and from 14 to 11 percent at the bottom, while reducing the top capital gains tax rate from 28 to 20 percent. The U.S. Treasury later estimated that these measures depressed federal revenues by 9 percent, causing the budget deficit to soar.

This combination of tight monetary and loose fiscal policies was an effective way of suppressing inflation while limiting unemployment.[43] Much as the textbooks predicted, high interest rates slowed price increases, while budget deficits supported the continued growth of spending. But a second textbook prediction was that this policy mix would push up the dollar exchange rate. Reagan's expansionary fiscal policy fueled the demand for domestic goods, since American households spent their incomes mainly on goods and services produced at home. The dollar had to strengthen to shift some of this demand toward less expensive imported goods and thereby prevent an excess demand for domestic production from developing.

In mid-1981, with signs that the fever of inflation had finally broken, the FOMC began lowering the federal funds rate. Members of Congress and even Reagan administration officials concluded that tax reductions had been excessive, leading them to reverse out portions of those earlier cuts starting in 1982. The hope was that these adjustments would relieve the pressure on the now over-strong dollar.

Turning Point

Instead, the dollar kept soaring, even though policy impetus for its appreciation had faded. It may simply be that the trend continued because foreign exchange traders, like all traders, tend to extrapolate the past. This practice, dressed up by finance specialists as "momentum-based trading strategies," was profitable for much of the 1970s and 1980s—with the exception of key turning points when, for obvious reasons, extrapolating the past could result in large losses.[44] Between 1981 and 1985, however, there was nothing to precipitate a turning point. Monetary policy remained tight, fiscal policy loose, just not quite as tight and loose as before. Ronald Reagan's Treasury secretary, Donald Regan, and Beryl Sprinkel, who had taken Solomon's place as undersecretary for monetary affairs, believed in leaving the markets to their own devices. They rejected outright foreign exchange market intervention and any tailoring of policies to influence exchange market outcomes.

Thus, a change in approach required a change in personnel. This occurred in 1985, when James A. Baker III, the president's chief of staff, traded jobs with Regan. Baker had been dispirited by White House infighting and yearned for a more visible public position. When Regan made an offhand remark about exchanging jobs, Baker pounced. Baker was less bombastic than John Connally, the fellow Texan who had preceded him as Treasury secretary, but no less astute politically. And unlike Regan, he was not wedded to free market ideology. Baker understood that an over-strong dollar created headwinds for manufacturing that could damage Republican prospects in upcoming midterm elections.

Once the Volcker-Reagan policy mix started pushing up the dollar, Congress saw a veritable "flood of bills" to limit imports of shirts, shoes, lumber, and telecommunications equipment, in what amounted to the single largest surge of protectionist legislation since World War II.[45] This congressional activism did not jibe with an administration committed to free trade. But in the same way Connally in 1971 had used his import surcharge to wring concessions from foreign governments, Baker now used the threat of congressional protectionism to press other countries to revalue their currencies. Over the summer of 1985, he and his assistant at Treasury, Richard Darman, engaged in furtive discussions with their G-5 counterparts. Their conversations culminated in a meeting of G-5 finance ministers at the Plaza Hotel in New York on Sunday, September 22. The meeting was supposed to be secret, though the news somehow leaked one day prior—a standard Baker tactic to ratchet up pressure on attendees to conclude an agreement.

As background for the negotiations, G-5 deputies circulated a paper pointing to the need for a "ten to twelve percent downward adjustment of the dollar from present levels," and suggested that this could be accomplished with $18 billion of concerted foreign exchange market intervention.[46] These recommendations were too prescriptive for the politicians, who disputed even generalities. Germany worried that Japan would not allow the yen to appreciate against the dollar, while Japan feared the same about Germany. Baker wanted to avoid the implication that the United States had abandoned its policy of leaving the exchange rate to the market, much less that the administration was actively attempting to push the currency down. Thus, the G-5 communique referred obliquely not to the need for dollar depreciation but to the desirability of "some further orderly appreciation of the main non-dollar currencies." It spoke of cooperation, not intervention. The form of such cooperation was left to the imagination.

This was weak soup, but in fact the tide had already turned by the time the agreement was reached. The dollar exchange rate had peaked and began falling seven months before the Plaza meeting, reflecting easing by the Federal Reserve. In May, Treasury staff had written Baker of the opportunity to "go with the flow"—to capitalize on and reinforce developing dollar weakness by crafting an international agreement.[47] By the time of the Plaza meeting, the dollar had already declined by 7 percent.[48] The Plaza communique gave this fall another fillip. By the end of October, the dollar had depreciated by an additional 12 percent against the yen and 9 percent against European currencies. By February 1986, it was fully 25 percent below its levels twelve months earlier. Evidently, momentum traders had all now switched to betting on dollar depreciation.

By early 1986, the desired adjustment had been achieved. But flow being what it is, the dollar's decline did not stop there. A decade earlier, the MIT economist Rudiger Dornbusch had published an influential analysis of the tendency for exchange rates to overshoot their equilibrium values. Overshooting was what the dollar now did.[49] In early 1987 this reversal of trajectory prompted yet another emergency meeting, this one at the ornate Louvre Palace, home of the French Finance Ministry. The Louvre Agreement committed governments to holding their exchange rates at prevailing levels. Another unpublished paper specified target zones surrounding those levels within which currencies would fluctuate. This time, in contrast to the Plaza, officials accepted the numerical recommendations of their experts. But they kept the details to themselves, raising questions about the depth of their commitment.[50] Volcker, for one, interpreted the Louvre Agreement as "soft," meaning that if the limits of the specified target zones were breached, the ranges in question would be modified rather than defended.[51]

Again, it quickly became evident that interventions unaccompanied by domestic policy adjustments would not do. U.S. budget and trade deficits triggered continued anxiety among investors, who persisted in driving down the dollar. Baker had promised his G-5 colleagues that the

United States would reduce its budget deficit for 1988 to 2.3 percent of GDP. This turned out to be more than the Congress could swallow. Germany and Japan had promised to increase spending as a means to suppress their chronic external surpluses. But German opposition to fiscal profligacy ran deep; the Bundestag agreed only to very modest augmentation of a tax cut already scheduled for the coming year. Japan too faced domestic political constraints; Prime Minister Yasuhiro Nakasone had campaigned on a platform of fiscal consolidation, and Ministry of Finance officials opposed fiscal expansion. The Japanese government offered a fiscal stimulus of 1.7 percent of GDP, significantly less than the United States wished for.[52] The U.S. external deficit, and its mirror-image surpluses in Germany and Japan, persisted through 1987.

Good Policy or Good Luck

Eventually, the dollar stabilized. Once more, the key change lay not in more extensive intervention or policy coordination. The years after 1987 were known as the Great Moderation, when macroeconomic fluctuations became less pronounced. With GDP fluctuating less, exchange rates, including that of the dollar, fluctuated less. Scholars debate whether the Great Moderation derived from good policy or good luck.[53] Whatever its cause, a corollary was a less volatile dollar.

These dollar fluctuations were a vivid reminder of Connally's dictum ("our currency, your problem"). Again, however, if they provoked complaints from foreign officials, they did nothing to diminish the dollar's international role. Between 1971 and 1985, despite the greenback's roller coaster ride, the dollar holdings of foreign central banks quadrupled. Dollars still accounted for 70 percent of global foreign exchange reserves.[54] More than 50 percent of world trade, according to Otmar Emminger of the Bundesbank, was priced in dollars.[55] More than 80 percent of the external debts of developing countries were issued in dollars. More countries pegged their exchange rates to the dollar than to all other currencies combined.[56] By the end of the 1980s, the dollar still accounted for 90 percent of foreign exchange market turnover.[57] The dollar was still the currency in which some two-thirds of the offshore assets and liabilities of banks reporting positions to the Bank for International Settlements were denominated.[58]

This experience suggested that what mattered for a currency's international role was not simply its stability or volatility. Exchange-rate stability per se was not as important as the assurance that the authorities would not opportunistically push the currency up or, especially, down.[59] What mattered was the depth and liquidity of the markets in which it was traded, and whether those markets were backstopped by a lender and liquidity provider of last resort. Throughout the period, the United States possessed a central bank prepared to backstop the markets. This was true under Volcker but even more visibly after 1987, when Alan Greenspan took the reins at the Fed.[60] The Fed had negotiated dollar swap lines with foreign central banks already in the 1960s, as we saw in chapter 8, and in the 1970s it used these to stabilize the dollar. Starting in 2007, in response to the Global Financial Crisis, it expanded these swap lines still further. These liquidity lines enabled foreign central banks to backstop their own commercial banks when the latter incurred dollar-denominated obligations. This in turn rendered those foreign authorities more relaxed about allowing local banks to hold and use dollars. The U.S. Treasury Department for its part took a hands-off policy toward the exchange rate when Robert Rubin took over as Treasury secretary in the 1990s and eschewed his predecessors' efforts to talk down the currency.[61]

The Search for Alternatives

The other thing sustaining the continuing dominance of the dollar was the absence of alternatives. There would be no more SDR allocations for three decades following the second allocation in 1979–81. There was no shortage of international liquidity to prompt additional SDR issuance. The United States ran current account deficits throughout the period, making dollars available to the rest of the world.[62] As issuer of the incumbent international currency, it attached no urgency to an allocation. And the U.S. government, reflecting its dominant position at the Bretton Woods Conference, still had a veto in the IMF.[63]

Japan was by this time the second largest economy, but the yen did not challenge or even significantly supplement the dollar as an international currency. Starting in 1983, the Japanese government took steps to foster an international role for the yen "commensurate with the share of the Japanese economy in the world and Japan's status as the world's largest net creditor nation," in the aspiring words of the Japanese Ministry of Finance.[64] It focused on liberalizing financial markets as a way of providing yen-denominated instruments to nonresidents, and on building the infrastructure needed for Tokyo to develop as an international financial center. It moved quickly on financial liberalization, partly for domestic reasons and partly to assuage the United States, which hoped that liberalization would produce a stronger yen and smaller Japanese current account surplus. There was also progress on the financial center front. By 1990, Tokyo was the third leading global banking center, behind London and New York as measured by foreign bank presence.[65]

Then, however, yen internationalization was set back by other events. Japan experienced first a banking crisis, next a deflation crisis, and finally an extended period of economic stagnation. U.S. experience in the 1930s, when banking crises had reversed the dollar's international gains, underscored how banking and financial instability, together with economic stagnation, could slow and even reverse progress at currency internationalization. The disarray in Japan's banking system did not now reassure foreign investors. Nor did it help that successive Japanese governments waited a decade to reorganize and recapitalize the banks. Earlier, the Japanese economy's rapid ascent had lent modest impetus to international use of the yen by Japan's own firms.[66] Now, however, the platform stopped growing. In the course of the 1990s the share of the yen in international financial transactions stagnated or declined (depending on whether one considers cross-border bank positions or external bond issuance). The yen's share of official foreign reserves, having doubled from 4.4 percent in 1980 to 8.5 percent in 1993, declined to 3.9 percent by 2003. At this point, "the international status of the yen essentially remained where it had started two decades earlier..."[67]

The deutschmark was the other logical substitute for the dollar, given its reputation for holding its value. Some measures suggested that it was making headway as an international currency. In 1988, when central banks worldwide held 7.2 percent of their foreign exchange reserves in yen, 16.2 percent were held in deutschmarks. This was a far cry from the dollar's 63.3 percent share, but it was not nothing. An estimated 12.4 percent of world exports were invoiced and denominated in deutschmarks, well behind the dollar's share but again far from negligible.[68]

In financial transactions, however, the deutschmark punched below its weight. Its share of Eurobond issues (bonds issued outside the borrower's home country) lagged even the share of the yen. Holdings abroad of deutschmark-denominated Treasury bills and other short-term claims were insignificant. In the 1970s, fearing that capital inflows would undermine price stability, the German authorities had prohibited sales of money market paper to nonresidents and banned the payment of interest on foreigners' bank deposits. They now limited bond issuance to fixed rate securities, where international investors preferred variable rate instruments given the uncertain prospects of the global economy. A turnover tax on secondary market transactions in bonds and equities and a withholding tax on interest income further diminished foreign appetite for deutschmark-denominated instruments.[69]

A further complication was the deutschmark's role as anchor of the European Monetary System. In the early 1970s, responding to the failure of global reform, the European Community had gone its own way. It established a regional system of currency pegs, in the manner of Bretton Woods, while floating against the dollar.[70] Capital controls insulated European currencies from market pressures, making it easier for central banks and governments to hold their exchange rates stable. But since this insulation was incomplete, so was the stability of those currencies. Britain was forced out of Europe's currency system in mid-1972, as we have seen. Denmark followed, though it was eventually able to return.[71] Italy left in 1973; in this case there would be no return. Especially humiliating was when France, having claimed leadership in Europe's monetary affairs, was forced out in 1974. The French rejoined in 1975 but were expelled again 1976.

The European Monetary System (EMS) established in 1979 was designed to put an end to this chaos. Although officially a symmetric system in which each European currency was held within a band against an average of the others, the EMS was effectively an asymmetric fixed-rate system centered on Germany and the deutschmark.[72] This created a dilemma for the Bundesbank. Limiting the pressure on weak European currencies and preserving the EMS might require the German central bank to loosen monetary policy, threatening inflation. But staying the monetary course could lead to speculative attacks and currency crises elsewhere in Europe, creating financial and political volatility in Germany's neighborhood. Ultimately, no one doubted which way the Bundesbank would jump if forced to choose between price stability and exchange rate stability. Experienced observers were thus not surprised in 1990 when the Bundesbank, responding to increased spending and inflation following German reunification, opted to tighten. The result was the 1992–93 crisis, when speculative attacks forced the pound sterling out of the EMS and came within a hair's breadth of toppling the French franc, the second most important currency in the system.

Great Powers, Great Currencies

This experience reinforced the commitment of European Community member states to the course on which they had just embarked—namely creating a regional currency, what became the euro. A shared currency had practical value for a European Community seeking to deepen integration among its members, and symbolic value for a Europe striving to secure a place on the global stage. "Great powers have great currencies," as Robert Mundell, Nobel laureate and intellectual father of the euro, put it.[73] More concretely, the EMS had been shown as fragile and unstable. Each outbreak of instability led governments to point their fingers accusingly at Germany, which hardly made for European solidarity.[74]

Not least, the euro afforded an opportunity to create a full-fledged rival to the dollar. Economically, the European Union was as large as the

United States. The extra-EU exports of its fifteen members exceeded U.S. exports. The EU was unified economically and financially. Ever since the days of Charles De Gaulle and Valéry Giscard d'Estaing, European leaders were critical of the dollar's international role. So if global monetary reform was off the table, regional reform might offer a way forward.

Faced with resistance to his efforts to reform the global monetary system, Triffin had contemplated a regional approach already in the 1950s, crafting proposals for a European Reserve Fund and a European currency unit that might free the continent from the dollar's thrall. Now the Frenchman Jacques Delors, who chaired the committee crafting the blueprint for the euro, saw the single currency as advancing Europe's political project but also as an opportunity to challenge the dollar.[75] In the words of Daniel Gros and Niels Thygesen, two economists who worked on the Delors Report, "the most visible effect of [European Monetary Union] at the global level will be the emergence of a second global currency."[76] Informed observers, including Americans, saw the development as epochal. C. Fred Bergsten, who headed the Washington, D.C.-based Institute for International Economics, anticipated in 1997 that "a successful euro will be the first real competitor to the dollar since it surpassed sterling as the world's dominant money during the interwar period."[77] Patricia Pollard of the Federal Reserve System warned her colleagues that "with the creation of the euro, for the first time the dollar has a potential rival for the status as the primary international currency."[78]

It did not turn out that way. Following its creation in 1999, there was little change in the international role of the euro relative to the national currencies it replaced. The share of those earlier currencies in the foreign exchange reserves of central banks was 15.9 percent prior to the changeover. At the outset, the euro's share was only very slightly lower, at 14 percent.[79] Actually, this modest decline was a statistical artifact: what had been the Bank of France's deutschmark reserves and the Bundesbank's French franc reserves were now redenominated as euros and reclassified as domestic-currency assets. Still, the point stands: there was no dramatic reshuffling of global reserve portfolios toward the euro. A similar stasis was evident on foreign exchange markets. The 2001 triennial survey of the Bank for International Settlements showed that the euro accounted for 37.6 percent of global foreign exchange transactions in April of the year, essentially unchanged from the 35.2 percent share of the deutschmark and franc in the preceding survey.[80]

More time, conceivably, had to pass before market participants came to appreciate the merits of the euro and assigned it a greater international role.[81] Again, it was not to be. By 2025, more than a quarter of a century had passed, yet the euro still ranked far behind the dollar on all relevant dimensions.[82] Where the dollar accounted for nearly 60 percent of foreign exchange reserves worldwide, the euro accounted for barely 20 percent, little changed from 1999. The dollar's advantage was still greater when it came to the currency denomination of international debt securities, international loans, and international deposits. The euro accounted for just 30 percent of global foreign exchange transactions—again, little changed from 1999—compared to the dollar's 90 percent.[83]

What then held the euro back? For over a decade, traders harbored doubts about the currency's survival. The specter of "Grexit" (that Greece's 2010 debt crisis might force the country to abandon the euro and reinstate the drachma) suggested that adoption of the euro was reversible. If so, the Greek crisis might spread to other heavily indebted member states such as Italy, splintering the currency area. These existential doubts were put to rest in 2012 when European Central Bank President Mario Draghi committed the ECB to "do whatever it takes to preserve the euro," and in August when its governing council authorized the purchase of unlimited numbers of government bonds in the secondary market.[84] Thirteen years into the euro experiment, after a long period of uncertainty, the single currency finally possessed a central bank prepared to act as lender and liquidity provider of last resort. Historical experience—from that of Britain and the pound sterling in the nineteenth century to the counterexample of the U.S. and the dollar in the 1930s—demonstrated that the acquisition and maintenance of international currency status presupposed the presence of a central bank prepared to backstop financial markets, guaranteeing the stability required by international investors. In this respect the euro was no different than its predecessors. Like the dollar in the 1930s, the early euro lacked a lender and liquidity provider of last resort. And the absence of that lender and liquidity provider frustrated Europe's international aspirations.

Dollar Dominance

Thus, the dollar's international position was not significantly challenged by the creation of the euro, nor for that matter by anything else. Its dominance reflected the absence of viable alternatives. But that dominance also rested on the fundamental factors responsible for the dollar's emergence as the leading international currency. The market in U.S. Treasury securities remained the single deepest and most liquid financial market in the world. The access of foreign investors to that market remained unimpeded. Price stability was restored by Volcker and maintained under his successors Greenspan, Ben Bernanke, and Janet Yellen. The United States remained the single largest economy, and the period following the fall of the Berlin Wall and collapse of the Soviet Union was its unipolar moment of maximum economic, financial, and geopolitical influence. It remained the world's largest exporter until being overtaken by China in 2009.

Importantly, the Federal Reserve was quick to step in and stabilize U.S. financial markets when these were threatened by events, be they the 1987 stock market crash, the 2001 attack on the Twin Towers, or the 2007–8 banking and financial crisis. The Fed and Treasury Department acknowledged and acted on their international obligations. They organized and extended financial support to Mexico in 1994–95 and South Korea in 1997–98, keeping these partners rooted in the dollar system. The Fed provided foreign central banks with dollar swap lines—collateralized loans of dollars for other currencies—giving those central banks the resources needed to act as dollar lenders of last resort. In turn this rendered those foreign central banks more sanguine about their local banks and firms' continued reliance on dollars in international transactions.

Together these factors bolstered the dollar's safe-haven status. When in September 2008 global financial markets were roiled by the bankruptcy of the U.S. investment bank Lehman Brothers, investors fled to the safety of the dollar, even though American policymakers had committed the missteps responsible for Lehman's chaotic failure. When COVID-19 erupted, creating high anxiety about the economic and financial future, investors once more fled to the safety of dollars. The market in U.S. Treasury securities remained the single deepest and most liquid. The Fed's support for U.S. banks and markets was unequivocal. The American government was prepared to take extraordinary steps to stabilize the U.S. economy but also to support its foreign partners. For all these reasons, the dollar continued to reign supreme.

There of course being no guarantee that what was true in the past would be true in the future.

PART III
What Comes Next

10

Outside Options

FOR HALF A CENTURY, the dollar has defied predictions of an imminent loss of international currency status. But past performance is no guarantee of future returns. So why might the future be different?

As mentioned in chapter 1, for the first time, competitors have entered the ring, from the euro and the Chinese renminbi to digital platforms enabling the cross-border use of central bank digital currencies. For the moment, none of these alternatives is ready for prime time. None is positioned to act as a full-fledged rival to the dollar. Instead, we must ask what it will take for them to move from potential to actual alternatives, and how long it will take to get there.

Euro Struggles

Even after Mario Draghi and the European Central Bank put to rest investors' existential doubts about the euro, there remained—and remains—a shortage of high-quality, liquid, euro-denominated securities for international investors to hold and use. Borrowing by the European Commission is a drop in the bucket by international monetary standards: outstanding EU debt is less than €0.5 trillion overall. Only three euro area sovereigns—Germany, Luxembourg, and the Netherlands—have AAA ratings from all three major credit rating agencies.[1] Only the bonds of these three euro area sovereigns therefore qualify as safe assets—as substitutes for U.S. Treasuries in the portfolios of central banks. At the end of 2024, the three countries' collective debt totaled

€3.5 trillion, or a tenth the outstanding public debt of the United States, and barely a quarter of global foreign exchange reserves. Aggravating the shortfall is the fact that the bonds of these three investment-grade countries are held by their own banks to meet capital and liquidity requirements or have been vacuumed up by the European Central Bank during its asset-purchase programs. Central banks and financial institutions in other parts of the world consequently do not have access to them.[2] Meanwhile, official foreign investors have as little appetite for holding the sub-investment grade bonds of the government of Greece as for holding the municipal bonds of the fiscally troubled city of Los Angeles.

Overall, of course, euro area debt is lower relative to GDP than that of the United States. The lack of creditworthiness of other euro area governments thus reflects how this debt is unevenly spread, with alarmingly high debt ratios and poor credit ratings for Greece, Italy, and certain other European countries. The euro area has no Treasury to underwrite governmental functions at a uniform cost and to issue bonds backed by the full faith and credit of euro area countries as a group. It also lacks a dedicated source of revenue it can use to service bonds such a Treasury might issue. No integrated capital market exists to fund public and corporate borrowing at the same cost regardless of where the governments and corporations in question are located.[3] President Draghi may have solved the problem created by the euro area's lack of a lender and liquidity provider of last resort, but the absence of a common Treasury and inadequate progress in creating an integrated capital market continue to frustrate the ambitions of those who seek a larger international role for Europe's currency.

A major shock could conceivably transform this situation. Jean Monnet, the *pater familias* of the European Union, famously argued that this is how Europe advances. ("Europe will be forged in crisis and will be the sum of the solutions adopted for those crises," he wrote in his memoirs.) The COVID-19 crisis stimulated renewed talk of creating an EU Treasury. COVID-19, blue-blooded Europeanists trumpeted, could be Europe's Hamiltonian moment; by reminding the residents of different European countries that "they were all in it together," COVID overcame nationalistic resistance to an EU bond issue to address the continent's health crisis. In the end, all that happened, however, was a one-off EU bond issue, not the creation of a permanent fiscal capacity (where permanent fiscal capacity means statutory authorization for the European Union to recurrently issue bonds, together with the assignment of permanent revenue streams, including transfers of fiscal revenues from the member states, to service those bonds). For member states jealous of their fiscal sovereignty, that EU fiscal capacity was a bridge too far.

Donald Trump's cozying up to Vladimir Putin and the realization that the United States can no longer be relied upon as an alliance partner have conceivably served as the tipping point for creating such a fiscal capacity to fund the defense spending that Europe now desperately requires. Thus, in March 2025, following the Trump administration's suspension of U.S. aid to Ukraine, the European Commission proposed borrowing €180 billion to lend to member states for defense-related purposes. But €180 billion makes only a small dent in the €1 trillion European governments committed to spending over the next decade to ramp up their defense and military capacity. It is small potatoes by the standards of an installed base of more than $30 trillion of U.S. Treasury securities. Again, the small scale of the initiative indicates the reluctance of EU member states to pool their fiscal resources to back the creation of safe assets by the European Union.

To be sure, an increase in defense spending might provide the European Union a lever with which to encourage extra-EU countries—in Eastern Europe, North Africa, and elsewhere—to rely more on the euro. History, from the ancient Greek and Roman empires to the twentieth-century United States, shows that geopolitical power and international currency status go together. At the same time, the failure to create a European Defense Community in the 1950s and the presence today of pro-Russian leaders in countries like Hungary and Slovakia caution against jumping to this conclusion. With different EU member states pursuing different foreign, defense, and military policies, the leverage exerted by those policies, when it comes to influence the international monetary policies and practices of other countries, will be correspondingly less.[4]

Enter the Dragon

Beijing has made concerted efforts to promote cross-border use of the renminbi since 2009, when People's Bank of China Governor Zhou Xiaochuan spoke of the shortcomings of the dollar-based international monetary order.[5] Although Zhou initially suggested substituting SDRs for dollars in a reformed international monetary system, it quickly became evident that any attempt to expand the role of the SDR would run up against the same obstacles to reaching international agreement that derailed Robert Triffin's plans in the 1960s and the Substitution Account in the 1970s. Chinese officials therefore pivoted toward internationalizing the renminbi.[6] They loosened restrictions on using the currency in trade settlements, permitting Shanghai and Guangdong to settle their trade in renminbi. When this trial proved successful, permission was then extended to other provinces. Officials encouraged Chinese enterprises to invoice and settle their trade in renminbi. Here Chinese officials followed the playbook of the early Federal Reserve, which sought to encourage international use of the dollar starting in 1914 first by promoting its use as a vehicle for trade settlement and then, once this practice was commonplace, encouraging its adoption for purely financial transactions. More generally, the Chinese authorities were following a centuries-long pattern, where currency internationalization begins with the adoption of a currency for financing and settling cross-border commodity and merchandise trade before its use is extended to financial transactions.

Subsequent programs enabled select Chinese enterprises to invest renminbi funds in foreign countries and select foreign investors to purchase renminbi-denominated assets in China. The Belt & Road Program, the global infrastructure project the Chinese government put forward in 2013, supported direct investment by Chinese enterprises abroad. Countries receiving renminbi in payment for China's foreign investments used them to purchase Chinese exports. Where Belt & Road projects took the form of infrastructure investment, renminbi were used to purchase the services of Chinese construction companies.

The first experiments in building markets in renminbi securities with international investor participation were initiated offshore. Starting in 2009, financial institutions in Hong Kong were allowed to issue renminbi-denominated bonds. When these early experiments proved successful, they were brought onshore; the authorities worked to cultivate domestic stock and bond markets, again with foreign investor participation. The Shanghai-Hong Kong Stock Connect, a trading link between the Shanghai and Hong Kong stock exchanges, opened in 2014. A Bond Connect giving overseas investors access to fixed income markets was added in 2017.[7] The Qualified Foreign Institutional Investor program allowed foreign investors to buy and sell renminbi-denominated shares of select Chinese companies. The authorities continually fine-tuned regulation with the goal of enhancing the stability, liquidity, and transparency of onshore markets, making the securities traded there more attractive to foreign investors.[8]

Still other measures sought to construct the infrastructure needed for a larger volume of transactions. Officials designated one or more of China's four big banks to act as official renminbi clearing bank in each of the world's international financial centers. By 2025, thirty-three official clearing banks were operating in twenty-seven financial centers around the world. Their role is to serve as correspondents for foreign banks wishing to exchange other currencies for renminbi and transfer funds to and from China.[9] This is not unlike how U.S. banks went abroad in 1914 to originate foreign financial business in dollars, or how the great merchant houses of Florence set up foreign branches in the fourteenth and fifteenth centuries with the same objective in mind. The People's Bank of China (PBoC) negotiated renminbi swap agreements with foreign central banks, more than forty in number, assuring foreign regulators that they would be able to provide renminbi liquidity to banks and firms under their authority, and thereby encouraging them to permit those entities to use the currency.[10] This directly parallels the Fed's dollar swaps. The Chinese central bank also sought to foster direct trading of the renminbi against the Russian ruble, the Japanese yen, the British pound, and other currencies, avoiding the need to first purchase dollars. Again, this was analogous to how the

Fed, starting in 1914, took steps to eliminate the need for U.S. exporters to purchase sterling as an intermediate step when making payment in other currencies.

China also worked to develop a clearinghouse for interbank transfers of renminbi as an alternative to the dollar-based Clearing House Interbank Payments System (CHIPS), together with a proprietary messaging system as an alternative to the Society for Worldwide Interbank Financial Telecommunication (SWIFT). Launched in 2015, its Cross-Border International Payments System (CIPS) has signed on more than 170 direct participants, including both commercial and central banks, who use the platform to transfer renminbi funds among themselves. In addition, 1,500 indirect participants use a direct participant as correspondent bank for transferring renminbi.[11] As of June 2025 this system was processing thirty-three thousand transactions daily, with an average daily value of RMB 758 billion, or $105 billion.[12]

While this sounds impressive, the idea that the renminbi currently has the strength to pose a serious challenge to the dollar remains dubious. The renminbi surpassed the dollar in early 2023 as the currency most used in China's own international payments, as efforts to promote its use by Chinese importers and exporters bore fruit. But in other respects, it languished. Globally, less than 2 percent of total trade is invoiced in renminbi, compared to more than 40 percent in dollars.[13] As of spring 2025, the renminbi was used in just 2.9 percent of global interbank payments, the dollar in 48 percent.[14] On foreign exchange markets, the dollar accounts for nearly 90 percent of turnover by value, the renminbi just 7 percent.[15] Fifty-eight percent of foreign exchange reserves worldwide was held in dollars, just 2.18 percent in renminbi as of the end of 2024.[16] Where CIPS processed a daily average of $105 billion of transactions, the dollar-based Clearing House settled more than $2 trillion a day, roughly 20 times as much by value. Average daily turnover of cash trading in all renminbi bond markets averaged $209 billion in 2024; the U.S. Treasury market alone: more than $1.1 trillion. And when central banks in emerging markets drew on their renminbi swap lines, many did so not to enable local banks and firms to undertake additional renminbi-denominated transactions, but out of desperation to obtain foreign currency reserves, borne of their exclusion from international capital markets.[17]

These disparities are no mystery. Internationalization of the dollar began more than a century ago. Renminbi internationalization, in contrast, has been underway for barely a decade. Whereas the United States has been investing in financial development for centuries, financial development of the People's Republic dates back only to the 1990s. The renminbi is starting out leagues behind. Even if the currency's use in interbank payments and foreign exchange transactions continues to rise at double-digit rates, decades will pass before the miracle of compound interest brings it within hailing distance of the dollar. Because the country faces demographic and financial headwinds, too, double-digit increases in Chinese financial aggregates are not to be taken for granted.

Earlier chapters recounted how Britain in the nineteenth century and the United States in the twentieth used geopolitical leverage to encourage other countries to hold and use a currency. China too is a geopolitical power. No one questions its ability to project military might. But China has not formed friendly alliances and mutual defense pacts with other economies, comparable to U.S. security agreements with West Germany and Japan after World War II. Its alliances are not obviously of the sort that would encourage its partners to embrace and support the renminbi's international role. A document published by the Chinese Embassy in the United States lists twenty-eight countries that have "established partnerships, cooperative relations or strategic relations of mutual benefit with China." While these range alphabetically from Afghanistan to Vietnam, they tend mostly to be small developing countries and emerging markets.[18]

Further, for centuries, virtually every leading international currency has been the currency of a political democracy or republic, where checks and balances limit the ability of the state to arbitrarily expropriate investors. This was true of the Netherlands and the guilder in the eighteenth century, Britain and the pound sterling in the nineteenth, and the United States and the dollar in the twentieth. Not only was there a separation of powers—not only did there exist a parliament or legislature where investors sat and whose consent was required for consequential changes in taxes and public spending—but there was an autonomous central bank to preserve the stability of the currency. When central bank autonomy was compromised, so too was the international dominance of its currency (a principle with obvious relevance also to the United States today). The PBoC, for its part, does not enjoy statutory independence. There is nothing to prevent the president and the State Council from arbitrarily replacing its management or changing the rules of the monetary game.[19] This uncomfortable fact discourages other central banks from holding reserves in Shanghai and foreign entities from relying on China for financial services.

To be sure, a benign dictator who values a currency's international role can sometimes take steps to reassure international investors. Successive Roman emperors preserved the value of the imperial coinage for centuries. Spanish kings clamped down on the emission of debased coin by the royal mint at Potosí, protecting the reputation of pieces of eight. Absolute leaders with absolute power can respond absolutely. But nothing ensures that they will respond positively.

For the foreseeable future, then, the renminbi will play an international financial role comparable to that of the dollar only in a geopolitically bifurcated world. Russia holds a significant share of its foreign reserves in renminbi and does a significant fraction of its cross-border transactions in the currency because China is not party to Western sanctions against Moscow. Russia is thus prepared to overlook questions about Chinese monetary and financial governance. If more countries find themselves in Russia's position, more countries will follow Russia's financial example. In a new Cold War, countries will have to choose with which rival power to do business and, correspondingly, in which currency to do it. The world would then divide into two monetary camps, organized respectively around the dollar and renminbi.[20]

So far, both Beijing and Washington have indicated that they wish to avoid this outcome. China has studiously avoided becoming a target of U.S. financial sanctions to retain access to the dollar, the U.S. banking system, and SWIFT. Within weeks of "Liberation Day," April 2, 2025, when President Trump escalated his trade war against China, his Treasury secretary Scott Bessent acknowledged that the complete economic decoupling of the two countries was "unsustainable," and tariffs were negotiated back down, at least for the moment. Beijing's temporary export controls made clear America's dependence on Chinese supplies of refined rare earth minerals that are key inputs into all manner of electronics. As a result, American and Chinese economic and monetary camps continue to overlap. Whether this will remain the case in the future is necessarily uncertain. More aggressive moves against Taiwan by China could aggravate tensions between the two countries, leading to U.S. sanctions against Beijing or worse. Even more aggressive U.S. trade policy toward China could push Beijing to retaliate by liquidating its dollar reserves, depressing the prices of U.S. Treasury bonds. This would destabilize the U.S. Treasury market, inflict financial losses on China, whose residual holdings of dollar bonds would lose value, and render international transactions more costly and difficult. It would be disastrous all around.

Nontraditional Reserve Currencies

If not the euro or renminbi, then what other currency might supplement or supplant the greenback? To the extent that the dollar has lost share in the global market for foreign exchange reserves, the principal beneficiaries have been not the euro or the renminbi, but in fact the currencies of a handful of relatively small, open, well-managed economies—those of Canada, Australia, New Zealand, South Korea, Singapore, Denmark, Sweden, and Norway.[21] These have in common that their financial markets are open to foreign investors. Their currencies provide central bank reserve managers with diversification, since they do not move in lockstep with the U.S. dollar. Several of their economies rely heavily on Chinese demand for their products, so they offer "China exposure." That is, their exchange rates and financial markets rise and fall with the Chinese economy, providing renminbi-like returns without requiring investors to hold renminbi-denominated deposits and bonds.

This rise of nontraditional reserve currencies was not anticipated a quarter-century ago, when the presumption was that country size and scale of issuance were key determinants of the market liquidity sought by international investors. At that time, a reserve manager seeking to add Australian dollars to a central bank foreign exchange portfolio faced bid-ask spreads fully three times those in markets for established reserve currencies like the Japanese yen, the British pound, and the deutschmark or euro.[22] It thus made sense for reserve managers wishing to diversify away from the U.S. dollar to diversify toward these other established reserve currencies.

Reel forward a couple of decades, and Aussie dollar spreads had fallen to where they were indistinguishable from those on the pound, the yen, and the euro.[23] The same was true of other nontraditional reserve currencies. As a result, nontraditional reserve currencies currently account for upwards of 10 percent of known foreign exchange reserves ("known" because certain central banks still do not publicly disclose the currency composition of their reserves).

What had changed was the advent of electronic trading of foreign exchange, which cut costs and increased the speed and efficiency of transactions. Through the early 1990s, the only way for dealers to obtain quotes, which they passed on to their customers, was by telephoning other dealers. The smaller a country and less frequently its currency traded, the harder it was to obtain a competitive quote. In 1992–93 Reuters and Electronic Broking Services then introduced broking systems using computer screens to provide "best bid and ask prices." These systems enabled dealers to offset foreign currency positions (that is, to match sales of a currency to one customer against purchases from another) and pass the savings to their clients. In the 2000s, large global banks developed electronic trading platforms on which their clients could trade currencies directly while receiving streaming price quotes, guaranteed liquidity, and low-cost execution. Next came multi-bank platforms streaming prices from multiple sources, heightening competition among dealers and further narrowing spreads; and retail aggregators—digital platforms that pooled small foreign exchange transactions—passing on lower wholesale prices to retail customers. As these platforms were opened to computer-driven transactions, manual trading gave way to electronic market-making and liquidity-provision algorithms, again lowering costs and improving liquidity. All this made it more attractive to buy, sell, and hold what had previously been lightly traded currencies.[24]

The fact that scale has dropped in importance is not entirely good news for the dollar and the United States. That said, these new reserve currencies can only compete with the dollar on the margin. Small size and limited issuance mean that they cannot replace the dollar in its entirety. And while these currencies are more prominent in central bank reserve portfolios, they have not begun to replace the dollar in other domains such as trade invoicing, settlement, and payments.

Yet another idea, worth passing mention, is a BRICS (Brazil, Russia, India, China, South Africa, Egypt, Ethiopia, Iran and the United Arab Emirates) basket currency or even a single BRICS currency, as suggested by Brazilian President Luiz Inácio Lula da Silva.[25] The problem is that BRICS members have very different economic structures and monetary preferences from one another—much more different even than the members of the Euro Area—which rules out a single currency in practice. Experience with the International Monetary Fund's Special Drawing Rights, a currency basket that still has no commercial use after more than half a century, suggests that a basket currency is no country's preference.

Stablecoins

This could change, however, as electronic platforms spread to payments, and specifically to payments for goods and services. A currency's use for cross-border payments is the first stage, history tells us, in the acquisition of international currency status. Some observers have suggested that cross-border payments might be executed with cryptocurrencies such as Bitcoin. But plain-vanilla cryptos are too volatile to provide the unit of account, store of value, and means of payment services of international money.

Another option might be stablecoins: cryptocurrencies pegged one-to-one to national currencies. In principle, these could be used to make payments by transferring cryptocurrency tokens, without exposure to variability in the value of those tokens and without having to go through the U.S. correspondent banking system.[26] To ensure their stability, regulators might require the issuer, perhaps a tech company, perhaps a bank, to hold backing equal to its outstanding stablecoin circulation.[27] The issuer would hold this collateral in the form of liquid assets such as Treasury bills.

The "equal to" proviso is important. If the issuer ran out of liquid assets with which to redeem every stablecoin token, the value of those tokens could vary. Aware that the issuer had only enough liquid collateral to pay off holders who were first in line, investors might rush to redeem their stablecoins while redemption was still possible. The analogy with a bank run would be direct. The value of the coin could collapse. The crisis of confidence might spread contagiously from one coin to another, destabilizing the stablecoin ecosystem. It might even destabilize the market in Treasury bills if multiple issuers had to simultaneously sell off their collateral.

Regulation requiring all stablecoins to be 100 percent backed would eliminate these problems, in theory.[28] But this assumes that regulations are effectively enforced. Issuers have incentives to cut corners—to hold less than the requisite amount of collateral, or to hold it in the form of risky assets that promise a higher rate of return. Banks have long since been regulated. Regulators have had decades to refine their procedures, but bank runs and failures still occur. Moreover, a regime where regulators license issuers and enforce collateral rules would lend the government's imprimatur to the stablecoins in question. Regulation could quickly shade into a government guarantee of stablecoin holdings, with all the costs this entails, not least to the taxpayer.

Yet even if tech firms in each of the 180 countries with its own currency issued a stablecoin pegged to that currency, this would do nothing to diminish the dominance of the dollar. South Korean exporters of DRAM (Dynamic Random Access Memory) chips to South Africa would have no more interest in accepting payment in a rand-linked stablecoin than they would in taking payment in the form of a rand bank deposit—which is to say, they would have no interest at all. There being no direct market for trading the rand for the won, the South African importer would still have to exchange his rand-linked stablecoin for a dollar-linked stablecoin which could then be used to pay the South Korean exporter in dollars, or else to purchase a won-linked stablecoin. One can imagine online cryptocurrency exchanges such as Binance and Coinbase extending the range of tokens traded on their platforms to additional stablecoins. But these platforms would have to hold huge, costly inventories of the stablecoins in question, both Korean won and South African rand stablecoins in the present example, to create a market for directly trading these tokens against one another and eliminate the intermediating role of the dollar.

The point is reinforced by the fact that the dominant stablecoins, Tether and USDC, are U.S. dollar linked. At present, 99 percent of all stablecoins, by value, are dollar linked. In practice these are used as on-ramps and off-ramps for purchasing and selling other cryptocurrencies, and to a limited extent for international remittances.[29] Were they more widely accepted and utilized, they would only reinforce the dollar's dominant position.[30]

Central Bank Digital Currencies

Alternatively, payment platforms facilitating the exchange of local currencies while eliminating the need to go through the dollar might follow on the creation of central bank digital currencies (CBDCs). CBDCs are digital tokens providing a direct claim on the central bank. To put it another way, CBDCs are effectively interchangeable with central bank money, where central bank money means cash and freely convertible credit balances at the central bank. CBDCs may circulate on a blockchain or other distributed ledger-based platform, but they also may use bespoke encryption administered by the central bank. More than a hundred central banks are trialing or studying CBDCs.[31]

They are exploring two variants: retail CBDCs, where individuals download digital wallets or apps into which central bank tokens are dropped; and wholesale CBDCs, where the central bank distributes digital claims to commercial banks and other regulated financial institutions, which use them to settle transactions among themselves. Retail CBDCs hold out promise, say their proponents, of enhancing financial inclusion, since users need only a smartphone and an app, not an account at a commercial bank. They will simplify and streamline payments when they are as ubiquitous as dollar bills. They offer instant settlement and a low-cost end-run around the fees charged by banks, credit-card companies, and commercial payment apps such as PayPal, Alipay, and WeChat Pay.

Of course, there are other ways of fostering financial inclusion, such as the no-frills bank accounts mandated by the Reserve Bank of India, which entitle holders to open and maintain a commercial bank account with a zero balance, receive a debit card, and use ATMs regardless of income and employment.[32] Instant payment platforms that transfer funds between bank accounts of individuals and companies instantaneously, without requiring issuance of a central bank digital currency, have been successfully launched by central banks (think PIX in Brazil) and consortia of commercial banks (think PayNow of the Association of Banks in Singapore).[33] Thus, retail CBDCs, where tokens are dropped into the digital wallets of individuals for use in everyday payments, are already redundant.

For now, in any case, retail CBDCs can only be used domestically. A case in point is the e-CNY (digital renminbi) issued by PBoC. The PBoC is at the forefront of CBDC development, having researched the question since 2014. It issues its e-CNY to commercial banks and other financial institutions, which distribute it to the public for use in transactions. The e-CNY can be used offline and is interoperable with mobile payment platforms such as Alipay and WeChat Pay. But users must reside in China and transact with domestic merchants.[34] Relaxing these restrictions would make the e-CNY a channel for evading China's capital controls. Individual and daily transactions are capped at low levels, limiting the information the PBoC is compelled to harvest about the user and their transaction when enforcing anti-money-laundering and know-your-customer rules. While this preserves a modicum of anonymity, it also prevents the currency from being used in large-value business transactions.

Other Chinese financial entities have gone abroad, and one can imagine the e-CNY similarly expanding overseas.[35] UnionPay, a credit-card company, serves Chinese travelers in 180 countries. Alipay+ has teamed with local partners to enable Chinese tourists to make in-store and online purchases abroad using digital Alipay wallets. But these initiatives likewise permit only small retail transactions, given China's capital controls and know-your-customer rules. There is reason to think that any cross-border use of the e-CNY by retail customers will similarly be allowed for small transactions only.[36]

Wholesale CBDC balances, on the other hand, would resemble the reserve accounts that commercial banks hold with central banks. The central bank would issue its CBDC to commercial banks and other regulated financial institutions with direct access to central bank money. Those commercial banks and financial institutions would use the CBDC in transactions among themselves. Unlike current arrangements, where the central bank intermediates a transaction between banks by transferring funds between their respective reserve accounts, banks would be able to transfer funds directly, without intermediation by the central bank or another institution. The central bank could add programs to its CBDC ("smart contracts" that provide for execution of a transaction only when the counterparty and transaction meet certain restrictions) to ensure compliance with know-your-customer and anti-money-laundering rules.

Foreign banks could maintain a CBDC wallet or account at one of these regulated commercial banks, just as foreign banks maintain dollar accounts with commercial banks in New York. This would streamline cross-border payments, which currently require up to five days when completed by wire transfer. At some point, however, a foreign bank with a CBDC wallet or account in a country issuing a digital currency would want to repatriate its funds, on its own behalf or on behalf of its client. It could do so by converting its CBDC balance into a conventional bank balance, before converting that balance into dollars and transferring it back home using the correspondent banking system, SWIFT or CHIPS. In this case, however, the existence of the CBDC does nothing to diminish the role of SWIFT, the U.S. banking system, or the dollar in executing the cross-border transaction.

mBridge to Nowhere

More ambitiously, one can envisage linking the CBDCs of different countries directly. This link might be a shared interface, where central banks hold accounts with one another, or single platform, where multiple CBDCs run on a single distributed ledger, or blockchain.[37] Project mBridge is the leading experiment along these lines. It started in 2021 as a collaboration of the central banks of China, Hong Kong, Thailand, and the United Arab Emirates, with logistical support from the Bank for International Settlements (BIS). Saudi Arabia's central bank joined up in 2024.

This platform enables central banks and commercial banks in the participating countries to transact with one another by directly exchanging their CBDCs. The participants' wholesale CBDCs are exchanged for one another on a permissioned blockchain. Central banks verify transactions through the blockchain's so-called validator nodes.[38] Commercial banks update their ledgers.

This technology has been extensively tested. In mid-2024 the BIS announced that Project mBridge had reached minimum viable product stage, meaning that it had enough features and reliability to attract adopters. Officials of the PBoC indicated that a limited number of actual payments were being executed on the platform by the end of the year.

When this project is scaled up, banks, firms, and governments of the participating countries will be able to directly exchange their CBDCs with one another. When undertaking cross-border transactions, they will no longer have to go through SWIFT, the U.S. banking system, and the dollar. In principle, transactions will be faster (settled within seconds), safer (since they would be settled in central bank money), cheaper (owing to streamlined processes), final (in contrast to correspondent bank transactions, where questions about the solvency and survival of the counterparty linger until settlement is complete), and out of the reach of U.S. authorities. One can imagine additional countries participating on an equal footing, exchanging their CBDCs quickly and at low cost without the need for the correspondent services of U.S. banks or having to go through the dollar.

That said, important technical questions remain to be answered. One is how to determine the exchange rates between the respective CBDCs. Conceivably, central banks could obtain foreign exchange quotations off-platform, in the conventional foreign exchange market, simply using mBridge as a set of payment rails for executing cross-border transactions. The problem is that direct markets between the currencies of many countries tend to be small, illiquid, and even nonexistent. There might be no available exchange rate quotation for direct trades of, say, the South African rand for the South Korean won. It would still be possible for the South African importer to infer the exchange rate from triangular arbitrage, taking the buying rate for dollars in terms of rand and dividing this by the selling rate for dollars in terms of won. But this rate would be unattractive, since it would incorporate payment of two bid-ask spreads—which is precisely why so many international transactions use dollars instead. Traders using an mBridge would be paying a price for bypassing the dollar and U.S. banking system, which might still appeal to countries such as Russia under sanction, but not more generally.

Alternatively, the exchange rate could be determined on platform.[39] An automated market maker could algorithmically set the exchange rate at which transactions are settled. The algorithm might be calibrated to replicate observed exchange-rate movements in historical market data. Commercial banks would contribute CBDCs to a pre-funded liquidity pool and be compensated with fees proportional to their contribution. If the past is an accurate guide to the future, then the liquidity pool would receive and possess enough of each CBDC to meet transactions at the algorithmically determined exchange rate. But market structures and outcomes do not remain unchanged over time or develop linearly. Whether the past would in fact be an accurate guide is a question, likely a question with a negative answer.[40]

Political Fly

A political fly in this ointment is the withdrawal of the BIS from Project mBridge in late 2024. This came about when Western governments belatedly recognized that Project mBridge was a Chinese-led project,

China being the largest participant and the software having been developed by the PBoC.[41] There was a realization that China could conceivably invite Russia to join, creating a mechanism through which Moscow could channel international payments despite its exclusion from SWIFT and Western banking systems.[42] The BIS's withdrawal coincided with a BRICS summit in Kazan, Russia, where Putin mulled the idea of a BRICS Bridge, or BRICS Cross-Border Payment Initiative, over which the BRICS countries' CBDCs might be directly exchanged.[43] This suggested the possibility that mBridge technology might be redeployed to facilitate transactions among the BRICS and allied countries.[44] Worried that the technology might be used as a sanctions-busting device, Western countries, starting with the United States, registered their disapproval, leading the BIS to exit the scheme.[45]

This points to the fundamental constraint on scaling up Project mBridge and other projects of similar ilk. This constraint is not the availability of proven digital technology but the politics of governance. Participating central banks would have to agree on who regulates the platform. They will have to agree on whom to admit as additional members and when. They will have to decide between one-country-one-vote as in the United Nations General Assembly, and weighted voting by country size in the manner of the IMF. Reaching decisions by consensus, yet another option, would become harder as participation grew. Originally, the architects of Project mBridge imagined a steering committee in charge of formulating strategies, overseeing business management, and guiding design and operation.[46] But how this steering committee would be constituted and what decision-making procedures it would adopt were left to the imagination.

Such governance problems are formidable when they require agreement among countries of different geopolitical persuasions. One need only recall the governance problems that have hamstrung the World Trade Organization since the geopolitical split between China and the United States. Contrast the case of SWIFT, whose governance is in the hands of a group of like-minded G-10 banks and governments whose geopolitical interests are traditionally aligned, and that cooperated extensively in the 1970s when the organization was formed.[47] Governance has remained in the hands of those like-minded founders even as participation was opened up to banks from additional countries.

Project mBridge includes no central bank from a NATO country. Given tensions between Russia and the West, and between China and the West, it is hard to conceive that a large membership could agree on how to govern an mBridge-like platform with an economic and geographical span as internationally encompassing as that of the dollar. This is an indication that this kind of digital platform is unlikely to have global reach. Like the renminbi itself, it will play a significant role only in a geopolitically bifurcated world. In the event of an irreparable rupture between the United States and China, other countries would have to choose which of the two economies to trade with, which set of payment rails to use, and on which of their respective currencies to rely.

Whether or not such a rupture occurs, and hence the fate of the dollar, is not entirely in the hands of the United States. But the country can do much to shape the consequences, for better or worse.

11

Our Currency, Our Problem

WHAT EUROPE and China do will matter for the future of the dollar. How technology evolves will be important. In addition, however, the United States can shape the consequences. To turn John Connally on his head: it's our currency and our problem.

To start, there is uncertainty about the prospects of the American economy and its weight in the world. The United States no longer commands the global stage as it did after World War II, or even in the 1970s when Bretton Woods met its maker. This implies that the country can less reliably supply safe and liquid assets, in the form of U.S. Treasury securities, on the scale needed to meet the demands of the rest of the world.[1] America's share of global GDP, at market prices, has dropped from 40 percent in 1960 to 26 percent today. This rebalancing makes sense, as there is no intrinsic reason why other countries should permanently lag the United States in per capita GDP. The post–World War II period saw reconstruction and catch-up growth in Western Europe and Japan. Subsequent decades saw opening and growth in successful emerging markets, notably in East Asia. There is nothing abnormal or unhealthy about this process of convergence, including for the United States itself. But there will likely be implications for the dollar.[2]

One may object that if the share of the United States in global GDP could fall from 40 to 26 percent without negative repercussions for the dollar, then there is no reason to anticipate anything different from a further fall.[3] The network effects of the dollar's widespread international use still exert a strong gravitational pull. But there may come a point.

More precisely, there may come a tipping point where agents move, en masse, to the currency of another country.

One can object further that America continues to outperform other advanced economies. It is home to many of the world's leading high-tech firms. It conducts vast amounts of basic and applied research. It is at the forefront of research in artificial intelligence. It has a start-up-friendly culture where serial entrepreneurs are forgiven their failures and draw on the world's leading venture capital industry. It is a magnet for foreign talent.

But, as ever, there is no guarantee that what was true in the past will be true in the future. In part, the United States has grown faster because of more rapid labor force growth, and its labor force has grown more rapidly because of immigration. This is something many of the country's politicians and much of its voting public, it would appear, are no longer willing to tolerate. And while the United States has done well—compared to other advanced economies—in terms of productivity growth, the productivity of the business sector depends on basic research conducted by government and universities and on public-private sector cooperation. Whether these sources of productivity growth will survive the Trump administration's cuts to public-sector R&D and university research overhead is yet to be seen. Both U.S. labor productivity growth and total factor productivity growth have been trending downward since the early twenty-first century. Cuts to the country's basic research capacity, far from making America great, threaten to deal them another blow.

Whether artificial intelligence will significantly boost U.S. productivity is uncertain. Earlier advances in information technology disproportionately benefited early adopters, large incumbent firms that were able to expand their market share and scale their operations across multiple product markets. This handful of large firms was able to deter entry by new competitors. With the rise in market concentration came an increase in markups of prices over costs, higher profits for dominant firms, declining firm entry rates, falling job reallocation, declining rates of innovation and adoption by potential competitors, and a growing gap in labor productivity between leading and lagging firms—bad signs all.[4]

Consequently, the impact on U.S. productivity growth of earlier advances in information technology was not entirely positive.

Productivity growth has fared even worse in Europe, of course, supporting the "cleanest dirty shirt in the pile" logic for continued dollar dominance. Europe's failure to grow its economy is one factor preventing the euro from challenging the dollar as the dominant international currency, in other words. In 2025, a new resolve to ramp up defense spending was seen as applying a healthy dose of fiscal stimulus that might stimulate faster growth in Europe. The positive reaction of stock markets to defense spending announcements indicated that investors anticipated that this would be the case. But evidence of sustained positive spillovers from defense spending, as opposed to an immediate sugar rush, is mixed. Moreover, Europe's governments and societies show a stubborn reluctance to adopt the deeper productivity-enhancing structural reforms suggested by Mario Draghi in his 2024 report to the European Commission.[5]

For their part, emerging markets such as China are experiencing a breathtakingly fast demographic transition. In the past they grew not just through increases in productivity but also through rapid growth of the labor force. The falling birth rates that come with higher incomes mean that the labor force is no longer growing rapidly, if at all.[6] Looking forward, there is therefore less reason for the U.S. share of global GDP to fall owing to faster growth in emerging markets.

Trading Places

What is true of the U.S. share of global output—that it has declined over time—is even truer of the country's share of trade. More emerging markets and low-income countries have adopted export-focused economic development strategies, and countries smaller than the United States necessarily specialize in particular sectors and naturally engage in more trade. The U.S. share of global exports has fallen by half since the early 1950s, from more than 18 percent to less than 9 percent.[7]

Again, there is nothing intrinsically unhealthy about these trends: they reflect the postwar reconstruction of the global economy, and growth fueled by economic opening and export orientation of countries around the world. Trade is not zero sum, or so most economists believe. The United States is among the beneficiaries.

But a further decline in the U.S. share of global trade engineered by the restrictive tariff policies of politicians convinced otherwise would be decidedly unhealthy for the U.S. economy. To be sure, there is an argument for selective tariffs to reduce the country's dependence on imports of critical dual-use products and technologies from unreliable partners. No less an authority than Adam Smith acknowledged this national security exception to the argument for free trade. As he wrote in *The Wealth of Nations*, "If any particular manufacture was necessary, indeed, for the defence of the society, it might not always be prudent to depend upon our neighbours for the supply; and if such manufacture could not otherwise be supported at home, it might not be unreasonable that all the other branches of industry should be taxed in order to support it."[8]

The Biden and first Trump administrations shared this view with respect to U.S. imports from China. But blunt across-the-board tariffs on all U.S. imports could prompt America's trade partners to negotiate deals among themselves that reorient their trade away from the country. The implications for the dollar's international status would not be pretty. The currency of the leading trading nation is a natural habitat for its own exporters and importers, who loom large in global markets. This creates an incentive for exporters and importers elsewhere seeking to do business with this country to use its currency, given its convenience for their customers and suppliers. The incentive is similar for foreign entities seeking to borrow and lend on this country's financial markets. It follows that as the weight of an economy in global trade and finance declines, the market forces supporting widespread use of its currency tend to weaken. The commercial struggles of Florence, as the city-state was overtaken by larger regional economies, ended the florin's rein as the leading unit used in cross-border transactions. The decline of Dutch commercial supremacy, with the mounting problems of the VOC, effectively sealed the fate of the guilder as a currency used in Northern European and intercontinental trade and finance. An "America First" tariff policy destructive of the country's commercial links would have the same negative implications for the dollar.

Stability in the Balance

Then there is America's troubled fiscal and financial outlook. The dollar has been attractive to central banks as foreign reserves, and to corporate treasurers, sovereign wealth fund managers, and other international investors because it is available in ample amounts while broadly holding its value. The United States has skated on the edge of the Triffin dilemma—it has successfully provided a steady supply of dollars to meet the liquidity needs of an expanding world economy without supplying so many as to erode confidence in their value. But if this has been true until now, it is still possible that U.S. fiscal and financial woes could push the dollar over the edge. Congressional Budget Office (CBO) forecasts of the evolution of federal government debt as a share of GDP vary over time, with changes in federal spending and revenues and with what is assumed about future interest rates and the growth of the economy. Overall, however, these forecasts all paint the same gloomy picture. The CBO's long-term budget outlook for 2025 shows debt in the hands of the public as leaping from 100 percent of GDP at the end of the year to 118 percent in 2035, 136 percent in 2045, and 156 percent in 2055, reflecting chronic federal government budget deficits.[9] In thirty years, interest payments will absorb more than a quarter of federal revenues.[10] Doubts about whether the United States has the willingness and ability to service its debt in full will raise questions about the safe-asset character of the dollar and the willingness of foreign official and private investors to hold it.

This rise in debt servicing costs points to the possibility that the government will press the Fed to aid in this effort. The central bank will feel pressure to keep interest rates down by acting as buyer of last resort of Treasury securities.[11] The additional cash it injects into circulation to finance those purchases, while putting downward pressure on interest rates, will put upward pressure on prices. This is a polite way of saying that the Fed will be asked to inflate away a portion of the debt. This is not a pleasant scenario for investors, who will incur losses on their Treasury holdings. They will logically seek to liquidate those positions in advance.

2055 may seem like a long way off. But investors act in advance of events. They have an incentive to exit prior to a crisis and, in so doing, bring that crisis forward in time. There is no set-in-stone numerical value for the debt-to-GDP ratio where investors automatically conclude that a sustainable debt has become unsustainable. But there can come a point where what were previously regarded as safe assets are abruptly rerated as unsafe.[12] History is littered with examples, from third-century Rome to twentieth-century Britain, where excessive deficits and heavy debts caused governments to resort to debasement and inflation that undermined confidence in their currencies. The longer America's chronic deficits persist, and the higher its debt levels rise, the harder it becomes to rule out the scenario where the dollar suffers a similar fate.

But if this scenario is impossible to rule out, neither is it inevitable. Congress could reform tax laws to boost revenues: loopholes could be closed; marginal rates could be raised on high earners. The U.S. could means test entitlement programs such as Social Security to limit their cost. Payments could be reduced for individuals with incomes above a certain level. The retirement age at which workers become eligible for benefits could be raised. Other budgetary outlays could be cut. But by every indication, the United States is moving in the opposite direction of these policies with the 2024 electoral victory of Trump and Congress's passage of his One Big Beautiful Bill Act in 2025.[13]

This is not just a Republican Party problem; in fact, neither political party shows much of an appetite for fiscal consolidation, or specifically for the entitlement reform that is a prerequisite for achieving that goal. Political polarization is an obstacle, always and everywhere, to the adoption and maintenance of painful if necessary fiscal measures, and the United States exhibits unusually high and rising levels of political polarization.[14] Fiscal reforms are easier to sustain when supported by a broad coalition of interest groups and embraced across the political spectrum.[15] Otherwise reforms are apt to be reversed when the party in power is replaced by the not-so-loyal opposition.

The ideological gulf between America's two parties limits the scope for forming and maintaining any such coalition.[16] Americans who oppose expansive government on ideological grounds—and there are many such Americans—object to any and all tax increases, preferring a starve-the-beast approach to constraining the public sector. Progressives object equally emphatically to cutting entitlements and social programs, and the higher taxes they favor, focused narrowly on the very wealthy, are inadequate for closing the revenue gap. Hence the scenario where the dollar loses the confidence of investors, and thus its international role, not because of America's economic limitations but because of its political disfunction.

Sanctions Bite Back

Another danger to the dollar lies in prolific U.S. use of sanctions. When the government imposes financial sanctions, foreign property within its reach is blocked or frozen. Although title remains with the owners, they lose access, and income accruing to the asset is held in a blocked account at a U.S. financial institution. The sanctioned entity is barred from doing business with American financial institutions and other U.S. entities. U.S. sanctions bite because foreign governments, banks, firms, and individuals are accustomed to holding liquid balances in U.S. Treasuries, U.S. commercial bank deposits, and custodial accounts at Federal Reserve Banks, all of which an executive order can block at any time.[17]

Even before Russia's attack on Ukraine and the United States's subsequent sanctions on Russian entities, America had taken increasing recourse to this financial weapon. The number of individuals subject to U.S. sanctions rose from 912 in 2000 to more than 9,400 in 2021.[18] Sanctions imposed on Russia in 2022 upped the stakes because of the possibility that Russia's assets might not only be frozen but also garnished and repurposed for Ukrainian reconstruction, setting a precedent for treatment of other countries. This weaponization of the dollar, as aggressive U.S. use of financial sanctions is known, pointed up the possibility that other countries with even the slightest notion that they too at some point might fall under U.S. sanctions would look for alternatives to U.S. Treasuries, U.S. bank deposits, and SWIFT.[19] China is a case in point, given that China and the United States see one another as geopolitical rivals, and that they might come to blows over Taiwan.

In the past, countries in this position have had few places to look, since the issuers of other internationally used currencies such as the euro, the pound sterling, and the yen cooperate with the United States and bless its sanctions. Again, however, past may not be prologue. European countries were not on board with the first Trump administration's policy of "maximum pressure" sanctions on Iran. The decline of transatlantic cooperation in Trump's second term underscores the possibility, indeed the likelihood, of other such disagreements. Trump in his second term has not been cautious in threatening to unleash economic and financial weapons, be they tariffs, taxes, sanctions, or other measures. His administration has not cooperated with other countries in their application—quite the contrary. If the United States continues to go its own way, then other currencies, those of countries that do not participate in U.S. sanctioning efforts, will benefit from diversification away from the dollar.

Golden Constant

In response to the specter of sanctions, some central banks, in emerging markets in particular, have added to their gold reserves.[20] Central banks have held reserves in this form, of course, for as long as there have been central banks. This need was immediate under the gold standard, when they were obliged to convert their other obligations into gold at a fixed rate of exchange.

But the practice has persisted, inertia being what it is, and increased further in recent years. Gold vaulted at home is safe from attachment; central bank reserve managers, being prudent, can be expected to shift their portfolios toward gold in advance of future sanctions. Venezuela repatriated gold held abroad in 2011, five years after the initial targeted sanctions of the George W. Bush administration but prior to the additional sanctions of Barack Obama. The Bank of Russia began shifting from dollars to gold even before Russia's invasion of Crimea and the application of U.S. sanctions in 2014, and before sanctions were extended to the Russian central bank in 2022.[21]

The major drawback is that gold lacks the other defining characteristic of an international currency: it is not suitable for settling commercial and financial transactions. It can be borrowed, lent, and used as collateral for financial transactions only when vaulted at the London Metal Exchange, the Bank of England, the Federal Reserve Bank of New York, or another recognized global repository, exposing it to expropriation risk.

Using it to pay for goods and services entails additional risks, as the Florentines recognized already in the thirteenth century when, acknowledging the cost of hiring armed guards, they devised ways of transferring funds without having to physically move specie. In 2019 the Venezuelan government of President Nicolás Maduro, a regime subject to U.S. sanctions, hired a Boeing 777 owned by a Russian air charter company to ferry 7.4 tons gold to Uganda, where it was refined and evidently resold. Venezuela received $300 million worth of euros in return, which it used to pay for imports of merchandise that would have otherwise been unavailable to the country. In 2022 the Maduro government then paid for oil-field equipment and services from Iran, also sanctioned, by hiring a fleet of 747s to transport gold bars.[22] These exceptions highlight the costs and risks of making payment in this form.[23]

Unsafe Haven

Dollar-denominated bank deposits and Treasury securities thus remain a more practical store of value and means of payment. But dollar claims are attractive only insofar as they hold their value and that value is guaranteed by an independent, stability-oriented central bank. Steps by the Trump administration, or a future U.S. administration, to tamper with the independence of the Fed would therefore dim the dollar's luster. In spring 2025 President Trump criticized Federal Reserve Chair Jerome Powell in terms widely interpreted as indicating the president's belief that he could fire Powell at will. ("If I want him out, he'll be out of there real fast, believe me.") Then in August of the year, Trump sought to "fire"

Fed Governor Lisa Cook for cause. That members of the Federal Reserve Board serve long terms in office and cannot be terminated at will is a cornerstone of the Fed's independence. Investors with dollar positions are certain to be watching.

There is plenty to watch. In February 2025 Trump signed Executive Order 12866 asserting that "officials who wield vast executive power must be supervised and controlled by the people's elected president." He instructed all "so-called independent agencies" to submit their regulatory proposals for review by the White House. While this order included the Fed's supervisory and regulatory policies, it exempted its monetary policies for the time being. Also in February, Trump's acting solicitor-general, Sarah Harris, informed the Senate that the Justice Department would no longer defend provisions requiring the president to provide cause when dismissing an independent agency head, citing "a variety of independent agencies" in this context.

The Supreme Court already in 2020 had overturned these "for cause" protections for agencies with a single person in charge, arguing that they violated the separation of powers. In May 2025 the court then upheld Trump's firing of officials at the multi-member National Labor Relations and Merit Systems Boards, while exempting the Fed on the grounds that it "is a uniquely structured, quasi-private entity that follows in the distinct historical tradition of the First and Second Banks of the United States" (the proto-central banks that operated in the United States from 1791 to 1836).[24] This logic is peculiar. Whereas the First and Second Banks of the United States were majority private corporations, Federal Reserve Banks have commercial bank shareholders but also directors representing the public, including directors appointed by the public officials of the Federal Reserve Board.[25] As the justices penning the minority opinion observed, the Fed's independence fundamentally rests on "the same constitutional and analytical foundations" as that of other independent agencies. If the Supreme Court overturns Humphrey's Executor v. United States, the 1935 case in which the Court determined that the president could fire commission members prior to expiry of their terms only in cases of "neglect of duty, or malfeasance in office," the Fed's independence could come back into the crosshairs.

In addition to whether U.S. Treasury securities are inflation-proof, there is the fundamental question of whether holders will be treated fairly. Scott Bessent, Trump's Treasury secretary, has mulled the idea of converting 5- and 10-year Treasury bonds into 100-year securities bearing low interest rates, whether investors like it or not.[26] During the 2024 presidential campaign, advisors to Trump such as Robert Lighthizer mooted the possibility of taxing foreign purchases of U.S. securities as a way of driving down the dollar, or at least of preventing foreign investors from driving it up, in the name of enhancing U.S. export competitiveness.[27] Trump's choice to head his Council of Economic Advisers, Stephen Miran, in his earlier incarnation as investment strategist, endorsed such a policy and described its implementation. Miran suggested withholding a portion of interest payments to foreign official holders of Treasury securities by imposing a "user fee."[28] Labeling the measure a user fee instead of a tax would avoid running afoul of international tax treaties. But it would run afoul of expectations that domestic and foreign investors should be treated comparably, something that is central to the dollar's international acceptance.

Miran proposed starting with a low tax rate to avoid triggering a deluge of Treasury liquidations and then gradually ramping up the tax to engineer a significant devaluation of the dollar. This again ignores the fact that central bank reserve managers, like other investors, look to the future when making financial decisions. Focusing the tax on geopolitical adversaries such as China, as Miran also proposed, runs up against the same problem as selective financial sanctions, namely that countries alert to the possibility that they too might be on the outs with the United States in the future will have an incentive to begin diversifying out of dollars in anticipation.[29] If interest rates spike as a result of large outflows from the Treasury market, Miran suggested that the Fed could cap those rates by buying what foreign investors sell. Having argued elsewhere for limits on Federal Reserve independence, he may believe that the White House and the Treasury will be able to compel the Fed to make such purchases.[30] But this would just be another way of opening the door to the inflation that foreign investors already fear. By fatally compromising the independence of the central bank, it would doom the dollar as an international currency.

At a practical level, the appeal of U.S. Treasury bonds as an international store of value and hence the appeal of the dollar as an international means of payment rest on the smooth operation of the market in Treasury securities. Central bank reserve managers, corporate treasurers, and other investors regard Treasuries as the bedrock of their portfolios because of their stability but also because of their ability to buy and sell them at stable and predictable prices. The importance of a smoothly functioning money market, backed by a lender and liquidity provider of last resort, is another iron law of international currencies seen everywhere from eighteenth-century Amsterdam to nineteenth-century London and twentieth-century New York.

Again, this is not something to be taken for granted. Bid-ask spreads, which measure the cost of getting in and out of the Treasury market, spiked in March 2020 with the outbreak of COVID-19, and again in March 2023 with the failure of Silicon Valley Bank.[31] In both cases, investors rushed to convert Treasuries into cash. Primary dealers, the large banks and investment firms that hold inventories of bonds and execute the orders of buyers and sellers, saw their cash depleted when multiple sellers showed up on their doorstep all at the same time. Their mass sales caused dealers to hit regulatory limits on the Treasury securities they could buy and hold. Bid-ask spreads gapped out, and price volatility surged. This fueled anxiety that the price of Treasuries would collapse, given a shortage of willing buyers and depletion of dealer liquidity, and that this could bring down banks and leveraged funds that had invested in these securities.[32]

Fortunately, the Fed intervened as faithful lender and liquidity provider of last resort. Between March and June 2020, it purchased $1 trillion of Treasuries, a significant fraction of the outstanding stock.[33] Still, the episode exposed the fragility of the U.S. Treasury market. It was a reminder of the essential role of the central bank.

Whether a future Federal Reserve Board, populated by appointees of a different political and ideological ilk, will respond similarly is uncertain. We can hope, but we cannot be sure.

Dollar Swaps and Dollar Politics

Another dimension of the Fed's liquidity-provision function, equally important for the dollar's global role, is the currency swap lines it provides foreign central banks. Foreign central banks hesitate to let banks and firms for which they are responsible buy, hold, and use dollars if those central banks are unable to act as dollar lenders of last resort. They hesitate when they are unable to supply dollars in a crisis, thereby enabling those banks and firms to meet their obligations.[34] The Fed's currency swap lines, by providing dollars on demand, offer the requisite liquidity and reassurance.[35]

Moreover, even when central banks possess an adequate supply of U.S. Treasuries, they may have to sell them in a crisis to mobilize the cash needed by the entities they oversee, with further destabilizing consequences for the Treasury market. In March 2020, with the outbreak of COVID-19, foreign central banks sold $109 billion of Treasuries, a one-month record. Had they been forced to sell even more, the squeeze facing brokers and dealers and the explosive widening of bid-ask spreads would have been paralyzing. In the face of these events, the Fed's dollar swap lines played a stabilizing role by relieving the pressure on foreign central banks to sell.[36]

Seasoned Federal Reserve officials understand these issues. The same is not uniformly true of their political masters, however. Members of Congress, in hearings on the Global Financial Crisis, erroneously criticized the Fed's swap lines for squandering the hard-earned dollars of U.S. taxpayers. Their criticisms were erroneous because the dollars provided to foreign central banks were and are fully collateralized by the currencies swapped in return. Future members of the Federal Reserve Board nominated by a nationalistic U.S. president might echo these reservations about helping foreign countries, either because they erroneously believed that currency swaps put U.S. tax dollars at risk or because they objected to the U.S. providing global public goods.[37] In 2025, following Trump administration tariff threats and Vice President JD Vance's remarks to the Munich Security Conference questioning the transatlantic alliance, European officials reportedly expressed doubts about whether they could still rely on the Fed to provide dollar funding in times of market stress.[38]

Then there is the fact that the Fed provides dollar swaps to America's friends but few others. Only the Bank of Canada, the Bank of England, the European Central Bank, the Swiss National Bank, and the Bank of Japan have permanent dollar swap lines. The nine central banks granted temporary access during the COVID-19 crisis were again selected to avoid exciting congressional sensibilities.[39] Countries not on the best terms with the United States thus have another reason to limit their dependence on the dollar, since they may not count on receiving swap lines in a crisis. And in a world where they are forced to choose between being friends with the United States or friends with China, additional countries may find themselves not on the best of terms.

Geopolitical Foundations

This reminds us that geopolitical alliances and power matter for international currency status. The Dutch guilder came into widespread use in Asia when the Dutch East India Company was established not just to trade but also to undertake military operations. Sterling was the invoicing and settlement currency for the world's trade and the dominant unit in global financial transactions when Britannia ruled the waves. The German and Japanese governments supported the dollar in the 1960s, helping to preserve its international currency role, because of the value they attached to their defense alliance with the United States. Saudi Arabia agreed to accumulate and hold U.S. Treasuries in the 1970s because of the value it attached to U.S. military support. Today the Bank of Korea holds a larger share of its foreign reserves in dollars than its trade and financial connections with the United States would lead one to expect, again as an implicit quid pro quo for U.S. troops stationed on the peninsula and America's broader security guarantee.

In the German, Japanese, and South Korean cases, official support was encouraged by the implicit threat that the United States might cut back its military commitments if its balance of payments and dollar exchange rate weakened further. This shows how a country possessing geopolitical leverage can nudge its allies and dependencies to hold and use its currency. It shows how, even without the explicit application of such leverage, they may willingly opt to use that currency, insofar as they are most comfortable relying on the currency and financial markets of an ally.[40] Russian opposition to the U.S. invasion of Iraq in 2002 and to U.S. air strikes against Syria in 2012, which prompted the Bank of Russia to begin diversifying its foreign reserves away from the dollar, illustrates the converse, namely the reluctance of a country to hold and use the currency of a geopolitical rival.

A less powerful United States would command less monetary and financial support from its alliance partners. U.S. defense spending, which undergirds that power, is constrained by the same budgetary imperatives, a combination of limited revenues and costly entitlement programs, impinging on other public programs.[41] Defense Secretary Pete Hegseth's 2025 plan to cut the U.S. defense budget by 8 percent in each of the following five years is indicative of those pressures.

The dollar's international role would also suffer were the United States decisively perceived as turning its back on those alliances, already on shaky ground. Trump in his 2017–21 presidential term cast doubt on continued U.S. participation in NATO. In early 2025, Vance, again at the Munich Security Conference, shocked America's allies by challenging the Western values providing the basis for North Atlantic alliance. Hegseth warned his European audience that the continent could no longer rely on the United States to guarantee its security. Trump allied himself with Vladimir Putin, imperiling Ukraine and alarming European countries bordering Russia. Next came the disastrous Oval Office blowup between Trump and Ukrainian President Volodymyr Zelenskyy, leading European governments to conclude that the United States was no longer a dependable alliance partner. European governments stepped up their military spending and support for Ukraine in recognition that they could no longer count on their old friend. The notion that alliance politics are important for international currency status was about to receive a real-time test.

In the end, the fate of the dollar will rest on the willingness of America's leaders to uphold the rule of law, respect the separation of powers, and honor the country's commitments to its foreign partners. It will depend on the readiness of the Congress, the courts, and the public to hold their feet to the fire. Ironically, it had been questions about the separation of powers and the ability of an autocratic leader to arbitrarily change the rules of the financial and political game that have held back the renminbi as a challenger to the dollar. The tables turn.

1930s All Over Again

Isolationism is having a moment. The same currents that cause U.S. commentators to question the desirability of America's contribution to NATO and argue that the costs of the alliance exceed its benefits similarly cause them to question the value of the dollar's international currency role and again suggest that the costs exceed the benefits. The Western defense alliance and the dollar's role in facilitating international transactions are global public goods. They benefit not just the United States, the country that as the leading economic and military power is disproportionately tasked with providing them, but also its partners in NATO and the global economy. Other things equal, U.S. policymakers would prefer a world in which other beneficiaries bore a greater share of the cost of supplying these security and financial services. This is what debates over NATO burden sharing and U.S. international economic competitiveness are all about.

But this is different from saying that the United States would be better off without NATO, or that it would be better off were the dollar to lose its international currency role, as sometimes contended by those who worry about the costs to the United States of providing these global public goods. The dollar's status as the leading international currency allows U.S. banks and firms to do cross-border business in dollars. This offers convenience but also a competitive edge, since it eliminates the need to account for exchange rate changes when doing international business or to buy financial instruments as hedges against currency risk.

It allows the Treasury Department to borrow at lower cost, given foreign demand for dollar-denominated securities. It provides the U.S. with built-in insurance against economic and financial shocks. So long as the liquidity of the U.S. Treasury bond market is unsurpassed, making the dollar a safe haven, foreign investors will rush into dollars in times of turbulence, supporting U.S. financial markets when they most need support. U.S. strategic leverage is enhanced insofar as foreigners rely on the dollar, since this reliance is what causes U.S. financial sanctions to bite.

Against this are the costs to U.S. exporters from a dollar exchange rate that is stronger than otherwise. But a stronger exchange rate is way down the list of factors affecting the international competitiveness of U.S. firms. It ranks below the modernity of the capital stock, the skills and training of American workers, the quality of entrepreneurship and management, and investment in research and development. If the level of the dollar creates headwinds for U.S. exporters, they can take other steps—invest more in plant and equipment, train their workers better, develop new products and processes—that offset those headwinds. It is much less clear how to offset loss of the dollar's global role, which would create other problems, such as a need to purchase hedging instruments, raise Treasury borrowing costs, add to the volatility of U.S. financial markets, and lessen the effectiveness of financial sanctions. While attempting to quantify this wide range of factors is daunting, there is little doubt that the benefits of the dollar's international currency status swamp the costs.

No other currency, now or in the foreseeable future, is positioned to fill the dollar's shoes. While backed by a capable central bank, the euro still lacks a European Treasury and a supply of safe assets adequate for the needs of an expanding world economy. There are technical fixes for these problems, but implementing them requires political will and consensus, which in Europe are in short supply. China has the economic size, and the renminbi has the international reach, required of a global currency. But while the renminbi is used to invoice and pay for a majority of China's own imports and exports, the currency is a bit player globally. It can be questioned whether China's political system, which assigns unchecked power to the president and State Council and denies full independence to the central bank, is compatible with elevating the renminbi to global currency status. A multi-currency platform supporting the interoperability of central bank digital currencies could in principle provide an alternative to the dollar and the U.S. banking system for settling cross-border transactions. But to constitute a full-fledged alternative to the dollar, global agreement would have to be reached on the architecture of that platform and on its governance, something that remains far-fetched. The leading candidate, Project mBridge, is a China-led project, in which the United States and its allies would likely not participate. Rather than providing a global contender to the dollar, this platform would only appeal to countries with which China is geopolitically aligned.

What then happens if, for reasons rooted as much in U.S. politics as economics, there is a crisis of confidence causing the dollar to lose its safe-haven status and international currency role? Central banks, no longer regarding dollars as safe and liquid, would no longer willingly hold them as reserves. Lacking the wherewithal to act as dollar lenders of last resort, they would not permit banks and firms under their purview to borrow and use dollars for financing investments and making cross-border payments. If the stability and terms of access to those dollars were uncertain, banks and firms would move away from relying on dollars of their own volition. With no other currency able to fill the void, central banks would hold fewer reserves, limiting their ability to intervene in international financial markets. Banks would be less able to lend across borders. Firms and governments would be less able to borrow. There would be downward pressure on the volume of cross-border transactions of all kinds. This would spell the end of globalization as we know it.

There is a precedent for this scenario—the disastrous 1930s. Three successive U.S. banking crises sparked a crisis of confidence in the dollar, causing central banks around the world to liquidate their dollar reserves, as described at the end of chapter 7. They attempted to shift from dollars into gold, but found that there was only so much gold to go around. Sterling still served as a source of foreign reserves, mainly to the bloc of British allies and trading partners known as the Sterling Area, but this was not enough to prevent downward pressure on supplies of global liquidity. That pressure in turn compressed the volume of cross-border trade and lending, helping to spawn the Great Depression. This is a scenario that no one, not U.S. policymakers, not policymakers in the rest of the world, should want to see repeated.

ACKNOWLEDGMENTS

WHEN A SCHOLAR STEPS OUT of his intellectual comfort zone, he depends, even more than usual, on the goodwill and generosity of others. I am especially grateful therefore to the many specialists who generously welcomed a trespasser onto their terrain. Charikleia Papageorgiadou of the National Hellenic Research Foundation and Cleo Papaevangelou of the Bank of Greece provided feedback on, you guessed it, ancient Greece numismatics. Darel Engen provided good advice on the ancient Greek economy generally. Kevin Butcher kindly offered comments on Republican and Imperial Rome, Guido Alfani on early modern Florence. Alejandra Irigoin and Carlos Marichal educated me on the intricacies of Spanish silver. Stephen Quinn and Will Roberds answered repeated queries about the Bank of Amsterdam and ledger money. Ron Liesching provided original thoughts on the economics of foreign exchange markets (and financial markets generally). Rafael Auer and Ousmène Mandeng provided reactions to the material on central bank digital currencies and multiple-CBDC platforms. Pierre Yared contributed thoughtful comments where our work on the connections between monetary and military matters overlapped. I am grateful to them all, although they will see instances where, contrary to their advice, I have stubbornly clung to my positions.

I exposed these ideas at conferences and seminars too many to name or even remember. Among those I recall, I am grateful to audiences at the University of Vienna, the University of Manchester, the Bank of Greece, the annual conference of the Portuguese Association of Economic Historians, the Central Bank of Peru and Reinventing Bretton Woods Committee conference in Cusco, and the Middle East Council on Global Affairs Istanbul CBDC roundtable. I also had the opportunity of exposing these ideas to actual central bank reserve managers at HSBC's Hong Kong Investor Conference, Credit Suisse's (final!) Asian Investment Conference, and UBS's Reserve Management Seminar.

The Bank of Greece facilitated a visit during which I was able to put the finishing touches on the manuscript, appropriately for a story that begins with Aristotle and his observations on coinage. I thank Andreas Kakrides and Bank of Greece Governor Yannis Stournaras for the opportunity. Thanks also to the Numismatic Museum of Athens, where it is possible to view all the coins mentioned in this book.

My coauthors of various articles and books will recognize here echoes of their analysis and evidence. My arguments have been greatly informed by collaborations with Serkan Arslanalp, Tamim Bayoumi, Livia Chiţu, Giancarlo Corsetti, Asmaa El-Ganainy, Rui Esteves, Marc Flandreau, Daniel Gros, Galina Hale, Ricardo Hausmann, Masahiro Kawai, Domenico Lombardi, Timothy Marple, Arnaud Mehl, Kris Mitchener, Eric Monnet, Alain Naef, Ugo Panizza, Chima Simpson-Bell, Nathan Sussman, Peter Temin, Charles Wyplosz, and John Zysman. Authoring books may be a solitary task, but research in economics increasingly is a collective endeavor. My collaborators will forgive me, I hope, for drawing so extensively on their work.

As always, Andrew Wylie provided valuable support in helping to place the manuscript. At Princeton University Press, I am grateful to three referees and especially Joe Jackson for valuable comments and suggestions. Holly LaFon provided especially careful and thoughtful copyediting, in conjunction with Angela Piliouras of Westchester Publishing Services.

In finalizing the manuscript, Ayden Chi provided invaluable help, checking facts, figures, dates, and references.

And this book, like all my books, is for Michelle.

NOTES

Preface

1. There are of course exceptions to this generalization. One thinks for example of the euro, where the national governments of European Union member states have ceded to a transnational institution, the European Central Bank, control over their common currency. Or the case of the United States in the first half of the nineteenth century, when Spanish pieces of eight had legal tender status alongside the U.S. dollar. Going forward, some imagine that privately issued cryptocurrencies will compete with national monies. I consider each of these cases in what follows.

2. This is the view of President Trump's 2025 Council of Economic Advisors chair Stephen Miran (2024), whose arguments figure in chapter 11.

Chapter 1: Introduction

1. Cited in Office of the Federal Register (1972), p. 887.

2. Congress included the provision in the Economic Stabilization Act attached to the amended Defense Production Act. Nixon was thus forced to sign the bill, notwithstanding his opposition to controls, to avoid a break in defense procurement.

3. Experts attributed the anchovy shortage, variously, to an unusually strong El Niño and overfishing by the Peruvian fleet.

4. Abrams and Butkiewicz (2017) discuss Nixon's motives in opting for controls, which included deflecting attention from the embarrassing possibility of an impending dollar devaluation.

5. Kindleberger (1976), p. 35.

6. This is according to the criteria used to identify anchor currencies by Ilzetzki, Reinhart, and Rogoff (2021). The authors include currencies where the authorities announce a peg to the dollar but also those that move by less than 2 percent against the greenback in more than 80 percent of months.

7. This includes not only the foreign exchange reserves of central banks but also foreign bonds and equities held by sovereign wealth funds, the majority of which, insofar as composition can be gleaned from published reports and mandates, is denominated in dollars.

8. The phrase is due to French Finance Minister Valéry Giscard d'Estaing, who in the 1960s was critical of the advantages accruing to the United States from the international role of the dollar. Giscard makes an appearance in chapter 8.

9. Connally made his remark at a Group of Ten meeting in London in September 1971 following the U.S. decision to close the gold window (suspending the right of foreign governments to redeem their dollars for gold at a fixed price), as described in chapter 8.

10. Proof by counterexample is the case of Russia, which has become increasingly aligned with China following its attack on Ukraine and the imposition of Western sanctions. In the first half of 2023, the renminbi was used in three-quarters of Russia's trade with China and fully a quarter of its trade with the rest of the world, while dominating trading on the Russian foreign exchange market (Glover 2023).

11. Early Roman coin hoards have also been unearthed in Japan, though they were found in a twelfth-century fortress, suggesting that they may have arrived later.

12. The guilder was also referred to as the florin, reflecting the earlier spread of Florentine coin and credit to the Low Countries, conveyed there in the course of commercial and financial transactions. For clarity I use florin for Florentine money and guilder for Dutch money.

13. Although there is no direct evidence of a causal relationship between democracy and coinage in the Athenian case, Trevett (2001) argues that passages from Aristotle's *Politics* are suggestive of a link. In the case of the Roman Republic, Crawford (1974) suggests that the public applied pressure for issuance of a uniform, stable coin, the denarius, that eventually gained widespread circulation beyond the borders of the Republic itself. Barnard (2018) points to expansion of Roman agriculture and commerce in the mid-Republican period and the political influence of this new class of holders of "movable wealth" when explaining the rise of the denarius system and, by implication, accounting for the unit's stability over time.

14. Veseth (1990) describes how the Cambio guild imposed severe punishments on members who failed to remove debased coins from circulation.

15. Uniformity has the additional advantage of deterring counterfeiting, insofar as every coin must be exactly alike. Helleiner (2003) and Redish (2000) associate such uniformity with the Industrial Revolution and the adoption of steam-powered machinery by the mint in the nineteenth century, but as we will see the importance of uniformity in the context of cross-border use goes back much further.

16. Here Rome refers to a political authority rather than a place. The Roman authorities minted coins not only in the city itself but at multiple locations around the Republic and Empire. Julius Caesar famously traveled with a mobile mint for use in producing coin to pay his legions (see chapter 2).

17. An introduction to the literature on safe assets is Gourinchas and Jeanne (2012). Pflueger and Yared (2024) focus specifically on the connections between military might and a currency's safe-asset status. Conversely, economists fret about the dangers of a safe-asset shortage when these fiscal, administrative, and military capacities are lacking, and specifically that such a shortage will depress the volume of international transactions (see Caballero, Farhi, and Gourinchas 2017).

18. See Eichengreen, Mehl, and Chiţu (2019); Weiss (2022), Goldberg, and Hannaoui (2024); and Brüggen, Georgiadis, and Mehl (2025).

19. It is sometimes asserted that the Saudis also agreed to price their oil exports in dollars as part of this agreement. Spiro (1999) suggests that Jimmy Carter's Treasury secretary, Michael Blumenthal, negotiated such an agreement, basing the assertion on a briefing book prepared for Blumenthal that emphasized the Carter administration's commitment to a strong dollar. But this emphasis could have been intended, equally, to reassure the Saudis about investing in U.S.

Treasuries and might have had nothing to do with the pricing of oil per se. Adinolfi (2024) concludes that there is no direct evidence of such an agreement.

20. Helleiner (2003) dates this phenomenon from the mid-nineteenth century, but as the history that follows shows one can find similar practices earlier in time.

21. At least this was the case after an initial phase when coinage was not yet widespread and pay for the army was weighed out rather than paid out. Again, see chapter 2.

22. Even here the role of the state is not absent, since some kind of police or military action may be needed to ensure the security of traders. The Athenian navy's protection of merchants in the Republican period and the British navy's protection of English merchants in the nineteenth century, in each case coinciding with the era when their respective currencies were internationally dominant, both illustrate the point, which is discussed more fully later.

23. Moreover, both economic theory (Bulow and Rogoff 1989) and extensive historical experience raise questions about whether this desire to maintain reputation and market access will necessarily be enough to deter opportunistic borrowers.

24. This distinction between Middle Eastern and European practice is the subject of Rubin (2010).

25. That said, there are those who worry that technical glitches adversely affecting the market are growing more frequent, which raises questions about the continued attractions of the dollar. For more on these glitches, see chapter 11.

26. This in the memorable words of Avaro (2024), by which she means that the currency could be held but no longer freely used.

Chapter 2: Aristotelian Beginnings

1. A review of these practices is Balmuth (1980).

2. Aristotle, *Politics*, 1.9 1257a31-41. Aristotle's emphasis on the growth of international or long-distance trade reflects the fact that early coins were too valuable for everyday retail transactions. Schaps (2004, p. 97) disputes the inference, observing that long-distance trade had been taking place for centuries without coin, and that there is no evidence of this early coinage circulating far from its place of issue. Kraay (1964) invokes the utility of such coins for other purposes, such as paying mercenaries, making payments to the state, and providing gifts.

3. Herodotus quotes Xenophanes as attributing the invention to the Lydians. Porteous (1980) and Goetzmann (2016) argue that the Chinese independently invented coins, which began circulating around this time. These authors argue that Chinese coinage was an independent invention, and not simply an imitation of Lydian or Greek coin finding its way to the East, on the grounds that Chinese coin looked very different. The earliest Chinese coins were knife- and hoe-shaped descendants of actual knives and hoes used in transactions (so-called utensil currencies) and made of cast bronze. Next came disk-shaped coins with square holes, permitting them to be strung on necklaces. Because Chinese coins continued to be cast out of base metals such as iron, large numbers were required for substantial transactions, posing an obstacle to widespread adoption. Another four centuries would pass before coined money was widely used throughout the country. China also pioneered paper currency, albeit at a later date. Because China's currency and coin were not widely used outside China itself, and cross-border transactions being the question at hand, their discussion is consigned to this footnote.

In addition, there were contemporaneous Indian coins, rectangular pieces of silver stamped on both sides, though dating these is difficult.

4. Kroll (2008), p. 18.

5. Where to draw the line between a lump or disk of bronze or silver and a bronze or silver coin is not obvious, to be sure. How should one classify lumps or chips of silver of standard weight (a fixed metallic unit), or lumps of silver inscribed with a group or leader's name or mark, for example? Prior to the minting of coins featuring the stamp of the Lydian king, silver rings and disks had circulated for centuries in Mesopotamia and Egypt. Schaps (2001) describes the transition from a monetary economy where money took the form of precious metal whose value depended on its weight and fineness to a monetary economy where money was coined.

6. This view, prominently associated with Bücher (1893) and Finley (1973), is discussed further in what follows.

7. Martin (1985) and more recently Engen (2005) make arguments to this effect.

8. This point is emphasized by Kim (2001). See also the related discussion in Engen (2004).

9. Howgego (1995), p. 53; Engen (2005), p. 363.

10. Woolmer (2015), p. 68; Davies (2015), p. 308.

11. An alternative standard adopted initially by Attica and Euboea also proved popular.

12. Such trades were subject to adjustments for wear, clipping, and parity which were familiar to specialized money changers, the bankers who set up tables in or near temples and other public buildings. The detection of counterfeits, whose prevalence would have undermined demand for the real thing, was overseen by so-called *doki-mastai* (testers), publicly owned slaves who operated in the agora (central marketplace) and Piraeus. Woolmer (2015), p. 84; Bresson (2016), p. 271.

13. Krugman (1980) and Devereaux and Shi (2013) describe the role of vehicle currencies in international markets.

14. Migeotte (2009), p. 123.

15. Schaps (2022), p. 239.

16. Psoma (2015), pp. 97–101; Bresson (2016), p. 272. In addition, there was an international role in large-value transactions for the gold daric of the Persian Achaemenid Empire, although Schaps (2002, p. 238) argues that this was more commonly used for bribes and hoarding than trade.

17. Even earlier there was adoption of the Lydian standard in Rhodes and the Cycladic islands (Psoma 2015, p. 91).

18. Kraay (1976), p. 55.

19. The latter two ports were both in Corinth, of course.

20. Kwon (2015, p. 358–59) goes on to observe that even following the defeat of Athens in the Peloponnesian War, the trade of Piraeus was comparable in value (measured in units of wheat) to the later trade of Venice at its height, when international monetary leadership had shifted to Italy.

21. Engen (2005), pp. 367–68. While various meanings have been attached to the phrase in quotation marks, as noted in chapter 1, here it means the ability of the issuer of an international currency to exchange financial assets for goods, services and foreign investments. We will see in what follows that their singular uniformity and reputation led other commodity currencies,

such as the Spanish pieces of eight described in chapter 4, to similarly be valued at more than their intrinsic commodity content.

22. Goetzmann (2016), p. 97.

23. The earliest Alexanders featured a portrait of Hercules, since it would have been seen as excessive hubris for a living king or emperor to put his own portrait on a coin; it might have been taken to indicate that the emperor put himself above the gods. Once Alexander became great, however, hubris was no deterrent.

24. The royal portrait that adorned the front of the coin might differ from king to king, but they were all "variation[s] on the theme of Alexander's original royal coinage." Thonemann (2015), p. 23.

25. For the two sides of the debate, contrast Kraay (1976), pp. 249–50 and Martin (1985), pp. 127–31.

26. Thonemann (2015), pp. 26, 32.

27. Crawford (1985), pp. 17–20; Kroll (2008), p. 12.

28. Migeotte (2009), p. 125.

29. Crawford (1985), p. 33.

30. There is disagreement regarding the year when minting commenced, some historians preferring earlier dates (Greene 1986, p. 48).

31. Hannibal himself had minted Carthaginian coin in Spain, but he appears not to have brought it along with his army, or so is suggested by the absence of hoards. Instead, Hannibal and rebel cities in Italy allied with him minted coins in the region they controlled during the war.

32. Termeer (2022), p. 92.

33. The quarter denarius was produced in limited quantities under the republic. In imperial times it was replaced by the brass sestertius (Butcher and Ponting 2015a, p. 23).

34. The main gold coin, the aureus, was introduced in significant numbers only under Julius Caesar (see below).

35. Lo Cascio (2008) refers to documents whose authors occasionally also quoted prices in gold aurei in connection with high-value transactions, although such mentions are rare.

36. Naismith (2023), pp. 206–8.

37. As analyzed by Redish (2000) and Flandreau (2004), among others.

38. The numismatic specialist Christopher Howgego attributes the difference in rates of diffusion to these cultural factors (Howgego 1995, p. 58).

39. Burnett (1980), p. 69.

40. Harney (2024), p. 17.

41. The definitive statement of this view is Polanyi (1944), on which Finley (1973) builds. A retrospective on their work, on which I draw, is Morris (1999).

42. This view lives on: for a more recent statement see Hendy (1985), pp. 262–63.

43. This according to an article by an anonymous author, "Roman Coins Found in China," in The American Journal of Numismatics, and Bulletin of the American Numismatic and Archaeological Society 20 (January 1886), pp. 60–62.

44. Greene (1986), pp. 24–25; Sidebotham (2011), pp. 216–17.

45. Howgego (1995), p. 90; Lo Cascio (2008), p. 166. Specifically, these practices anticipated subsequent innovations by the Florentines and others to settle payments across space, including across borders, using accounting (bank) transfers. See chapter 3.

46. Crawford (1985), p. 173–74.

47. Nappo (2018), p. 571. Some scholars have used these Asian hoards to infer the overall volume of trade. These estimates are spurious, since the Romans exported other things, including wine, oil, textiles, and glass, taking payment in their own coin and repatriating it. Such estimates fail to distinguish net and gross flows, in other words. For discussion see Cobb (2015).

48. Ptolemy I instituted a new, lighter standard for his silver coins, and to support it he banned the use of foreign currency. Thonemann (2015, p. 123) speculates that Ptolemy may have decided to run a closed currency system because Egypt lacked abundant silver of its own; if Hellenic silver had been allowed to enter the country, it would also have been able to exit, undermining the silver-based monetary economy. This changed only with Diocletian's monetary reform (see below), which introduced the gold aureus into Egypt around 301 CE. Some scholars suggest that limited quantities of denarii and aurei circulated in Egypt in the second century CE but not before (Butcher and Ponting 2015a, p. 609–10), for payment of troops at Alexandria.

49. This was likely a strategic decision by Emperor Augustus, who treated Egypt as his private estate, not unlike how the much later King Leopold of Belgium treated the Congo. To limit profiteering by private adventurers in his personal kingdom, Augustus might have resorted to arrest and deportation, but he could more easily freeze the currency, preventing profiteers from repatriating their ill-gotten gains and prodding them to seek their fortunes elsewhere. Imperial coinage might be exchanged for Egyptian coins, but only by authorized moneychangers at banks or at the main mint in Alexandria, and only for eligible transactions. See Milne (1952), p. 10; Howgego, Butcher, Ponting, and Heuchert (2010), p. 3–4. One thinks, by way of analogy, of the financial sanctions imposed on Russia following its 2022 attack on Ukraine, intended to prevent Moscow from using its gold reserves outside the country and from gaining access to the Russian government's foreign exchange.

50. The sealed bags are alluded to in the Muziris Papyrus, a second century CE customs and loan contract for an Indian cargo (according to the interpretation of De Romanis 2020). Nappo (2018), p. 565, provides ancillary evidence consistent with this interpretation.

51. Nappo (2018), pp. 564–65. Along with denarii, certain hoards also include gold aurei suggestive of high-value transactions.

52. Hoard evidence suggests that Indian merchants preferred the pure silver issues of the mint of Lugdunum (modern-day Lyon, France), indicative of an awareness that, official guarantees notwithstanding, the bullion content of Roman coin could vary. On the other hand, there is evidence that the Kusana kings of Northern India melted down Roman coin and struck new coins bearing their own insignia but with precisely the same weight, as if they recognized them not as bullion but monetary units (Cunningham 1891).

53. This as of the mid-fourth century CE according to Bernardi (1970), p. 55.

54. See Harper (2017).

55. See McConnell et al. (2025). The authors infer levels of lead in the air from their presence in ice cores in Greenland and the Russian Artic in the period of the Empire. They then invoke modern research to estimate the impact of these levels of lead emission on brain functioning. In addition, some historians have speculated that the use of lead pipes for urban plumbing created health problems, though continuous water flow and hard water deposits may have helped to limit lead dissolution.

56. Otherwise, the old denarii would have driven the new denarii out of circulation according to Gresham's Law, given the obligation of Roman citizens to accept denarii.

57. Griffin (1984), p. 198; Butcher and Ponting (2015a), p. 203. Estimates differ because written records are absent, and surviving coins vary in weight.

58. For example, Bernardi (1970), p. 39.

59. Wassink (1991), p. 465.

60. See Mickwitz (1965), cited in MacMullen (1988), p. 37. Butcher (2010) offers additional reasons for questioning pronounced effects.

61. Keynes (1919), p. 220.

62. This statement is strictly correct only in a world without significant international capital flows. Thus, while it is incorrect to apply it to the world today, it may be appropriate in the context of ancient Rome.

63. Mac Dowell (1991), p. 146. Gupta (1991), p. 127 questions this interpretation, suggesting that Indian merchants had no way of knowing of Nero's debasement, and argues instead that, the value of trade having risen, Roman merchants simply decided that making payment in gold aurei was more convenient. To an economist it seems implausible that Indian merchants were too lazy to assay Roman coins or that they were so impressed by Nero's reputation that he was able to pull the wool over their eyes.

64. Harney (2024), p. 238.

65. Some accounts suggest that renewed debasement began earlier, under the Emperor Trajan. Butcher, and Ponting (2015b) dispute the claim.

66. As imperial resources contracted, mint output of silver coin slowed to a trickle. By this time the denarius had been replaced by the coin known to numismatists as the antoninianus, minted first out of silver (with approximately 1.5 times the silver of the denarius) but progressively debased until it was all but entirely bronze. Gold coin still minted was reduced in size.

67. Duncan-Jones (2004), p. 46.

68. Morrison (2002), p. 919. The Greeks referred to the coin as nomisma (Greek for "coin" or "currency"), and certain modern literature follows that convention. Seventy-two coins were struck per pound of gold; the resulting weight of one-seventy-second of a pound was also referred to as twenty-four keratai or (Anglicized) carats. Readers will hear echoes in the modern term "twenty-four-carat gold."

69. This was part of a bungled monetary reform undertaken at the same time when Diocletian doubled the face value of gold and copper issues. Diocletian is better known for his price controls—his Edict on Maximum Prices—which in the end were no more successful than his monetary reforms at taming inflation.

70. As Runciman (1952, p. 133) put it, "In Byzantine eyes a good emperor was an emperor who left behind him a well-stocked treasury." Kaldellis (2023, p. 4) ascribes this fiscal probity to the structure of the Byzantine, or New Roman, state, whose "political legitimacy derived from the stewardship of the public good."

71. Thus, Prigent (2014, p. 182) refers to Byzantium as a "tax-based state *par excellence*."

72. Runciman (1952), p. 163.

73. In contrast, goldsmiths, silversmiths, and jewelers all belonged to the guild of the *argyropratai*, anticipating the gold- and silversmith origins of the bankers who figured prominently in the development of subsequent financial centers, such as London. Maniatis (2016), 111–19.

74. Harper (2017), p. 179.

75. That said, with the final collapse of the Western Roman Empire and Western Europe's descent into the Dark Ages, the volume of trade in the West declined.

76. Morrison (2002), pp. 963–64.

77. Runciman (1952), p. 134.

78. Even when its weight was reduced in the tenth century, its fineness remained unchanged.

79. Lopez (1951), p. 211.

80. See Grierson (1960).

81. 'Abd al-Malik may have been provoked by the decision of the Emperor Justinian II in 690 to place an image of Christ on the front of his coins while moving his imperial image to the back.

82. Previously, 'Abd al-Malik had briefly issued a gold coin bearing an image of a man holding a sword and a Muslim legend. When the image was removed, the Muslim legend was replaced by an Arab legend. Kaldellis (2023), p. 415–16.

83. Cipolla (1956) writes that it had been customary in Arab lands to refer to foreign gold coin, including that of Byzantium, as dinars.

84. The precise text might vary slightly from mint to mint and coin to coin; the text quoted appears on Umayyad dinars minted in Damascus in 694–95. Mourad (2001), p. 228.

85. The constituent parts of this Islamic declaration of faith appear at various points in the Quran, but not in this combined form.

86. For comparison, see chapter 4 on the Dutch defeat at the hands of the French and the end of the guilder as an international currency.

87. Blankinship (1994, p. 6) explains how "the expansionist policy was a fundamental pillar of the state ideology, informed as it was by the belief in *jihād*, the military struggle against the non-Muslims until they either embraced Islam or agreed to pay tribute on their persons in exchange for protection . . . a belief derived originally from the Qur'ān itself."

88. Again quoting Blankinship (1994), p. 6.

89. Runciman (1952), p. 165; Laiou and Morrison (2007), p. 160.

90. Diehl (1970), p. 100; Laiou and Morrison (2007), p. 142.

91. Treadgold (1995), pp. 198.

92. There had been an earlier "creeping" debasement of the coinage, dating to the 950s, but at a very slow rate of 0.04 percent a year (Laiou and Morrison 2007, p. 148).

93. Treadgold (1997), p. 595. In 1053, as a further economy measure, Constantine demobilized about a fifth of the standing army, compensating them with regular cash payments.

94. Kaplanis (2003), p. 768.

95. Lopez (1951), p. 213.

Chapter 3: Renaissance of Credit

1. Just as the solidus had a rival in the Islamic dinar, the florin had a rival in the Venetian ducat, though the florin, like the solidus, was first among equals. Proud Venetians will of course disagree. Pond (1940), a neutral arbitrator, compares the two units.

2. There was a very minor change in its weight in 1422 (Grierson 1981), but no matter.

3. Mueller (1997), pp. 4–5. Scholars have in fact traced the origins of the bill of exchange back to Babylonian clay tablets inscribed as early as the ninth and eighth centuries BCE, although there is no evidence that these claims were sold or traded (Du 2020, p. 240).

4. Where Eurodollar deposits are physically held, as opposed to where their title resides, is a subtle issue discussed in chapters 8 and 9, which provides background on the development of the Eurodollar market.

5. They had to do so, at least, prior to acquiring Porto Pisano from Genoa in the fifteenth century, after which Florence became a significant seafaring power (Hunt and Murray 1999, pp. 181–82). When seafaring circumstances were difficult, wool could also be transported overland, albeit at higher cost and even greater risk. Fryde (1983), pp. 298–99.

6. This as of the early thirteenth century. Najemy (2006, p. 96) describes how Florence had lagged Venice, Genoa, and Pisa in commercial development in earlier centuries.

7. Goldthwaite (2008), pp. 5–6.

8. Robert Lopez, who we met in chapter 2, traced the origins of what is known as the Commercial Revolution to the eleventh century CE and placed the Italian Peninsula and Byzantium at its center (Lopez 1971).

9. A historical note on the origins of the industry is Dixon (1898).

10. Goldthwaite (2008), p. 27.

11. Lane and Mueller (1987), p. 257 and passim.

12. Stahl (2000, p. 17) reports accounts that minting of the grosso commenced before the Fourth Crusade, which casts doubt on the connection with shipwrights' wages.

13. Spufford (2014), p. 273.

14. There is controversy about the date, as explained by Lopez (1956).

15. In conducting transactions with the Levant, Venetian merchants had customarily used Byzantine gold coin and other units indigenous to the region. Now in addition they had gold coin minted at home, which consequentially came into circulation in the eastern Mediterranean.

16. Spufford (2014), pp. 234–35.

17. See Spufford (2008), p. 234. Locatelli (2025, p. 85) questions this story on the grounds that the price of cloth in terms of gold florin surely varied over time and that the gold coins allegedly received by weavers would then have had little practical use in everyday transactions.

18. Lopez (1956), p. 219. Or in the more modern terminology of Richard Goldthwaite (2008, p. 48), "international money."

19. Goldthwaite (2008), p. 53. The author suggests that there may have been cases where the contents of the purse did not correspond to its stated value. But the fact that the communal authorities adopted legislation governing the practice and that they stood behind it discouraged merchants from shortchanging suppliers and encouraged acceptance.

20. The practice may have been adapted from similar arrangements practiced earlier by Islamic traders in North Africa. In Venice these were known as *colleganza* contracts.

21. Abraham Udovitch, the authority on such matters, argued that the *commenda* derived from similar Byzantine and Islamic practices (Udovitch 1970). Pryor (1977) questions this conventional wisdom.

22. An analogy is with sharecropping contracts in agriculture, where effort similarly tends to be undersupplied.

23. It might still be possible for the *commendator* to reduce risk through diversification if he possessed resources sufficient to invest in multiple *commendae*, although this strategy was available only to the wealthiest.

24. This is argued by Walker (1931). Schmitthoff (1939) disputes his claims.

25. De Roover (1963a), p. 43. Edwards and Ogilvie (2012) argue that the fairs also declined because of deteriorating property rights and contract enforcement once the French crown annexed the county of Champagne in 1285 and limited these privileges to those favored by the royal court.

26. The origins of these labels are described by Padgett and McLean (2006). Early recognition of the importance of the organizational form in the context of the Medici can be found in de Roover (1963b).

27. Strathern (2021), p. 39.

28. When he died, Datini specified that his papers be preserved in his house. Rediscovered in 1870, they include 150,000 letters, fifty account books and ledgers, and three hundred partnership deeds. These documents can now be consulted at his home, Palazzo Datini. Origo (1960) builds her biography on these records. A recent treatment is Alfani (2023).

29. Padgett and McLean (2011), p. 1478.

30. Hunt (1994) and Hunt and Murray (1999) argue that these business enterprises were so exceptionally large as to deserve a name of their own: "super-companies." One can see here a family resemblance to the modern multidivisional corporation, whose separate divisions are each overseen by a manager reporting to a chief executive and board of directors (Chandler 1994). There is a further resemblance to the Japanese zaibatsu/keiretsu form, within which multiple units are separately incorporated but operate under a common corporate umbrella (as described by Morikawa 1994). It follows that the advantages of these Florentine partnership systems are understood in the same way that economists understand the advantages of multidivisional corporations and Japanese zaibatsu.

31. Analyses of this hold-up problem, citing vertical integration as a solution, are Williamson (1975) and Klein, Crawford, and Alchian (1978).

32. Limited liability, another Florentine innovation, would come later, with the advent of the *accomandite* partnership in the fifteenth century. No less an authority than Max Weber, in his first publication (Weber 1889 [2003]), traced the progressive evolution of partnership agreements from the *commenda* to the *accomandite*. Weber devoted an entire chapter to the case of Florence.

33. There is dispute over the exact role of these loans in the failure of the Bardi and Peruzzi. For more on Edward III and the fallout from his borrowing, see below.

34. This argument is developed by Padgett and McLean (2002, 2011). Readers will be reminded of the post–World War II Japanese main-bank system in which the constituent companies are effectively linked to a common credit provider.

35. Goldthwaite (1985) focuses on the role of these local bankers, arguing that they were unduly neglected by historians fixated on Florence's better-known international bankers.

36. There is no evidence that these domestic deposits bore interest. See, however, the contrasting case of foreign deposits below.

37. That bankers held substantial amounts of coin and invested in security meant that they had sidelines as pawnbrokers, since they were able to securely store jewelry and other valuables.

In this respect there was a resemblance to the English goldsmith bankers discussed in chapter 6.

38. Usury doctrine in Western Europe took hold in an earlier period when lending was for "consumption" purposes: loans were to individuals living hand to mouth, desperate to put food on the table, who then became trapped in a downward spiral, increasingly indebted to their creditors. By the late medieval period, however, lending for productive mercantile and commercial purposes had become important, rendering usury restrictions increasingly onerous. A discussion is Hunt and Murray (1999), p. 71–72.

39. The Monte delle doti was a public fund established to provide dowries for prospective brides. Fathers typically invested starting when their daughters were five. The Monte delle doti offered generous rates of return, which made it a vehicle for financial speculation (Kirshner and Molho 1978).

40. Partners, in contrast, expected a higher return—in the case of the Peruzzi, 11 to 18 percent—reflecting the fact that they were residual claimants. They received the profits that were left after payments to depositors, in other words. See Najemy (2006), p. 115.

41. In this case, the currency in question would have been the groat of Flanders.

42. See chapter 2, p. 35.

43. Goldthwaite (2008, pp. 210–11) provides an example of such a transaction undertaken by the Datini merchant bank in the late fourteenth century.

44. Bills payable in other centers might be executed after slightly different periods, reflecting differences in travel time. By the 1330s the Florentines had standardized their loans such that the maturity of credits was exactly two months regardless of the center involved. The next step was "dry exchange," where currencies were exchanged for one another at specified intervals, but an actual bill of exchange was not drawn up. De Roover (1944) describes the mechanics.

45. See for example Mueller (1997), chapter 7, on the Venetian case.

46. Spufford (2008), pp. 277–78.

47. Some historians have suggested that by the 1340s, their loans to the English crown had swelled to as much as a third of the total liquid assets of the entire Florentine economy. See for example Goldthwaite (2008), p. 231. Hunt (1990) questions whether the Bardi could have mobilized such large sums even with the help of foreign deposits, concluding that these estimates are exaggerated.

48. Slater (2018), p. 20; Eichengreen, El-Ganainy, Esteves, and Mitchener (2021), p. 22.

49. More precisely, no merchandise could be shipped or landed other than that which was smuggled.

50. Actually, Edward never repudiated his debts; he simply stopped paying (Hunt 1990).

51. Again, this is for the thirteenth and fourteenth centuries. See Bell, Brooks, and Moore (2009).

52. Compare the interest rate of 8 to 10 percent paid on time deposits with Florentine banks. Stasavage (2011) compares realized returns on sovereign loans with land rents, reaching the same conclusion.

53. In addition to this signaling effect, economists in the tradition of Jensen and Meckling (1976) argue that long-term borrowing encourages risk taking, since the borrower benefits from successful outcomes, while losses from unsuccessful outcomes are borne by the lender. Short-term debt, in contrast, mitigates this moral hazard (Leland and Toft 1996).

54. This is described by Kaeuper (1973).

55. On the Genoese and Philip II, see Drelichman and Voth (2011). That said, the atomized structure of Florentine merchant-banking, with multiple small banking houses, made collective action of this sort more difficult.

56. Munro (2012), pp. 74–75.

57. Fryde (1984), p. 301.

58. Alum was used in the textile industry for removing impurities from wool and for fixing dyes. The papacy had previously formed a partnership with the discoverer of the Tolfa deposits in the hope that their development might free Europe from dependence on supplies from Asia Minor controlled by the Turks. To this end, Pope Paul II banned imports of alum from Muslim countries into any part of Christendom. But this left the papacy with the problem of financing and marketing the alum, which is where the Medici came in.

59. Goldthwaite (1987), pp. 28, 237.

60. Goldthwaite (2008), p. 246; Locatelli (2025), p. 168. In this connection the Florentines had their ups and downs. From 1305 they instead transferred funds to Avignon. They did so until 1376, when Pope Gregory XI placed Florence under interdict and expelled the entire Florentine colony, including the bankers, in response to an armed revolt of the Central Italian cities (prompted by a bad harvest and a decree by the Papal Legate in Romagna forbidding the export of wheat from Romagna to Tuscany). Florentines then reestablished themselves as bankers to the pope once Urban VI restored the papacy to Rome in 1378, as recounted below, and relaxation of papal sanctions on Florence in 1381.

61. Locatelli (2025), p. 170–72. In this context Locatelli refers to the florin as the Florentine bankers' "unique selling proposition."

62. De Roover (1963b, p. 197) and Bullard (1980, pp. 104–12) describe the operation of the depository.

63. Holmes (1968), p. 364–66; Bullard (1980), p. 115. Owing to prohibitions against usury, interest payments were disguised by inflating the principal of the loan.

64. De Roover (1963b), p. 202.

65. The business relationship was smoothed, no doubt, by the fact that the pope at the time, Clement VII, was himself a Medici. Partner (1999), pp. 374–75.

66. Morrison, Kirschner, and Molho (1985) use the records of the Monte delle doti to infer death rates.

67. Some date this relative decline from the fifteenth century. Accounts suggesting this earlier timing may be overly focused on the difficulties of the Medici bank following Cosimo de' Medici's death in 1464. Other bankers and merchants, by comparison, did better.

68. Bullard (1980), p. 9.

69. See for example Brucker (1983), p. 261–62.

70. Cochrane (1970), p. 55. Bergier (1979), p. 111 similarly alludes to "all the signs of a smoothly operating capitalism, but the spirit is lacking" and to how the Italian bankers "from the middle of the fifteenth century, if not before . . . had settled down into a comfortable routine." On p. 114 he indicts the Florentines for "a simple lack of imagination, a habit that had grown up during more than a century of good business, of easy business on a short-term basis." The wool industry was in decline already in the late fourteenth century.

71. Cochrane (1973), p. 113; Munro (2012), pp. 55, 78.

72. Malanima (1988), pp. 67–68.
73. Veseth (1990), p. 69.
74. Strieder (1966), pp. 7–8 and passim.
75. Collateral descendants, actually; Jakob's most important inheritors on the business side were his nephews Anton and Raymund (Haberlein 2012). On the business practices in question, see Ehrenberg (1928), pp. 65–72. For more on the Fuggers, see Walter and Kalus (2013) and Steinmetz (2015).
76. Melanchthon, quoted in Herre (2009), p. 19.
77. See for example the discussion in Marks (1960).
78. Alfani and Ammannati (2017) document these inequality trends.

Chapter 4: The First Global Currency

1. Currency substitution being use of a foreign currency instead or in addition to the domestic currency. Introductions to the modern literature on currency substitution include Calvo and Vegh (1992) and Giovannini and Turtelboom (1992).
2. Munro (2003), p. 11.
3. See L'Hértier and Téreygeol (2010).
4. More precisely, the peak was reached in 1526–35 according to the estimates of Nef (1941).
5. Irigoin (2020), p. 385.
6. *Haifuki* dates from the early sixteenth century, as explained by Keiji and Yamamura (1988, p. 81–82).
7. Miyamoto and Shikano (2003), p. 172.
8. The statistics here are from Irigoin (2020).
9. Contemporaries were aware of the connection, as documented by Giráldez (2015, p. 31).
10. Stein and Stein (2000), p. 20. In addition, these methods resembled rudimentary refining techniques used by indigenous Andeans, who had refined silver in *guayras*, inverted-cone-shaped smelters three feet in height, heated by llama dung and with holes in the sides to admit wind. Use of these native smelters persisted through the colonial period (TePaske and Brown 2010, pp. 69–70), which may have further inspired Spanish mine operators.
11. The statement applies strictly to the periods 1571–75 and 1576–85.
12. What follows is a compressed version of the description in Bakewell (1994).
13. Until the early eighteenth century, the fee was 20 percent at Potosí, levied on the value of refined, assayed, stamped output, but 10 percent elsewhere.
14. The royal authorities in fact defined the real's fineness as 930.5/1000, which exceeded the precision manufacturing capacity of the mints.
15. In 1728 the fineness of the peso was reduced slightly, but its size and weight remained the same (see below).
16. Moisés (2005), p. 76. It no doubt helped that the high output of the mines and mints provided ample amounts of income to the Crown even in the absence of debasement.
17. These blanks were known as cobs. Initially this was hand work using a hammer and die. Eventually the process was mechanized, with twelve hammers raised and lowered using a cammed axle connected to a mill wheel. Lane (2023), p. 85.
18. Lane (2023), p. 390. Recall that the Crown paid officials in proportion to mint output of coin.

19. Lane (2017), p. 35.

20. Lane (2019), p. 133. Other officials, who also served as civil judges of the Royal Audiencias (the High Courts of Justice), were found to have been complicit in the scheme. Although they were too powerful to be executed, they were required to pay substantial fines or transferred to positions elsewhere in the empire.

21. This is according to Lohmann Villena (1976), cited in Sato (2023), p. 361.

22. O'Rourke and Williamson (2002), Table 1. Their estimate pertains to trade other than in silver itself; they exclude silver (and gold) because of their "monetary role" (fn. 4).

23. TePaske and Brown (2010), p. 8.

24. Irigoin (2020), p. 391.

25. From the 1730s, scope for counterfeiting diminished further with the application of horse or mule-driven rolling mills and screw presses in place of the hammer and die, making for greater uniformity. Use of the screw press facilitated the addition of milled edges (hence "milled dollars"), making it easier to detect clipping and shaving. These technological changes were accompanied by administrative changes that ended the selling of mint offices and shifted responsibility for mint operations to administrators appointed by the Crown.

26. Also involved were the houses of Hope and Baring, who we encounter in chapters 5 and 6, respectively. Marichal (2007), pp. 164–68. On the Fuggers, see chapter 3.

27. Stein and Stein (2000), pp. 51–52.

28. González (2003), p. 110. In addition to the treasure fleet, occasional single private ships sailed at other times, and there was also a small handful of royal ships.

29. Bolialian (2023) shows that the galleons carried not only Mexican silver but Peruvian silver as well, silver from Potosí having made its way northward to Acapulco. On the westward leg the galleons also sometimes carried tobacco, sweet potato, and other goods sourced in the Americas, as well as European manufactures shipped from Seville to Veracruz and then overland to Acapulco. Silver, however, dominated the cargo by value.

30. Copper coin was also used in Asia for day-to-day transactions but was impractical for higher-value trade. Nonetheless, copper coin produced in the period of the Song dynasty (960 to 1279) was used in transactions with other parts of East Asia (Yang 1952, p. 38), until a severe copper shortage caused the Song to shift to paper currency.

31. Von Glahn (1996), p. 127.

32. Von Glahn (2003, p. 197 et seq.) describes how gold was China's most important export to the West from the sixteenth through eighteenth centuries. Why arbitrage took the form of silver flowing east rather than gold flowing west presumably reflected the fact that silver had greater utility in the East as a means of payment. In Europe, in contrast, there was no shortage of precious metal, given large inflows from the New World. In addition, higher incomes meant that Europeans could afford Asian spices and other merchandise, which they imported in lieu of gold.

33. Irigoin (2020), p. 395.

34. Fisher (2003), pp. 124–25.

35. Just why this was the case only deepens the mystery, since the Chinese had been among the very earliest producers of coined money, as we saw in chapter 2.

36. Song emperors went as far as to ban the export of scarce gold and silver coin (Du 2020, p. 243). Merchants used ingots ("sycee") in long-distance trade, but these were subject to the

same limitations as ingots elsewhere. Paper money, pioneered by China in the ninth century CE, was sporadically used in trade along the Silk Road from the twelfth through sixteenth centuries, a practice that gave rise to associated bills of exchange. But detecting and preventing the counterfeiting of paper notes was difficult with existing technology. In addition, there was nothing to prevent the emperors at the apex of a hierarchical political regime from printing paper notes in excess. An underdeveloped revenue system and pressing fiscal needs repeatedly tempted them go down this road. Xu (2021) and Guan, Palma, and Wu (2024) provide details.

37. Mann (2011), p. 138.
38. Irigoin (2019), p. 273.
39. Chaudhury (2003), p. 160.
40. Cipolla (1989) provides another explanation for the premium. He writes that silver ingots could be subject to customs duties when crossing borders, whereas pieces of eight were not. Note, however, that differential treatment of ingots and coined silver was not universally the case.
41. Miyamoto and Shikano (2003), p. 173.
42. Busschers (1999), pp. 33–34.
43. Marichal (2006), p. 41.
44. Irigoin (2019), p. 280.
45. Pond (1941), pp. 14–15. See also McCusker (1978).
46. Seijas and Frederick (2017), pp. 23–24.
47. Muhl (2001) provides details.
48. The immigrants in question came from multiple German states, each with its distinctive if unfamiliar money, and from Scandinavia, Italy, and Russia, among other places (Kraft 2019, pp. 241–47).
49. See for example Flynn (1982), p. 139.
50. Fisher (1975), pp. 38–39.
51. For details see Ficker (2022), pp. 258–59.

Chapter 5: Fiat Lux

1. Mooij (2019), p. 29.
2. This is described in chapter 3. Similarly, opportunities for diversification (for investing in multiple ships as a way of hedging the risk that one or more might fail to return) were few in the era of limited partnerships, much as they had been under *commenda* contracts.
3. Jonker and Sluyterman (2001), p. 30.
4. In 1576, the Pacification of Ghent had sought to establish a common exchange rate between the coins of the different provinces but proved impossible to enforce.
5. Van Dillen (1934), p. 81.
6. Quinn and Roberds (2005) explain how local officials, to reduce uncertainty and transactions costs, adopted ordinances setting official prices for these coins, enabling debtors to settle their accounts at these artificial prices and in turn creating additional incentive for depreciated coinage.
7. Dehing and 't Hart (1997), p. 40.
8. Van Dillen (1934), p. 83.

9. VOC is shorthand for the less wieldy Vereenigde Oostindische Compagnie.

10. The same activity was undertaken by the Dutch West Indies Company, which operated less successfully between West Africa and the Americas (de Vries and van der Woude 1997, pp. 464–66).

11. In addition, the VOC minted small-denomination copper coins and large-denomination gold coins (Bucknill 1931). Whereas it conducted transactions within Asia using these distinctive coins, transactions between the VOC's offices in the Netherlands and its outposts in Asia were settled with bills of exchange. This was a rare exception to the rule that trade between continents required the actual movement of coin, whereas only trade within Europe could be settled with bills.

12. An exception was the West African slave trade, in which the Dutch West India Company "purchased" slaves to work on its plantations in the Caribbean and Brazil with "manilas," horseshoe-shaped bracelets of copper, brass, or bronze produced in Amsterdam (Einzig 1949, pp. 151–52).

13. The leeuwendaalder was introduced at the federal level starting in 1606, the dukaat and ducaton both in 1659.

14. Gherardi and Pelsdonk (2025) use X-ray fluorescence spectroscopy to identify the source of silver used in Dutch coin in the seventeenth and early eighteenth centuries and show that mints in the Dutch Republic still relied on recycling older coins and importing silver from Central European mines, in addition to coining Spanish silver.

15. Glamann (1958), pp. 69.

16. Previously, clearing and payment transactions had been spread amongst a range of independent moneychangers and cashiers, effectively fragmenting the market.

17. This is documented by Flandreau, Galimard, Jobst, and Nogues-Marco (2009).

18. Dehing and 't Hart (1997), p. 48.

19. Heckscher (1950), p. 221. Heckscher also notes a role for Hamburg and the mark.

20. Gillard (2019), p. 114, quoting an estimate of the British business historian Charles Wilson.

21. This is according to the 2022 Triennial Central Bank Survey of Foreign Exchange and Over-the-Counter Derivatives Markets (BIS 2022).

22. At times bank money might trade at a premium over current money (coin), given its superior convenience. This premium was known as the "agio." The agio was generally limited to 5 percent or less.

23. Since receipts were provided for deposits of high-quality coin only, the bank could reduce its withdrawal fees, since it no longer had to melt down and remint the coin so deposited, lowering its costs. A receipt had to be redeemed within six months, although the depositor could roll over or "prolong" the six-month term on payment of a fee (van Dillen 1934, p. 103). Quinn and Roberds liken this to the repurchase ("repo") transactions of modern central banks.

24. Another scenario was where the purchaser of the receipt had insufficient funds at the bank but borrowed these from a third party also with an account, against an IOU.

25. Quinn and Roberds (2014), p. 2.

26. In contrast to plain-vanilla bills of exchange, which were unsecured and therefore subject to counterparty risk, this endorsement provided an extra layer of protection, rendering these acceptances, as they came to be known, still easier and cheaper to buy and sell, including across borders. Quinn and Roberds (2024), p. 120.

27. Precious metal so imported could then be sold to the bank, giving the Amsterdam metals dealer a balance in bank money with which to settle the bill. The metals dealer meanwhile acquired a receipt that could be sold to other parties seeking a long position in trade coins. Berre and Kosmetatos (2024) discuss these dealers.

28. Van Dillen (1934), p. 104; Quinn and Roberds (2023), p. 2.

29. Jonker and Sluyterman (2001), p. 94.

30. Securitization was associated with excesses, as is often the case. Berre and Kosmetatos (2024) describe how speculation in West Indian mortgage securities contributed to the 1772–73 credit crisis in Amsterdam.

31. Like the earlier sovereign loans of the Florentines, these were secured by liens on mining or other natural resource concessions and, eventually, on the general revenues of the Crown. Van Dillen (1934), p. 106; Dehing and 't Hart (1997), p. 57; Jonker and Sluyterman (2001), p. 122.

32. Berre and Kosmetatos (2024), p. 2.

33. Van Dillen (1934), p. 105.

34. Flandreau, Galimard, Jobst, and Nogues-Marco (2009), p. 159.

35. Boxer (1970), p. 255.

36. Israel (1995), pp. 998–1008.

37. Hay (2024, p. 48–50) describes the house's origins.

38. Van Dillen (1934), p. 112. This contrasted with loans to the city, which were regularly forgiven.

39. This history is recounted by Quinn and Roberds (2014).

40. Bolt, Frost, Shin, and Wierts (2023), p. 8.

Chapter 6: The World's Banker

1. Consols were perpetual in the sense that they paid interest but never matured (there was no date by which the principal amount had to be repaid by the borrower).

2. This is the famous argument of North and Weingast (1989).

3. On this, see Stasavage (2003), pp. 6–7.

4. Neal (1987) and Berre and Kosmetatos (2024) document the high degree of integration of the two financial markets in this period.

5. The example is from Chapman (1984), p. 4.

6. Both quotes are from Baster (1937), p. 294.

7. Jenks (1927), p. 6.

8. Roberts (1992), pp. 18–19.

9. Mayhew (1999), p. 141.

10. We saw this in chapter 3.

11. Relying on copper coinage valued at more than its metallic content, yet another potential alternative, created an incentive for counterfeiting. While this might help to relax the constraint of inadequate coin circulation, it did not enhance confidence or encourage widespread acceptance of the resulting circulation.

12. Loan and overdraft facilities came later, as described below.

13. See the discussion in de Roover (1963b), pp. 94–100.

14. Accominotti and Ugolini (2020), p. 10.

15. This was not unlike how Florentines centuries earlier had begun using pairs of offsetting bills of exchange to undertake credit transactions (see again chapter 3).

16. An introduction to the development and spread of the real bills doctrine is Mints (1945).

17. Rogers (1995), pp. 225–36.

18. The first two figures are from Mayhew (1999), p. 108, the third from Nishimura (1971), p. 86.

19. Broadberry, Campbell, Klein, Overton, and van Leeuwen (2015), Table 5.04, p. 201.

20. Quinn (1997), p. 411.

21. King (1936), p. 37.

22. Hansard (1826), vol. 14, cols. 15–20 (February 2). Liverpool was prime minister from 1812 to 1827. A half-century later, Walter Bagehot's view was that the modest origins of these banks were actually healthy. It made sense, in his view, that country banking services should be provided by merchants and shopkeepers known to the local community and knowledgeable of local trade and industry. Bagehot (1873), pp. 252–53.

23. Qualifying country banks could issue one-pound and two-pound notes without relation to their gold reserves. The Bank of England and two Scottish banks were exempt from the six-partner rule intended to protect the bank's market dominance and to subsidize the services it provided the government. This dictated that London, where the Bank of England was available to provide liquidity, would become the intermediary between country banks with excessive and inadequate liquid reserves, respectively. An indication of the light-touch nature of regulation is that only from 1808 were note-issuing banks required to obtain a license. The Bank Charter Act of 1844, in response to the 1825 crisis, gave the Bank of England a monopoly of note issue by fixing the maximum note issues of other banks at their levels just prior to the act's passage and mandating that banks give up their note-issuing rights when merging or being absorbed by other banks.

24. The 5 percent usury ceiling on bills of exchange of three months or less was eliminated in 1833. Elimination was in response to the 1825 crisis, when the Bank of England, to attract gold and restrain demand, was unable to raise its discount rate above that level (see later). Residual usury restrictions were finally removed in 1854.

25. With the suspension of convertibility in 1797 and expansion of the Bank of England's note issue, interest rates fell, leading city banks to stop paying interest on the balances of country banks. This gave the latter an incentive to look for other outlets, which they found in the discount market (King 1936, p. 9). In addition, the Bank of England, the largest player in the market, did not discount bills of more than sixty-five days maturity (such "long bills" being typical of provincially drawn paper). Other London banks similarly hesitated to discount them, given their inability to rediscount them at the Bank of England. Bill brokers found willing takers in country banks, whose long liabilities matched these long assets. Cassis and Cottrell (2015), p. 101.

26. Again, we see here the catalytic role of the French and Napoleonic Wars in British financial development.

27. The commission was paid by the banker offering bills for discount. Richardson describes it in his 1811 testimony before the Select Committee on the High Price of Bullion (reprinted in *The Belfast Monthly Magazine* 1811, p. 194), from where other details in this paragraph are also drawn.

28. Truptil (1936), p. 111.
29. Thus, the bank was uncomfortably both a competitor and supporter of other city banks.
30. Van Dillen (1934), p. 106.
31. Turner (2014), pp. 67–69.
32. Hilton (1977), p. 209.
33. Jackson (2022), p. 241. In addition, there was the negative impact on commodity-trading firms of weak cotton, coffee, and sugar prices, which had risen in the earlier lax-money boom, and the collapse of the bubble in Latin American loans, which endangered banks that had extended advances to customers on the security of bonds purchased on margin. It can be argued, however, that defaults by Latin American governments were more a consequence than a cause of the 1825 crisis (again, see later).
34. Most observers ascribe the problems of the country banks to their reckless lending during the boom. Pressnell (1956, pp. 477–99) attributes the timing to the need for the banks to remit taxes to the government.
35. Hilton (1977), p. 215.
36. Dawson (1990), p. 116; Neal (1998), p. 64.
37. Jenks (1927), p. 57.
38. Mayhew (1999), p. 155.
39. Kynaston (2017), p. 121.
40. Fetter (1956), p. 116. Hilton (1977), pp. 217–18.
41. Olmstead-Rumsey (2019) looks closely at the transmission of financial distress to real economic activity in England. She concludes that the nontradables sector was hit disproportionately, and that the mechanism was a decline in demand and spending owing to the destruction of household wealth, reflecting the reduced value of claims on now-failed country banks.
42. This preferential access meant that the London discount market remained more concentrated, in the hands of a small number of dealers, than the Amsterdam market described in the preceding chapter. It can be argued that the Bank of England's gatekeeper function prevented excessive competition leading dealers to discount inferior, low-quality bills, discrediting the market. For the contrast with Amsterdam, see Berre and Kosmetatos (2024), pp. 14–15.
43. Acceptance houses managed the risks of extending this guarantee by limiting leverage to three or four times the value of capital and reserves (Accominotti, Lucena-Piquero, and Ugolini 2021, p. 896).
44. King (1936), p. 45 notes that such guarantees became commonplace only after 1836, which puts a date on the rise of the modern acceptance house.
45. Especially important in this connection were Anglo-American acceptance houses that financed trade across the Atlantic (more on which later).
46. Michie (2012), p. 20. By 1913 these overseas banks had grown to twenty-five in number.
47. Other such bank offices and branches in London were founded by British expatriates in India and the Far East. Strictly speaking, banks founded by British expatriates, even when possessing London offices, do not qualify as overseas banks as the term is used by Michie (2012), p. 22.
48. These foreign banks worked with rather than competed against British banks, since the Bank of England did not discount bills of foreign banks unless they were first endorsed by a British financial institution.

49. Michie (2007), p. 53. An extended discussion of correspondent banking is Easton (1908).

50. Nishimura (1971), Table 15, p. 93.

51. It also reflected a tendency for firms to obtain working capital and credit from sources other than the bill market and a corresponding decline in the importance of inland bills. Relaxing the six-partner limit permitted the formation of joint-stock banks with transferable shares, enabling producers to avail themselves of the loan and overdraft facilities of large clearing banks (Scammell 1968, p. 29). This 1826 reform was a response to the 1825 crisis, which laid bare the fragility of small provincial banks. It allowed joint-stock banks to be formed outside a radius of sixty-five miles around London that was preserved for the Bank of England. An 1833 law then allowed the formation of joint-stock banks in London itself so long as these did not issue notes. These banks attracted a growing volume of deposits and moved money around the country via their extensive branch networks. Nishimura (1971) objects that the decline in rediscounting inland bills in London preceded the creation of nationwide branch networks. He points instead to the fact that banks in industrial cities opened branches in the suburbs, enabling them to attract deposits and permitting them to hold to maturity the bills they discounted, as opposed to sending them to London. He points to improvements in transportation and communication enabling British firms to economize on inventories, which in turn reduced discounting to finance inventory investment. Exporters and importers, in contrast, faced longer delivery and shipment lags, requiring them to maintain the traditional practice of holding extensive inventories. Hence the importance of the foreign bill.

52. Cassis (2006), p. 45; Cassis and Cottrell (2015), p. 121.

53. Farhi and Maggiori (2019) and Gopinath and Stein (2021) emphasize the role of similar complementarities in supporting the dollar's dominance in the early twenty-first century.

54. Details are from King (1936), pp. 275–78.

55. Buchan (1960), p. 232.

56. Saunders (1928), p. 35.

57. Exchequer bills meanwhile went into decline and were abolished in 1897.

58. Masayoshi appreciated that this sterling might be converted into gold or used as backing for the operation of a gold-exchange standard. Japan went onto the gold standard two years later, using its holdings at the Bank of England. See Metzler and Bytheway (2016).

59. When Hong Kong and Shanghai Bank and Deutsch-Asiatische Bank took over from Russia finance of the indemnity in 1896, they underwrote Chinese payments by floating two £16 million loans for the Chinese government, again on the London market. Metzler and Bytheway (2016), pp. 10–11.

60. Michie (1992), pp. 77–78.

61. Chapman (1984), pp. 105–6.

62. Carter (1953) notes earlier estimates that the Dutch held 43 percent of British government debt circa 1777. Riley's (1980) estimate for 1762 is half that level. For more on the question, see Oppers (1993). Britain's own foreign lending had been limited to a personal loan to the Austrian emperor in 1706, a loan to the emperor of Prussia by a group of London merchants in the 1730s, and a small Danish credit in 1753. That so much English debt was placed with Dutch investors while being denominated in sterling was a harbinger of things to come.

63. The quote, originally from an advertisement to the second edition of *Letter to Pitt* (Drennan 1799), is reproduced in Wedmore (1886), p. 101.

64. Uglow (2014), pp. 94–96.

65. There was the further problem that Boyd, Benfield had made large loans to one Alexander Houston & Co, which imported sugar and coffee from the West Indies. As if the French Revolution was not enough, in more bad luck a slave revolt in Grenada and St. Vincent destroyed the sugar crop and associated infrastructure, putting paid to the Houston loans. Cope (1983), pp. 124–25.

66. Helleiner (1965) is a detailed account of diplomatic maneuverings and parliamentary debates around the guarantees, which the British extended in return for an Austrian commitment to undertake more extensive anti-French military operations. Parliamentary opposition to the guarantee was intense, on the grounds that the Austrians might be unable to repay. The Dutch had provided similar guarantees for foreign government loans in the eighteenth century. Again, the British were following their example.

67. That is to say, they commanded a modest premium relative to the bonds of the British government.

68. Nichols (1958), p. 329.

69. The Amsterdam office of Hope & Co. was involved in managing the transaction as well, but the London office was key for coordinating with the London-based Baring Brothers. The most extensive treatment of the transaction is Hay (2024), chapter 4. See also Ziegler (1988), pp. 71 and Kynaston (1994), p. 23.

70. Uglow (2014), p. 93

71. Cassis (2006), p. 21.

72. By this time the Hopes had reestablished their house in Amsterdam, though they still did extensive business in London. In 1816, Barings had rebuffed an earlier approach by the French government, worried that the Chamber of Deputies might default on already outstanding debt. A new election brought a more moderate Chamber in 1817, which made it more attractive to market bonds on its behalf.

73. White (2001), p. 346. Eventually, in the 1820s, with the entry of additional underwriters, commissions came down to 8 percent. Still, underwriting remained a highly lucrative line of business.

74. Tranches were issued in Amsterdam, Vienna, Hamburg, Frankfurt, and Berlin as well as London.

75. Dawson (1990), p. 20; Ferguson (1998), 124–25.

76. This was both because of restrictions on what securities could be traded on the Stock Exchange and because of crowding on the trading floor. Michie (1999), p. 55. What started as a separate Foreign Funds market was eventually incorporated as the "foreign room" of the consolidated Exchange.

77. Rothschild and Barings were at least peripherally involved the Latin American bonanza. Barings was involved in an 1824 loan to Buenos Aires but only as marketer and issuer (receiving requests for payment of the interest coupon), as opposed to underwriting the loan (Flandreau and Flores 2009, p. 655), the difference being that an underwriter advanced the balance to the borrower and bore the risk of successfully or unsuccessfully marketing the bonds. Rothschild for its part participated in a small loan for the Brazilian Empire in 1825 (Cassis and Cottrell 2015, p. 119). Both banks invested in Mexican and Colombian bonds on the secondary market (Jackson 2022, p. 227).

78. Marichal (1989), p. 22.

79. Recall the discussion in chapter 4.

80. Flandreau and Flores (2009), pp. 658–59.

81. On the contrast with Amsterdam, see Riley (1980), p. 198. In this way, London banks were essentially reviving the methods of Florentine bankers, who had drawn funding from abroad as well as at home, as described in chapter 3.

82. The first syndicates in the London market were formed in the late 1860s to fund loans to Egypt and Turkey. Rothschild and Barings did not lend their names to the practice until the turn of the century (Cottrell 1991, p. 37).

83. Listing of foreign bonds had commenced in 1823. Conversely, when a borrower fell into arrears, its bonds were delisted, which made them less attractive and prevented the borrower from accessing the market until it settled on acceptable terms, as defined by the bondholders committee conducting negotiations.

84. Cassis and Cottrell (2015), p. 132.

85. Feis (1930), p. 17 and passim.

86. The Deutsche Bank was established to provide trade credit for German exports and imports, renationalizing transactions for which German firms relied on London (Flandreau 1998, p. 112). Thus, the same synergy between trade credit and foreign lending characteristic of British experience was also evident in Germany.

87. M. M. Warburg reappears in chapter 7 in a different light.

88. For instance, an issue might be underwritten by a British bank but partially distributed in another country. Principal might be denominated in sterling while periodic interest payments were in the currencies of each investing country. While new bond issues are straightforward to aggregate, tracking the retirement of existing bonds, through the operation of sinking funds, is less straightforward. Platt (1989) emphasizes the problems.

89. See Woodruff (1967).

90. Government support refers to the fact that the British government, unlike its continental counterparts, did not place political conditions on loan flotations to foreign powers or discourage capital exports. Feis (1930) and Born (1977) discuss these foreign government interventions. Political interference elsewhere was thus another reason foreign funds flowed toward London, from where they might be reexported without prejudice. King (1936), p. 267. Notice the parallel here with the Eurodollar market discussed in chapter 8.

91. Wilgress (1912–13), p. 212.

92. Wilgress (1912–13), p. 211.

93. This was permissible under the country's "limping" gold standard. Although silver was legal tender, it was no longer freely coined. Paying out silver increased the volatility of the franc exchange rate, since arbitrage to limit exchange rate fluctuations, effected by shipping precious metal from where it was cheap to where it was costly, was more expensive for high-weight-to-value silver. The National Banks of Belgium and Switzerland did likewise, given their monetary union agreement with France. This was the Latin Monetary Union, dating from 1865, under which France, Italy, Belgium, and Switzerland agreed to standardize their silver and gold coinage on French lines. Greece joined subsequently, and other countries adopted the standard without formally joining. Willis (1901) is an account of the limping gold standard and Latin Union. Madden and Nadler (1931) argue that this limping standard was a primary reason for the

underdevelopment of the Paris money market before World War I and its lack of head start in the 1920s, when the French government sought to develop that market further.

94. The definitive account of the gold devices remains Bloomfield (1959).

95. "Little" rather than "no" use, because the bank did occasionally change its bid and ask prices for various kinds of foreign coin, which might make it slightly more expensive to export or more attractive to import precious metal in that form. See Scammell (1965) and Ugolini (2012).

96. Thus, the British authorities shunned the easy option of devaluation. Devaluation would have enhanced the competitiveness of exports and raised the sterling value of the Bank of England's gold reserves, easing the subsequent process of financial management. But it would have undermined the credibility of the new parity.

97. Bordo and Kydland (1995) is fundamental to this interpretation. Eichengreen (1992) emphasizes the role of credibility in the smooth operation of the gold-sterling standard.

98. See, for example, the indictment of Overend & Gurney's risk management practices in Sowerbutts, Schneebalg, and Hubert (2016).

99. Sowerbutts, Schneebalg, and Hubert (2016), p. 99.

100. An analysis of these inter-firm dynamics is Flores (2010). Here "Argentina" should be understood to encompass not only the national government but also the Province of Buenos Aires, the Buenos Ayres Water Supply & Drainage Company (a private enterprise), and sundry and assorted other entities.

101. In addition, the Bank of England organized a consortium of other banks to support Barings, in a move not unlike that engineered by J. P. Morgan during the 1907 financial crisis in the United States, as described in chapter 7.

102. Barings, for its part, lived to see another day (or, more precisely, another century—it failed in 1995). Under the direction of the Bank of England, it was split into a new Barings, which took over the bank's day to day operations, and an old Barings, tasked solely with selling off the securities and other assets of the former bank.

103. Walter Bagehot, the architect of the Treasury market, is widely credited with formalizing this idea that the central bank should lend freely at a penalty rate. However, the Bank of England's actions in 1866 (and for that matter in 1825) predated publication of *Lombard Street*, where Bagehot described the practice. The underlying ideas go back to Henry Thornton (1802), who credits Francis Baring for the insight, and whose son Henry Sykes deserves credit for bringing the issue to Bagehot's attention (see above).

104. Previously, the Bank of England had outsourced the screening of discounters to the discount houses. But Overend & Gurney's problems in 1866 demonstrated the dangers of delegation and led the bank to take a proactive role. Flandreau and Ugolini (2013, 2014) show how the Bank of England evaluated the condition of borrowers as well as the quality of their collateral. Along with avoiding adverse selection, these practices limited moral hazard by signaling that not everyone would be bailed out. Allowing Overend & Gurney to fail lent credibility to the position, albeit at a cost.

105. Limiting the loss of reserves and export of gold in turn removed pressure to devalue.

106. Impatient investors would have converted their sterling into French francs, invested in Paris, and repurchased sterling bills six months later once conditions normalized. Flandreau and Ugolini (2014), pp. 90–92 compare the returns of the two classes of investors.

107. Burk (1992), p. 360. Brezis (1995) suggests that Britain financed a portion of its French and Napoleonic War expenses by borrowing abroad. But these borrowings were small by comparison.

108. Incomes and savings were high and rising relative to domestic investment, that is, allowing for investment abroad. Eichengreen (2000, pp. 467–68) details the shift.

109. The latter were enthusiastically promoted by Jacob Schiff of the U.S. investment bank Kuhn, Loeb, who saw Japan as a useful counterweight to an antisemitic Russian regime (Eichengreen, El-Ganainy, Esteves, and Mitchener 2021, p. 75). For details on these bonds, see chapter 7.

Chapter 7: Engineering an International Currency

1. Chernow (1990), p. 127. Whether the elderly Morgan left out of exhaustion, locking his precious library to protect its contents, or whether he had in mind forcing the occupants to reach an agreement, is unclear. It is not implausible that both elements were at work.

2. The publication in question was Warburg (1910).

3. There were changes between the Aldrich Plan for a central bank and the Federal Reserve Act, as described by Wicker (2005, chapter 7).

4. Data on dollar and sterling acceptances in the 1920s are in Eichengreen, Mehl, and Chițu (2018).

5. The London firm for which the young Warburg worked, Samuel Montagu & Co., had started in 1853 as a bullion broker but moved subsequently into discounting bills of exchange, a fact that is relevant for what follows.

6. Naclerio (2018), p. 66. Warburg's brother, Felix, was married to Schiff's daughter Frieda, deepening the connection. Paul met Nina when serving as best man at Felix's wedding, where Nina served as maid of honor.

7. While the 1904 Japanese issue was the first significant foreign loan in the United States, there had been a small loan on behalf of Mexico in 1899, and further small issues on behalf of Mexico and Cuba coinciding with the Japanese issue. Schiff, as it happened, had been seated next to Korekiyo Takahashi, Japan's chief loan negotiator, at a dinner party in London in 1904. Conscious of czarist oppression of the Jews and anxious to do what he could to aid Japan's campaign against Russia, Schiff arranged for Kuhn, Loeb and National City Bank to underwrite Japanese government bonds and market them to American investors. More Japanese imperial loans followed in 1905. A tranche was marketed in Germany by none other than M. M. Warburg & Co. See Best (1972) and Rosenbaum and Sherman (1979).

8. "Defects and Needs of our Banking System" having been the title of Warburg's January 6, 1907, article in *The New York Times*.

9. Madden and Nadler (1935), p. 161.

10. Warburg (1930), volume 2, p. 186.

11. Myles (2023), p. 7.

12. The financial expert Edwin Kemmerer highlighted this pattern in yet another study for the National Monetary Commission (Kemmerer 1910).

13. This had been standard practice since at least 1899. Supple (1970), p. 246.

14. Royal Exchange Assurance could trace its origins back to 1720 and the South Sea Bubble. When it began underwriting policies in the United States in the 1890s, it focused on San Francisco, which was a lucrative market given its fire hazards and maritime trade.

15. See Cockrell and Green (1994). The British fire insurance industry can be seen as growing out of the shipping insurance activities described in chapter 5, together with appreciation of the need to insure urban property in the wake of the Great London Fire of 1666 and then the fire risks of furnaces and engines associated with early industrialization.

16. Details are provided by Odell and Weidenmier (2004). See also Fink (2019), p. 17.

17. Quoted in Malone (1981), p. 49.

18. Technically, the Heinzes sold out to the Butte Coalition Mining Company, a holding company controlled by Amalgamated.

19. Trust companies were state-chartered financial institutions that provided wealth-management services, competed with banks for demand deposits, and extended loans to brokers on the New York Stock Exchange. By 1907 they were major financial players; their assets were comparable to those of national banks (Tabor, Di Lucido, and Zhang 2021). But as state-chartered institutions they were not subject to the same reserve requirements and investment restrictions as national banks. Specifically, they were required to hold reserves equal to only 5 percent of customer deposits and allowed to make riskier loans than commercial banks. Lack of restrictions permitted them to branch abroad to originate foreign business, in contrast to limitations placed on banks under the National Banking Act. A few did so, starting with the Equitable Trust Company, which opened an office in London in 1895. But the foreign operations of trust companies were too few to significantly diminish the dependence of U.S. exporters and importers on foreign financial institutions.

20. Bruner and Carr (2007), p. 86.

21. O'Sullivan (2016), pp. 247–48.

22. Jackson (1983), p. 264.

23. "Barney's Successor Puts All on Morse," *The New York Times* (November 16, 1907), p. 1.

24. James (2020), p. 305.

25. Of existing banking crisis chronologies, the most comprehensive is Jalil (2015).

26. American banks had begun establishing these correspondent relationships in the mid-nineteenth century with the expansion of U.S. wheat exports, exporters needing trade credit as well. First National Bank of Chicago was the first mover, establishing a standing relationship with a London correspondent in 1873. Abrahams (1976), p. 2.

27. "The risks of exchange fluctuations were borne by American trading interests," in the words of Reed (1922, p. 155). See also Abrahams (1976), p. 6.

28. Parrini (1969), pp. 102–3.

29. Doubts were raised not just by the events of 1907 but also by a run on the U.S. Treasury's gold reserves in 1894–95 and the presidential campaigns of William Jennings Bryan in 1896, 1900, and 1908. On the events of 1894–95, see Simon (1968) and Garber and Grilli (1986). On Bryan, see Cherny (1985) and Eichengreen (2018).

30. The structure and dynamics of this coalition are detailed by Broz (1997).

31. This they did on August 3.

32. The last time had been in the Overend-Gurney crisis in 1866. Prior to the 1914 suspension, the Bank of England had been authorized to issue notes only up to a specified ceiling without also holding matching gold backing. This was the so-called fiduciary issue, which was capped at roughly £19 million in 1914 (Bank of England 1969). Above that, notes had to be backed pound for pound, as it were, in gold.

33. The initial moratorium was for a month. It was later extended into November.

34. Scammell (1968), p. 195.

35. In addition, much of what was imported was purchased by the government itself and financed by issuing foreign bonds and Treasury bills (more on which below).

36. Michie (2024, p. 112) notes that Asian banks turned to Tokyo, Bombay, and Shanghai, in addition to now sourcing trade credit in the United States.

37. Abrahams (1976), p. 52.

38. Michie (2024), p. 103.

39. Higgins (1949), p. 21.

40. This ceiling was then raised to 100 percent of capital and surplus in 1919.

41. Reed (1922), p. 161.

42. This amendment was adopted in September 1916. In addition, Reserve Banks were authorized to accept bills to supply dollars for transactions with countries where bank checks were not used.

43. Roberts (2002), p. 153. Even earlier, National City had invested in subsidiaries and affiliates in the Caribbean to service U.S. companies active in Cuba and Haiti. In 1915 it then acquired the International Banking Corporation (IBC), a state-chartered bank set up in 1901 to promote U.S. trade with the Philippines and related parts of Asia (state-chartered banks being permitted to branch abroad, though those not expressly set up for this purpose typically lacked the scale). This acquisition jumpstarted its network of foreign branches. See Bridges (2024).

44. Morgan's foreign branches sometimes operated through affiliated state banks, mirroring the connection between National City Bank and IBC. Parrini (1969), p. 116.

45. Hudson (2017), pp. 151–52. In 1919 the Edge Amendment to the Federal Reserve Act sought to broaden participation in foreign acceptance business by allowing Federal Reserve member banks engaging in foreign business to also accept domestic deposits tied to international business, thereby funding themselves more extensively, something that the AFBC and Mercantile Bank of the Americas were essentially prohibited from doing.

46. Madden and Nadler (1935), pp. 212–13.

47. Miron (1985) compares the periods ending in 1908 and beginning in 1919 and documents a sharp decline in U.S. interest rate seasonality between the two, which he ascribes to the founding of the Fed. Clark (1986) identifies 1914 as the breakpoint, uncomfortably since this was before the Fed initiated large-scale operations in acceptances and other financial instruments. Clark also shows that interest rate seasonality declined simultaneously in other countries, suggesting that more than just the founding of the Fed was responsible for the shift. While not offering direct evidence, he suggests that a global factor, such as the breakdown of the classical gold standard, could have been the operative factor.

48. The value of acceptances outstanding fell even more dramatically starting in 1930, albeit without a subsequent recovery, for reasons analyzed below.

49. This refers to end-of-year figures, from Eichengreen and Flandreau (2010).

50. As Melchior Palyi, writing in the 1930s, observed, "In practice the English broker not only guarantees the ultimate conversion of the paper but is also ready to take it back from the banks at any moment, so to speak; the liquidity policy of the banks rests largely on this function of the brokerage house, backed in turn by the Bank of England and by an internationally communicating money market. Nothing equal or comparable to this has grown up in the United States." Palyi (1937), p. 110. See Michie (2024, p. 113) on the view from London.

51. Madden and Nadler (1935), p. 165; Abrahams (1976), pp. 174–75.

52. Moreover, a majority of bills bought by Reserve Banks in 1934 were payable in foreign currency; these purchases were designed to relieve pressure on the foreign exchange market, as opposed to maintaining the liquidity of bills. This was different from the situation through 1931, when 90 percent and more of the bills purchased by Reserve Banks were payable in dollars. See Board of Governors (1943), pp. 331–32.

53. Ferderer (2003), pp. 679–80.

54. The co-sponsor was Senator Robert Owen, Democrat from Oklahoma.

55. *Time* (June 10, 1946), p. 26. Glass's grating personality did not prevent Wilson from appointing him Treasury secretary in 1918; he served until 1920.

56. Chernow (1993), pp. 136–37. Warburg's own account is Warburg (1930), vol. 1, pp. 91–92. Warburg also pushed for allowing a subset of members of the Board of Governors to be appointed by the banking community, as opposed to by politicians. In this he failed, although the bankers, as shareholders in their respective Reserve Banks, retained a voice in selecting regional bank governors.

57. Glass (1927), p. 210. Fink (2019) provides detail on the serial revisions of the original legislation.

58. Adam (2020), p. 4.

59. In the case of Germany, acceptances also had to be endorsed by the Gold Discount Bank, a subsidiary of the German Reichsbank. The Gold Discount Bank was created to provide credit to German exporters and capitalized with a $50 million loan from a consortium organized by Warburg. Adam (2020), p. 6.

60. Adam (2020), p. 13.

61. Glass also saw the New York Fed's activism as favoring New York banks, which were consequently able to dominate the acceptance market at the expense of other financial institutions. This further excited the Southern Democrat's suspicion of concentrated financial power.

62. James (2020), p. 309.

63. Glass was appointed to the Senate in 1920 to fill an unexpired term; he served until 1946. The report of the investigation was U.S. Senate (1931).

64. Although these de facto finance bills might be disguised as commodity transactions, they were serially rolled over as they matured (Madden and Nadler 1935, p. 59). Scammell (1968), p. 204 suggests that this was also standard practice in London, ascribing it to competition for business between the London and New York discount markets. Accominotti (2012) describes the consequences.

65. Bridges (2024, pp. 98–99) reaches the same conclusion.

66. Parrini (1969), p. 125.

67. It was if anything too steadfast, Scammell (1968, p. 205) suggests, citing complaints that the Bank lowered its standards for the quality of bills it was prepared to discount.

68. Such was the conclusion of Conway (1946, p. 62), that "although London received severe and seemingly permanent setbacks in the field of acceptance financing during this period, the available evidence all indicates that the city's relative position of leadership in this field was not seriously threatened."

69. It did so as a gesture of good faith and to counter the impression that the United States was a second-rate financial power. Abrahams (1976), p. 32.

70. Mintz (1951), p. 19.

71. Eichengreen and Portes (1986), Figures 1 and 2.

72. Loan proceeds were used to finance purchases of commodities and armaments in the United States.

73. Intergovernmental lending declined to negligible levels after mid-1920.

74. Lewis (1938), p. 374. This was 4.5 percent of foreign government securities issued in the UK in this five-year period.

75. Annual issuance in the two markets and currencies is from Mintz (1951), p. 19. Values are computed in common currency using annual average exchange rates.

76. For details see Moggridge (1971). The Bank of England's arm twisting worked because of the Bank's dual role as rediscounter of acceptances (see chapter 6), a power that it could use to penalize the recalcitrant (Royal Institute of International Affairs 1937, p. 77).

77. Lending in 1928 was concentrated in the first half of the year, for reasons analyzed below.

78. U.S. Senate (1932), p. 1324.

79. The Open Market Investment Committee was succeeded by the now more familiar Federal Open Market Committee in 1933. The Fed's 150 basis point increase was implemented between January and July of 1928. Federal Reserve officials' preoccupation with the stock market is much remarked upon, their concern with gold losses less so. Hamilton (1987) links U.S. gold losses in 1927–28 to monetary and fiscal stabilization in France following a period of rapid inflation, and to an improved investment climate there. The Federal Reserve Bank of New York noted in its annual report for 1928, "The heavy gold export movement of the second half of 1927 was continued in the first half of 1928, largely in connection with the French program of monetary stabilization, which required additions to that country's gold reserve" (Federal Reserve Bank of New York 1929, p. 7).

80. In contemporary parlance, they sought to make the central bank's higher policy rates "effective."

81. Here "post-war inflation period" refers to 1919–20. Burgess (1929), p. 19.

82. See Mintz (1951), p. 55.

83. Royal Institute of International Affairs (1937, p. 22) estimated that, as of early 1935, 35 percent of British capital invested in the bonds of foreign governments were not being serviced in full. Kindersley (1934) is careful to distinguish British capital from foreign capital invested in these sterling obligations, noting that a substantial share of sterling loans was held abroad, indirectly affirming the currency's international status.

84. Kindersley (1937), p. 645. An exception was Australia, which was heavily indebted and chose to pay down its sterling debt instead of engaging in additional borrowing.

85. Accominotti (2012) documents the phenomenon.

86. Grossman's (1994) cross-country comparisons suggest that Britain's abandonment of the gold standard, by facilitating lender-of-last-resort intervention, explains why no British banks failed in the 1930s.

87. Conway (1946, p. 19) and Michie (1992, p. 81) go as far as to suggest that London came to be regarded as a safe haven.

88. Michie (1992), pp. 81–82.

89. Unlike U.S. commercial banks, British banks were not prevented from doing so by new banking and securities-market regulation. In the United States, the Glass-Steagall Act of 1933 prevented commercial banks from underwriting bonds, whether through their securities affiliates or otherwise.

90. This group of countries came to be known as the Sterling Area. Vicquéry (2022) shows that sterling gained ground in the 1930s as an anchor currency to which other countries pegged, first at the expense of the dollar and then, once the so-called Gold Bloc collapsed in 1936, at the expense of the French franc.

91. Triffin (1964), Appendix 2. The estimate for the late 1920s is from Eichengreen, Mehl, and Chițu (2018), p. 47.

Chapter 8: Dollar Dominance

1. There is disagreement, including among family members, about the father's name (Weissnovitz or Weit) and his date of landing in the United States (1885 or 1888).

2. Morgenthau himself had no banking experience, a fact that caused his appointment to be viewed critically on Wall Street. The secretary's compensating strengths were his access to FDR and able aides such as Viner (Meier 2022, pp. 241, 243–44).

3. The May 1933 Thomas Amendment to the Agricultural Relief Act authorized the president to reduce the gold content of the dollar by up to half. When Roosevelt's gold-buying program reduced the gold value of the dollar to 59 percent of its earlier level, FDR acknowledged the writing on the wall and stabilized the price by signing the Gold Reserve Act of January 1934.

4. Friedman and Schwartz (1963), Bloomfield (1950), and Romer (1992) emphasize the safe-haven aspect of these flows.

5. The literature on the Bretton Woods Conference is vast. A classic analysis is Gardner (1956). Two more recent treatments are Steil (2013) and Conway (2015).

6. The 1867, 1878, 1881, and 1892 conferences were held to set standards for weight and fineness of the gold and silver coins of participating nations. When superficially similar coins with different metallic contents were emitted by different countries, the light ones would depreciate against their heavier rivals, disturbing exchange rates, prices, and trade flows. In the limit, the light ones would drive the heavy ones out of circulation, frustrating mint officials and fueling inflation. In the event, no agreement on a common standard was reached. France provided invitations for the 1867 conference, but Britain rejected its proposals. In 1878 Germany refused to attend. The 1933 conference was intended, again with French impetus, to put in place a reformed gold standard. But again, there was no agreement on directions for reform. The United States and Britain prioritized monetary autonomy, while Germany, having made the transition to exchange control and National Socialism, had no interest in collaborating.

7. White's connection to the Soviet Union—whether he was a spy, a fellow traveler, or unwitting collaborator—continues to be debated. A review of the evidence is Craig (2004). Steil (2013) makes the case for the prosecution, Boughton (2021) that for the defense.

8. The Gold Reserve Act of 1934, noted above, had transferred the Federal Reserve's gold to the U.S. Treasury, which was provided gold certificates denominated in dollars in return.

9. Cited in Steil (2013), p. 129.

10. White (1933), pp. 302–13.

11. A representative warning to this effect was Młyanarski (1929).

12. *Time* (April 28, 1941), p. 14.

13. Bankson (1971), p. 145.

14. Beyond their interest in liquid refreshment, the Soviets wished to maximize the role of gold in postwar monetary arrangements, since they anticipated being a leading gold producer.

15. Recalling Lord Halifax's doggerel from the period: "They have all the moneybags, but we have all the brains."

16. The question of what exactly was meant by gold-convertible currencies was raised by A. D. Shroff of India, who represented an economy understandably concerned that the blocked sterling it accumulated during the war might not be convertible into gold. Here it mattered that Britain was represented on the subcommittee by Dennis Robertson, an economist rather than a diplomat who valued clarity over well-justified ambiguity; Robertson took up Shroff's challenge and proposed substituting "gold or U.S. dollars."

17. Technically, their initial subscriptions were equal to 10 percent of their official holdings of gold and U.S. dollars or 25 percent of their quotas (how much they were entitled to draw), whichever was smaller.

18. In the event, the transition to full current account convertibility would take even longer, until the end of 1958 for Western Europe and 1964 for Japan.

19. Thus, an article in the *Federal Reserve Bulletin* in April 1948 noted that foreign holdings of gold and dollars at the end of 1947 were less than half 1938 levels (Federal Reserve Board 1948, p. 371).

20. Formally this was the Economic Recovery Program. The historical literature is vast, starting with Harris (1948) and continuing through Mee (1984), Hoffman and Maier (1984), Hogan (1987), Killick (1997), and Steil (2018).

21. To prevent the recipients from double-dipping and undercutting American influence over their policies, the United States prohibited them from concurrently drawing on the Fund.

22. Not everyone agreed that the postwar disequilibrium was accurately characterized as a dollar shortage. Contrasting perspectives include Graham (1949), Kindleberger (1950), and MacDougall (1954). Hoffmeyer (1958) lent precision to the concept. On p. 20 he explained that "the concept of a dollar shortage is another word for disequilibrium in the U.S. balance of payments either because it is not possible to restore equilibrium by acceptable means or because equilibrium is constantly being disturbed with a bias in favor of the U.S."

23. An account emphasizing the discriminatory aspect of these policies is Hieronymi (1973). Hoffmeyer (1958) analyzes the impact on U.S. export competitiveness. Related to the European Coal and Steel Community was the European Payments Union, established in 1950, through

which European countries collectively cleared their payments obligations vis-à-vis one another, facilitating the liberalization and expansion of intra-European trade (Kaplan and Schleiminger 1990; Eichengreen 1993).

24. These measures were put in place at the end of 1949. Details are in Mendershausen (1950).

25. Polak (1951), p. 1. The particular "short period" to which Polak was referring was September 1949 to mid-1951.

26. It helped that reconstruction and recovery continued apace. Even Polak acknowledged the "improved European supply position." Also helpful was a resurgent U.S. economy, whose demand for imports rose strongly from mid-1950 when the country joined the Korean War.

27. Hirschman (1960), p. 100.

28. Thus, Hirschman in the quotation just cited referred to the balance of payments, including financial flows, and not just the balance of trade.

29. Moscow Narodny Bank was declared state property in December 1917 and then nationalized and transformed into a department of the People's Bank in December 1918. In 1919 the London subsidiary, established in 1915 to facilitate trade with Russia, was reorganized as an independent bank under English law. Another version of the origins of the Eurodollar market has the Chinese government moving a portion of its dollar deposits to a Soviet financial institution in Paris following the outbreak of the Korean War to avoid having them frozen by the U.S. government (Mayer 1974; Garson 2001). Still another traces the deep origins to National City Bank opening a branch in Buenos Aires in 1914 (as described in chapter 7) and accepting dollar deposits (Zweig 1995, p. 112).

30. This imbroglio stretched on for another third of a century, until the Czech government finally agreed to compensate expropriated U.S. property owners and the United States surreptitiously flew the gold to Zurich, from where it was transferred to Prague.

31. At least they were placed out of reach of U.S. financial diplomacy, given the provisions of international law. The dollar deposits in question remained physically in the United States (insofar as financial balances can be physical). That is, Moscow Narodny Bank kept them on deposit with a U.S. correspondent bank. But because the Soviet deposits were now legally held by an English limited liability company, they were thought to be insulated from sanctions potentially applied by the United States to the USSR.

32. Triffin served with, among other agencies, the Federal Reserve Board, the IMF, the Organisation for European Economic Cooperation, and the Economic Cooperation Administration administering the Marshall Plan. Recall how we already encountered him at the end of chapter 7.

33. If one considered total foreign dollar holdings, both private and official, the problem was even worse. This total might be more appropriate insofar as private holders, while unable to convert their dollars with U.S. authorities, could exchange them for other currencies, including with their own national authorities, who might then cash them in.

34. In practice, the United States pursued various expedients to reassure central banks with heavy dollar exposures. In 1961 the United States and a consortium of European central banks established the Gold Pool. Participating central banks agreed to coordinate their purchases and sales of gold to stabilize its dollar price and to share any profits and losses (Bordo, Monnet, and

Naef 2019). Starting in 1962 the Federal Reserve negotiated swap lines to provide forward cover—an insurance guarantee—to foreign banks with unwanted dollar positions (Bordo, Humpage, and Schwartz 2014). This was the origin of the twenty-first-century swap lines discussed in chapters 10 and 11.

35. See Triffin (1964). The title of the relevant chapter, "Myth and Realities of the So-Called Gold Standard," says it all. On Belgium's troubled return to the gold standard in 1926 and its consequences, see van der Wee (2012).

36. In advancing ideas for reforming the international monetary system, Triffin acknowledged his intellectual debt to Keynes. Triffin (1957), p. 107; Maes and Pasotti (2021), p. 131.

37. Triffin (1967), p. 134.

38. Triffin (1960), p. 10.

39. This, Triffin imagined, could involve increasing the stock of IMF deposits by 3 to 5 percent a year. The Fund might augment the supply by allocating additional reserves in proportion to countries' quotas, or it might engage in expansionary open market operations (purchasing the Treasury securities of various countries) and expand its own lending activities (Federal Reserve Bank of New York 1979, p. 41).

40. The president's memo is reproduced in Johnson (1971, p. 315). Gavin (2004, p. 126) describes the constitution and deliberations of Fowler's committee.

41. *Time* (September 10, 1965).

42. Gavin (2004), p. 127. The United States regarded talk of devaluing the dollar as unhelpful, since such talk could become a self-fulfilling prophesy. There was also the fact that an increase in the gold price would disproportionately benefit Soviet Russia and apartheid South Africa, which were the two principal gold producers.

43. The Group of Ten had been established in 1962 by the governments of eight industrial countries and the central banks of two others to provide the IMF with an additional $8 billion of lendable resources.

44. Odell (1982), pp. 163–64.

45. A detailed reconstruction of the negotiations is Wilkie (2012).

46. How exactly this measure could be enforced is an interesting question, given the availability of dollar bills at U.S. banks and their ready acceptance abroad. In the event, Fowler's proposal was never pursued.

47. This step was taken in March 1968.

48. It did in fact fall below $35 for a time, before recovering to above that level.

49. Gavin (2002), p. 209; Lanoszka (2018), p. 68. Blessing's commitment was part of a larger U.S. effort, tracing back as far as 1961, to compel West Germany to offer "offset commitments," whereby it offset U.S spending on Europe's defense by purchasing a matching amount of American-produced military equipment and taking other steps to support the U.S. economy, including not converting dollars into gold. Blang (2004) describes how problems developed in the mid-1960s, when the Vietnam War strained the U.S. budget, with negative implications for the dollar. Dudley and Passell (1968) and Collins (1996) link Vietnam War spending to the weakness of the U.S. balance of payments and the dollar. As Posen (2008, pp. 88–89) notes, other German officials tempered Blessing's commitment subsequently, but there were no significant official sales of German dollar holdings until 1979.

50. Unemployment in mid-1971 was hovering around 6 percent, high for the period, though it would trend even higher in later years.

51. As recounted by John Connally in Connally and Herskowitz (1993), p. 237.

52. Subsequent authors concluded that the British were in fact asking for compensation for potential losses, not payment of the entire principal in gold. See Combs (1976), p. 218.

53. Volcker (2018), p. 70.

54. Matusow (1998), pp. 87.

55. Reston (1989), p. 405.

56. As additional prerequisites, other countries might be required to take steps to enhance the access of American exporters to their markets and agree to finance a larger share of NATO expenditures.

57. The gold window was not reopened, although most U.S. officials had believed at the time of its closure that it eventually would be reactivated. Garten (2021), p. 180.

58. See de Vries (1976), chapter 26.

59. Countries in weaker positions, such as Italy, allowed their exchange rates to decline relative to the dollar.

Chapter 9: Meet the New Boss

1. Hughes (2014), p. 144. In his diary (Ferrell 2010, p. 48), Burns voiced suspicions that the president was behind the leaks.

2. Between 1971 and 1972, the budget deficit was up slightly in absolute dollar terms, and down only marginally, by three-tenths of one percent, as a percentage of GDP.

3. In current prices, the trade gap quadrupled between 1971 and 1972. This was the notorious "J-curve," whereby a devaluation first worsens the trade balance before improving it once spending patterns and the volume of imports and export began to adjust. Contemporaries were aware of the phenomenon. Google Books' Ngram Viewer shows an up-tick in the frequency of references to the J-curve in 1971.

4. So it wrote on Senate passage of the bill (Dale 1972, p. 1). *The Times* again used identical language when the House passed the bill and sent it to the president.

5. In the more convoluted words of an IMF spokesman, the SDR "had previously been valued by reference to a fixed quantity of gold, via the par value of the U.S. dollar. [But] after 1973 par values were no longer observed." Byrne (1982), p. 31.

6. Eventually, in 1974, there would be an agreement to value the SDR with reference to a basket of currencies used widely in international transactions. But not yet.

7. Kindleberger (1976), p. 35.

8. The government required German firms borrowing abroad above certain ceilings to first obtain the approval of the Bundesbank; it also prohibited sale of fixed-interest-rate, deutschmark-denominated bonds to non-residents. See Bakker and Chapple (2002).

9. Specifically, the Japanese authorities limited such purchases to amounts sold by other foreign investors. In addition, a reserve requirement was placed on nonresident yen accounts, and controls were tightened on the receipt of advances of export proceeds. Fukao (2003) provides details.

10. It took time for the trade balance to turn around, but by 1970–71 the transformation was complete (Cairncross and Eichengreen 1983, p. 198).

11. Sandbrook (2012), p. 9.

12. Hansard, vol. 33: debated on Tuesday, March 21, 1972: Budget Statement.

13. The band was ±2.25 percent against the currencies of European Community countries that established their own regional exchange rate arrangement following the widening of bands at the Smithsonian (for more on this see below). While the UK was not yet a member of the community, it participated in the European currency arrangement.

14. Ireland left the system along with the UK, the Irish pound (as it was then known) having been pegged to sterling since its creation in 1928 and Britain remaining Ireland's most important trading partner.

15. Entering the European Monetary System and pegging the pound to the deutschmark was meant as an inflation-control strategy (Stephens 1996; James 2020b). The decision was fateful in that it led to currency overvaluation and a costly speculative attack that drove sterling out of the system in the summer of 1992 (Eichengreen 2003; Naef 2022).

16. The record figure for calendar year 1972 was released the following January. In addition to the demoralizing annual number, the report included an alarmingly large monthly deficit for December, suggesting ongoing deterioration of the trade balance. This figure was inaccurate; it was revised downward subsequently. But the damage to confidence was done. All this occurred against the backdrop of pressure on the Italian lira, which incited capital flows from Italy to Switzerland, leading the Swiss National Bank to allow the franc to appreciate out of its Smithsonian band, encouraging speculation that Germany might follow.

17. Coombs (1976), pp. 226–27.

18. Resources were in the Treasury's Exchange Stabilization Fund, created in 1934 as part of the Gold Reserve Act (as described in chapter 8) to stabilize the dollar price of gold following the conclusion of FDR's gold-buying program. The fixed dollar price of gold was now history, so the fund was used instead to finance interventions in the foreign exchange market. Paul Volcker, then at Treasury but subsequently at the Fed, noted that the central bank possessed foreign exchange of its own and was empowered by the Federal Reserve Act to intervene in the foreign exchange market by purchasing and selling trade acceptances (as described in chapter 7). But Volcker also explained that Treasury was mainly responsible for the international dimension of monetary policy, rendering the Fed reluctant to intervene over Treasury objections, since doing so would cause political problems. Volcker and Gyohten (1992), pp. 232–33.

19. This according to the Bundesbank's *Monthly Report* for March 1973. More precisely, it was the largest single-day intervention up to this time. There would be larger interventions in 1992 during the crisis of the European Monetary System (see below).

20. There were actually sixty representatives of twenty countries, for each country the finance minister, the central bank governor, and a senior civil servant. A factor in the decision to create this committee rather than deliberating within the IMF Executive Board was that the United States was feuding with IMF Managing Director Pierre-Paul Schweitzer over his criticism of the decision to close the gold window and America's Vietnam War. The managing director oversaw meetings of the Executive Board but played a less prominent role in this new committee.

21. In 1999 the Interim Committee was finally transformed into a permanent International Monetary and Financial Committee to advise the Board of Governors of the IMF on

"management and adaptation of the international monetary and financial system" (quoting a resolution of the IMF Executive Board).

22. This, in 1977, was the second time the Articles were amended, the first time having been in 1969 when the SDR was created.

23. In addition to liquidity and returns, there was a role for security concerns. Saudi Arabia invested in U.S. Treasury securities as a quid pro quo for promises of U.S. military hardware and security guarantees, as described in chapter 1. See also Wong (2016).

24. The earlier deposit inflow now being matched by a foreign lending outflow, the greenback gave back the ground it had gained at the end of 1973.

25. This refers to the change in the exchange rate on a trade-weighted basis.

26. With benefit of hindsight, Solomon (1999, p. 3) writes of a depreciation of the dollar "of near crisis proportions." Contemporary accounts dispensed with the word "near."

27. Blumenthal himself denied that he had the intent of weakening the dollar (Solomon 1981, p. 346).

28. Bordo, Humpage, and Schwartz (2015), p. 239. The Fed already had a separate swap line with the Bundesbank.

29. Greene (1984), p. 12.

30. Volcker and Gyohten (1992), p. 149.

31. An expected future change in policies might be enough—this is the so-called "signaling channel" through which foreign exchange market intervention might have lasting effects. A survey of the literature on the signaling channel is Watanabe (2010). In any case, U.S. policymakers, from Blumenthal on down, signaled to the contrary that they had no intention of changing policy.

32. See for example *Time* (November 13, 1978), pp. 18, 21.

33. Quoted in Eizenstat (2018), p. 327.

34. In addition, they increased the interest rate paid on SDRs to make holding them more attractive.

35. Among other things, there was the danger that dollars paid into the Substitution Account would depreciate against SDRs (now backed by a basket of dollars, deutschmarks, French francs, Japanese yen, and British pounds) that were the account's liabilities, and that interest on U.S. Treasury bills would be insufficient for maintaining the account's solvency. This raised delicate technical and political questions of how losses should be apportioned across countries, which officials were unable to answer (McCauley and Schenk 2015).

36. Eizenstat (2018), p. 328.

37. Clymer (1979), p. 1.

38. This famously came to be known as the "malaise" speech, although Carter never used the word.

39. In addition, they suspected Blumenthal of insufficient loyalty. The Treasury Department was responsible for investigating banking irregularities that arose in conjunction with the business affairs of Office of Management and Budget Director and presidential confidant Bert Lance. By his own account, Blumenthal remained studiously neutral in Treasury's investigation, but he was inevitably the bearer of bad news, causing White House staff to suspect him, in the secretary's own words, of "overzealousness, deliberate press leaks and scheming to harm Lance" (Blumenthal 2013, p. 300).

40. The president of the Federal Reserve Bank of New York has a permanent seat on the Federal Open Market Committee, while other Reserve Bank presidents rotate. Volcker's reputation as an inflation fighter led Carter's advisors, including Lance, to oppose his nomination on the grounds that a Volcker Fed's restrictive policies would damage the president's reelection bid, as in fact turned out to be the case.

41. This refers to the narrow effective exchange rate for the United States, which rose from an index value of 102.7 in September 1979 to 150.5 in March 1985 (sourced from the website of the Federal Reserve Bank of St. Louis).

42. Latin American countries, accustomed to importing rather than exporting capital, learned this to their chagrin. They soon found it impossible to roll over and repay their previous borrowings. The Latin American debt crisis can be said to have formally started on August 20, 1982, when Mexican Finance Minister Jesús Silva-Herzog announced a three-month moratorium on payments due on bank loans to the public sector.

43. This was precisely the argument of, among others, Sachs (1985).

44. On the profitability of momentum trades in the foreign exchange market, see Okunev and White (2003).

45. The "flood of bills" quotation is from Farnsworth (1985), p. D1.

46. Volcker and Gyohten (1992), p. 254.

47. Cohen (2000), p. 217.

48. This again refers to the narrow effective exchange rate for the United States.

49. The citation is to Dornbusch (1976). According to Google Books' Ngram Viewer, references to "overshooting" peaked in 1986, coinciding with these events.

50. The genesis of those recommendations and the Louvre negotiations are analyzed by Funabashi (1988).

51. Volcker and Gyohten (1992), p. 282.

52. To be fair, the Japanese government had already expanded fiscal policy in 1986, responding to the economic slowdown caused by the yen's post-Plaza appreciation and pressure from the United States. But this was not enough to significantly affect the country's external surplus (and the U.S. external deficit) or to slow the dollar's decline.

53. The good-luck school suggests that shocks hitting the U.S. and global economies were milder and fewer (no oil shocks or productivity slowdowns as sharp as those of 1973–74). The good-policy school would point to the adoption of inflation targeting and related improvements in the conduct of monetary policy. See Blanchard and Simon (2001); Ahmed, Levin, and Wilson (2002); and Bernanke (2004) for discussions of the competing views.

54. There was in fact a decline in the dollar share of identified foreign exchange reserves from 78.6 percent at the end of 1972 to 65.8 percent at the end of 1984, exactly matched by the increase in the combined share of deutschmarks and yen (12.8 percent). But this was almost entirely due to the United States' own reserve accumulation over the period (U.S. foreign reserves necessarily being in currencies other than the dollar), slower reserve accumulation by Germany and Japan (which traditionally held the bulk of their reserves in dollars), and faster reserve accumulation by emerging markets (which customarily held a larger share of their reserves in nondollar form). Horii (1986) concludes that no more than 1.2 percentage points of the 12.8 percentage point decline in the share of dollars in reserves reflected active diversification away from the dollar.

55. Emminger (1985), p. 19.

56. The IMF provides tabulations of de jure exchange rate arrangements in its Annual Report on Exchange Arrangements and Exchange Restrictions. While there exist alternative tabulations of de facto arrangements, all point to the dominance of dollar pegs in the late 1980s. See for example Ilzetzki, Reinhart, and Rogoff (2019), p. 616.

57. This according to the BIS triennial survey of foreign exchange activity as of April 1989. Note that foreign exchange market shares total 200 percent, given that foreign exchange transactions involve two currencies.

58. This is according to the 60th Annual Report of the BIS (1990), p. 134.

59. In fact, the effective dollar exchange rate was almost the same at the beginning of floating, in March 1973, as when the Louvre Agreement was reached in February 1987.

60. Some thought Greenspan went too far—hence popular and scholarly references to the "Greenspan put" (Bornstein and Lorenzoni 2017; Mullin 2023).

61. Rubin took over as Treasury secretary in 1995. He became known, when queried about the dollar exchange rate, for reiterating that "we believe in a strong dollar," and leaving it at that.

62. The sole exception was calendar year 1991.

63. A new SDR allocation requires approval by 85 percent of IMF voting power, giving the U.S. an effective veto, and requiring the expenditure of political capital by the U.S. administration. It took the Global Financial Crisis to break this logjam in 2009.

64. The quote is from Japanese Ministry of Finance (1999), cited in Takagi (2012, p. 75), who provides detail on measures undertaken by the authorities to promote yen internationalization.

65. Choi, Park, and Tschoegl (1996), Table 2.

66. This is like how the rapid ascent of the Chinese economy in the early decades of the twenty-first century encouraged cross-border use of that country's currency, the renminbi, by China's own firms (see chapter 10).

67. Takagi (2012), p. 83. Takagi is similarly the source of details earlier in this paragraph.

68. The estimate is for calendar year 1987 for the six largest industrial economies and OPEC members (Tavlas 1991).

69. Certain restrictions were abolished at the end of the 1980s (Tavlas 1991), but their retention for an extended period limited international use of the deutschmark.

70. This European system known as the Snake was adopted in 1972 to limit the variability of intra-European currencies following the December 1971 widening of Bretton Woods bands. The Europeans were especially averse to exchange rate volatility, recalling how beggar-thy-neighbor devaluations had fanned international tensions in the 1930s.

71. Denmark competed with Ireland in product markets (such as those for dairy), and Ireland had depreciated its exchange rate along with the UK (as noted).

72. This reflected the fact that the deutschmark was regularly the strongest currency in the European system. Observers thus referred to the EMS as a "Greater Deutschmark Area" (see, e.g., Herz and Rőger 1992).

73. Mundell (1993), p. 10.

74. Erratic exchange-rate changes also threatened the operation of the community's Common Agricultural Policy (as explained by Hill 1984) and political support for its recently established Single Market (Thygesen 2016).

75. As Delors put it, "le petit euro deviendra grand" (Grekou 2020).
76. Gros and Thygesen (1998), p. 373.
77. Bergsten (1997), p. 83.
78. Pollard (2001), p. 17.
79. This as of March 1999.
80. Recall again that a 35 percent share is one-sixth of the global total, since two currencies are involved in every foreign exchange transaction (since currency shares sum to 200 percent). The one place where an increase in use was noticeable was international bond issuance, where the euro gained ground on earlier currencies (Moss 2012).
81. This was argued at the outset by, among others, Henning (1996).
82. Statistics here are from the European Central Bank's June 2025 report on the international role of the euro (ECB 2024). This was the twenty-fifth such annual report, a regularity that is itself indicative of the hopes of European officials that their currency might assume a larger global role.
83. Again, foreign exchange market shares sum to 200 percent, since two currencies are involved in each transaction.
84. This program was known as Outright Monetary Transactions (since the ECB was prepared to purchase bonds on the market "outright"). In the event, it never proved necessary to activate the program, its announcement being enough.

Chapter 10: Outside Options

1. This as of early 2025. A fourth country, Austria, was rated AAA by Morningstar DBRS but not by other rating agencies.
2. Restrictive mandates and convention prevent central banks and private institutions from holding the sub-investment-grade bonds of other euro area countries.
3. The European Commission acknowledged this problem when it launched its capital markets union project (European Commission 2015). But progress has been slow, given the reluctance of banks and securities exchanges to open their national financial preserves to international competition.
4. There is also the awkward fact that any European initiative to ramp up military spending in support of Ukraine is likely to involve non-EU countries such as the UK. Both the UK desire to opt in and the preference of certain EU countries to opt out make it more likely that resources and government guarantees of borrowings on the markets will be pooled by a "special purpose financial vehicle" rather than a permanent EU or euro area fund.
5. See Zhou (2009). Some would date the internationalization drive to 2004, when banks in Hong Kong were allowed to offer deposits, currency exchange, remittance, and credit card services in renminbi to individual clients.
6. There is a large literature on these initiatives and on renminbi internationalization more broadly. A sampling is Zhaodong and Yong (2014), Eichengreen and Kawai (2015), and Li (2015).
7. Whereas the Stock Connect enables two-way trading between the Hong Kong and Shanghai markets, the Bond Connect initially handled only northbound trading, that is, overseas investors buying and selling bonds on the mainland. Southbound trading was added in 2021.

8. Like most regulatory initiatives, success was mixed; there was a notable spike in financial volatility in 2015, for example. But Chinese regulators stayed the course.

9. Currently there are thirty-four offshore clearing banks in thirty-two countries. Certain of the renminbi clearing banks in question are foreign banks rather than foreign subsidiaries of Chinese banks. In the United States the two official renminbi clearing banks are JPMorgan-Chase and a subsidiary of Bank of China.

10. In 2010, in addition, China, Japan, South Korea, and the ten members of the Association of Southeast Asian Nations agreed to the Chiang Mai Initiative Multilateralization, under which participants established a multilateral network of currency swaps. The earlier Chiang Mai Initiative, initialed in 2000, was a system of bilateral swaps.

11. Indirect participants in CIPS still rely on SWIFT to send payment instructions to the system's direct participants, notwithstanding China's efforts to develop its own messaging system (Eichengreen 2022).

12. Figures are from CIPS's official website, accessible at https://www.cips.com.cn/en/index/index.html.

13. Figures are for the end of 2023, from Brüggen, Georgiadis, and Mehl (2025).

14. This is according to SWIFT's RMB Tracker for June 2025 (SWIFT 2025), which reported data for May.

15. Again, these figures summed across all countries add up to 200 percent, since two currencies are involved in every foreign exchange transaction.

16. Percentages here refer to "allocated" reserves—that is, those for which a government discloses information on their currency composition. In the fourth quarter of 2024, about 7 percent of the reserves of IMF member countries were unallocated (unidentified).

17. See Bahaj and Reis (2022), p. 111. Argentina is an example of a country whose poor credit and troubled economy prevented it from accessing international capital markets, leading it to draw on its renminbi swap line instead (Arnold 2023).

18. See Embassy of China (2023). The other twenty-six are Pakistan, North Korea, Timor-Leste, Russia, the Philippines, Kazakhstan, Kyrgyzstan, Cambodia, Laos, Maldives, Malaysia, Mongolia, Bangladesh, Myanmar, Nepal, Sri Lanka, Tajikistan, Thailand, Turkmenistan, Brunei, South Korea, Uzbekistan, Singapore, India, Japan, and Indonesia. A notable entry on this list is Russia, which has been drawing closer to China geopolitically and which, given Western sanctions, now uses the renminbi for the bulk of its cross-border transactions. Obviously, India does not qualify as small, while Singapore, South Korea, and Japan are developed rather than developing. Still, none of these large and/or developed countries qualifies as a close geopolitical ally of China.

19. Thus, the PBoC's governing law does not specify a term of office for officials or require citation of reasons or cause for their removal. As Jin (2022, pp. 232) puts it, "the State Council may change leaders at will due to political factors, which provides a legal loophole for the State Council to interfere with the PBC's [sic] functions."

20. Chahrour and Valchev (2023) model this scenario.

21. The trend is detailed in Arslanalp, Eichengreen, and Simpson-Bell (2022).

22. This refers to spreads against the U.S. dollar, since the issue is the cost of exchanging dollars for the currency in question.

23. Heath and Whitelaw (2011), p. 44.

24. On the (generally positive) impact of algorithmic trading on market liquidity, see Hendershott, Jones, and Menkveld (2011) and Hendershott and Riordan (2012). Looking ahead, the latest iterations of artificial intelligence may deepen market liquidity yet further and move currency trading and reserve holding in the same direction. Abbas, Cohen, Grolleman, and Mosk (2024) speculate about the impact of AI on financial markets spreads and efficiency, along with other financial variables.

25. The basket currency proposal is laid out in Nogueira-Batista (2023).

26. Or, for that matter, any other country's banking system.

27. The GENIUS (Guiding and Establishing National Innovation for U.S. Stablecoins) Act passed by the U.S. Congress and signed by President Trump in July 2025 authorizes U.S. financial regulators to license not only banks but also tech companies, retailers and others to issue stablecoins, so long as they meet certain qualifications. Amazon and Walmart, among others, have expressed interest.

28. The GENIUS Act provides for exactly this kind of regulation.

29. Other current use cases include illicit transactions such as tax evasion and money laundering, which strict regulation could—in principle—eliminate.

30. Moreover, insofar as most stablecoins are dollar linked and backed by the issuers' holdings of U.S. Treasury securities, their more widespread adoption would only reinforce the U.S. Treasury's ability to borrow at a lower cost than otherwise.

31. The Atlantic Council maintains a CBDC tracker at https://www.atlanticcouncil.org/cbdctracker/, where these initiatives can be followed.

32. In 2012, to remove the stigma attached to the term "no frills," these were renamed Basic Savings Bank Deposit Accounts (BSBDAs). In 2014 the Prime Minister's People's Wealth Scheme charged public sector banks with offering zero-balance, low-cost bank accounts to rural residents. The government also launched a mobile app enabling smartphone users to locate bank branches, ATMs, and post office banking facilities near their villages.

33. This points to yet another possibility for enhancing the efficiency of cross-border payments, namely linking fast retail payments systems such as Singapore's PayNow and Malaysia's DUITNOW. There in fact exists a network of such linked systems; see Minesso, Mehl, Bagur, and Vansteenkiste (2025). Distributed ledger technology (discussed further below) could be used to boost the speed and efficiency of such systems. But these systems rely on commercial bank money, which is only good as the commercial bank providing the payment, whereas CBDCs are central bank money, with attendant advantages in terms of financial stability and counterparty risk (Mayer 2024).

34. An exception was in late 2023 when state-owned PetroChina International Co. bought an undisclosed amount of crude oil from an undisclosed foreign seller using a digital wallet at the state-owned Bank of Communications (Central Banking 2023). The CBDC collected by the foreign supplier may still be in a digital wallet at the Bank of Communications, in the same manner that international oil transactions settled in dollars result in a credit to the U.S. bank account of the seller. Or it might have been converted into another currency and repatriated, with the approval of the authorities responsible for China's capital controls. The e-CNY also provides further evidence that there may be less progress on renminbi internationalization than

meets the eye. As of mid-2023, the e-CNY accounted for only 0.16 percent of the stock of high-powered money (central bank reserves and cash in circulation). Chinese consumers prefer the commercial apps and wallets of Alipay and WeChat Pay, since these provide a one-stop shop for not just payments but also the purchase of train tickets, parking spaces, and the like. That these additional services are not something central banks are likely to offer is another reason promoting widespread use of CBDCs may be an uphill fight.

35. This assumes of course that a Chinese government-run payment system is welcomed by foreign authorities. It would not be so welcomed were the e-CNY seen as a potential mechanism for surveillance, in the manner of Huawei telephonics equipment, or as a vehicle for money laundering or busting sanctions.

36. One can also imagine retail CBDCs linked to one another on a common platform. Project Icebreaker, involving the central banks of Norway, Sweden, and Israel, has conducted experiments along these lines (Reslow, Soderberg, and Tsuda 2024). In practice, however, this approach would raise technical and governance issues, which are discussed below in the context of wholesale CBDCs.

37. Auer, Haene, and Holden (2021) describe these alternatives.

38. Validators are nodes on a blockchain that verify transactions, authorizing their verification. On public blockchains, validators are compensated in proportion to the amount of work or computing they do (these are known, for straightforward reasons, as "proof of work" mechanisms) or the amount of their holdings of the associated digital currency ("proof of stake" mechanisms). Project mBridge is a private blockchain on which only central banks function as validators. The PBoC has developed what it calls the Dashing Protocol, which requires less validation for smaller transactions, enhancing the efficiency of this process. It is anticipated that Project mBridge will eventually deploy zero-knowledge proofs (Goldwasser, Micali, and Rackoff 1989), cryptographic means of validating information without showing it, eliminating the need for validator nodes.

39. Mayer (2024) describes this option.

40. Note that this more ambitious automated alternative resembles the operation of algorithmically backed stablecoins, where in lieu of collateral an algorithm mints or burns the coin in question in response to deviations from the stablecoin's parity value. The record of algorithmically backed stablecoins is not reassuring.

41. Rosa and Larsen (2024), pp. 186–87.

42. This was noted in reporting by Benrath-Wright, Schroers, and Randow (2024).

43. Russian Finance Minister Anton Siluanov had already described the proposal earlier in the year.

44. For discussion see Long (2024).

45. Digital enthusiasts have noted that the Fed has been slow off the mark, and that its reluctance to move faster in developing a CBDC could jeopardize the dollar's international standing, as other central banks speed ahead in creating digital currencies and building shared platforms. Although the Federal Reserve System (specifically the Federal Reserve Bank of Boston) is exploring CBDC technology, it is moving slowly, given congressional suspicion of big government, and of CBDCs on privacy and confidentiality grounds. In addition, there is the opposition of the cryptocurrency industry, which sees a central bank-backed digital currency

as unwelcome competition and has a friend in the White House. Fast or slow is not the issue, however. Even if the Fed moved faster, issuing a CBDC for use in wholesale transactions and becoming a full partner in a platform such as Project mBridge, the latter could still offer other countries the ability to complete bilateral transactions in their respective currencies at the same speed and at or near the same cost without going through the dollar.

46. See BIS (2023), pp. 8–9.

47. The European Central Bank, not exactly the central bank of a G-10 country but closely aligned, now participates in that governance.

Chapter 11: Our Currency, Our Problem

1. Gourinchas, Rey, and Sauzet (2019) explain the logic. The demand for safe assets is proportional to the growth of the rest of the world. The ability of the United States to supply them, in contrast, is limited by the growth of its fiscal revenues, which provide the backing for U.S. Treasuries, revenues that are proportional to the more slowly growing U.S. economy.

2. Whereas the U.S. share of global GDP is down to 26 percent, China's share at current prices and market exchange rates is pushing 17 percent. Figures here are for 2025, from the IMF's *World Economic Outlook* database. Economists sometimes prefer international prices (purchasing power parities) for comparisons across countries, since local prices vary (the prices of nontraded goods and services will be lower in low-income countries). This makes the comparison even more striking: at purchasing power parities China's share is 19 percent, where that of the United States is just 15 percent. Arguably, market exchange rates and prices are preferable for present purposes, since international trade in goods and services is what is relevant for international currency status, and the prices of internationally traded goods and services have a strong tendency to converge across countries. Comparisons here are for aggregate as opposed to per capita GDP, since a small economy is unlikely to engage in large volumes of cross-border trade and finance even when its residents have high incomes. The importance of economic scale for international currency status may now be changing, however, as discussed in the preceding chapter.

3. Again, the 40 percent figure for 1960 is at current prices, this time from the World Bank's data bank.

4. On the connection between rising concentration and falling productivity growth, see Aghion, Bergeaud, Boppart, Klenow, and Li (2023). Facts about declining business dynamism in the United States are from Philippon (2021) and Akcigit and Ates (2023). Insofar as these ills are causally connected to the rise in market concentration, a vigorous competition policy might reverse declining business dynamism. But a robust antitrust policy is not something to which the United States is obviously inclined, at least currently.

5. An illuminating if not especially encouraging study of the impact of U.S. military spending during World War II is Field (2022). Saeed (2025) analyzes the experience of 133 countries, distinguishing the impact of military spending from other conflict-related economic impacts, and finds negative effects on growth. The published version of the Draghi Report referred to in the text is European Commission (2024).

6. In China, demographic stagnation also reflects the legacy of the country's one child policy. But the fact that fertility rates have fallen across the emerging-market world suggests that economic factors, such as higher incomes, are strongly at work.

7. China, in contrast, accounts for fully 14 percent of global exports.

8. Smith (1776 [1981]), Para. IV.5.36.

9. Debt in the hands of the public, as opposed to all debt outstanding, is the relevant metric, since the difference is made up of debt held by governmental entities, such as the Social Security Trust Fund, on which the government is paying interest to itself.

10. This is on the optimistic assumption that interest rates on 10-year Treasury notes remain steady over the period and that interest rates on all federal debt rise only modestly (CBO 2025). More pessimistic assumptions about the evolution of interest rates lead to more dire scenarios. As for the deficit as a share of GDP, the CBO's forecast shows this rising from 5.6 percent of GDP in 2024 to 8.5 percent of GDP in 2054 due to a combination of rising entitlement spending and rising interest payments.

11. "Fiscal dominance" is the technical term for this pressure on the monetary authority to aid the government in servicing the debt (Sargent and Wallace 1981; Leeper 1991).

12. Gómez-Cram, Kung, and Lustig (2024) provide theory and evidence on this process.

13. Committee for a Responsible Federal Budget (2024, 2025) costs Trump's campaign proposals and the One Big Beautiful Bill [Budget] Act of 2025.

14. Cross-country comparisons and trends in political polarization are described by Boxell, Gentzkow, and Shapiro (2024).

15. Arslanalp and Eichengreen (2024) study episodes when high debts have been stabilized and significantly reduced. They find that low levels of political polarization, together with a growing economy, are the main variables distinguishing sustained debt reductions.

16. Grechyna (2016) describes the data used by social scientists in international comparisons of political polarization. She finds that social trust and income inequality are the two robust determinants of political polarization, an observation that helps one understand why the United States stands out.

17. In addition, the Federal Reserve Bank of New York holds substantial amounts of monetary gold on behalf of foreign governments and central banks, more on which below.

18. These 9,400 sanctions on governments, banks, firms, and individuals were part of thirty-seven national sanctions programs (U.S. Treasury 2021). Mulder (2022, p. 293) refers to the United States as the world's "most avid user" of economic sanctions.

19. As for why the United States has resorted increasingly to economic and financial sanctions, one factor may be growing economic integration and financialization of the economy, which increases the power of sanctions. Another may be America's reluctance to commit troops; this leaves sanctions as the alternative to doing nothing. Assertions that the United States is unable to resist recourse to sanctions may be overdrawn. U.S. officials are aware that excessive resort to sanctions could accelerate movement away from the dollar, knowledge that encourages those officials to limit recourse to the weapon. See Singh (2024) and Agence France Presse (2023).

20. On the impact of sanctions on the accumulation of gold by central banks, and the distinctive behavior of emerging markets, see Arslanalp, Eichengreen, and Simpson-Bell (2023).

21. Using historical data, Arslanalp, Eichengreen, and Simpson-Bell (2023) document a small effect of sanctions on the share of reserves held in gold. In other words, only a small portion of recent central bank gold purchases are obviously attributable to actual or preemptive sanctions busting. The balance reflects a combination of central banking tradition and portfolio-diversification motives.

22. The first episode is described by Steinhauser and Bariyo (2019), the second by Pourmohsen (2022).

23. There also exist reports of Russia using gold bars to purchase military equipment from Iran and North Korea (Kennedy, Grossfeld, Wolford, and Kenchington 2024), but no details are available.

24. Supreme Court of the United States (2025), p. 2. The quotation from the three dissenting justices cited immediately below is from the same document.

25. Class C directors, who represent the public, are appointed by the Federal Reserve Board. Class A and B directors, who represent member banks and the public, respectively, are elected by member banks of the district in question.

26. Discussion is in Sandbu (2025).

27. Lighthizer (2024, p. 317) refers to an "adjustable fee" that would rise in periods of large-scale foreign purchases of U.S. securities.

28. This document, Miran (2024a), dates from November 2024.

29. The efficacy of such measures is unclear. McCauley (2025) argues that official reserve managers and other investors could simply shift their dollars offshore to custodians in Europe, such as Euroclear and Clearstream, preventing the U.S. Treasury from tracing the beneficial owner. Perhaps for related reasons, China has already increased its reliance on such offshore custodians.

30. On this see Miran (2024b).

31. The same was true of other measures of market dysfunctionality such as declining order book depth (the average quantities of securities available for sale or purchase). See Duffie et al. (2023) and Fleming (2023).

32. An explanation for this plumbing problem is the large volume of additional Treasury issuance together with tightened bank capital regulation following the Global Financial Crisis. New regulations constrain the ability of bank dealers to acquire and hold inventories of Treasury bonds to meet fluctuating demands. While there has been a tendency for hedge funds and high-speed traders to step into the market as additional sources of liquidity, these entities are highly leveraged, a characteristic that can amplify price volatility, as well as being less transparent than banks. A compact discussion of Treasury market structure and dynamics is Ashcroft and Mercer (2025). This is not to question the case for strengthened bank regulation but to observe that even when bank regulation is effective—most of all when bank regulation is effective—excessive Treasury issuance can undermine the international role of the dollar by eroding Treasury market liquidity and stability, quite apart from questions raised about debt sustainability and the safe-asset attribute of the dollar.

33. In the 2023 episode, the Fed relied instead on lending directly to the banks to avoid forcing them to liquidate their Treasury holdings.

34. Das, Gopinath, Kim, and Stein (2022) show that foreign central banks anticipate this need, accumulating dollar reserves when local corporations incur obligations denominated in dollars. But holding additional dollar reserves is costly, given that the interest rate earned on U.S. Treasuries is below that paid by emerging markets on their own sovereign debt. Hence the need in addition for dollar swap lines.

35. One might think that foreign central banks, and the commercial banks and corporations that are their clients, could simply obtain those dollars on the foreign exchange market, outside

the United States if necessary, when strained conditions in the United States leave dollars in short supply. Here too, however, tightened regulation following the Global Financial Crisis is an obstacle. Central banks typically obtain dollars by borrowing foreign currency offshore and converting this into U.S. dollars using swap contracts (that is, converting the foreign currency into dollars in the spot market and simultaneously entering a forward contract to convert them back into the foreign currency at a future date). In a liquidity crunch, however, the cost of synthetic borrowing, as this practice is known, can shoot up, given the narrowness of offshore and swap markets and regulations limiting the scope of those markets.

36. The value of dollar swaps on the Fed's balance sheet rose from essentially zero at the beginning of March 2020 to $160 billion on March 19 and almost $450 billion by the end of April. See Davis and Sagnanert (2024). March 19 was nine days after regulators intervened to close Silicon Valley Bank. In addition to swap lines, in March 2020 the FOMC created a Foreign and International Monetary Authorities (FIMA) Repo Facility, enabling foreign central banks to sell U.S. Treasuries to the Fed overnight in exchange for cash, together with an agreement to repurchase them the next day. Applications to utilize this facility are similarly subject to the approval of the Federal Reserve (Choi, Goldberg, Lerman, and Ravazzolo 2022, p. 102).

37. Thus, Miran (2024a) points to the international role of the dollar and U.S. international security arrangements as global public goods for which the country is inadequately compensated.

38. See the reporting in Martinuzzi, Aguado, Koranyi, Spezzati, and O'Donnell (2025).

39. Cassetta (2022) shows that the provision of dollar swap lines is positively associated with geopolitical alignment with the United States as measured by the alignment of votes in the United Nations General Assembly.

40. McDowell (2023), p. 42.

41. U.S. defense spending has trended steadily downward from 14 percent of GDP during the Korean War to 10 percent in the second half of the 1950s and barely 3.5 percent today, reflecting these pressures. This otherwise steady trend was interrupted by the Vietnam War, for a second time in the Reagan years, and for a third time during America's early twenty-first-century involvement in wars in Afghanistan and Iraq. But the basic point stands.

REFERENCES

Abbas, Nassira, Charles Cohen, Dirk Jan Grolleman, and Benjamin Mosk (2024), "Artificial Intelligence can Make Markets More Efficient—and More Volatile," *IMF Blog*, October 15, https://www.imf.org/en/Blogs/Articles/2024/10/15/artificial-intelligence-can-make-markets-more-efficient-and-more-volatile.

Abrahams, Paul (1976), *The Foreign Expansion of American Finance and its Relationship to the Foreign Economic Policies of the United States, 1907–1921*, New York: Arno Press.

Abrams, Burton and James Butkiewicz (2017), "The Political Economy of Wage and Price Controls: Evidence from the Nixon Tapes," *Public Choice* 170, pp. 63–78.

Accominotti, Olivier (2012), "London Merchant Banks, the Central European Panic, and the Sterling Crisis of 1931," *The Journal of Economic History* 72, pp. 1–43.

Accominotti, Olivier, Delio Lucena-Piquero, and Stefano Ugolini (2021), "The Origination and Distribution of Money Market Instruments: Sterling Bills of Exchange during the First Globalization," *Economic History Review* 74, pp. 892–921.

Accominotti, Olivier and Stefano Ugolini (2020), "International Trade Finance from the Origins to the Present: Market Structures, Regulation and Governance," in *The Oxford Handbook of Institutions of International Economic Governance and Market Regulation*, edited by Eric Brousseau, Jean-Michel Glachant, and Jérôme Sgard, Oxford: Oxford University Press.

Adam, Marc (2020), "Liquidating Bankers' Acceptances: International Crisis, Doctrinal Conflict and American Exceptionalism in the Federal Reserve 1913–1932," Economics Discussion Paper No. 2020/4, School of Business & Economics, Freie Universität Berlin.

Adinolfi, Joseph (2024), "Reports of the Petrodollar System's Demise are 'Fake News'—Here's Why," *MarketWatch* (June 17), https://www.marketwatch.com/story/reports-of-the-petrodollar-systems-demise-are-fake-news-heres-why-4e712804.

Agence France Presse (2023), "Yellen Says Sanctions May Risk Hegemony of US Dollar," *Agence France Presse*, April 16, https://www.barrons.com/news/yellen-says-sanctions-may-risk-hegemony-of-us-dollar-479c564f.

Aghion, Philippe, Antonin Bergeaud, Timo Boppart, Peter Klenow, and Huiyu Li (2023), "A Theory of Falling Growth and Rising Rents," *Review of Economic Studies* 90, pp. 2675–702.

Ahmed, Shaghil, Andrew Levin, and Beth Anne Wilson (2002), "Recent U.S. Macroeconomic Stability: Good Policies, Good Practice, or Good Luck?" International Finance Discussion Paper No. 2002-740, Washington, D.C.: Board of Governors of the Federal Reserve System (July).

Aitkin, John (2005), *The Foreign Exchange Market of London: Development Since 1900*, London: Routledge.

Akcigit, Ufuk and Sina Ates (2023), "What Happened to US Business Dynamism?" *Journal of Political Economy* 131, pp. 2059–124.

Alfani, Guido (2023), *As Gods Among Men: A History of the Rich in the West*, Princeton: Princeton University Press.

Alfani, Guido and Francesco Ammannati (2017), "Long-Term Trends in Inequality: The Case of the Florentine State, c. 1300–1800," *Economic History Review* 70, pp. 1072–102.

Arnold, Vincient (2023), "Argentina: Emergency Liquidity Support through Chinese Central Bank Swap Line and Qatari SDR Loan," Program on Financial Stability, Yale School of Management (August).

Arslanalp, Serkan and Barry Eichengreen (2024), "Living with High Public Debt," in *Structural Shifts in the Global Economy*, Federal Reserve Bank of Kansas City, , Kansas City, MO: Federal Reserve Bank of Kansas City.

Arslanalp, Serkan, Barry Eichengreen, and Chima Simpson-Bell (2022), "The Stealth Erosion of Dollar Dominance and the Rise of Nontraditional Reserve Currencies," *Journal of International Economics* 138, https://www.sciencedirect.com/science/article/abs/pii/S0022199622000885.

Arslanalp, Serkan, Barry Eichengreen, and Chima Simpson-Bell (2023), "Gold as International Reserves: A Barbarous Relic No More?" *Journal of International Economics* 145, https://www.sciencedirect.com/science/article/abs/pii/S0022199623001083.

Ashcroft, Merlene and Julian Mercer (2025), "Preserving the Safe Haven Attributes of US Treasury Markets," *American Journal of Management and Economics Innovations* 7, pp. 1–7.

Auer, Raphael, Philipp Haene, and Henry Holden (2021), "Multi-CBDC Arrangements and the Future of Cross-Border Payments," Bank for International Settlements Paper No. 115 (March).

Avaro, Maylis (2024), "Zombie International Currency: The Pound Sterling 1945–71," *The Journal of Economic History* 48, pp. 917–52.

Bagehot, Walter (1873), *Lombard Street: A Description of the Money Market*, London: Henry S. King & Co.

Bahaj, Saleem and Ricardo Reis (2022), "The Workings of Liquidity Lines Between Central Banks," in *Research Handbook of Financial Markets*, edited by Refet Gurkaynak and Jonathan Wright, Cheltenham: Edward Elgar Publishing.

Bakewell, Peter (1994), "The First Refining Mills in Potosí: Design and Construction," in *In Quest of Mineral Wealth: Aboriginal and Colonial Mining and Metallurgy in Spanish America*, edited by Alan Craig and Robert West, Baton Rouge: Louisiana State University Press.

Bakker, Age and Bryan Chapple (2002), "Advanced Country Experiences with Capital Account Liberalization," IMF Occasional Paper 2002/009 (September).

Baldassarri, Monica and Stefano Locatelli (2018), "Genoa, Florence and the Mediterranean: New Perspectives on the Return to Gold in the 13th Century," *Revue Numismatique* 175, pp. 433–75.

Ball, Michael and David Sunderland (2001), *An Economic History of London 1800–1914*, London: Routledge.

Balmuth, Miriam (1980), "Money before Coinage," in *Coins: An Illustrated Survey, 650 BC to the Present Day*, edited by Martin Jessop Price, London: Methuen.

Bank of England (1969), "The Bank of England Note: A Short History," *Bank of England Quarterly Bulletin* 11, pp. 211–22.

Bank for International Settlements (1990), *60th Annual Report*, Basel: Bank for International Settlements.

Bank for International Settlements (2022), "Triennial Central Bank Survey of Foreign Exchange and Over-the-Counter Derivatives Markets," Basel: Bank for International Settlements (November).

Bank for International Settlements, Innovation Hub (2023), "Project mBridge Update: Experimenting with a Multi-CBDC Platform for Cross-Border Payments," Hong Kong: Bank for International Settlements (October).

Bankson, Marjory (1971), "The Isolationism of Senator Charles W. Tobey," Master's thesis, University of Alaska (June).

Barnard, Seth (2018), "The Social History of Early Roman Coinage," *Journal of Roman Studies* 108, pp. 1–26.

Baster, Albert Stephen James (1935), *The International Banks*, London: P. S. King & Son.

Baster, Albert Stephen James (1937), "The International Acceptance Market," *American Economic Review* 27, pp. 294–301.

Belfast Monthly Magazine (1811), "The Examination of Thomas Richardson, esq.," *Belfast Monthly Magazine* (September), pp. 192–98.

Bell, Adrian, Chris Brooks, and Tony Moore (2009), "Interest in Medieval Accounts: Evidence from England, 1272–1340," *History* 94, pp. 411–33.

Benrath-Wright, Bastian, Mark Schroers, and Jana Randow (2024), "BIS Debates Ending Project Eyed by Putin to Undermine Dollar," *Bloomberg* (October 28), https://www.bloomberg.com/news/articles/2024-10-28/bis-debates-ending-project-eyed-by-putin-to-undermine-dollar.

Bergier, Jean-Francois (1979), "From the Fifteenth Century in Italy to the Sixteenth Century in Germany: A New Banking Concept?" in *The Dawn of Modern Banking*, edited by Robert Lopez, New Haven: Yale University Press.

Bergsten, C. Fred (1997), "The Dollar and the Euro," *Foreign Affairs* 76, pp. 83–95.

Bernanke, Ben (2004), "The Great Moderation," Remarks by Governor Ben Bernanke at the Meetings of the Eastern Economic Association, Washington, D.C. (February 20), https://www.federalreserve.gov/boarddocs/speeches/2004/20040220/.

Bernardi, Aurelio (1970), "The Economic Problems of the Roman Empire at the Time of its Decline," in *The Economic Decline of Empires*, edited by Carlo Cipolla, London: Methuen.

Berre, Stein and Paul Kosmetatos (2024), "Anglo-Dutch Financial Connections and Contrasts in the Late Eighteenth Century: The Amsterdam Phase of the 1772–3 Credit Crisis," *Economic History Review* 77, pp. 1–27.

Best, Gary (1972), "Financing a Foreign War: Jacob H. Schiff and Japan, 1904–05," *American Jewish Historical Quarterly* 61, pp. 313–24.

Blanchard, Olivier and John Simon (2001), "The Long and Large Decline in U.S. Output Volatility," *Brookings Papers on Economic Activity* 1, pp. 135–64.

Blang, Eugenie (2004), "A Reappraisal of Germany's Vietnam Policy, 1963–1966: Ludwig Erhard's Response to America's War in Vietnam," *German Studies Review* 27, pp. 341–60.

Blankinship, Khalid Yahya (1994), *The End of the Jihâd State: The Rein of Hisham Ibn 'Abd Al-Malik and the Collapse of the Umayyads*, Albany: State University of New York Press.

Bloomfield, Arthur (1950), *Capital Imports and the American Balance of Payments, 1934–39*, Chicago: University of Chicago Press.

Bloomfield, Arthur (1959), *Monetary Policy under the International Gold Standard: 1880–1914*, New York: Federal Reserve Bank of New York.

Blumenthal, W. Michael (2013), *From Exile to Washington: A Memoir of Leadership in the Twentieth Century*, New York: Overlook.

Board of Governors of the Federal Reserve System (1943), *Banking and Monetary Statistics, 1914–1941*, Washington, D.C.: Board of Governors of the Federal Reserve System.

Bolialian, Mariano (2023), "The Silver of Potosí, 1580–1630: The Beating and Pumping of One of the Hearts of Early Globalization," in , *Potosí in the Global Silver Age (16th–19th Centuries)*, edited by Rossana Barragán and Paula Zagalsky, Leiden: Brill.

Bolt, Wilko, Jon Frost, Hyun Song Shin, and Peter Wierts (2023), "The Bank of Amsterdam and the Limits of Fiat Money," Working Paper No. 1065, Bank for International Settlements (November).

Bordo, Michael, Owen Humpage, and Anna Schwartz (2014), "The Evolution of the Federal Reserve Swap Lines Since 1962," Working Paper No. 20755, National Bureau of Economic Research (December).

Bordo, Michael and Finn Kydland (1995), "The Gold Standard As a Rule: An Essay in Exploration," *Explorations in Economic History* 32, pp. 423–64.

Bordo, Michael, Eric Monnet, and Alain Naef (2019), "The Gold Pool (1961–1968) and the Fall of the Bretton Woods System: Lessons for Central Bank Cooperation," *The Journal of Economic History* 79, pp. 1027–59.

Borer, Mary Cathcart (1977), *The City of London: A History*, New York: David McKay.

Born, Karl Erich (1977), *International Banking in the 19th and 20th Centuries*, Oxford: Berg Publishers.

Bornstein, Gideon and Guido Lorenzoni (2017), "Moral Hazard Misconceptions: The Case of the Greenspan Put," Working Paper No. 24050, National Bureau of Economic Research (November).

Boughton, James (2001), *Silent Revolution: The International Monetary Fund 1979–1989*, Washington, D.C.: IMF.

Boughton, James (2021), *Harry White and the American Creed: How a Federal Bureaucrat Created the Modern Global Economy (and Failed to Get the Credit)*, New Haven: Yale University Press.

Boxell, Levi, Matthew Gentzkow, and Jesse Shapiro (2024), "Cross-Country Trends in Affective Polarization," *Review of Economics and Statistics* 106, pp. 557–65.

Boxer, Charles (1970), "The Dutch Economic Decline," in *The Economic Decline of Empires*, edited by Carlo Cipolla, London: Methuen.

Bresson, Alain (2016), *The Making of the Ancient Greek Economy: Institutions, Markets and Growth in the City-States*, Princeton: Princeton University Press.

Brezis, Elise (1995), "Foreign Capital Flows in the Century Before Waterloo: New Estimates, Controlled Conjectures," *Economic History Review* 48, pp. 46–67.

Bridges, Mary (2024), *Dollars and Dominion: US Bankers and the Making of a Superpower*, Princeton: Princeton University Press.

Broadberry, Stephen, Bruce Campbell, Alexander Klein, Mark Overton, and Bas van Leeuwen (2015), *British Economic Growth 1270–1870*, Cambridge: Cambridge University Press.

Broz, Lawrence (1997), *The International Origins of the Federal Reserve System*, Ithaca, NY: Cornell University Press.

Brucker, Gene (1983), *Renaissance Florence*, Berkeley: University of California Press.

Brüggen, Anja, Georgios Georgiadis, and Arnaud Mehl (2025), "Global Trade Invoicing Patterns: New Insights and the Influence of Geopolitics," in *The International Role of the Euro*, Frankfurt: European Central Bank.

Buchan, Alastair (1960), *The Spare Chancellor: The Life of Walter Bagehot*, East Lansing, Michigan: Michigan State University Press.

Bücher, Karl (1893 [1919]), *Die Entstehung der Volkswirtschaft*, Tübingen: H. Laupp.

Bucknill, John (1931), *The Coins of the Dutch East Indies: An Introduction to the Study of the Series*, London: Spink & Son Ltd.

Bullard, Melissa Meriam (1980), *Filippo Strozzi and the Medici: Favor and Finance in Sixteenth-Century Florence and Rome*, Cambridge: Cambridge University Press,

Bulow, Jeremy and Kenneth Rogoff (1989), "A Constant Recontracting Model of Sovereign Debt," *Journal of Political Economy* 97, pp. 155–78.

Burgess, W. Randolph (1929), "The Money Market in 1928," *Review of Economics and Statistics* 11, pp. 19–25.

Burk, Kathleen (1992), "Money and Power: The Shift from Great Britain to the United States," in *Finance and Financiers in European History, 1880–1960*, edited by Youssef Cassis, Cambridge: Cambridge University Press.

Burnett, Andrew (1980), "Rome and the Hellenistic World," in *Coins: An Illustrated Survey: 650 BC to the Present Day*, edited by Martin Jessop Price, London: Methuen.

Busschers, J. (1999), *The Mexican Pieces of Eight and their Domination in South-East Asia: A Historic Survey of More than Three Centuries of a Trading Coin*, Driebergen, Netherlands: ONS Press.

Butcher, Kevin (2010), "Debasement and the Decline of Rome," unpublished manuscript, University of Warwick, https://warwick.ac.uk/fac/arts/classics/intranets/staff/butcher/debasement_and_decline.pdf.

Butcher, Kevin and Matthew Ponting (2015a), *The Metallurgy of Roman Silver Coinage from the Reform of Nero to the Reform of Trajan*, Cambridge: Cambridge University Press.

Butcher, Kevin and Matthew Ponting (2015b), "The Reforms of Trajan and the End of the Pre-Neronian Denarius," *Annali dell'Instituto Italiano di Numismatica* 61, pp. 21–42.

Byrne, William (1982), "Evolution of the SDR, 1974–81: Changes in the Basket, Interest Rate, and Use of the SDR," *Finance and Development* 19 (September), pp. 31–35.

Caballero, Ricardo, Emmanuel Farhi, and Pierre-Olivier Gourinchas (2017), "The Safe Assets Shortage Conundrum," *Journal of Economic Perspectives* 31, pp. 29–46.

Cairncross, Alec and Barry Eichengreen (1983), *Sterling in Decline: The Devaluations of 1931, 1949 and 1967*, Oxford: Blackwell.

Calomiris, Charles, Marc Flandreau, and Luc Laeven (2016), "Political Foundations of the Lender of Last Resort: A Global Historical Narrative," *Journal of Financial Intermediation* 28, pp. 48–65.

Calvo, Guillermo and Carlos Végh (1992), "Currency Substitution in Developing Countries: An Introduction," Working Paper WP/92/040, International Monetary Fund (May).

Carstens, Agustin and Nandan Nilekani (2024), "Finternet: The Financial System for the Future," Working Paper No. 1178, Bank for International Settlements (April).

Carter, Alice Clair (1953), "The Dutch and the English Public Debt in 1777," *Economica* 20, pp. 159–61.

Cassetta, John (2022), "The Geopolitics of Swap Lines," Working Paper No. 181, Mossavar-Rahmani Center for Business and Government, Cambridge, MA: Harvard Kennedy School (April).

Cassis, Youssef (2006), *Capitals of Capital: A History of International Financial Centres, 1780–2005*, Cambridge: Cambridge University Press.

Cassis, Youssef and Philip Cottrell (2015), *Private Banking in Europe: Rise, Retreat, and Resurgence*, Oxford: Oxford University Press.

Central Banking (2023), "Digital Yuan Used to Settle Crude Oil Trade," *Central Banking* (November 3), https://www.centralbanking.com/fintech/cbdc/7960119/digital-yuan-used-to-settle-crude-oil-trade.

Chahrour, Ryan and Rosen Valchev (2023), "The Dollar in an Era of International Retrenchment," Working Paper No. 31405, National Bureau of Economic Research (June).

Chandler, Alfred (1994), *Scale and Scope: The Dynamics of Industrial Capitalism*, Cambridge, MA: Belknap Press for Harvard University Press.

Chapman, Stanley (1984), *The Rise of Merchant Banking*, London: Allen & Unwin.

Chaudhury, Sushil (2003), "The Inflow of Silver to Bengal in Global Perspective, c. 1650–1757," in *Global Connections and Monetary History, 1470–1800*, edited by Dennis Flynn, Arturo Giráldez, and Richard von Glahn, Aldershot: Ashgate.

Cheong, W. E. (1979), *Mandarins and Merchants: Jardine Matheson & Co., A China Agency of the Early Nineteenth Century*, Monograph Series No. 26, Copenhagen: Scandinavian Institute of Asian Studies.

Chernow, Ron (1990), *The House of Morgan: An American Banking Dynasty and the Rise of Modern Finance*, New York: Simon & Schuster.

Chernow, Ron (1993), *The Warburgs: The Twentieth-Century Odyssey of a Remarkable Jewish Family*, New York: Vintage.

Cherny, Robert (1985), *A Righteous Cause: The Life of William Jennings Bryan*, Boston: Little, Brown.

Choi, Mark, Linda Goldberg, Robert Lerman and Fabiola Ravazzolo (2022), "The Fed's Central Bank Swap Lines and IMFA Repo Facility," *Federal Reserve Bank of New York Economic Policy Review* 28, pp. 93–113.

Choi, Sang Rim, Daekeun Park, and Adrian Tschoegl (1996), "Banks and the World's Major Banking Centers, 1990," *Weltwirtschaftliches Archiv* 132, pp. 774–93.

Cipolla, Carlo (1956), *Money, Prices and Civilization in the Mediterranean World: Fifth to Seventeenth Century*, Princeton: Princeton University Press.

Cipolla, Carlo (1989), "American Treasure and the Florentine Coinage in the Sixteenth Century," in *Precious Metals, Coinage and the Changes of Monetary Structures in Latin-America, Europe and Asia (Late Middle Ages—Early Modern Times)*, edited by Eddy Van Cauwenberghe, Leuven: Leuven University Press.

Clark, Truman (1986), "Interest Rate Seasonals and the Federal Reserve," *Journal of Political Economy* 94, pp. 76–125.

Clymer, Adam (1979), "Carter's Standing Drops to New Low in Times-CBS Poll," *New York Times* (June 10), p. 1, https://www.nytimes.com/1979/06/10/archives/carters-standing-drops-to-new-low-in-timescbs-poll-approval-falls.html.

Cobb, Matthew (2015), "Balancing the Trade: Roman Cargo Shipments to India," *Oxford Journal of Archaeology* 34, pp.185-203.

Cochrane, Eric (1970), "A Case in Point: The End of the Renaissance in Florence," in *The Late Italian Renaissance 1525–1630*, edited by Eric Cochrane, London: Macmillan.

Cochrane, Eric (1973), *Florence in the Forgotten Centuries 1527–1800: A History of Florence and the Florentines in the Age of the Grand Dukes*, Chicago: University of Chicago Press.

Cockrell, H.A.L. and Edwin Green (1994), *The British Insurance Business 1547–1970: A Guide to its History and Records*, Sheffield: Continuum International Publishing Group.

Cohen, Stephen (2000), *The Making of United States International Economic Policy: Principles, Problems, and Proposals for Reform*, Westport, CT: Praeger.

Collins, Robert (1996), "The Economic Crisis of 1968 and the Waning of the 'American Century,'" *American Historical Review* 101, pp. 396–422.

Committee for a Responsible Federal Budget (2024), "The Fiscal Impact of the Harris and Trump Campaign Plans," Washington, D.C.: Committee for a Responsible Federal Budget (October 28).

Committee for a Responsible Federal Budget (2025), "Breaking Down the One Big Beautiful Bill," Washington, D.C.: Committee for a Responsible Federal Budget (May 21).

Congressional Budget Office (2025), "The Long-Term Budget Outlook: 2025 to 2055," Washington, D.C.: Congressional Budget Office (March).

Connally, John, with Mickey Herskowitz (1993), *In History's Shadow: An American Odyssey*, New York: Hyperion.

Conway, Ed (2015), *The Summit: Bretton Woods, 1944: J. M. Keynes and the Reshaping of the Global Economy*, New York: Pegasus Books.

Conway, Leonard (1946), "The International Position of the London Money Market, 1931–1937," PhD thesis, University of Pennsylvania.

Coombs, Charles (1976), *The Arena of International Finance*, New York: John Wiley & Sons.

Cope, S. R. (1983), *Walter Boyd: A Merchant Banker in the Age of Napoleon*, Gloucester: A Sutton.

Costigliola, Frank (1977), "Anglo-American Financial Rivalry in the 1920s," *The Journal of Economic History* 37, pp. 911–34.

Cottrell, Philip (2005), "Established Connections and New Opportunities: London as an International Financial Centre, 1914–1958," in *London and Paris as International Financial Centres in the Twentieth Century*, edited by Youssef Cassis and Eric Bussiere, Oxford: Oxford University Press.

Cottrell, Philip (1991), "Great Britain," in *International Banking 1870–1914*, edited by Rondo Cameron and V. I. Bovykin, New York: Oxford University Press.

Craig, R. Bruce (2004), *Treasonable Doubt: The Harry Dexter White Spy Case*, Lawrence, KS: University of Kansas Press.

Crawford, Michael (1970), "Money and Exchange in the Roman World," *Journal of Roman Studies* 60, pp. 40–48.

Crawford, Michael (1974), *Roman Republican Coinage,* Cambridge: Cambridge University Press.

Crawford, Michael (1985), *Coinage and Money under the Roman Republic: Italy and the Mediterranean Economy*, London: Methuen.

Cunningham, Alexander (1891), *Coins of Ancient India from the Earliest Times Down to the Seventh Century A.D.*, London: B. Quaritch.

Dale, Edwin (1972), "Gold Price Rise Approved by Senate in 86-to-1 Vote," *The New York Times* (March 2), https://www.nytimes.com/1972/03/02/archives/gold-price-rise-approved-by-senate-in-86to1-vote-senate-approves.html.

Das, Mitali, Gita Gopinath, Taehoom Kim, and Jeremy Stein (2022), "Central Banks as Dollar Lenders of Last Resort: Implications for Regulation and Reserve Holdings," Working Paper No. 30787, National Bureau of Economic Research (January).

Davies, John (2015), "Towards a General Model of Long-Distance Trade: Aromatics as a Case Study," in *The Ancient Greek Economy: Markets, Households and City-States*, edited by Edward Harris, David Lewis, and Mark Woolmer, Cambridge: Cambridge University Press.

Davis, J. Scott and Pon Sagnanert (2024), "Swap Lines Curbed Global Dollar Shortages, Appreciation During COVID-19 Crisis," Dallas Fed Economics, Dallas: Federal Reserve Bank of Dallas (May 21), https://www.dallasfed.org/research/economics/2024/0521.

Dawson, Frank (1990), *The First Latin American Debt Crisis: The City of London and the 1822–25 Loan Bubble*, New Haven: Yale University Press.

Dehing, Pit and Marjolein 't Hart (1997), "Linking the Fortunes: Currency and Banking, 1550–1800," in *A Financial History of the Netherlands*, edited by Marjolein 't Hart, Joost Jonker, and Jan Luiten van Zanden, Cambridge: Cambridge University Press.

De Romanis, Federico (2020), *The Indo-Roman Pepper Trade and the Muziris Papyrus*, Oxford: Oxford University Press.

De Roover, Raymond (1944), "What is Dry Exchange? A Contribution to the Study of English Mercantilism," *Journal of Political Economy* 52, pp. 250–266.

De Roover, Raymond (1963a), "The Organization of Trade," in *The Cambridge Economic History of Europe, Volume III: Economic Organization and Policies in the Middle Ages*, edited by M. M. Postan, E. E. Rich, and Edward Miller, Cambridge: Cambridge University Press.

De Roover, Raymond (1963b), *The Rise and Decline of the Medici Bank 1397–1494*, Cambridge, MA: Harvard University Press.

Devereaux, Michael and Shouyong Shi (2013), "Vehicle Currency," *International Economic Review* 54, pp. 97–133.

De Vries, Jan and Ad van der Woude (1997), *The First Modern Economy: Success, Failure, and Perseverance of the Dutch Economy, 1500–1815*, Cambridge: Cambridge University Press.

De Vries, Margaret (1976), *The International Monetary Fund, 1966–71: The System Under Stress*, Washington, D.C.: IMF.

De Vries, Margaret (1985), *The International Monetary Fund, 1972–1978: Cooperation on Trial*, Washington, D.C.: IMF.

Diehl, Charles (1970), "The Economic Decay of Byzantium," in *The Economic Decline of Empires*, edited by Carlo Cipolla, London: Methuen.

Dixon, E. (1898), "The Florentine Wool Trades in the Middle Ages: A Bibliographical Note," *Transactions of the Royal Historical Society* 12, pp. 151–79.

Dornbusch, Rudiger (1976), "Expectations and Exchange Rate Dynamics," *Journal of Political Economy* 84, pp. 1161–76.

Drelichman, Mauricio and Hans-Joachim Voth (2011), "Lending to the Borrower from Hell: Debt and Default in the Age of Philip II," *Economic Journal* 121, pp. 1205–27.

Du, Dan (2020), "'Flying Cash': Credit Instruments on the Silk Roads," in *Silk Roads: From Local Realities to Global Narratives*, edited by Jeffrey Lerner and Taohua Shi, Oxford: Oxbow Books.

Duca, John (2009), "Preventing a Repeat of the Money Market Meltdown of the Early 1930s," Working Paper 0904, Research Department, Federal Reserve Bank of Dallas (November).

Dudley, Leonard and Peter Passell (1968), "The War in Vietnam and the United States Balance of Payments," *Review of Economics and Statistics* 50, pp. 437–42.

Duffie, Darrell, Michael Fleming, Frank Keane, Claire Nelson, Or Shachar, and Peter Van Tassel (2023), "Dealer Capacity and US Treasury Market Functionality," Working Paper No. 1138, Bank for International Settlements (October).

Duncan-Jones, Richard (2004), "Economic Change and the Transition to Late Antiquity," in *Approaching Late Antiquity: The Transformation from Early to Late Empire*, edited by Simon Swain and Mark Edwards, Oxford: Oxford University Press.

Easton, Harry Tucker (1907), *Money, Exchange and Banking in their Practical, Theoretical and Legal Aspects: A Complete Manual for Bank Officials, Business Men and Commercial Students*, London: Sir I. Pitman & Sons.

Edwards, Jeremy and Sheilagh Ogilvie (2012), "What Lessons for Economic Development Can We Draw from the Champagne Fairs?" *Explorations in Economic History* 49, pp. 131–48.

Ehrenberg, Richard (1928), *Capital & Finance in the Age of the Renaissance*, New York: Harcourt, Brace & Company.

Eichengreen, Barry (1992), *Golden Fetters: The Gold Standard and the Great Depression, 1919–1939*, New York: Oxford University Press.

Eichengreen, Barry (1993), *Reconstructing Europe's Trade and Payments: The European Payments Union*, Manchester: Manchester University Press.

Eichengreen, Barry (2000), "U.S. Foreign Financial Relations in the Twentieth Century," in *The Cambridge Economic History of the United States, Volume III: The Twentieth Century*, edited by Stanley Engerman and Robert Gallman, Cambridge: Cambridge University Press.

Eichengreen, Barry (2003), "The EMS Crisis in Retrospect," in *Capital Flows and Crises*, Cambridge: MIT Press.

Eichengreen, Barry (2011), *Exorbitant Privilege: The Rise and Fall of the Dollar and the Future of the International Monetary System*, New York: Oxford University Press.

Eichengreen, Barry (2018), *The Populist Temptation: Economic Grievance and Political Reaction in the Modern Era*, New York: Oxford University Press.

Eichengreen, Barry (2022), "Sanctions, SWIFT, and China's Cross-Border Interbank Payments System," CSIS Brief, Washington, D.C.: Center for Strategic & International Studies (May).

Eichengreen, Barry, Asmaa El-Ganainy, Rui Esteves, and Kris James Mitchener (2021), *In Defense of Public Debt*, New York: Oxford University Press.

Eichengreen, Barry and Marc Flandreau (2010), "The Federal Reserve, the Bank of England, and the Rise of the Dollar as an International Currency, 1914–1939," *Open Economies Review* 23, pp. 57–87.

Eichengreen, Barry and Masahiro Kawai, eds. (2015), *Renminbi Internationalization: Achievements, Prospects, and Challenges*, Washington, D.C.: Brookings Institution.

Eichengreen, Barry, Arnaud Mehl, and Livia Chiţu (2018), *How Global Currencies Work, Past, Present and Future*, Princeton: Princeton University Press.

Eichengreen, Barry, Arnaud Mehl, and Livia Chiţu (2019), "Mars or Mercury? The Geopolitics of International Currency Choice," *Economic Policy* 34, pp. 315–63.

Eichengreen, Barry and Richard Portes (1986), "Debt and Default in the 1930s: Causes and Consequences," *European Economic Review* 30, pp. 599–640.

Einzig, Paul (1949), *Primitive Money in its Ethnological, Historical and Economic Aspects*, London: Eyre & Spottiswoode.

Eizenstat, Stuart (2018), *President Carter: The White House Years*, New York: Thomas Dunne Books.

Embassy of the People's Republic of China in the United States (2023), "Outlook on China's Foreign Policy on Its Neighborhood in the New Era," Washington, D.C.: Embassy of the People's Republic (October 24), http://us.china-embassy.gov.cn/eng/zgyw/202310/t20231024_11167100.htm.

Emminger, Otmar (1985), "The International Role of the Dollar," *Economic Review of the Federal Reserve Bank of Kansas City* (September/October), pp. 17–24.

Engen, Darel (2004), "The Economy of Ancient Greece," Economic History Net Encyclopedia, https://eh.net/encyclopedia/the-economy-of-ancient-greece/.

Engen, Darel (2005), "'Ancient Greenbacks': Athenian Owls, the Law of Nikophon, and the Greek Economy," *Historia: Zeitschrift für Alte Geschichte* 54, pp. 359–81.

European Central Bank (2025), *The International Role of the Euro*, Frankfurt: ECB.

European Commission (2015), "Action Plan on Building a Capital Markets Union," Document 52015DC0468, Brussels: European Commission.

European Commission (2024), "The Future of European Competitiveness: A Competitiveness Strategy for Europe," Brussels: European Commission (September).

Farhi, Emmanuel and Matteo Maggiori (2019), "China Versus the United States: IMF Meets IPS," *American Economic Association Papers and Proceedings* 109, pp. 476–81.

Farnsworth, Clyde (1985), "Tide of Protectionism in Congress," *The New York Times* (July 4), https://www.nytimes.com/1985/07/04/business/tide-of-protectionism-in-congress.html.

Federal Reserve Bank of New York (1929), "Fourteenth Annual Report of the Federal Reserve Bank of New York for the Year Ended January 31, 1928," New York: Federal Reserve Bank of New York.

Federal Reserve Bank of New York (1979), "A Substitution Account: Precedents and Issues," *Federal Reserve Bank of New York Quarterly Review* (Summer), pp. 40–48.

Federal Reserve Board (1948), "The Postwar Drain on Foreign Gold and Dollar Reserves," *Federal Reserve Bulletin* 34 (April), pp. 371–81.

Feis, Herbert (1930), *Europe, the World's Banker 1870–1914*, New Haven: Yale University Press.

Ferderer, Peter (2003), "Institutional Innovation and the Creation of Liquid Financial Markets: The Case of Bankers' Acceptances, 1914–1934," *The Journal of Economic History* 63, pp. 666–94.

Ferguson, Niall (1998), *The House of Rothschild: Money's Prophets, 1798–1848*, New York: Viking.

Ferrell, Robert (2010), *Inside the Nixon Administration: The Secret Diary of Arthur Burns, 1969–1974*, Lawrence, KS: University Press of Kansas.

Ficker, Sandra Kuntz, "The Universal Mint: Mexico's Silver and the World Economy (1821–1870)," *Capitalism: A Journal of History and Economics* 3, pp. 257–300.

Field, Alexander (2022), *The Economic Consequences of U.S. Mobilization for the Second World War*, New Haven: Yale University Press.

Fink, Matthew (2019), *The Unlikely Reformer: Carter Glass and Financial Regulation*, Charlottesville: University of Virginia Press.

Finley, Moses (1973), *The Ancient Economy*, Berkeley: University of California Press.

Fisher, John (1975), "Silver Production in the Viceroyalty of Peru, 1776–1824," *Hispanic American Historical Review* 55, pp. 25–43.

Fisher, John (2003), "Mining and Imperial Trade in Eighteenth Century Spanish America," in *Global Connections and Monetary History, 1470–1800*, edited by Dennis Flynn, Arturo Giráldez, and Richard von Glahn, Aldershot, England: Ashgate Publishing.

Flandreau, Marc (1998), "Does Integration Globalize? Elements of Nineteenth-Century Financial Geography," in *Finance and the Making of the Modern Capitalist World, 1750–1931*, edited by Clara Eugenia Núñez, Seville: Universidad de Sevilla Press.

Flandreau, Marc (2004), *The Glitter of Gold: France, Bimetallism, and the Emergence of the International Gold Standard, 1848–1873*, Oxford: Oxford University Press.

Flandreau, Marc and Juan Flores (2009), "Bonds and Brands: Foundations of Sovereign Debt Markets, 1820–1830," *The Journal of Economic History* 69, pp. 646–84.

Flandreau, Marc, Christophe Galimard, Clemens Jobst, and Pilar Nogues-Marco (2009), "Monetary Geography before the Industrial Revolution," *Cambridge Journal of Regions, Economy and Society* 2, pp. 149–71.

Flandreau, Marc and Stefano Ugolini (2013), "Where It All Began: Lending of Last Resort at the Bank of England: Monitoring during the Overend-Gurney Panic of 1866," in *The Origins, History and Future of the Federal Reserve*, edited by Michael Bordo and William Roberds, Cambridge: Cambridge University Press.

Flandreau, Marc and Stefano Ugolini (2014), "The Crisis of 1866," in *British Financial Crises since 1825*, edited by Nicholis Dimsdale and Anthony Hotson, Oxford: Oxford University Press.

Fleming, Michael (2023), "How Has Treasury Market Liquidity Evolved in 2023?" *Liberty Street Economics*, New York: Federal Reserve Bank of New York (October 17).

Flynn, Dennis (1982), "Fiscal Crisis and the Decline of Spain (Castile)," *The Journal of Economic History* 42, pp. 139–47.

Friedman, Milton and Anna Schwartz (1963), *A Monetary History of the United States 1867–1960*, Princeton: Princeton University Press.

Fryde, Edmund (1955), "Loans to the English Crown 1328–31," *English Historical Review* 70, pp. 198–211.

Fryde, Edmund (1984), *Studies in Medieval Trade and Finance*, London: Hambledon Press.

Fukao, Mitsuhiro (2003), "Capital Account Liberalization: The Japanese Experience and Implications for China," in *China's Capital Account Liberalisation: International Perspectives*, Paper No. 15, pp. 35–57, Bank for International Settlements.

Fulmer, Sean (2022a), "United Kingdom: Bank of England Lending during the Panic of 1825," *Journal of Financial Crises* 4, pp. 1037–52.

Fulmer, Sean (2022b), "United Kingdom: Bank of England Lending during the Panic of 1866," *Journal of Financial Crises* 4, pp. 1053–73.

Funabashi, Yoichi (1988), *Managing the Dollar: From the Plaza to the Louvre*, Washington, D.C.: Institute of International Finance.

Garber, Peter and Vittorio Grilli (1986), "The Belmont-Morgan Syndicate as an Optimal Investment Banking Contract," *European Economic Review* 30, pp. 649–77.

Gardner, Richard (1956), *Sterling-Dollar Diplomacy: Anglo-American Collaboration in the Reconstruction of Multilateral Trade*, New York: Columbia University Press.

Garson, Barbara (2001), *Money Makes the World Go Around*, New York: Penguin Books.

Garten, Jeffrey (2021), *Three Days at Camp David: How a Secret Meeting in 1971 Transformed the Global Economy*, New York: Harper.

Gavin, Francis (2002), "Ideas, Power, and the Politics of America's International Monetary Policy During the 1960s," in, *Monetary Orders: Ambiguous Economics, Ubiquitous Politics*, edited by Jonathan Kirschner, Ithaca, NY: Cornell University Press.

Gavin, Francis (2004), *Gold, Dollars, and Power: The Politics of International Monetary Relations, 1958–1971*, Chapel Hill: University of North Carolina Press.

Gherardi, Francesca and Jan Pelsdonk (2025), "Investigating the Sources of Silver in 17th- and 18th-Century Silver Coins from the *Rooswijk* Shipwreck by Compositional Studies," *Materials* 18, pp. 1–24.

Gillard, Lucien (2009), "The International Role of the Bank of Amsterdam," in *The Bank of Amsterdam: On the Origins of Central Banking*, edited by Marcus van Nieuwkerk and Cherelt Kroeze, Amsterdam: Sonsbeek Publishers.

Giovannini, Alberto and Bart Turtelboom (1992), "Currency Substitution," Working Paper No. 4232, National Bureau of Economic Research (December).

Giráldez, Arturo (2015), *The Age of Trade: The Manila Galleons and the Dawn of the Global Economy*, New York: Rowman & Littlefield.

Glamann, Kristof (1958), *Dutch-Asiatic Trade: 1620–1740*, Gloucester: A. Sutton.

Glass, Carter (1927), *An Adventure in Constructive Finance*, Garden City NY: Doubleday, Page & Co.

Glover, George (2023), "Russia Is Using China's Yuan to Settle 25% of Its Trade With the Rest of the World," *Business Insider* (September 28), https://markets.businessinsider.com/news/currencies/dedollarization-dollar-dominance-russia-china-ruble-yuan-war-in-ukraine-2023-9.

Goetzmann, William (2006), *Money Changes Everything: How Finance Made Civilization Possible*, Princeton: Princeton University Press.

Goldberg, Linda and Oliver Hannaoui (2024), "Drivers of Dollar Share in Foreign Exchange Reserves," Staff Report No. 1087, New York: Federal Reserve Bank of New York (August).

Goldthwaite, Richard (1985), "Local Banking in Renaissance Florence," *Journal of European Economic History* 14, pp. 5–55.

Goldthwaite, Richard (1987), "The Medici Bank and the World of Florentine Capitalism," *Past & Present* 114, pp. 3–31.

Goldthwaite, Richard (2008), *The Economy of Renaissance Florence*, Baltimore: Johns Hopkins University Press.

Goldwasser, Shafi, Silvio Micali, and Charles Rackoff (1989), "The Knowledge Complexity of Interactive Proof Systems," *SIAM Journal on Computing* 18, pp. 186–208.

Gómez Cram, Roberto, Howard Kung, and Hanno Lustig (2024), "Government Debt in Mature Economies: Safe or Risky?" paper prepared for the Economic Policy Symposium, Jackson Hole WY: Federal Reserve Bank of Kansas City (August).

González, A. García-Baquero (2003), "American Gold and Silver in the Eighteenth Century: From Fascination to Accounting," in *Global Connections and Monetary History, 1470–1800*, edited by Dennis Flynn, Arturo Giráldez, and Richard von Glahn, Aldershot, England: Ashgate.

Gopinath, Gita and Jeremy Stein (2021), "Banking, Trade, and the Making of a Dominant Currency," *Quarterly Journal of Economics* 136, pp. 783–830.

Gordon, Peter and Juan José Morales (2017), *The Silver Way: China, Spanish America and the Birth of Globalization*, New York: Penguin.

Gourinchas, Pierre-Olivier and Olivier Jeanne (2012), "Global Safe Assets," Working Paper No. 399, Bank for International Settlements (December).

Gourinchas, Pierre-Olivier, Hélène Rey, and Maxime Sauzet (2019), "The International Monetary and Financial System," *Annual Review of Economics* 11, pp. 859–93.

Graham, Frank (1949), "The Cause and Cure of 'Dollar Shortage,'" *Essays in International Finance* no. 10, International Finance Section, Department of Economics, Princeton University (January).

Grechyna, Daryna (2016), "On the Determinants of Political Polarization," *Economics Letters* 144, pp. 10–14.

Greene, Kevin (1986), *The Archaeology of the Roman Economy*, Berkeley: University of California Press.

Greene, Margaret (1984), "U.S. Experience with Exchange Market Intervention," Staff Study No. 127, Washington, D.C.: Board of Governors of the Federal Reserve System (August).

Greengrass, H. W. (1930), *The Discount Market in London: Its Organization and Recent Development*, New York: Sir I. Pitman & Sons.

Grekou, Carl (2020), "Un dollar contesté, mais toujours pas détrôné," in *L'économie mondiale 2021*, Paris: Éditions La Découverte.

Grierson, Philip (1960), "The Monetary Reforms of 'Abd Al-Malik: Their Metrological Basis and Their Financial Repercussions," *Journal of the Economic and Social History of the Orient* 3, pp. 241–64.

Grierson, Philip (1981), "The Weight of the Gold Florin in the Fifteenth Century," *Quaderni ticinesi di numismatica e antichità classiche* 10, pp. 421–31.

Griffin, Miriam (1984), *Nero: The End of a Dynasty*, London: B. T. Batsford.
Gros, Daniel and Niels Thygesen (1998), *European Monetary Integration: From the European Monetary System to European Monetary Union*, second edition, London: Longman.
Grossman, Richard (1994), "The Shoe That Didn't Drop: Explaining Banking Stability During the Great Depression," *The Journal of Economic History* 54, pp. 654–82.
Guan, Hanhui, Nuno Palma, and Meng Wu (2024), "The Rise and Fall of Paper Money in Yuan China, 1260–1368," *Economic History Review* 77, pp. 1222–50.
Gupta, Parmeshwari (1991), "Coins in Rome's Indian Trade," in *Coinage, Trade, and the Economy*, edited by A. K. Jha, Maharashtra, India: Indian Institute of Research in Numismatic Studies.
Haberlein, Mark (2012), *The Fuggers of Augsburg; Pursuing Wealth and Honor in Renaissance Germany*, Charlottesville & London: University of Virginia Press.
Hamilton, James (1987), "Monetary Factors in the Great Depression," *Journal of Monetary Economics* 19, pp. 145–69.
Harfield, Henry and Wilbert Ward (1958), *Bank Credits and Acceptances*, New York: Ronald Press.
Harney, Gareth (2024), *A History of Ancient Rome in Twelve Coins*, New York: Atria Books.
Harper, Kyle (2017), *The Fate of Rome: Climate, Disease, and the End of Empire*, Princeton: Princeton University Press.
Harris, Seymour (1948), *The Economic Recovery Program*, Cambridge, MA: Harvard University Press.
Hay, Mark Edward (2024), *Transatlantic Finance in the Age of Revolutions: Hope, Baring, and the Financing of the Sale and Purchase of Louisiana*, Cham, Switzerland: Palgrave Macmillan.
Heath, Alexandra and James Whitelaw (2011), "Electronic Trading and the Australian Foreign Exchange Market," *Reserve Bank of Australia Bulletin* (June Quarter), pp. 41–48
Heckscher, Eli (1950), "Multilateralism, Baltic Trade, and the Mercantilists," *Economic History Review* 3, pp. 219–28.
Helleiner, Eric (2003), *The Making of National Money: Territorial Currencies in Historical Perspective*, Ithaca, NY: Cornell University Press.
Helleiner, Karl (1965), *The Imperial Loans: A Study in Financial and Diplomatic History*, Oxford: Clarendon Press.
Hendershott, Terrance, Charles Jones, and Albert Menkveld (2011), "Does Algorithmic Trading Improve Liquidity?" *The Journal of Finance* 66, pp. 1–33.
Hendershott, Terrance and Ryan Riordan (2012), "Algorithmic Trading and the Market for Liquidity," *Journal of Financial and Quantitative Analysis* 48, pp. 1001–24.
Hendy, Michael (1985), *Studies in the Byzantine Monetary Economy c. 300–1450*, Cambridge: Cambridge University Press.
Henning, C. Randall (1996), "Europe's Monetary Union and the United States," *Foreign Policy* 102, pp. 83–100.
Herre, Franz (2009), *The Life and Times of the Fuggers*, Augsburg, Germany: Wißner.
Herz, Bernhard and Werner Röger (1992), "The EMS is a Greater Deutschmark Area," *European Economic Review* 36, pp. 1413–25.
Hieronymi, Otto (1973), *Economic Discrimination Against the United States in Western Europe (1945–1958): Dollar Shortage and the Rise of Regionalism*, Paris and Geneva: Librairie Droz.

Higgins, Benjamin (1949), *Lombard Street in War and Reconstruction*, New York: National Bureau of Economic Research.
Hill, Brian (1984), *The Common Agricultural Policy: Past, Present and Future*, London: Methuen.
Hilton, Boyd (1977), *Corn, Cash, Commerce: The Economic Policies of the Tory Governments 1815–1830*, Oxford: Oxford University Press.
Hirschman, Albert (1960), "Invitation to Theorizing About the Dollar Glut," *Review of Economics and Statistics* 42, pp. 100–102.
Hoffman, Stanley and Charles Maier eds. (1984), *The Marshall Plan: A Retrospective*, Cambridge, MA: Center for European Studies, Harvard University.
Hoffmeyer, Erik (1958), *Dollar Shortage and the Structure of U.S. Foreign Trade*, Copenhagen: E. Munksgaard.
Hogan, Michael (1987), *The Marshall Plan: America, Britain, and the Reconstruction of Western Europe, 1947–1952*, New York: Cambridge University Press.
Holmes, George (1968), "How the Medici Became the Pope's Bankers," in *Florentine Studies: Politics and Society in Renaissance Florence*, edited by Nicolai Rubinstein, Evanston: Northwestern University Press.
Hopkins, Keith (1978), "Economic Growth and Towns in Classical Antiquity," in *Towns in Societies: Essays in Economic History and Historical Sociology*, edited by Philip Abrams and E. A. Wrigley, Cambridge: Cambridge University Press.
Horii, Akinari (1986), "The Evolution of Reserve Currency Diversification," BIS Economic Papers No. 18 (December).
Howgego, Christopher (1994), "Coin Circulation and the Integration of the Roman Economy," *Journal of Roman Archeology* 7, pp. 5–21.
Howgego, Christopher (1995), *Ancient History from Coins*, London: Routledge.
Howgego, Christopher, Kevin Butcher, Matthew Ponting, and Volker Heuchert (2010), "Coinage and the Roman Economy in the Antonine Period: The View from Egypt," unpublished manuscript, University of Oxford.
Hudson, Peter (2017), *Bankers and Empire: How Wall Street Colonized the Caribbean*, Chicago: University of Chicago Press.
Hughes, Ken (2014), *Chasing Shadows: The Nixon Tapes, the Chennault Affair, and the Origins of Watergate*, Charlottesville: University of Virginia Press.
Hunt, Edwin (1990), "A New Look at the Dealings of the Bardi and Peruzzi with Edward III," *The Journal of Economic History* 50, pp. 149–62.
Hunt, Edwin (1994), *The Medieval Super-Companies: A Study of the Peruzzi Company of Florence*, Cambridge: Cambridge University Press.
Hunt, Edwin and James Murray (1999), *A History of Business in Medieval Europe, 1200–1550*, Cambridge: Cambridge University Press.
Ilzetzki, Ethan, Carmen Reinhart, and Kenneth Rogoff (2019), "Exchange Rate Arrangements Entering the Twenty-First Century: Which Anchor Will Hold?" *Quarterly Journal of Economics* 134, pp. 599–646.
Ilzetzki, Ethan, Carmen Reinhart, and Kenneth Rogoff (2021), "Rethinking Exchange Rate Regimes," NBER Working Paper No. 29347, National Bureau of Economic Research (October).

International Monetary Fund (2011), "Did the Plaza Accord Cause Japan's Lost Decades?" in *World Economic Outlook*, Washington, D.C.: IMF (April).

Irigoin, Alejandra (2009), "Gresham on Horseback: The Monetary Roots of Spanish American Political Fragmentation in the Nineteenth Century," *Economic History Review* 62, pp. 551–75.

Irigoin, Alejandra (2019), "The New World and the Global Silver Economy, 1500–1800," in *Global Economic History*, edited by Tirthankar Roy and Giorgio Riello, London: Bloomsbury.

Irigoin, Alejandra (2020), "Rise and Demise of the Global Silver Standard," in *Handbook of the History of Money and Currency*, edited by Stefano Battilossi, Youssef Cassis, and Kazuhiko Yago, Singapore: Springer.

Israel, J. (1995), *The Dutch Republic: Its Rise, Greatness and Fall, 1477–1806*, Oxford: Oxford University Press.

Jackson, Stanley (1983), *J. P. Morgan: A Biography*, New York: Stein and Day.

Jackson, Trevor (2022), *Impunity and Capitalism: The Afterlives of European Financial Crises, 1690–1830*, Cambridge: Cambridge University Press.

Jacobs, Lawrence (1910), *Bank Acceptances*, Washington, D.C.: U.S. Government Printing Office.

Jalil, Andrew (2015), "A New History of Banking Panics in the United States, 1825–1929: Construction and Implications," *American Economic Journal: Macroeconomics* 7, pp. 295–330.

James, Harold (2020), "Networks and Financial War: The Brothers Warburg in the First Age of Globalization," *Financial History Review* 27, pp. 303–18.

Japanese Ministry of Finance (1999), "Internationalisation of the Yen for the 21st Century," Council on Foreign Exchange and Other Transactions (April), www.mof.go.jp/english/if/e1b064a.htm.

Jenks, Leland (1927), *The Migration of British Capital to 1875*, New York: Alfred A. Knopf.

Jensen, Michael and William Meckling (1976), "Theory of the Firm: Managerial Behavior, Agency Costs and Ownership Structure," *Journal of Financial Economics* 3, pp. 305–60.

Jin, Wenhui (2022), "Research on the Legal Status of the People's Bank of China from the Perspective of Independence," *Advances in Economics and Management Research*, pp. 227–34.

Johnson, Lyndon Baines (1971), *The Vantage Point: Perspectives on the Presidency 1963–1969*, New York: Holt, Rinehart and Winston.

Jones, A.H.M. (1974), *The Roman Economy: Studies in Ancient Economic and Administrative History*, Oxford: Oxford University Press.

Jones, Geoffrey (1995), *British Multinational Banking, 1830–1990*, New York: Oxford University Press.

Jonker, Joost and Keetie Sluyterman (2001), *At Home on the World Markets: Dutch International Trading Companies from the 16th Century until the Present*, Toronto: McGill-Queen's University Press.

Kaeuper, Richard (1973), "The Frescobaldi of Florence and the English Crown," *Studies in Medieval and Renaissance History* 10, pp. 41–95.

Kaldellis, Anthony (2023), *The New Roman Empire: A History of Byzantium*, New York: Oxford University Press.

Kaplan, Jacob and Günther Schleiminger (1990), *The European Payments Union: Financial Diplomacy in the 1950s*, Oxford: Oxford University Press.

Kaplanis, Costas (2003), "The Debasement of the 'Dollar of the Middle Ages,'" *The Journal of Economic History* 63, pp. 768–801.

Katsari, Constantina (2011), *The Roman Monetary System: The East Provinces from the First to the Third Century AD*, Cambridge: Cambridge University Press.

Keiji, Nagahara and Kozo Yamamura (1988), "Shaping the Process of Unification: Technological Progress in Sixteenth- and Seventeenth-Century Japan," *Journal of Japanese Studies* 14, pp. 77–109.

Kemmerer, Edwin (1910), *Seasonal Variations in the Relative Demand for Money and Capital in the United States, a Statistical Study*, Washington, D.C.: Government Printing Office.

Kennedy, John, Elena Grossfeld, Zsofia Wolford, and Thomas Kenchington (2024), "Gold Rush: How Russia Is Using Gold in Wartime," Cambridge, UK: RAND Europe.

Keynes, John Maynard (1913), *Indian Currency and Finance*, London: Macmillan.

Keynes, John Maynard (1919), *The Economic Consequences of the Peace*, London: Macmillan.

Keynes, John Maynard (1923), *A Tract on Monetary Reform*, London: Macmillan.

Keynes, John Maynard (1930), *A Treatise on Money*, two volumes, London: Macmillan.

Killick, John (1997), *The United States and European Reconstruction*, Edinburgh: Keele University Press.

Kim, Henry (2001), "Archaic Coinage as Evidence for the Use of Money," in *Money and Its Uses in the Ancient Greek World*, edited by Andrew Meadows and Kirsty Shipton, Oxford: Oxford University Press.

Kindersley, Robert (1934), "British Overseas Investments in 1932 and 1933," *The Economic Journal* 44, pp. 365–79.

Kindersley, Robert (1937), "British Oversea Investments in 1935 and 1936," *The Economic Journal* 47, pp. 642–62.

Kindleberger, Charles (1950), *The Dollar Shortage*, Cambridge, MA: MIT Press.

Kindleberger, Charles (1976), "Systems of International Economic Organization," in *Money and the Coming World Order*, edited by David Calleo, New York: New York University Press.

King, Wilfred (1936), *History of the London Discount Market*, London: Routledge.

Klein, Benjamin, Robert Crawford, and Armen Alchian (1978), "Vertical Integration, Appropriable Rents, and the Competitive Contracting Process," *The Journal of Law and Economics* 21, pp. 297–326.

Kraay, Colin (1964), "Hoards, Small Change and the Origin of Coinage," *The Journal of Hellenistic Studies* 84, pp. 76–91.

Kraay, Colin (1976), *Archaic and Classical Greek Coins*, Berkeley: University of California Press.

Kraft, Jesse (2019), "The Circulation of Foreign Coinage: An American Response, ca. 1750–1857," Ph.D. diss., University of Delaware.

Kroll, John (2008), "The Monetary Use of Weighed Bullion in Archaic Greece," in *The Monetary Systems of the Greeks and Romans*, edited by W. V. Harris, Oxford: Oxford University Press.

Krugman, Paul (1980), "Vehicle Currencies and the Structure of International Exchange," *Journal of Money, Credit and Banking* 12, pp. 513–26.

Kwon, Geoffrey (2015) "Classical Greek Trade in Comparative Perspective," in *The Ancient Greek Economy: Markets, Households and City-States*, edited by Edward Harris, David Lewis, and Mark Woolmer, Cambridge: Cambridge University Press.

Kynaston, David (1994), *The City of London: Volume 1: A World of its Own 1815–1890*, London: Chatto & Windus.

Kynaston, David (1995), *The City of London, Volume II: Golden Years 1890–1914*, London: Chatto & Windus.

Kynaston, David (2017), *Till Time's Last Stand: A History of the Bank of England 1694–2013*, London: Bloomsbury.

Laiou, Angeliki and Cécile Morrisson (2007), *The Byzantine Economy*, New York: Cambridge University Press.

Lane, Frederic and Reinhold Mueller (1985), *Money and Banking in Medieval and Renaissance Venice, Volume 1: Coins and Moneys of Account*, Baltimore: Johns Hopkins University Press.

Lane, Kris (2017), "From Corrupt to Criminal: Reflections on the Great Potosí Mint Fraud of 1649," in *Corruption in the Iberian Empires: Greed, Custom, and Colonial Networks*, edited by Christoph Rosenmüller, Albuquerque: University of New Mexico Press.

Lane, Kris (2019), *Potosí: The Silver City that Changed the World*, Oakland: University of California Press.

Lane, Kris (2023), "The Hangover: Global Consequences of the Great Potosí Mint Fraud, c. 1650–1675," in *Potosí in the Global Silver Age (16th–19th Centuries)*, edited by Rossana Barragán and Paula Zagalsky, Leiden: Brill.

Lanoszka, Alexander (2018), *Atomic Assurance: The Alliance Politics of Nuclear Proliferation*, Ithaca: Cornell University Press.

LaRoche, Robert (1993), "Bankers Acceptances," *Federal Reserve Bank of Richmond Economic Quarterly Review* 79, pp. 75–85.

Leeper, Eric (1991), "Equilibria under 'Active' and 'Passive' Monetary and Fiscal Policies," *Journal of Monetary Economics* 27, pp. 129–47.

Leland, Hayne and Klaus Toft (1996), "Optimal Capital Structure, Endogenous Bankruptcy, and the Term Structure of Credit Spreads," *Journal of Finance* 51, pp. 987–1019.

Lewis, Cleona (1938), *America's Stake in International Investments*, Washington, D.C.: Brookings Institution.

L'Hértier, Maxime and Florian Téreygeol (2010), "From Copper to Silver: Understanding the *Saigerprozess* through Experimental Liquidation and Drying," *Historical Metallurgy* 44, pp. 136–52.

Li, Ruogu (2015), *Reform of the International Monetary System and Internationalization of the Renminbi*, Singapore: World Scientific Publishing.

Lighthizer, Robert (2024), *No Trade is Free: Changing Course, Taking on China, and Helping America's Workers*, New York: Harper Collins.

Lo Cascio, Elio (1981), "State and Coinage in the Late Republic and Early Empire," *Journal of Roman Studies* 71, pp. 76–86.

Lo Cascio, Elio (2008), "The Function of Gold Coinage in the Monetary Economy of the Roman Empire," in *The Monetary Systems of the Greeks and Romans*, edited by W. V. Harris, Oxford: Oxford University Press.

Lo Cascio, Elio (2018), "Market Regulation and Transactions Costs in the Roman Empire," in *Trade, Commerce, and the State in the Roman World*, edited by Andrew Wilson and Alan Bowman, Oxford: Oxford University Press.

Locatelli, Stefano (2025), *The Florentine Florin: The Politics and Culture of Money in the Middle Ages*, Manchester: Manchester University Press.

Lohmann Villena, Guillermo (1976), "La Memorable Crisis Monetaria de Mediados del Siglo XVII y sus Repercusiones en el Virreinato del Perú," *Anuario de Estudios Americanos* 33, pp. 579–639.

Long, Kimberly (2024), "BIS Backs Out of CBDC Project mBridge," *The Banker* (October 31), https://www.thebanker.com/Explainer-BIS-backs-out-of-CBDC-project-mBridge-1730397190.

Lopez, Robert (1951), "The Dollar of the Middle Ages," *The Journal of Economic History* 11, pp. 209–34.

Lopez, Robert (1956), "Back to Gold, 1252," *Economic History Review* 9, pp. 219–40.

Lopez, Robert (1971), *The Commercial Revolution of the Middle Ages*, Englewood Cliffs, NJ: Prentice-Hall.

Lovell, Michael (1957), "The Role of the Bank of England as Lender of Last Resort in the Crises of the Eighteenth Century," *Explorations in Entrepreneurial History* 10, pp. 8–21.

MacDougall, Donald (1954), "A Lecture on the Dollar Problem," *Economica* 21, pp. 185–200.

MacDowall, D. W. (1991), "Indian Imports of Roman Silver Coins," in *Coinage, Trade and the Economy*, edited by A. K. Jha, Maharashtra, India: Indian Institute of Research in Numismatic Studies.

MacMullen, Ramsay (1988), *Corruption and the Decline of Rome*, New Haven: Yale University Press.

Madden, John and Marcus Nadler (1931) *The Paris Money Market*, New York: Investment Bankers Association of America and New York University.

Madden, John and Marcus Nadler (1935), *The International Money Markets*, New York: Prentice Hall.

Maddison, Angus (2001), *The World Economy: A Millennial Perspective*, Paris: OECD Publishing.

Maes, Ivo and Ilaria Pasotti (2021), *Robert Triffin: A Life*, Oxford: Oxford University Press.

Malanima, Paolo (1988), "An Example of Industrial Reconversion: Tuscany in the Sixteenth and Seventeenth Centuries," in *The Rise and Decline of Urban Industries in Italy and the Low Countries (Late Middle Ages—Early Modern Times)*, edited by Herman Van der Wee, Leuven: University of Leuven Press.

Malone, Michael (1981), *The Battle for Butte: Mining and Politics on the Northern Frontier, 1864–1906*, Seattle: University of Washington Press.

Maniatis, George (2016), "The Impact of Financial Institutions on the Development of the Byzantine Economy (10th–12th Centuries)," *Zbornik Radova Vizantoloskog Instituta (Journal of the Serbian Institute of Byzantine Studies)* 53, pp. 101–25

Mann, Charles (2011), *1493: Uncovering the New World Columbus Created*, New York: Alfred A. Knopf.

Marichal, Carlos (1989), *A Century of Debt Crises in Latin America: From Independence to the Great Depression, 1820–1930*, Princeton: Princeton University Press.

Marichal, Carlos (2006), "The Spanish-American Silver Peso: Export Commodity and Global Money of the Ancien Régime, 1550–1800," in *From Silver to Cocaine: Latin American Commodity Chains and the Building of the World Economy, 1500–2000*, edited by Steven Topik, Carlos Marichal, and Zephyr Frank, Durham: Duke University Press.

Marichal, Carlos (2007), *Bankruptcy of Empire: Mexican Silver and the Wars Between Spain, Britain and France, 1760–1810*, Cambridge: Cambridge University Press.

Marks, L. F. (1960), "The Financial Oligarchy in Florence under Lorenzo," in *Italian Renaissance Studies*, edited by Ernest Fraser Jacob, London: Faber and Faber.

Martin, Thomas (1985), *Sovereignty and Coinage in Classical Greece*, Princeton: Princeton University Press.

Martinuzzi, Elisa, Jesús Aguado, Balazs Koranyi, Stefania Spezzati, and John O'Donnell (2025), "Some European Officials Weigh if They Can Rely on Fed for Dollars under Trump," *Reuters* (March 24), https://www.reuters.com/markets/some-european-officials-weigh-if-they-can-rely-fed-dollars-under-trump-2025-03-22/.

Matusow, Allen (1998), *Nixon's Economy: Booms, Busts, Dollars, and Votes*, Lawrence, KS: University Press of Kansas.

Mayer, Jörg (2024), "De-Dollarization: The Global Payment Infrastructure and Wholesale Central Bank Digital Currencies," FFM Working Paper No.102, Forum for Macroeconomics and Macroeconomic Policies, Hans-Böckler-Stiftung (May).

Mayer, Martin (1974), *The Bankers*, New York: Weybright and Talley.

Mayhew, Nicholas (1999), *Sterling: The Rise and Fall of a Currency*, London: Allen Lane.

McCauley, Robert (2025), "Will a 'User Fee' on US Treasuries Actually Work?" *FT Alphaville* (February 25), https://www.ft.com/stream/32f52354-d7e6-4adb-abab-25cb3bbf41f0.

McCauley, Robert and Catherine Schenk (2015), "Reforming the International Monetary System in the 1970s and 2000s: Would an SDR Substitution Account Have Worked?" *International Finance* 18, pp. 187–206.

McConnell, Joseph, Nathan Chellman, Andreas Plach and Andrew Wilson (2025), "Pan-European Atmospheric Lead Pollution, Enhanced Blood Lead Levels, and Cognitive Decline from Roman-Era Mining and Smelting," *Proceedings of the National Academy of Sciences*, 122, pp. 1–7.

McCusker, John (1978), *Money and Exchange in Europe and America, 1600–1775: A Handbook*, Chapel Hill: University of North Carolina Press.

McDowell, Daniel (2023), *Bucking the Buck: US Financial Sanctions and the International Backlash Against the Dollar*, New York: Oxford University Press.

Mee, Charles (1984), *The Marshall Plan: The Launching of the Pax Americana*, New York: Simon and Schuster.

Meier, Andrew (2022), *Morgenthau: Power, Privilege, and the Rise of an American Dynasty*, New York: Random House.

Melton, William and Jean Mahr (1981), "Bankers' Acceptances," *Federal Reserve Bank of New York Quarterly Review* 6, pp. 39–55.

Mendershausen, Horst (1950), "Dollar Shortage and Oil Surplus in 1949–1950," *Essays in International Finance* no.11, International Finance Section, Department of Economics, Princeton University (November).

Metzler, Mark and Simon Bytheway (2016), *Central Banks and Gold: How Tokyo, London and New York Shaped the Modern World,* Ithaca: Cornell University Press.

Meyer, David (1991), "The Formation of a Global Financial Center: London and its Intermediaries," in *Cities in the World System,* edited by Resat Kasaba, New York: Greenwood Press.

Michie, Ranald (1992), *The City of London: Continuity and Change, 1850–1990,* London: Macmillan.

Michie, Ranald (1999), *The London Stock Exchange: A History,* Oxford: Oxford University Press.

Michie, Ranald (2007), "The City of London as a Global Financial Centre, 1850–1939: Finance, Foreign Exchange and the First World War," in *Centres and Peripheries in Banking: The Historical Development of Financial Markets,* edited by Philip Cottrell, Even Lange, and Ulf Olsson, Aldershot: Ashgate.

Michie, Ranald (2012), "The Origins of International Banking in Asia: The Nineteenth and Twentieth Centuries," in *The Origins of International Banking in Asia,* edited by Shizuya Nishimura, Toshio Suzuki, and Ranald Michie, Oxford: Oxford University Press.

Michie, Ranald (2024), *Forex Forever: The City of London and the Foreign Exchange Market since 1850,* Oxford: Oxford University Press.

Mickwitz, Gunnar (1932), *Geld un Wirtschaft im Römischen Reich,* Helsinki: Helsingfors Centraltryckeri Och Bokbinderi.

Migeotte, Léopold (2009), *The Economy of Greek Cities: From the Archaic Period to the Early Roman Empire,* Berkeley: University of California Press.

Millar, Fergus (1981), "The World of the Golden Ass," *Journal of Roman Studies* 71, pp. 63–75.

Milne, J. G. (1952), "Roman Coinage in Egypt in Relation to the Native Economy," *Aegyptus* 32, pp. 143–51.

Minesso, Massimo, Arnaud Mehl, Olga Bagur, and Isabel Vansteenkiste (2025), "Geopolitics and Global Interlinking of Fast Payment Systems," Discussion Paper No. 20105, Centre for Economic Policy Research (April).

Mints, Lloyd (1945), *A History of Banking Theory in Great Britain and the United States,* Chicago: University of Chicago Press.

Mintz, Ilse (1951), *Deterioration in the Quality of Foreign Bonds Issued in the United States, 1920–1930,* New York: National Bureau of Economic Research.

Miran, Stephen (2024a), "A User's Guide to Restructuring the Global Trading System," Stamford, CT: Hudson Bay Capital (November).

Miran, Stephen (2024b), "The Fed Isn't as Independent as It Seems," *Barron's* (October 15), https://www.barrons.com/articles/fed-independence-trump-treasury-powell-ee680e8b.

Miron, Jeffrey (1985), "Financial Panics, the Seasonality of the Interest Rate, and the Founding of the Fed," *American Economic Review* 126, pp. 125–40.

Miyamoto, Matao, and Yoshiaki Shikano (2003), "The Emergence of the Tokugawa Monetary System in East Asian International Perspective," in *Global Connections and Monetary History, 1470–1800,* edited by Dennis Flynn, Arturo Giráldez and Richard von Glahn, Aldershot: Ashgate.

Młyanarski, Feliks (1929), *Gold and Central Banks,* New York: Macmillan.

Moggridge, Donald (1971), "British Controls on Long Term Capital Movements, 1924–1931," in *Essays on a Mature Economy: Britain After 1840,* edited by Donald McCloskey, Princeton: Princeton University Press.

Moisés, Rachel (2005), "The Rise of the Spanish Silver *Real*," *Sigma: Journal of Political and International Studies* 23, pp. 69–89.

Mooij, Jooke (2019), "The Bank of Amsterdam: The Beginning of a Phenomenon," in *The Bank of Amsterdam: On the Origins of Central Banking*, edited by Marius van Nieuwkerk and Cherelt Kroeze, Amsterdam: Sonsbeek Publishers.

Morikawa, Hidemasa (1992), *Zaibatsu: The Rise and Fall of Family Enterprise Groups in Japan*, University of Tokyo Press.

Morris, Ian (1999), Foreword to *The Ancient Economy*, by Moses Finley, Berkeley: University of California Press.

Morrison, Alan, Julius Kirschner, and Anthony Molho (1985), "Epidemics in Renaissance Florence," *American Journal of Public Health* 75, pp. 528–35.

Morrison, Cécile (2002), "Byzantine Money: Its Production and Circulation," in *The Economic History of Byzantium from the Seventh through the Fifteenth Century*, vol. 3, edited by Angeliki Laiou, Washington, D.C.: Dumbarton Oaks.

Moss, Frank (2012), "The Euro: Internationalised at Birth," in *Currency Internationalisation: Lessons from the Global Financial Crisis and Prospects for the Future in Asia and the Pacific*, BIS Paper No. 61, pp. 57–74.

Mourad, Suleiman (2019), "The *Shahada* and the Creation of an Islamic Identity," in *Geneses: A Comparative Study of the Historiographies of the Rise of Christianity, Rabbinic Judaism, and Islam*, edited by John Tolan, Abingdon, Oxon: Routledge.

Mueller, Reinhold (1997), *The Venetian Money Market: Banks, Panics, and the Public Debt, 1200–1500*, Baltimore: Johns Hopkins University Press.

Muhl, Gerard (2001), "When Foreign Coins Circulated Freely," *The Crooked Lake Review* (Spring), https://www.crookedlakereview.com/articles/101_135/119spring2001/119muhl.html.

Mulder, Nicholas (2022), *The Economic Weapon: The Rise of Sanctions as a Tool of Modern War*, New Haven: Yale University Press.

Mullin, John (2023), "The Fed, the Stock Market, and the 'Greenspan Put,'" *Federal Reserve Bank of Richmond Econ Focus* (First Quarter), pp. 10–13.

Mundell, Robert (1993), "EMU and the International Monetary System: A Transatlantic Perspective," Working Paper No. 13, Vienna: Austrian National Bank.

Munro, John (2003), "The Monetary Origins of the 'Price Revolution': South German Silver Mining, Merchant Banking, and Venetian Commerce," in *Global Connections and Monetary History, 1470–1800*, edited by Dennis Flynn, Arturo Giráldez, and Richard von Glahn, Aldershot: Ashgate.

Munro, John (2012), "The Rise, Expansion, and Decline of the Italian Wool-Based Cloth Industries, 1100–1730: A Study in International Competition, Transactions Costs, and Comparative Advantage," *Studies in Medieval and Renaissance History* 9, pp. 45–207.

Myers, Margaret, Benjamin Beckhart, James Gerald Smith, and William Adams Brown (1931-2), *The New York Money Market*, New York: Columbia University Press.

Myles, Jamieson (2024), "Trade Acceptances, Financial Reform, and the Culture of Commercial Credit in the United States, 1915–1920," *Enterprise & Society* 25, pp. 1079–109.

Naclerio, Richard (2018), *The Federal Reserve and its Founders: Money, Politics and Power*, Newcastle upon Tyne: Agenda Publishing.

Naef, Alain (2022), *An Exchange Rate History of the United Kingdom, 1945–1992*, Cambridge: Cambridge University Press.

Naismith, Rory (2023), *Making Money in the Early Middle Ages,* Princeton and Oxford: Princeton University Press.

Najemy, John (2006), *A History of Florence 1200–1575*, Oxford: Blackwell.

Nappo, Dario (2018), "Money and Flows of Coinage in the Red Sea Trade," in *Trade, Commerce, and the State in the Roman World*, edited by Andrew Wilson and Alan Bowman, Oxford: Oxford University Press.

Neal, Larry (1987), "The Integration and Efficiency of the London and Amsterdam Stock Markets in the Eighteenth Century," *The Journal of Economic History* 47, pp. 97–115.

Neal, Larry (1998), "The Financial Crisis of 1825 and the Restructuring of the British Financial System," *Federal Reserve Bank of St. Louis Review* (May–June), pp. 53–76.

Nef, John (1941), "Silver Production in Central Europe, 1450–1618," *Journal of Political Economy* 49, 575–91.

Nichols, Irby, Jr. (1958), "Britain and the Austrian War Debt, 1821–1823," *The Historian* 20, pp. 328–46.

Nishimura, Shizuya (1971), *The Decline of Inland Bills of Exchange in the London Money Market, 1855–1913*, Cambridge: Cambridge University Press.

Nogueira-Batista, Paulo (2023), "A BRICS Currency?" Speech given at the BRICS Seminar on Governance and Cultural Exchange Forum 2023, Johannesburg (August 19).

North, Douglass and Barry Weingast (1989), "Constitutions and Commitment: The Evolution of Institutions Governing Public Choice in Seventeenth-Century England," *The Journal of Economic History* 49, pp. 803–32.

Odell, John (982), *U.S. International Monetary Policy: Markets, Power, and Ideas as Sources of Change*, Princeton: Princeton University Press.

Odell, Kerry and Marc Weidenmier (2004), "Real Shock, Monetary Aftershock: The 1906 San Francisco Earthquake and the Panic of 1907," *The Journal of Economic History* 64, pp. 1002–27.

Office of the Federal Register ed. (1972), *Richard Nixon, Containing the Public Messages, Speeches and Statements of the President*, Washington, D.C.: US Government Printing Office.

Okunev, John and Derek White (2003), "Do Momentum-Based Strategies Still Work in Foreign Exchange Markets?" *Journal of Financial and Quantitative Analysis* 38, pp. 425–47.

Olmstead-Rumsey, Jane (2019), "Country Banks and the Panic of 1825," unpublished manuscript, Northwestern University, https://elischolar.library.yale.edu/cgi/viewcontent.cgi?article=13783&context=ypfs-documents.

Oppers, Stefan (1993), "The Interest Rate Effect of Dutch Money in Eighteenth-Century Britain," *The Journal of Economic History* 53, pp. 25–43.

Origo, Iris (1960), *The Merchant of Prato*, London: J. Cape.

O'Rourke, Kevin and Jeffrey Williamson (2002), "After Columbus: Explaining Europe's Overseas Trade Boom, 1500–1800," *The Journal of Economic History* 62, pp. 417–56.

O'Sullivan, Mary (2016), *Dividends of Development: Securities Markets in the History of U.S. Capitalism, 1865–1922*, Oxford: Oxford University Press.

Padgett, John and Paul McLean (2002), "Economic and Social Exchange in Renaissance Florence," Santa Fe Institute Working Paper 2002-07-32.

Padgett, John and Paul McLean (2006), "Organizational Invention and Elite Transformation: The Birth of Partnership Systems in Renaissance Florence," *American Journal of Sociology* 111, pp. 1463–568.

Padgett, John and Paul McLean (2011), "Economic Credit in Renaissance Florence," *Journal of Modern History* 83, pp. 1–47.

Palyi, Melchior (1937), *The Chicago Credit Market: Organization and Institutional Structure*, Chicago: University of Chicago Press.

Parrini, Carl (1969), *Heir to Empire: United States Economic Diplomacy, 1916–1923*, Pittsburg: University of Pittsburgh Press.

Partner, Peter (1999), "The Papacy and the Papal States," in *The Rise of the Fiscal State in Europe, c.1200-1815*, edited by Richard Bonney, Oxford: Oxford University Press.

Pflueger, Carolin and Pierre Yared (2024), "Global Hegemony and Exorbitant Privilege," Working Paper 32775, National Bureau of Economic Research (August).

Philippon, Thomas (2021), *The Great Reversal: How America Gave Up on Free Markets*, Cambridge, MA: Belknap Press for Harvard University Press.

Platt, D.C.M. (1989), *Mickey Mouse Numbers in World History: The Short View*, London: Palgrave Macmillan.

Polak, Jacques (1951), "Contribution of the September 1949 Devaluations to the Solution of Europe's Dollar Problem," *IMF Staff Papers* 2, pp. 1–32.

Polanyi, Karl (1944), *The Great Transformation*, New York: Rinehart.

Pollard, Patricia (2001), "The Creation of the Euro and the Role of the Dollar in International Markets," *Federal Reserve Bank of St. Louis Quarterly Review* (September/October), pp. 17–36.

Pond, Shepard (1940), "The Ducat: Once an Important Coin in European Business," *Bulletin of the Business Historical Society* 14, pp. 17–19.

Pond, Shepard (1941), "The Spanish Dollar: The World's Most Famous Silver Coin," *Bulletin of the Business Historical Society* 15, pp. 12–16.

Porteous, John (1980), "The Nature of Coinage," in *Coins: An Illustrated Survey, 650 BC to the Present Day*, edited by Martin Jessop Price, London: Methuen.

Posen, Adam (2008), "Why the Euro will Not Rival the Dollar," *International Finance* 11, pp. 75–100.

Pourmohsen, Mojtaba (2022), "Iran Smuggling Venezuelan Gold to Finance Hezbollah: Document," *Iran International* (December 12), https://www.iranintl.com/en/202212124467.

Prakaesh, Om (2003), "Precious-Metal Flows into India in the Early Modern Period," in *Global Connections and Monetary History, 1470–1800*, edited by Dennis Flynn, Arturo Giráldez, and Richard von Glahn, Aldershot: Ashgate.

Pressnell, Leslie (1956), *Country Banking in the Industrial Revolution*, Oxford: Clarendon Press.

Prigent, Vivien (2014), "The Mobilisation of Fiscal Resources in the Byzantine Empire (Eighth to Eleventh Centuries)," in *Diverging Paths? The Shapes of Power and Institutions in Medieval Christendom and Islam*, edited by John Hudson and Ana Rodríguez López, Leiden: Brill.

Pryor, John (1977), "The Origins of the *Commenda* Contract," *Speculum* 52, pp. 5–37.

Psoma, Selene (2015), "Choosing and Changing Monetary Standards in the Greek World during the Archaic and the Classical Periods," in *The Ancient Greek Economy: Markets, Households and City-States*, edited by Edward Harris, David Lewis, and Mark Woolmer, Cambridge: Cambridge University Press.

Quinn, Stephen (1997), "Goldsmith-Banking: Mutual Acceptance and Interbanker Clearing in Restoration London," *Explorations in Economic History* 34, pp. 411–32.

Quinn, Stephen and William Roberds (2005), "The Big Problem of Large Bills: The Bank of Amsterdam and the Origins of Central Banking," Working Paper No. 2005-16, Federal Reserve Bank of Atlanta, (October).

Quinn, Stephen and William Roberds (2014), "How Amsterdam Got Fiat Money," *Journal of Monetary Economics* 66, pp. 1–12.

Quinn, Stephen and William Roberds (2023), *How a Ledger Became a Bank: A Monetary History of the Bank of Amsterdam*, New York: Cambridge University Press.

Redish, Angela (2000), *Bimetallism: An Economic and Historical Analysis*, New York: Cambridge University Press.

Reed, Harold (1922), *The Development of Federal Reserve Policy*, Boston and New York: Houghton Mifflin Company.

Reslow, André, Gabriel Soderberg, and Natsuki Tsuda (2024), "Cross-Border Payments with Retail Central Bank Digital Currencies: Design and Policy Considerations," Fintech Notes No. 2024/002, Washington, D.C.: IMF (May).

Reston, James (1989), *The Lone Star: The Life of John Connally*, New York: Harper & Row.

Riley, James (1980), *International Government Finance and the Amsterdam Capital Market 1740–1815*, Cambridge: Cambridge University Press.

Roberts, Pricilla (2002), "Frank A. Vanderlip and the National City Bank during the First World War," *Essays in Economic and Business History* 20, pp. 145–66.

Roberts, Richard (1992), *Schroders: Merchants and Bankers*, Houndmills, Basingstoke, Hampshire: Macmillan.

Rogers, James (1995), *The Early History of the Law of Bills and Notes: A Study of the Origins of Anglo-American Commercial Law*, Cambridge: Cambridge University Press.

Romer, Christina (1992), "What Ended the Great Depression?" *The Journal of Economic History* 52, pp. 757–84.

Rosa, Brunello with Casey Larsen (2024), *Smart Money: How Digital Currencies Will Win the New Cold War—and Why the West Needs to Act Now*, London: Bloomsbury.

Rosenbaum, Eduard and Ari J. Sherman (1979), *M. M. Warburg & Co. 1798–1938: Merchant Bankers of Hamburg*, London: C. Hurst & Company.

Royal Institute of International Affairs (1937), *The Problem of International Investment*, London: Oxford University Press.

Rubin, Jared (2010), "Bills of Exchange, Interest Bans, and Impersonal Exchange in Islam and Christianity," *Explorations in Economic History* 47, pp. 213–27.

Runciman, Steven (1952), "Byzantine Trade and Industry," in *The Cambridge Economic History of Europe, Volume II: Trade and Industry in the Middle Ages*, edited by M. M. Postan and Edward Miller, Cambridge: Cambridge University Press.

Sachs, Jeffrey (1985), "The Dollar and the Policy Mix: 1985," *Brookings Papers on Economic Activity* 1, pp. 117–85.

Saeed, Luqman (2025), "The Impact of Military Expenditures on Economic Growth: A New Instrumental Variables Approach," *Defense and Peace Economics* 36, pp. 86–101.

Sandbrook, Dominic (2012), *Seasons in the Sun: The Battle for Britain, 1974–1979*, London: Allen Lane.

Sandbu, Martin (2025), "Can Europe Go It Alone on Russia Sanctions?" *FT Free Lunch* (February 27), https://www.ft.com/content/29799337-cbad-4b11-823a-a2fd6ee38ec0.

Sargent, Thomas and Neil Wallace (1981), "Some Unpleasant Monetarist Arithmetic," *Federal Reserve Bank of Minneapolis Quarterly Review* 5 (Fall), pp. 1–17.

Sato, Masaki (2023), "Local Links behind a Global Scandal: The Audiencia de Charcas and the Great Potosí Mint Fraud, ca. 1650," in *Potosí in the Global Silver Age (16th–19th Centuries)*, edited by Rossana Barragán and Paul Zagalsky, Leiden: Brill.

Saunders, Philip (1928), *Stuckey's Bank*, Taunton UK: Barnicott & Pearce.

Scammell, W. M. (1965), "The Working of the Gold Standard," *Bulletin of Economic Research* 17, pp. 32–45.

Scammell, W. M. (1968), *The London Discount Market*, New York: St. Martin's Press.

Schaps, David (2001), "The Conceptual Prehistory of Money and its Impact on the Greek Economy," in *Hacksilber to Coinage: New Insights into the Monetary History of the Near East and Greece*, edited by Miriam Balmuth, Numismatic Studies no.24, New York: American Numismatic Society.

Schaps, David (2004), *The Invention of Coinage and the Monetization of Ancient Greece*, Ann Arbor: University of Michigan Press.

Schaps, David (2022), "Money, Credit and Banking," in *The Cambridge Companion to the Ancient Greek Economy*, edited by Sitta von Reden, Cambridge: Cambridge University Press.

Schmitthoff, M. (1939), "The Origin of the Joint-Stock Company," *University of Toronto Law Journal* 3, pp. 74–96.

Seijas, Tatiana and Jake Frederick (2017), *Spanish Dollars and Sister Republics: The Money that Made Mexico and the United States*, New York: Rowman and Littlefield.

Sidebotham, Steven (2011), *Berenike and the Ancient Maritime Spice Route*, Berkeley: University of California Press.

Simon, Matthew (1968), "The Morgan-Belmont Syndicate of 1895 and Intervention in the Foreign-Exchange Market," *Business History Review* 42, pp. 385–417.

Singh, Daleep (2024), "Forging a Positive Vision of Economic Statecraft," Atlantic Council (February 22), https://www.atlanticcouncil.org/blogs/new-atlanticist/forging-a-positive-vision-of-economic-statecraft/.

Sissoko, Carolyn (2019), "The Monetary Foundations of Britain's Early 19th Century Ascendency," Economics Working Paper No. 1906, UWE Bristol.

Slater, Martin (2018), *National Debt: A Short History*, Oxford: Oxford University Press.

Smith, Adam (1776 [1981]), *An Inquiry into the Nature and Causes of the Wealth of Nations*, Indianapolis: Liberty Fund edition.

Solomon, Robert (1981), *The International Monetary System, 1945–1981*, New York: Harper & Row.

Solomon, Robert (1999), *Money on the Move: The Revolution in International Finance Since 1980*, Princeton: Princeton University Press.

Sowerbutts, Rhiannon, Marco Schneebalg and Florence Hubert (2016), "The Demise of Overend Gurney," *Bank of England Quarterly Bulletin* Q2, pp.94-106.

Spalding, William (1931), *The London Money Market: A Practical Guide to What it is, Where it is, and the Operations Conducted in it*, New York: Sir I. Pitman & Sons.

Spiro, David (1999), *The Hidden Hand of American Hegemony: Petrodollar Recycling and International Markets*, Ithaca, NY: Cornell University Press.

Spufford, Peter (2008), *Money and its Use in Medieval Europe*, Cambridge: Cambridge University Press.

Spufford, Peter (2014), "The Provision of Stable Moneys by Florence and Venice, and Northern Italian Financial Innovations in the Renaissance Period," in *Explaining Monetary and Financial Innovation: A Historical Analysis*, edited by Peter Bernholz and Roland Vaubel, London: Springer.

Stahl, Alan (2000), *Zecca: The Mint of Venice in the Middle Ages*, Baltimore: Johns Hopkins University Press in association with the American Numismatic Society.

Stasavage, David (2003), *Public Debt and the Birth of the Democratic State: France and Great Britain, 1688–1789*, New York: Cambridge University Press.

Stasavage, David (2011), *States of Credit: Size, Power, and the Development of European Polities*, Princeton: Princeton University Press.

Steil, Benn (2013), *The Battle of Bretton Woods: John Maynard Keynes, Harry Dexter White, and the Making of a New World Order*, Princeton: Princeton University Press.

Steil, Benn (2018), *The Marshall Plan: Dawn of the Cold War*, New York: Simon and Schuster.

Stein, Stanley and Barbara Stein (2000), *Silver, Trade and War: Spain and America in the Making of Early Modern Europe*, Baltimore: Johns Hopkins University Press.

Steinhauser, Gabriele and Nicholas Bariyo (2019), "How 7.4 Tons of Venezuela's Gold Landed in Africa—and Vanished," *Wall Street Journal* (June 18), https://www.wsj.com/articles/how-7-4-tons-of-venezuelas-gold-landed-in-africaand-vanished-11560867792.

Steinmetz, Greg (2015), *The Richest Man Who Ever Lived: The Life and Times of Jacob Fugger*, New York: Simon & Schuster.

Stephens, Philip (1996), *Politics and the Pound: The Conservatives' Struggle with Sterling*, New York, Trans-Atlantic Publishers.

Strathern, Paul (2021), *The Florentines from Dante to Galileo: The Transformation of Western Civilization*, New York: Pegasus Books.

Strieder, Jacob (1966), *Jacob Fugger The Rich: Merchant and Banker of Augsburg, 1459–1525*, Hamden, Conn.: Archon Books.

Supple, Barry (1970), *The Royal Exchange Assurance: A History of British Insurance 1720–1970*, Cambridge: Cambridge University Press.

Supreme Court of the United States (2025), "Donald J. Trump, President of the United States, et al, v. Gwynne A. Wilcox, et al, On Application for Stay" (May 22), https://www.supremecourt.gov/opinions/24pdf/24a966_1b8e.pdf.

SWIFT (Society for Worldwide Interbank Financial Telecommunication) (2025), "SWIFT RMB Tracker" (June), https://www.swift.com/sites/default/files/files/rmb-tracker_june-2025.pdf.

Sylla, Richard (2011), "Wall Street Transitions, 1880–1920: From National to World Financial Centre," in *Financial Centres and International Capital Flows in the Nineteenth and Twentieth Centuries*, edited by Laure Quennouëlle-Corre and Youssef Cassis, Oxford: Oxford University Press.

Tabor, Nicholas, Katherine Di Lucido, and Jeffery Zhang (2021), "A Brief History of the U.S. Regulatory Perimeter," Finance and Economics Discussion Paper No. 2021-051, Divisions of Research & Statistics and Monetary Affairs, Federal Reserve Board, Washington, D.C.

Takagi, Shinji (2012), "Internationalising the Yen, 1984–2003: Unfinished Agenda or Mission Impossible," in *Currency Internationalisation: Lessons from the Global Financial Crisis and Prospects for the Future in Asia and the Pacific*, BIS Paper No.61, pp. 75–92.

Tavlas, George (1991), "On the International Use of Currencies: The Case of the Deutsche Mark," *Essays in International Finance* No. 181, International Finance Section, Department of Economics, Princeton University (March).

TePaske, John and Kendall Brown (2010), *A New World of Gold and Silver*, Leiden: Brill.

Termeer, Marleen (2022), "The Political Culture of Coinage: The Introduction and Development of the Denarius System," in *A Community in Transition: Rome between Hannibal and the Gracchhi*, edited Mattia Balbo and Federico Santangelo, Oxford: Oxford University Press.

Thonemann, Peter (2015), *The Hellenistic World Using Coins as Sources*, Cambridge: Cambridge University Press.

Thorley, J. (1969), "The Development of Trade between the Roman Empire and the East under Augustus," *Greece & Rome* 16, pp. 209–23.

Thorley, J. (1971), "The Silk Trade between China and the Roman Empire at Its Height, 'Circa' A.D. 90–130," *Greece & Rome* 18, pp. 71–80.

Thornton, Henry (1802 [1939]), *An Inquiry into the Nature and Effects of the Paper Credit of Great Britain*, London: George Allen & Unwin.

Thygesen, Niels (2016), "Why Did Europe Decide to Move to a Single Currency 25 Years Ago?" *Intereconomics* 51, pp. 11–16.

Treadgold, Warren (1995), *Byzantium and Its Army, 284–1081*, Stanford, CA: Stanford University Press.

Treadgold, Warren (1997), *A History of the Byzantine State and Society*, Stanford, CA: Stanford University Press.

Trevett, Jeremy (2001), "Coinage and Democracy at Athens," in *Money and its Uses in the Ancient Greek World*, edited by Andrew Meadows and Kirsty Shipton, Oxford: Oxford University Press.

Triffin, Robert (1957), *Europe and the Money Muddle: From Bilateralism to Near-Convertibility 1947–1956*, New Haven: Yale University Press.

Triffin, Robert (1960), *Gold and the Dollar Crisis: The Future of Convertibility*, New Haven: Yale University Press.

Triffin, Robert (1964), "The Evolution of the International Monetary System: Historical Reappraisal and Future Perspectives," *Princeton Studies in International Finance* no. 12, International Finance Section, Department of Economics, Princeton University.

Triffin, Robert (1967), "The Coexistence of Three Types of Reserve Assets," *Banca Nazionale del Lavoro Quarterly Review* 20, pp. 107–134.

Truptil, Roger Jean (1936), *British Banks and the London Money Market*, London: Jonathan Cape.

Turner, John (2014), *Banking in Crisis: The Rise and Fall of British Banking Stability, 1800 to the Present*, Cambridge: Cambridge University Press.

Udovitch, Abraham (1970), *Partnership and Profit in Medieval Islam*, Princeton: Princeton University Press.

Uglow, Jenny (2014), *In These Times: Living in Britain through Napoleon's War, 1793–1815*, London: Faber & Faber.

Ugolini, Stefano (2012), "The Bank of England as the World Gold Market-Maker during the Classical Gold Standard Era, 1889–1910," Working Paper 15/2012, Norges Bank (October).

U.S. Senate (1931), "Operation of the National and Federal Reserve Banking Systems," *Hearings Before a Subcommittee of the Committee on Banking and Currency*, 71st Cong. 3rd sess., S. Res. 71, Washington, D.C.: Government Printing Office.

U.S. Senate (1932), "Sale of Foreign Bonds or Securities in the United States," *Hearings Before the Senate Committee on Finance*, 72 Cong., 1st sess., S. Res. 19, Washington, D.C.: U.S. Government Printing Office.

U.S. Treasury (2021), *Treasury 2021 Sanctions Review*, Washington, D.C.: U.S. Department of the Treasury, https://home.treasury.gov/system/files/136/Treasury-2021-sanctions-review.pdf.

Van der Wee, Herman (2012), "Belgian Monetary Policy under the Gold Standard during the Interwar Period," in *The Gold Standard Peripheries: Monetary Policy, Adjustment and Flexibility in a Global Setting*, edited by Anders Ögren and Lars Øksendal, Houndmills, Basingstoke: Palgrave Macmillan.

Van Dillen, Johannes Gerard (1934), *History of the Principal Public Banks Accompanied by Extensive Bibliographies of the History of Banking and Credit in Eleven European Countries*, The Hague: Martinus Nijhoff.

Veseth, Michael (1990), *Mountains of Debt: Crisis and Change in Renaissance Florence, Postwar Britain, and Postwar America*, New York: Oxford University Press.

Vicquéry, Roger (2022), "The Rise and Fall of Global Currencies over Two Centuries," Working Paper No. 882, Banque de France (July).

Volcker, Paul (2018), *Keeping At It: The Quest for Sound Money and Good Government*, New York: PublicAffairs.

Volcker, Paul and Toyoo Gyohten (1992), *Changing Fortunes: The World's Money and the Threat to American Leadership*, New York: Times Books.

Von Glahn, Richard (1996), *Fountain of Fortune: Money and Monetary Policy in China, 1000–1700*, Berkeley: University of California Press.

Von Glahn, Richard (2003), "Money Use in China and Changing Patterns of Global Trade in Monetary Metals, 1500–1800," in *Global Connections and Monetary History, 1470–1800*, edited by Dennis Flynn, Arturo Giráldez, and Richard von Glahn, Aldershot: Ashgate.

Walker, C. E. (1931), "The History of the Joint Stock Company," *Accounting Review* 6, pp. 97–105.

Walter, Rolf and Maximilian Kalus (2013), "Innovation in the Age of the Fuggers," in *The Two Sides of Innovation: Creation and Destruction in the Evolution of Capitalist Economies*, edited by Guido Buenstorf et al., Zurich: Springer International.

Warburg, Paul (1910), *The Discount System in Europe*, Washington, D.C.: Government Printing Office.

Warburg, Paul (1914), *Essays on Banking Reform in the United States*, New York: Academy of Political Science.

Warburg, Paul (1930), *The Federal Reserve System, Its Origin and Growth: Reflections and Recollections*, two volumes, New York: Macmillan.

Wassink, Alfred (1991), "Inflation and Financial Policy under the Roman Empire to the Price Edict of 301 A.D.," *Historia: Zeitschrift für Alte Geschichte* 40, pp. 465–93.

Watanabe, Tsutomu (2010), "The Signaling Effect of Foreign Exchange Intervention: The Case of Japan," in *Exchange Rate Policy and Interdependence: Perspectives from the Pacific Basin*, edited by Reuven Glick and Michael Hutchison, New York: Cambridge University Press.

Weber, Max (1889 [2003]), *The History of Commercial Partnerships in the Middle Ages*, Lanham, MD: Rowman and Littlefield.

Wedmore, Frederick (1886), "Walter Boyd (1754?-1837)," in *Dictionary of National Biography Vol. 6*, edited by Sir Leslie Stephen, New York: Macmillan.

Weiss, Colin (2022), "Geopolitics and the U.S. Dollar's Future as a Reserve Currency," International Finance Discussion Paper No. 1359, Washington, D.C.: Board of Governors of the Federal Reserve System (October).

Weissmann, Jordan (2024), "Could Donald Trump Break the Fed?" *The Atlantic* (August 21), https://www.theatlantic.com/politics/archive/2024/08/donald-trump-federal-reserve-independence/679535/.

White, Eugene (2001), "Making the French Pay: The Costs and Consequences of Napoleonic Reparations," *European Review of Economic History* 5, pp. 337–65.

White, Harry Dexter (1933), *The French International Accounts, 1880–1913*, Cambridge, MA: Harvard University Press.

Wicker, Elmus (2005), *The Great Debate on Banking Reform: Nelson Aldrich and the Origins of the Fed*, Columbus, OH: Ohio State University Press.

Wilgress, L. D. (1912/13), "The London Money Market," *Journal of the Canadian Bankers Association* 20, pp. 210–25.

Wilkie, Christopher (2012), *Special Drawing Rights: The First International Money*, New York: Oxford University Press.

Williamson, Oliver (1975), *Markets and Hierarchies: Analysis and Antitrust Implications*, New York: Free Press.

Willis, Henry Parker (1901), *A History of the Latin Monetary Union: A Study of International Monetary Action*, Chicago: University of Chicago Press.

Wong, Andrea (2016), "The Untold Story Behind Saudi Arabia's 41-Year U.S. Debt Secret," *Bloomberg* (May 30), https://www.bloomberg.com/news/features/2016-05-30/the-untold-story-behind-saudi-arabia-s-41-year-u-s-debt-secret.

Woodruff, William (1967), *Impact of Western Man: A Study of Europe's Role in the World Economy 1750–1960*, New York: St. Martin's Press.

Woolmer, Mark (2015), "Forging Links between Regions: Trade Policy in Classical Athens," in *The Ancient Greek Economy: Markets, Households and City-States*, edited by Edward Harris, David Lewis, and Mark Woolmer, Cambridge: Cambridge University Press.

World Bank (2021), "Central Bank Digital Currencies for Cross-Border Payments," Washington, D.C.: World Bank (November).

Xu, Jin (2021), *Empire of Silver: A New Monetary History of China*, New Haven: Yale University Press.

Yang, Lien-sheng (1952), *Money and Credit in China: A Short History*, Cambridge, MA: Harvard University Press.

Zhaodong, Sun (2014), *Renminbi: The Internationalization of China's Currency*, London and Beijing: Paths International Ltd.

Zhou, Xiaochuan (2009), "Reform of the International Monetary System," Shanghai: People's Bank of China (March 23), http://camlmac.pbc.gov.cn/english/130724/2842945/index.html.

Ziegler, Philip (1988), *The Sixth Great Power: A History of One of the Greatest of All Banking Families: The House of Barings, 1762–1929*, New York: Knopf.

Zweig, Philip (1995), *Wriston: Walter Wriston, Citibank, and the Rise and Fall of American Financial Diplomacy*, New York: Crown Books.

INDEX

Note: page numbers followed by n refer to notes, with note number.

'Abd al-Malik, 43–44, 252nn81–82
acceptance houses, as key financial infrastructure, 16
acceptances. *See* trade acceptances
Adams, John, 90–91, 94
Alexanders as international currency, 8, 249n23; spread through conquest, 11–12, 28; stable value and quality of, 28
Alipay+, 219
alliances between countries, international currencies and, 11, 12
American Acceptance Council, 16, 128, 141
American and Foreign Banking Corporation, 140
Arab merchants: early use of bills of exchange, 15; gold traded to Italian city-states, 52
Arellano, Juan Ramíez de, 76
Aristotle, 23, 24, 247n2
Arte del Cambio, 10, 58, 59
artificial intelligence, and U.S. productivity, 225–26
Asia: copper coins in, 258n30; scarcity of silver in, 79; trade using Spanish silver reals, 78–81
Athenian tetradrachm ("owls") as international currency, 8; Athenian form of government and, 246n13; Athens' high volume of trade and, 14, 27; Athens' military strength and, 27–28; quality and stability of Athenian coins, 26–27, 248n12
Azores, U.S.-French talks in, 175–76

Bagehot, Walter, 106, 110
Baker, James A. III, 190–93
bancor, 159, 161, 168–69
bankers, origin in goldsmiths and silversmiths, 102, 251n73
Bank for International Settlements (BIS), and mBridge, 220–22
bank money-based transactions, first modern system of, 50
Bank of Amsterdam: and appeal of stable and liquid guilder, 88, 89–91; loans to Amsterdam government and VOC, 94–95; as de facto central bank, 84, 91; and development of bank giro system, 87–88; exchange of precious metal deposits for fiat currency, 89–90; loss of ability to stabilize bank money value and liquidity, 94–95; receipt system for deposited specie, 89–90, 260n23, 260n26; and regularization of Dutch currency, 87
Bank of England: and Chinese war indemnity payments to Japan, 110–11; convertibility of funds into gold as key attraction of, 110, 117–18; convertibility into gold, suspensions and threats of suspension, 104–5, 106, 114, 118, 120, 137–39, 151, 262n25, 270n32; and crisis of 1825, 104–7, 263n33; Dutch investment in, 92; and financial firm failures of 1800s, 119–21, 267nn101–2; gold standard, post-World War I, 147–48; interwar

323

Bank of England (*continued*)
  policies to stabilize pound sterling, 150–52; as lender and discounter of last resort, 99, 107, 120–21; and San Francisco earthquake, 131
Bardi banking partnership, 17, 57, 58, 60, 63, 64, 65, 67, 163
Baring Brothers, 107, 112, 113–14, 116
Barney, Charles, 133–35
Belgium, and gold standard, 168
Bernanke, Ben, 200
Bessent, Scott, 212–13, 234
bills of exchange: and Amsterdam as financial hub, 88, 89–91; and development of international currencies, 15–16; function of, 61–62, 255n44; origins of, 49, 253n3
Blessing, Karl, 171, 276n49
Blumenthal, Michael, 185–87, 188, 279n39
Boyd, Benfield & Co., 112–13
Boyd, Walter, 98, 112–13
Bretton Woods Conference, 160–62; choice of location, 160; conferences prior to, 156, 273n6; U.S. Alternative A at, 162; and U.S. dollar as international currency, 159, 162–64
Bretton Woods system: British pound driven from system, 180–82, 196; collapse of, 183–85; and controls on international capital flows, 158, 161; and convertibility of currencies, 161; Denmark and France driven from, 196–97; exchange controls, 158; Marshall Plan and, 164; U.S. abandonment of, under Nixon, 3–4, 175–76, 177, 178–83. *See also* United States dollar as international currency, under Bretton Woods system
BRICS: Cross-Border Payment Initiative, 222; efforts to supplant U.S. dollar as international currency, viii, 215
Britain/England: consol perpetual bonds, 96; loans denominated in dollars, post-Bretton Woods, 167; Fourth Anglo-Dutch War and, 94, 95; GDP growth, financial infrastructure supporting, 102–4; mint's silver shortages of 18th century, 100–101; political checks and balances protecting investors, 96; stock exchange, international trading on, 111; and U.S. devaluation of dollar, 172–73. *See also* Bank of England
British East India Company: competition with Dutch East India Company, 93–95; Dutch investment in, 92
British pound sterling: driven from Bretton Woods system, 180–82, 196; and EMS crisis of 1992–93, 197
British pound sterling as international currency, 8–9; attraction of investment and foreign loans, 18; Bank of England as guarantor of value, 10; Bank of England interwar policies to stabilize, 150–52; Bretton Woods Conference and, 158; Britain's high volume of trade and, 14–15; British form of government and, 9; British Navy's dominance of seas and, 99; and circulation in bank money, 50; decline of, 12, 19, 137–39; duration of, 19; financial infrastructure allowing for, 16, 99; French and Napoleonic Wars and, 98; and gold standard, 9, 147–48; high number of overseas transactions, 97; international bonds and, 97; interwar competition with U.S. dollar, 145–48, 150–52, 272n83; interwar loan policies, 145–46; market liquidity and, 17; post-World War I loans to Europe, 147; rise in British international trade and, 99, 100; rise to international dominance, 97–99; spread with British financing of international trade, 109, 264n51; stable value of, 9; superior vetting of borrowers and, 150; trade in U.S. dollars and, 18; World War I and, 137–39. *See also* Bank of England; London as international finance center
brokers, as key financial infrastructure, 16
Bryan, William Jennings, 134, 142
Burns, Arthur, 173, 174, 178, 189

Byzantine Empire's soldus as international currency, 8, 251n68; administrative capacity to control money supply, 42; decline, factors in, 45–48; Empire's conquest by Pecheneg Turks and, 46–47; expansive trade network and, 42–43; other coins designed to imitate, 43, 44; reasons for, 42–43; rise of Italian currencies and, 48; spread through conquest, 42; stable value of, 9, 42, 43

Caesar, Julius, 8, 33
Carter, Jimmy, 185–90, 246–47n19
central bank digital currencies (CBDCs): direct digital exchange of, 220–21; as potential rival to U.S. dollar, 217–19, 241; retail, 217–19, 284–85n32–34; U.S. and, 285–86n36; wholesale, 217–18, 219
central banks: autonomy of, as guarantor of international currency stability, 10; as key financial infrastructure, 16, 211–12
Cerro de Pasco mine, 82
Champagne Fairs, 51–52, 254n25
Charles VIII (king of France), 67–68
China: coins, early, 247n3; and Cross-Border Interbank Payment System (CIPS), 17; European coins used in trade with, 83; falling birth rates and sluggish labor force growth, 226, 286n6; and financial market infrastructure, 16–17; gold exports, 16th-18th centuries, 79, 258–59n36, 258n32; and mBridge project, 220, 221–22, 241; paper money and bills of exchange in, history of, 258–59n36; and potential new Cold War, economic effects of, 212–13, 223; and risk of U.S. sanctions, 231; trade using Spanish silver reals, 78, 79–80
Chinese renminbi as international currency, 208–13; Belt & Road Program and, 208; China's growing global influence and, 6, 12; China's military power and alliances, 211, 283n18; Chinese officials' push for, 14, 208–10; digital renminbi (e-CNY) and, 218–19, 284–85nn34–35; direct trading of renminbi against other currencies, 209–10; international banking infrastructure, development of, 209–10; lack of political checks and balances and central bank autonomy, 211–12, 240–41; obstacles to, 210–12, 240–41; and potential new Cold War, economic effects of, 212–13; regional role for foreseeable future, 212; and renminbi-denominated securities, 209
Churchill, Winston, 155
Cipolla, Carlo, 43–44
CIPS. *See* Cross-Border Interbank Payment System
Claudius Gothicus (Roman emperor), 41
Clement VII (pope), 66–67
Coal and Steel Community, 165
coins: early standardization, to allow for exchange, 25; and facilitation of trade, 25; invention of, 23–24; as vehicle for taxation, 25
commenda contracts, 54–55
Committee of Twenty, 183, 278n20
Connally, John, 6, 173–78, 191
Constantine I, 41–42
Cook, Lisa, 232–33
Coombs, Charles, 182, 187
countries issuing international currency: attraction of investment and foreign loans, 17–18; benefits to, ix–x, 5; disadvantages for exporters and lenders, x; distortions in investment and excessive financialization, effects of, 19, 38; high volume of trade characteristic of, 14–15, 27, 34–37; risks inherent in, 47–48; spread of currency through foreign conquest or military bases, 11–12, 28, 31–32. *See also* international currency, core requirements for
countries issuing international currency, loss of dominance: economic and strategic decline and, 18–20, 37–39, 45–48; risks leading to, x; as typically gradual, 19–20; viable alternatives currencies as necessary for, 20

COVID-19 pandemic: and EU integration, 206–7; and Federal Reserve currency swap lines, 236–37, 289n36; and U.S. dollar as safe haven, 200–201
Croesus (king of Lydia), 24
Cross-Border Interbank Payment System (CIPS), 17, 210
cryptocurrencies as international currencies. *See* central bank digital currencies; stablecoins

de Gaulle, Charles, 170, 198
Delian League, 27
Delors, Jacques, 198
digital currencies as international currencies. *See* central bank digital currencies; stablecoins
Diocletian, 41, 251n69
double-entry bookkeeping, development of, 49, 69
Draghi, Mario, 199, 206, 226
Dutch East India Company (VOC): and Asian trade, 79, 80, 86–87; coins minted by, 260n11; collapse of, 93–95; and demand for silver, 79; and expansion of Dutch trading networks, 86; founding of, 86; use of bills of exchange in Asian trade, 260n11
Dutch financial firms: loans to fund American Revolution, 90–91, 94; move from acceptances to long-term loans, 90; securitization of loans, 90
Dutch guilders, as pure fiat currency, 84
Dutch guilders as international currency, 8; Amsterdam as financial hub and, 88, 89–91; Bank of Amsterdam as guarantor of value, 10; circulation in bank money, 50; duration of, 19; and Dutch ability to control money supply, 10; Dutch form of government and, 9; French and Napoleonic Wars and, 98; global expansion of, 89–91; interchangeability with Dutch bank money, 87; liquidity of, 17, 88; overshadowing of coin and bullion, 84; spread of, with expanding trade, 86–87; stable value of, 88, 91. *See also* Bank of Amsterdam
Dutch guilders as international currency, collapse of, 12; Dutch East Indies Company collapse and, 93–95; excessive financialization and, 92–93; fall of Dutch Republic and, 95; French and English competition and, 91–92, 93–95; lack of military power to defend trade routes and, 92; loss of dominance with economic decline, 18–19; loss of liquidity, 95; loss of stable value, 94–95
Dutch Republic: early monetary disarray, 85, 86; expansion of Dutch trading networks in, 86–87; fall of, 95; founding of, 85; merchant corporations, development of, 86; minting of gold coins for international trade, 86

Edward I (king of England), 65, 66
Edward II (king of England), 65, 66
Edward III (king of England), 58, 63, 64, 67; loan default, 58
Egypt: closed currency system of, 36–37, 250nn48–49; trade with Rome, 36–37
electronic market-making and liquidity-provision algorithms, 214–15, 284n24
electronic trading, and nontraditional reserve currencies as potential international currency, 214–15
electrum, early coins made from, 24
English East India Company, 79, 80
English Navigation Acts, 92
euro: lender of last resort for, 199–200; as potential international currency, 6–7, 197–200, 205–7, 226, 240; reasons for creation of, 197–98
European Central Bank, as lender of last resort, 199–200
European Economic Community, establishment of, 165
European Monetary System (EMS), 196–97

INDEX 327

European Payment Union, 274–75n23
European Union: bonds, limitations of, 205–6; and defense of Ukraine, 207, 282n4; lack of commitment to supranational financial institutions, 206–7; lack of geopolitical power, 207; recent defense spending increases, 226
exchange rate equilibrium values, tendency to overshoot, 192
"exorbitant privilege" of country with international currency, 5, 27, 37, 248–49n21

Federal Reserve, U.S.: CBDCs and, 285–86n36; creation of, ix, 128, 152; currency swap lines, 236–37, 288–89nn34–35; and dollars' evolution from commercial to financial use, 14; Glass-Owen Federal Reserve Act and, 142; as guarantor of U.S. dollar stability, 10; as lender of last resort, 235; policies leading to Great Depression, 149–50, 151–52, 272n79; successful market stabilization, 200–201; and U.S. financial infrastructure, 16; withdrawal from U.S. acceptance market, 141
Federal Reserve Act, U.S., 128, 136–37, 139, 143, 270n45
Federal Reserve Board: creation of, 142; Trump attacks on independence of, 232–33
fiat currency, Dutch introduction of, 84
financialization, in countries issuing international currency, 19, 38; and decline of British pound sterling, 122; and decline of Dutch guilder, 92–93; and decline of Florentine florins, 70; and decline of Roman denarius, 38; U.S. and, 287n19
Flandreau, Marc, 91
Florence: acquisition of Porto Pisano and sea access, 253n5; early international trade, 51–52, 53; influx of gold through trade, 52–53; merchants' early use of bills of exchange, 15; minting of gold coins for domestic commerce, 53, 59; as neither military nor commercial leader prior to florins' rise, 50–51
Florentine banks: accounting transactions and reduced risk of currency transfers, 61; development from partnership networks and holding companies, 49, 55–56; evolution into international banks, 60–63; and exchange rate risks, 62–63; financial services and loans to papacy, 65, 66–67, 256n58, 256n60; interbank transfers and bills of exchange, 61–62, 255n44; interest-bearing time deposits of, 60; interplay of banking and trade expansion, 62; liquidity provided by, 59–60; loans to merchants and monarchs, 81, 255n47; loans to royalty, risks and rewards of, 63–66; payment and credit services, 60–61; prominent families in, 60; reputation for security and good returns, 60; risk management practices, 65, 255n53; special privileges derived from loans to royalty, 65–66; syndicates formed by, 65; use of deposited funds to expand trade side of business, 60
Florentine florins as international currency, 8; attraction of investment and foreign loans, 17; duration of, 19; evolution from commercial to financial use, 14; Florence's form of government and, 9; Florence's wide-ranging trade network and, 49, 53, 54; Florentine institutions preserving stability of, 10, 58–59; imitations minted by other city-states, 53–54; liquidity of, 59–60; and loans to royalty, 63–66; officials' promotion of, 54; rivals to, 252n1; stable value of, 9, 49, 58; traders' preference for, 58. *See also* Florentine banks
Florentine florins as international currency, decline of, 67–70; excessive financialization and, 70; Florence's military setbacks and, 67–68; political and economic stagnation and decline and, 18, 68–69, 256n70; rise of competitors, 69, 70

Florentine florins' role in banking and finance: development of intangible bank money, 50; and international spread of florin-denominated assets, 49–50; as pioneering innovation, 49–51, 70

Florentine holding companies for legally-separate partnerships: advantages of, 57–58; development of, 56–57; division of labor in, 57; evolution into branched international banks, 49, 55–56, 60–63; expansive trade networks of, 57, 254n30; legal protections of separate partnerships, 56, 58; prominent families in, 57

Foreign Direct Investment Program, 171

Fourth Anglo-Dutch War, 94, 95

Fowler, Henry, 169–70, 171

France: driven from Bretton Woods system, 196–97; and EMS crisis of 1992–93, 197; and U.S. as international currency, 170, 175–76

French and Napoleonic Wars, and rise of British pound sterling, 98

French franc as regional currency, 117

French Revolution, 95

Fugger family, 69, 78

Genghis Khan, 45

Genoa: challenge to Florentine financial dominance, 69; coins minted by, 53; and development of international trade partnerships, 56; and Spanish New World silver, 78

German deutschmark: as alternative international currency, 196; and European Monetary System, 196–97

Germany: banks' competition with London, 117; rise of international commercial and financial leagues, 69; and Saiger process for silver purification, 72; support for U.S. dollar, 12, 237; and troubled U.S. dollar, 173, 174, 176, 178, 180, 185–87, 191, 193

Glass, Carter, 141–44, 271n61

Glass-Owen Federal Reserve Act, 142

Global Financial Crisis, maintenance of liquidity in, 194

gold, discovery in Brazil, 100

gold reserves: as hedge against U.S. sanctions, 231–32, 287n21; as impractical means of payment, 232

gold standard: Belgium and, 168; British pound sterling and, 9, 147–48; and definition of gold-convertible currencies, 274n16; and pressure on U.S. gold reserves, 159; Triffin's critique of, 167–69; U.S. abandonment of, under Roosevelt, 154; U.S. return to, in 1934, 155

Great Depression: events leading to, 149–50, 151–52, 272n79; repeat of, as likely consequence of collapse of U.S. dollar as international currency, 241–42; and U.S. acceptance market, 141; and U.S. dollar as international currency, 10–11, 17, 151–52

Greece, ancient, coins in, 24–25, 247n2, 248n5. *See also* Athenian tetradrachm ("owls") as international currency

Greenspan, Alan, 194, 200

Group of Five (G-5): exchange rate meetings of 1980s, 191–92; founding of, 183–84

Group of Seven (G-7), 184

Group of Ten (G-10): and Smithsonian Agreement, 176–77; and Special Drawing Rights (SDRs), 170–71; and SWIFT, 222; and U.S. fall from gold standard, 175

Gurney, Samuel and John, 103

Heinze, Fritz Augustus, 131–34

Hirschman, Albert, 165–66

Hope & Co., 92–93, 95, 96, 98, 113–14

Hungary, gold traded to Italian city-states, 52–53

India: Roman coins found in, 35–36, 250n52; trade using Spanish silver reals, 78

interest on loans, early circumvention of usury prohibitions, 59–60, 62, 255n38

Interim Committee, 183, 278–79n21
International Acceptance Bank of New York, 128
international capital flows, first modern system of, 50
international currencies: evolution from commercial to financial use, 13–15; government support necessary for, 164; history, overview of, 7–8; and international alliances, 11, 12; lifecycle of, ix–x; persistence over time of, 19, 47–48; tensions between national government and international interests, vii–ix, 5–6, 245n1
international currency, requirements for, 9–12; administrative capacity to control money supply, 10, 32, 42, 75–76, 246n15; capacity to ensure stability of banking and financial systems, 9, 10–11, 32; countries' power to defend its merchants, 247n22; currency's stable value and quality, assurance of, 9, 26–27, 28, 32, 35, 40, 42, 43, 58, 248n12; financial innovation and infrastructure as, 15–18; liquidity as, 17–18, 59–60; military power and security of issuing country as, 11–12, 27–28, 32, 42, 47–48, 207, 237–39; political checks and balances protecting currency as (typically democracy or republic), 9–10, 32, 39, 58–59, 211–12, 246n13
International Monetary Fund (IMF): and collapse of Bretton Woods system, 184; role of, 158; and Triffin's plan, 168–69; U.S. contribution to, 160–61; U.S. veto in, 194–95
international monetary policy, design of, 154–55. *See also* Bretton Woods Conference

Japan: bank branches in UK, 108, 145; Chinese war indemnity payments to, 110–11; financing of war with Russia, 122, 129; silver production in 16th century, 72–73; support for U.S. dollar, for security reasons, 11, 12, 237; trade in pounds sterling, 108; and troubled U.S. dollar, 173, 174, 176, 178, 180, 185–87, 191, 193; Yen as alternative international currency, 195
J. Henry Schröder & Co., 98
J. P. Morgan & Co., 140, 146, 148, 149

Keynes, John Maynard, 155, 158–59, 161–62, 168–69
Kindleberger, Charles, 3–4, 179
Knickerbocker Trust, 133–35
Kuhn, Loeb & Co., 129, 148

Latin America, capital flight from, 83
Lehman Brothers, 200–201
lender of last resort: development of concept, 105; as essential for international currency, 199–200; Rothschild as, in crisis of 1825, 106
Lend-Lease Act of 1941, 156, 161, 163
Liberty Loan Act (U.S.), 146
Lindbergh, Charles, 160
Loeb, Solomon, 129
London as international financial center, 107–8; acceptance houses' overseas branches and, 107; acceptance market, World War I damage to, 137–39; banks' origin in goldsmith firms, 102; Baring crisis of 1890, 119–20, 267nn101–2; bill brokers, 103–4; bills of exchange development into international instruments, 100–102; bills of exchange infrastructure, 102–4; British stock exchange and, 111; competition from French and German banks, 116–17, 120; convertibility of funds to gold as key attraction of, 110, 117–18; and crisis of 1825, 104–7, 115; discount houses, development of, 106–7; and dominance of pound sterling, 109; 18th-century financial cooperation with Amsterdam,

London as international financial center (*continued*) 97; foreign correspondent relationships and, 108; and foreign market for British Treasury securities, 109–10; government's political neutrality and, 266n90; and international arbitrage transactions, 111–12; large percentage of foreign bills, 108; loans to foreign governments, 112–16; loan to America for Louisiana Purchase, 113–14; network of local banks tied to, 102–4, 262n23, 264n51; origin and development of, 96–97; Overend & Gurney crisis of 1866 and, 118–19, 121; overseas banks with London branches, 107–8; rise to dominance, 97; safety as attraction of, 96, 98, 121

London as international finance center, decline of: factors in, 122; World War I and, 137–39

Lowell, Abbott Lawrence, 154

Lucca, 53, 56

Lula da Silva, Luiz Inácio, 215

Lydians, invention of coins by, 23–24, 247n3

Marshall Plan, 164

Medici, Piero de', 67–68

Medici family, 14, 56, 65, 67

Medina, Bartolomé de, 73

Mercantile Bank of the Americas, 140

Mercantile National Bank, 133

Mexico: capital flight to Europe, 83; coins minted in, post-Independence, 82–83

momentum-based trading strategies, 190

money: bank money, first system of, 50; international capital flows, first modern system of, 50; objects used as, before coins, 23; three canonical functions of, 23. *See also* coins

Mongol Empire, coins issued by, 45

Monnet, Jean, 206–7

Monte Comune, 60, 69

Monte delle doti, 60, 69, 255n39

Morgan, J. P., 127, 134–35

Morgenthau, Henry, 154

Morse, Charles W., 132–34

National Banking Act of 1863, U.S., 129

National City Bank, 140, 145, 146, 149, 270n43

National Monetary Commission, U.S., 128

Nero (Roman emperor), 39–41, 251n63

Nestares Marín, Francisco de, 75–76

Netherlands: as commercial backwater in 16th century, 84–85; late use of trading partnerships, 84–85. *See also entries under* Dutch

Newton, Isaac, 100–101

Nixon, Richard M.: efforts to curb gold outflow in 1970s, 172, 173–75; and fallout from dollar devaluation, 178–79; suspension of gold convertibility, 3–4, 175–76, 177, 178–83; and threat to U.S. dollar as international currency, 3–4, 6, 7; wage and price controls, 1–2, 3, 175

nontraditional reserve currencies as potential rivals to U.S. dollar, 213–15

OAPEC. *See* Organization of Arab Petroleum Exporting Countries

OPEC. *See* Organization of the Petroleum Exporting Countries

Open Market Investment Committee (OMIC), 149, 272n79

Organization of Arab Petroleum Exporting Countries (OAPEC), 184–85

Organization of the Petroleum Exporting Countries (OPEC), 18

Overend & Gurney, 103, 107

Papacy, Florentine international banks and, 65, 66–67, 256n58, 256n60

partnerships for international trade, development of, 55–56

Paul II (pope), 256n58

People's Bank of China (PBoC), 209, 211, 212, 218, 220, 222, 283n19

Peruzzi banking partnership, 17, 57, 58, 60, 63, 65, 67, 163
Philip II (king of Spain), 65, 85
Philip IV (king of Spain), 75, 76–77
Pole, Thornton & Co., 105
Pompidou, Georges, 175–76
Potosí silver mine, 73, 74; minting fraud, impact of, 75–77; minting of silver, 77; Spanish loss of, 82
Powell, Jerome, 232
Project Icebreaker, 285n36
Project mBridge, 220–21, 285n38; governance problems with, 222–23; political problems with, 221–22, 241; technical problems with, 221
promissory notes, 59
Putin, Vladimir, 207, 222, 238

Qualified Foreign Institutional Investor Program, 209

Reagan, Ronald W.: and Great Moderation, 193; tax cuts, and strength of dollar, 190–94, 280n53
real bills doctrine: accommodation papers and, 101–2; U.S. acceptance market and, 142–45
Regan, Donald, 190–91
Reuss, Henry, 186
R. G. Dun & Co., 130
Riccardi banking partnership, 65
Richardson, Thomas, 103
Rocha, Francisco Gómez de la, 75–76
Rockefeller, John D., 132
Roman denarius as international currency, 8; flow of currency between government and market, 35; primitivists' theory on early use of coins, 34; Roman administrative capacity to control money supply, 10, 32; Roman form of government and, 9–10, 32, 212, 246n13; and Roman trade deficits, 36–37, 41; Rome's economic and military power and, 32; Rome's extensive trade networks and, 34–37; spread through conquest, 12, 31–33; stable value and quality of, 35; trade with Asia and, 35–37, 250n47
Roman denarius as international currency, decline of, 37–41; cost of empire and taxation, 37–38; currency debasement pressures and, 39–41; denarius, replacement of, 251n66; drain of silver from empire and, 39, 41; excessive financialization and, 38; loss of political checks and balances and, 37, 39; loss of stable value and quality, and rising inflation, 39–41, 251n63; role of disease and pollution in, 38–39, 250n55
Rome: Aes rude, 29; aes signatum, 30; Antonine Plague, 38–39; bi-metallic system, 33, 39–40; denarius, introduction of, 29, 31; denarius' evolution from unit of account to currency, 31–32; early protocurrency and evolution of coins, 29–31; first mint, 30; splintering of empire, 41
Roosevelt, Franklin D.: economic policies, 154, 157; and Gold Reserve Act of 1934, 273n3; and gold standard, 154
Rothschild, Nathan Mayer, 98–99, 105, 106, 113, 114
Rothschild & Sons, 107, 112, 114, 116
Royal Exchange (England), 96
Russia: and Chinese renminbi, 212; and Project mBridge, 222; turn from U.S. dollar reserves, 238; use of Chinese renminbi in international trade, 246n10; U.S. sanctions on, viii, 230–32

sanctions, U.S. use of: gold reserves as hedge against, 231–32, 287n21; potential damage to U.S. dollar as international currency, viii, 230–31; reasons for increase in, 287n19
San Francisco earthquake, and financial crisis of 1907, 131

SDRs. *See* Special Drawing Rights
Shanghai-Hong Kong Stock/Bond Connect, 209
Shultz, George, 174–75, 178–79, 182, 183–85
silver mining: methods of indigenous Andeans, 257n10; Nevada silver rush, 81–82; patio process in, 73–74; prior to Spanish New World mines, 72–73; Saiger process in, 72. *See also* Spanish New World silver mines
small-economy currencies as potential rivals to U.S. dollar, 213–15
Smith, Adam, 101, 227
Smithsonian Agreement, 176–77, 183
Soviet Union, and U.S. dollar as international currency, 166–67, 275nn29–31
Spanish New World silver mines: destinations of silver from, 77–78; forced indigenous labor (*mita*) used in, 74; global impact of, 71, 76–77; and minting fraud, 74–76, 258n25; minting of silver from, 74–75, 77, 257n17, 258n25; public-private partnerships in, 74; silver processing methods, 73–74; silver sources prior to, 72–73; and Spanish influence, 73; transport of silver from, 78, 258n29; volume of silver produced, 73
Spanish silver reals as international currency, 8; administrative capacity to control money supply, 10, 75–76; also referred to as "pieces of eight," 74, 82; decline, 82–83; duration of, 19; as first global currency, 71, 80; and globalization of trade, 71, 76–77, 78–80; as preferred currency for international transactions, 80–81; Spain's loss of New World mines, 82–83; Spanish form of government and, 212; stable value of, 9, 74, 80; U.S. use of, 81–82; various names for, 80
Special Drawing Rights (SDRs): China and, 208; initial issue of, 171; limited impact of, 171–72; second issues of, 179, 187; third issue of, 194; value after U.S. abandonment of Bretton Woods system, 179

stablecoins, as potential international currency, 215–17, 284n27
Stuckey's Bank, 106, 110
Supreme Court, U.S., Trump's authority over bureaucracy and, 233
SWIFT (Society for Worldwide Interbank Financial Telecommunication): China and, 210, 212; digital efforts to circumvent, 219, 220, 222; U.S. sanctions and, 230–31

tariffs, U.S. trade and, 212–13, 227–28
trade, international: *commenda* contracts for, 54–55; and spread of international currency, positive feedback loop with finance, 5, 43, 62, 86–87, 109
trade acceptances: Dutch banks and, 90; and financial innovation, 15; London and, 16, 107, 109, 112, 137–39; and U.S. dollar as international currency, 14. *See also* United States as financial center, and acceptance market
trade deficits: in Ancient Roman, 36–37, 41; in Byzantine Empire, 43, 46; as consequence of international currency status, 41; U.S. and, 46, 179–80, 182, 185–86, 192
Treasury Bills Act of 1877, 110
Treasury securities, U.S.: equal treatment of foreign and domestic investors, importance of, 234; market depth and liquidity, importance of, 5, 17, 185, 200; threats to stability of, 5–6, 234–35
Triffin, Robert, 167–68, 198, 208, 228
Tripartite Agreement, 155
Trump, Donald J.: alliance with Putin, 207, 238; claimed authority over U.S. bureaucracy, 233; and EU defense spending, 207; policies on sanctions, 231; policies threatening U.S. dollar as international currency, viii, ix, x, 225, 227, 229, 231, 232–36, 238; and stablecoins, 284n27; tariff policies, 212–13, 227–28; as threat to Treasury securities' stability, 234–35; U.S. isolationism under, 239

INDEX 333

Tuscans, invention of partnership for international trade, 55–56

Ukraine, Trump policy on defense of, 238
Umayyad dinar as international currency, 43–44; collapse of, 45, 252n87; and spread of Islam, 44
UnionPay, 219
United Copper Company, plot to corner shares in, 131–35
United States: Coinage act of 1857, 81–82; financial crisis of 1907, 127–28, 129, 131–35; isolationism under Trump, 239; Mexican silver pesos in, 83; National Banking System, flaws in, 130–31; Spanish silver reals as currency in, 81–82; World War II flow of gold into, 156; World War I loans to allies, 146–47. *See also* sanctions, U.S. use of
United States banks: Fed's interwar policies tightening credit and, 149; interwar foreign lending, high volume and high default rates, 145–50; lack of experienced personnel to evaluate borrowers, 148, 150; loans to London for Boer War costs, 122; pre–World War I loans, 146
United States central bank: campaign for establishment of, 127–28, 135–36; lack of, and 1907 financial crisis, 127–28, 129, 131–35; need for, 127–28, 130–31, 134–35, 144–45. *See also* Federal Reserve, U.S.
United States debt levels: political polarization as obstacle to resolution of, 229–30; projected increases in, 228; and U.S. dollar as international currency, 5, 228–30, 287n10
United States dollar as international currency, vii–viii; advantages of, 5, 239–40; attraction of investment and foreign loans, 18; Bretton Woods Conference and, 159, 162–64; collapse, consequences of, 241–42; costs to exporters, 240; creation of U.S. acceptance market and, 128, 139–41; current status of, 4–5, 7; Great Depression and, 10–11, 17, 151–52; international leverage ("exorbitant privilege") provided by, 5; interwar competition from British pound sterling, 145–48, 150–52, 272n83; Marshall Plan and, 164; and military action abroad, 12; postwar strength and, 156–58, 163; and pressure on gold standard, 159; pre–World War II discussion of, 155–56; rise of, post–World War I, 147, 148; and tensions between U.S. and international interests, viii, 5–6; U.S. characteristics conducive to, 4–5; U.S. military power as incentive to use, 11, 237–38; U.S.'s high volume of trade and, 15. *See also* Bretton Woods Conference; gold standard

United States dollar as international currency, after Smithsonian Agreement: Bretton Woods system, collapse of, 183–84; British pound driven from Bretton Woods system, 180–82; and Carter administration inflation, 185–90; Carter's efforts to restore public confidence, 188–89; dollars' ongoing viability for cross-border capital flows, 185; fallout from dollar devaluation, 178–83, 277n3, 278n16, 278n18; lack of alternatives to, 194–97, 200, 240–41; market depth and liquidity, central importance of, 194, 200; petrodollar investments and, 184–85; prominent role in international finance and trade, 193–94, 280n54; Reagan administration impact on, 190–94, 280n53; safe haven status, importance of, 200–201

United States dollar as international currency, potential rivals to: BRICS basket currency, viii, 215; central bank digital currencies (CBDCs), 217–19, 241; Chinese renminbi, 208–13, 240–41; euro, 197–200, 205–7, 226, 240; lack of alternatives, 6–7, 194–97, 200, 240–41; nontraditional reserve currencies, 213–15; stablecoins, 215–17

United States dollar as international currency, threats to: decline in immigration as, 225; erosion of U.S. military dominance as, 237–39; loss of stability as, 232–35, 288n32; in Nixon administration, 3–4, 6, 7; trade deficits, 46, 179–80, 182, 185–86, 192; Trump's policies and, viii, ix, x, 225, 227, 229, 231, 232–36, 238; U.S. critics of costs to U.S. as, 239; U.S. debt levels as, 5, 228–30, 287n10; U.S. decline in research dominance and, 225, 286n4; U.S. declining share of global GDP and, 224–25, 286n2; U.S. declining share of global trade and, 226–28; U.S. overuse of sanctions and, viii, 230–31. *See also* Nixon, Richard M.

United States dollar as international currency, under Bretton Woods system, 176–77; dollar devaluation under Smithsonian Agreement, 176–77; dollar glut of 1950s, 165–67; and European loans denominated in dollars, 167; foreign currency devaluations, 165; initial dollars shortages, and U.S. policy, 164–65, 274n22; and potential run on U.S. gold reserves, 167–71, 275–76n34; Special Drawing Rights (SDRs) and, 171–72; suspension of gold convertibility, 3–4, 175–76, 177, 178–83; U.S. efforts to curb gold outflow in 1970s, 171–75, 276n49

United States as financial center, and acceptance market: creation of, through Federal Reserve Act, 14, 15, 136–37, 139; early lack of infrastructure to support, 16, 122–23, 127–28, 129–31; efforts to create, 127–28, 135–36; Fed withdrawal from, 141; growth prior to Great Depression, 140–41, 143; hampering of, by real bills doctrine advocates, 142–45; lack of developed infrastructure to support, 141, 145, 150, 271n50; liquidity problems in, 141; need for market maker of last resort, 144–45; overseas branches of U.S. banks and, 140, 270n43; problems caused by lack of, 129–35; retrenchment in early 1930s after Federal Reserve's withdrawal, 144; and U.S. dollar as international currency, 128, 139–41; U.S. trust companies and, 269n19; World War I growth of, 137

United States financial system reform, rationales for, 135–36

United States military power: erosion of, as threat to U.S. dollar dominance, 237–39; as incentive for countries to use U.S. dollar, 11, 12, 237–38; Trump defense budget cuts and, 238; and U.S. under Trump as unreliable ally, 238–39

United States trade, tariffs and, 212–13, 227–28

Urban VI (pope), 66–67

Vance, JD, 236–37, 238
vehicle currencies, early, 25
Venetian gold ducats as international currency, 48
Venice: coins minted by, 52; and development of international trade partnerships, 56; double entry bookkeeping, development of, 49; enrichment by Fourth Crusade spending, 52; as trade center, 51, 52–53
Viner, Jacob, 154, 157
VOC. *See* Dutch East India Company
Volcker, Paul, 173–75, 179, 182–83, 186, 188–89, 194, 200, 277n18, 280n40

Warburg, Paul Moritz, 127–29, 131, 135, 142–43, 145, 271n56
West Africa, gold traded to Italian city-states, 52
Western Schism, 66–67
White, Harry, 153–57, 161–62
Wilson, Woodrow, 128, 142